Populism, the Pandemic and the Media

Journalism in the age of Covid, Trump, Brexit and Johnson

EDITED BY
JOHN MAIR, TOR CLARK,
NEIL FOWLER, RAYMOND SNODDY
and
RICHARD TAIT

Published 2021 by Abramis academic publishing

www.abramis.co.uk

ISBN 978 1 84549 785 9

© John Mair, Tor Clark, Neil Fowler,
Raymond Snoddy and Richard Tait 2021

All rights reserved

This book is copyright. Subject to statutory exception and to provisions of relevant collective licensing agreements, no part of this publication may be reproduced, stored in a retrieval system, or transmitted in any form or by any means, without the prior written permission of the author.

Typeset in Garamond

This book is sold subject to the conditions that it shall not, by way of trade or otherwise, be lent, re-sold, hired out, or otherwise circulated without the publisher's prior consent in any form of binding or cover other than that which it is published and without a similar condition including this condition being imposed on the subsequent purchaser.

Abramis is an imprint of arima publishing.

arima publishing
ASK House, Northgate Avenue
Bury St Edmunds, Suffolk IP32 6BB
t: (+44) 01284 700321

www.arimapublishing.com

ebook version published by Routledge

Contents

Acknowledgements — ix

The Editors — x

Introduction: Journalism under pressure but still a force for good
Nick Robinson, presenter, Today *programme, BBC Radio Four* — 1

Section 1: January 6 and the end of Trumpism?
Dispatches and analysis from the heart of the 21st century American drama
Raymond Snoddy — 5

1. January 6 and the challenge to American television journalism
Robert Moore, US correspondent, ITV News — 10

2. Ego uber alles: Will the Trump brand play on?
Matt Frei, presenter, Channel 4 News — 18

3. Politics, pandemics and the race that Trumped all others
Jon Sopel, BBC North America Editor — 23

4. How close Donald Trump came to victory in 2020 – and what it means
David Cowling, King's College London, former BBC editor of political research — 31

5. Navigating the Trump storm
Bill Dunlop, former President and CEO of Eurovision Americas, Inc — 38

6. How Trump's abuse of the media has changed America forever
Philip John Davies, Emeritus Professor of American Studies,
De Montfort University, Leicester — 45

7. Donald Trump: Populist victim of partisan impeachment?
Clodagh Harrington, Associate Professor of American Politics,
De Montfort University. Leicester — 52

8. The lie in the machine: Truth, big tech and the limits of free speech
Mark Thompson, former Director-General of the BBC and CEO of the
New York Times — 59

Section 2: UK politics and the media
Reporting the populist wave
Richard Tait   67

9. Public reactions to Brexit and Covid-19
Sir John Curtice, Professor of Politics, Strathclyde University   70

10. When news broadcasters became critical workers
Gary Gibbon, Political Editor, Channel 4 News   83

11. Johnson and Oborne: Parallel lives, diverging views
Raymond Snoddy, media journalist   89

12. Johnson and journalism: Anonymous sources in senior journalists' social media feeds
David Smith and Julian Matthews, Lecturers in Media and Communication, University of Leicester   94

13. (Most) Populists aren't what they seem…
Peter York, cultural commentator, President of the Media Society   101

14. Must Labour lose?
Tor Clark, Associate Professor in Journalism, University of Leicester   110

15. The pursuit of truth… or not
Dorothy Byrne, former Head of News and Current Affairs, Channel 4   118

Section 3: Covid, journalism and society
The vaccine may be working on the population, but what about the health of the media?
John Mair   125

16. When the politics of science met the science of politics
Juliet Rix, science and current affairs journalist   129

17. The virus and journalism: Telling truth to the hacks?
Alan Rusbridger, Principal of Lady Margaret Hall, Oxford; former editor, The Guardian   135

18. The view from the hospital frontline
Dr Julian Barwell, Clinical Geneticist and Honorary Professor in Genomic Medicine at the University Hospitals of Leicester NHS Trust   139

19. Covering Covid reveals uncomfortable truths
Mark Easton, BBC Home Affairs Editor   143

20. Populism, anti-system politics and the media: A spotlight on Covid-19
Robert Dover, *Professor of Criminology, University of Hull* — 148

21. Now you see 'race', now you don't: The hyper-visibility and hyper-invisibility of race and Covid-19 in political and public health discourse
Paul Ian Campbell, *Lecturer in Sociology, University of Leicester* — 155

22. Messengers as well as messages in the spotlight
Raymond Snoddy, *media journalist* — 164

Section 4: Outside the metropolitan elite

Introduction: The future of this United Kingdom is in the hands of those far removed from those who think they rule us
Neil Fowler — 171

23. The pandemic and the provincial press
Tor Clark, *Associate Professor in Journalism, University of Leicester* — 174

24. How Britain ends
Gavin Esler, *former presenter, BBC* Newsnight — 180

25. Who was the godfather of the new populism? Archie Gemmill or Alex Salmond?
Maurice Smith, *Scottish business journalist* — 187

26. Political reality and the issue of perception between Boris and Nicola
John McLellan, *former editor of* The Scotsman, *director of communications for Scottish Conservatives 2012-13* — 193

27. Upper-case Unionism vs lower-case unionism: Populism on the streets of Northern Ireland
Gail Walker, *Editor-at-large,* Belfast Telegraph — 198

28. How populism turned against devolution in Wales
Martin Shipton, *Political Editor-at-large of the* Western Mail — 206

29. Life the other side of the Red Wall
David Banks, *former editor,* Daily Mirror — 212

30. A tale of two challenges: How did the media report Brexit and Covid in South Asian communities?
Barnie Choudhury, *Professor of Professional Practice, University of Buckingham and former BBC broadcast journalist* — 217

Section 5: Boris and Brexit

The role played by the beastly Europeans and their Euromyths
John Mair — 223

31. Are the 'beastly Europeans' really 'trying to do us in'?
James Mates, Europe Editor, ITV News — 226

32. How Britain was let down by its press over Brexit –
and how that can change
*Will Hutton, former Principal of Hertford College, Oxford and columnist,
The Observer* — 232

33. Did the British ever understand the European project?
Deborah Bonetti, UK correspondent, Il Giorno *and director of the
Foreign Press Association in London* — 238

34. Al promised you a miracle – Life under 'greased piglet' Johnson
*Steven McCabe, Associate Professor and Senior Fellow, Centre for Brexit Studies
and Institute of Design and Economic Acceleration, Birmingham City University* 242

35. Deceptively silly – the role of the cucumber in Boris Johnson's ideology
Imke Henkel, Senior Lecturer in Journalism, University of Lincoln — 250

36. Getting Brexit done and the future of the UK-EU relationship
Alistair Jones, Associate Professor in Politics, De Montfort University, Leicester — 256

Section 6: The new populism and the media

The undermining of truth in a changing and unreliable media environment
Raymond Snoddy — 263

37. Artificial intelligence and extremist content: a recipe for insurgency
*Alex Connock, Fellow in Management Practice (Marketing),
Said Business School, Oxford University* — 268

38. 'Enemies of the people?' Will populism be the death of
impartial journalism?
Richard Tait, Professor of Journalism, Cardiff University — 278

39. The populist press: Conservatism, 'common sense' and culture wars
Julian Petley, Professor of Journalism, Brunel University London — 290

40. Journalism ethics in a populist age
Sara McConnell, University Teacher in Journalism, University of Sheffield — 299

41. Journalism safety in the time of populism: A cautionary tale from the US
Elena Cosentino, director of the International News Safety Institute   305

42. Insurrection or over reaction? One afternoon in Manchester
Jim White, sports writer, the Daily Telegraph   314

43. Over here, over there: Lessons from the USA on why British TV journalism needs to stay fair and impartial
Clive Myrie, BBC BBC News journalist and presenter,
RTS Journalist of the Year, 2021   320

44. Misinformation and the decline of shared experience
Ken Goldstein, President of Communications Management Inc, based in Canada   325

Acknowledgements

This book is the third in a trilogy after *Brexit, Trump and the Media* in 2017 and *Brexit, Boris and the Media* in 2020. They have examined in great depth the rise of 'populists' especially in the UK and the USA. That phenomenon shows little sign of abating despite Donald Trump's loss of the office of president. Brexit is done, Covid has come and not gone and Boris Johnson is seemingly in the saddle for a long period. This book examines the media's role in all of this. Cheerleader, critic or what?

The book is the work of five editors working harmoniously week after week over various technology platforms.

We are, as ever, grateful to Richard and Pete Franklin at Abramis, our publishers, and Dean Stockton for designing another very stylish cover. We could not do it without them.

Enjoy the book.

John Mair, Oxford
Tor Clark, Leicester
Neil Fowler, Northumberland
Raymond Snoddy, London
Richard Tait, London

The editors

This is **John Mair**'s fortieth book as an editor. All have been 'hackademic' volumes mixing the work of leading journalists and academics. He invented the genre with Richard Keeble. In the last year he has edited 11 books, five on the pandemic, three on the future of the BBC, two on Boris and Brexit for Abramis and one on 'Oil Dorado' in Guyana. His previous books have covered a wide piste from the Arab Spring, the Leveson Inquiry, data journalism and the works of VS Naipaul. He invented the Coventry Conversations which attracted 350 media movers and shakers to Coventry University. Six million have downloaded the podcasts. Today he runs the weekly My Jericho events in Oxford (myjericho.co.uk) which attract local and national movers and shakers. In previous lives he was an award-winning producer/director for the BBC, ITV and Channel Four and a secondary school teacher.

Tor Clark is Associate Professor in Journalism, BA Journalism programme director, Deputy Head of the School of Media, Communication and Sociology at the University of Leicester, UK, and a Senior Fellow of the Higher Education Academy. After studying Politics and History at Lancaster University, he worked for the Northamptonshire Evening Telegraph, before becoming editor, first of the Harborough Mail in Leicestershire, and then of Britain's oldest newspaper, the Rutland & Stamford Mercury. Previously he was Principal Lecturer in Journalism and Associate Director of Learning and Teaching at De Montfort University in Leicester. As a political journalist he has covered eight UK general elections, the last four for BBC Leicester, where he is a regular commentator on politics and media.

Neil Fowler has been in journalism since graduation, starting life as trainee reporter on the Leicester Mercury. He went on to edit four regional dailies, including The Journal in the north east of England and the Western Mail in Wales. He was then publisher of the Toronto Sun in Canada before returning to the UK to edit Which? magazine. In 2010/11 he was the Guardian Research Fellow at Oxford University's Nuffield College where he investigated the decline and future of regional and local newspapers in the UK. From then until 2016 he helped organise the college's prestigious David Butler media and politics seminars. As well as being an occasional contributor to trade magazines he now acts as an adviser to organisations on their management, external and internal communications and media policies and strategies.

Raymond Snoddy OBE, after studying at Queen's University in Belfast, worked on local and regional newspapers, before joining The Times in 1971. Five years later he moved to the Financial Times and reported on media issues before returning to The Times as media editor in 1995. He is now a freelance journalist writing for a range of publications. He presented NewsWatch on the BBC from its inception in 2004 until 2012. His other television work has included presenting Channel 4's award-winning series Hard News. In addition, he is the author of a biography of the media tycoon Michael Green and of The Good, the Bad and the Ugly, which looked at the UK national press in the 1990s. He was awarded an OBE for his services to journalism in 2000.

Richard Tait CBE is Professor of Journalism at the School of Journalism, Media and Culture, at Cardiff University. From 2003 to 2012, he was director of the school's Centre for Journalism. He was editor of Newsnight from 1985 to 1987, editor of Channel 4 News from 1987 to 1995 and editor-in-chief of ITN from 1995 to 2002. He was a BBC governor and chair of the governors' programme complaints committee from 2004 to 2006, and a BBC Trustee and chair of the Trust's editorial standards committee from 2006 to 2010. He is a Fellow of the Royal Television Society and the Society of Editors, and a board member of the International News Safety Institute.

Introduction

Journalism under pressure but still a force for good

Broadcasting has long-term critics who may favour the US model of partisan programming, but public service news journalism serves the public best with facts, not opinions, says BBC *Today* programme host Nick Robinson

Are you a Leaver or a Remainer? For or against the lockdown? Woke or anti-woke? For or against Black Lives Matter? Do you call the Prime Minister Boris or Johnson? Are you a proud Scot or a proud Brit?

More and more our national debate is being reduced to a series of binary choices. Social media doesn't do nuance. It doesn't do explanation. It doesn't do a careful assessment of the merits of carefully balanced arguments. It is all too often summed up by a three-letter word – LOL, OMG or WTF. What really sums up so much of it, though, is a simple question: "Whose side you are on?" And an assertion that accompanies it: "If you're not with us you must be with them." That is the challenge facing the media – not just those like me, who work in broadcasting, but all of us.

I'm a little wary of the word 'populism' which appears in the title of this book as it's all too often used by people whose views are unpopular to sneer at those whose views do have popular support.

For years, decades indeed, there has been a power struggle between those with power and those who report on what they are doing. I've even written a book about it – *Live from Downing Street*. Throughout my career politicians have claimed the media – newspapers with huge circulations and broadcasters who commanded vast audiences – have too much power. Sometimes they've sought to flatter and ingratiate themselves with the media. At others they've sought to bully, control or regulate it.

The dramatic change in recent years is the rise of individual citizens and groups of them who have been empowered by the ability to publish and broadcast themselves without the need for the 'media' and at little or no cost. At the same time they have been able to consume news and information without relying on a publisher or broadcaster to provide it for them. The most successful politicians – the populists if you like – have exploited this and found ways to communicate directly without the interference of, or irritation created by, openness and transparency, questioning and accountability.

Those of us who earn our living reporting on the choices we face as a society should not respond with our own form of populism, i.e. measuring our success by the number of clicks, likes or shares we get, let alone by a claim that we should fall into line with this or that mood, opinion, party, faction or campaign which claims to speak for the public or this or that 'community'. We are not meant to be popular and must resist the clamour to take sides.

Yet you'd have to be a fool not to recognise that journalism is under pressure – from without and within – from those who are sworn enemies of independent journalism and those who proclaim they are supporters of it.

The behaviour of my own organisation – the BBC – has merely added to pressure that was on it long before the recent furore over Martin Bashir raised serious and legitimate questions about our journalistic standards. That self-styled master strategist Dominic Cummings published a plan to get a media more to his and the Conservatives' liking and did so many years before he entered Downing Street. It had three simple steps. First discredit the BBC. Second, establish an alternative news provider. Third, cut the licence fee. It is a plan worth keeping in mind as you listen to ministers express their regret that the reputation of 'this world-class institution has been highly damaged' and talk of this being 'one of those key moments in the history of the BBC'. Some in government see it as their duty to reform and improve a public institution. Others see it as an opportunity to weaken what they've always loathed.

However, it is the self-proclaimed friends of an independent media who also damage our standing by criticising us for not 'calling out' those they disagree with all or insisting we make a stand for this or against that cause they believe in. The journalism I believe in does not need to shout or grandstand. It should challenge and reveal, analyse and explain. If I'd wanted to wear badges, wave placards or to take sides on the big questions that face us all I wouldn't have taken the career path I did.

I have long argued there are real dangers in the popularity of views not news; opinions not facts; partisanship not impartiality. I continue to worry broadcasting is being allowed to follow the path of the United States in which people will choose which show or channel they watch or listen to according to the views they hold. I hope regulators and politicians will not come to regret the decisions they are taking now.

However, one thing the latest BBC crisis has reminded me of is the dangers of what Matthew Syed has called 'institutional narcissism', the need to recognise organisations devoted to public service – whether the BBC or the NHS or the

Catholic church – can attract upstanding people committed to uplifting values who fail to uphold them precisely because they believe they are more worthy, more virtuous, more interested in public service than anyone else.

So, I welcome the creation of new providers of news and the competition they will provide just as I welcome this book as a healthy self-examination of how well journalism has been performing. I welcome the next series of difficult and divisive challenges that look set to follow those of recent years – the debate about how to recover from this pandemic; about independence for Scotland and a border poll in Northern Ireland; about race, gender and gender identity and who knows what else. I do so believing the media in this country – for all its flaws and limitations – remains a force for good.

Section one

January 6 and the end of Trumpism?

***

Dispatches and analysis from the heart of the 21st century American drama

Raymond Snoddy

What better place to start a book on the media than with three working journalists, observing, reporting, analysing; in this case three television journalists who are household names, ITV's Robert Moore, Jon Sopel of the BBC and Matt Frei of Channel 4 News.

Frei recounts his one and only meeting with Donald J Trump and suggests what is likely to happen now. Sopel opens telling pages from his diary of the recent presidential election campaign.

Remarkably Moore tells it like it was from the heart of the mob, rioters or insurrectionists – call them what you will – who marched on the US Capitol on January 6, 2021. Moore was there in the midst of the attack with his camera crew. His coverage will probably win broadcasting awards but, as he explains, there was something far more remarkable than recording historic events breaking before his eyes – the fact that in a city with more television journalists than any in the world he was almost alone.

The US networks had reporters inside Congress but they were in front of fixed camera positions with constant commitments to do live analysis and with 'no remit to roam'. The networks sacrificed newsgathering to comment. The 24-hour news channels such as CNN and Fox chose to cover an attempt to overturn a presidential election by force with endless, polarised, studio-based panel discussions.

So it was that the primary task of reporting from the heart of the demonstration in Washington DC, events unprecedented in modern American history, fell largely to a television journalist from London. Moore argues there should now be a period of reflection by American television, which failed to find out what was happening in their own country, outside of Washington. January 6, Moore argues, raises even more questions for cable television news channels, not only over their coverage, or lack of it, on the day, but also 'the more consequential issue of whether the extreme partisanship which has dominated so much television, radio and online conversation during the Trump years was a factor in nurturing the extremism which led to the crisis'.

Moore believes American television journalism should go back to first principles, showcasing editorial balance and listening to people with diverse perspectives from far beyond the studio. "Above all we must remember we are newsgatherers or we are nothing but noise," he argues.

We choose two days from Sopel's election diary, the first day of Trump's re-election campaign and the last, more than 500 days later. Sopel was there in Orlando, Florida, on June 18, 2019, when Trump launched his campaign with thousands queuing to get into the Amway Center. One Trump supporter told Sopel his president is Jesus-like, here to do God's work. Another woman expressed pride at travelling all the way from California to attend. The Trump supporters chant their favourite slogans from last time such as Make America Great Again, Lock Her Up and Build the Wall before being steered by Trump away from MAGA, the greatest political slogan of all time according to Trump, to KAG – Keep American Great.

Roll forward to 'the tumultuous, astonishing' decisive day, November 7, 2020, the day when it became clear Trump had effectively lost. The call from CNN's Wolf Blitzer that Joseph R Biden Jr was the next President-elect of the US came at 11.15am. "They really do 'the moment' well," notes Sopel, who lovingly portrays the Trump campaign's press conference that was not held at Philadelphia's Four Seasons Hotel. "Let history record that the story which began with Donald Trump descending the gold elevator in his ritzy Manhattan apartment block on 5th Avenue to launch his presidential bid ends here in a scruffy suburb of Philly, five years later. And with the social media almost wetting itself laughing," Sopel writes.

At the time of his first and only interview with Donald Trump in 2013 Matt Frei saw Trump as a man with an opinion on everything but whose opinion was not necessarily worth seeking. "My bad," admits Frei who notes that while everyone was laughing at 'The Donald', they were missing the point; that in the seedbed of bitterness, resentment and fantasy even the most absurd lie could become a reality for enough people to rearrange the political firmament. In retirement, Frei believes, Trump is less likely to focus on a presidential library – there would be room for only one author – than on burnishing his brand, raising funds, causing trouble and being the Republican kingmaker. "The Grand Old Party can't live without him nor can they live with him. He is the parasite that has taken over the host," Frei argues.

Bill Dunlop, a former Channel 4 journalist who has spent years in the US working for the European Broadcasting Union, believes the Trump era has forced US journalism into a split which is reflective of US society as a whole. In the face of abuse, exaggeration and a string of falsehoods from Trump, the traditional media have come down firmly on the liberal side. Meanwhile Trump supporters turned to an increasingly rabid range of right-wing news channels and the free-for-all that is social media.

Trump's simmering resentment at Fox News intensified when owner Rupert Murdoch reportedly told associates Biden was going to win and exploded when Fox made an early call that the swing state of Arizona would be won by Biden. As Trump supporters increasingly turned to channels such as Newsmax, which grew its ratings from 58,000 to more than a million within a few weeks as Fox lost 20 per cent of its viewers, what was Murdoch to do? Fox decided to 'double down and compete with the fiction' (of electoral fraud) and more hours of 'opinion' programming rather than 'news programming', for Dunlop a missed opportunity by Murdoch to change for the better. Instead Chris Stirewalt, the Fox political editor who had accurately called Arizona for Biden on election night, was fired. Dunlop believes when a charismatic populist leader such as Trump, keeps a hold on millions and continues to disrupt social norms, journalism is stuck with it. "Like it or not, the media are still talking about Donald Trump today – and they will for years to come," argues Bill Dunlop.

Next we turn to the work of three academics for much needed analysis, background and context. Professor Philip John Davies, emeritus professor of American politics at De Montfort University in Leicester, a presidential watcher for more than half a century, believes after systematically undermining the main media outlets in the eyes of his supporters, Trump then benefited mightily from the alternatives springing up in their place.

Regular network news US election expert Clodagh Harrington, associate professor in American politics, also at De Montfort University, emphasises the 'potentially catastrophic downside' Trump has created for society – the undermining of objective truths. Even with populist rhetoric surrounding the impeachment of President Andrew Johnson in 1868, and the Watergate scandal of President Nixon, she says, 'the truth remained an objective entity'.

For David Cowling, a visiting senior research fellow at King's College London and former BBC editor of political research, the most remarkable thing about the 2020 presidential election was how close Trump came to winning a second term given all that had happened during his presidency. As Cowling argues, the figures speak for themselves. The 'relentless four-year crusade' against Donald Trump resulted in a 3.1 per cent increase in the Democratic vote and an 0.8 per cent rise in the Trump vote.

In no less than 31 states, plus Washington DC, Trump's vote share increased compared with 2016 while in 16 states his share fell, but by a mere one per cent in ten of them.

The most telling numbers of all come from an analysis of the increase in votes compared with 2016. In no less than ten states more of the extra votes went to the Republicans and Trump rather than Joe Biden's Democrats. Cowling also uncovers 'quite extraordinary' numbers by comparing swings to Joe Biden to that of Hilary Clinton. In six states, plus the District of Columbia, there were swings to Donald Trump and in two other states there was no swing at all. The remaining 42 states showed swings to Biden but in 25 they were of 2 per cent of less.

In the great bastions of Democratic support California and New York, California registered a small swing to Trump while New York recorded the smallest swing of any state to Biden of only 0.3 per cent. The more Trump's opponents ignore or disparage the reasons for his rise – their sense of being disenfranchised by the Democrat/Republican establishment – the more difficult will they find it to engage with the 74.2 million who voted for him, Cowling believes.

Prof Davies helps provide the explanation for Cowling's 'quite extraordinary numbers'. He cites research by Pew that around 30 per cent of respondents said they relied mainly on Donald Trump, the Trump campaign and the Trump White House as major sources of both election and coronavirus information. Research by the Election Integrity Partnership found a small number of social media account holders, including Trump and members of his family, generated most of the disinformation contributing to 'the Big Lie' that the presidential election was stolen.

Similarly Dr Harrington points to 'the most dangerous use' of the social media platforms, in promoting Trump's refusal to accept the outcome of the 2020 presidential election. Harrington notes on January 6 Trump engaged in what Congress termed 'incitement to insurrection' and tweeted messages of love to those at the Capitol and another, later deleted, stating 'we will remember this day forever'. "The populism of Trump came at a high price, not only in the lives lost that day (Jan 6), but in the undermining of public trust in the democratic process and a fracturing of political norms. And that is too high a price for any nation to bear," Harrington concludes.

Finally former director-general of the BBC and former chief executive of the New York Times Company, Mark Thompson, makes a weighty contribution on truth, big tech and the limits of free speech. It's hard to imagine, Thompson argues, of a more thorough debunking of the conspiracy theory that led to a one-man armed mission to rescue children supposedly being held and tortured by paedophiles in secret tunnels under the basement of the Comet Ping Pong restaurant in Washington. Apart from everything else the restaurant didn't even have a basement. Yet five years on 'the underlying myth' of Pizzagate is still alive and well. "It's central to the QAnon conspiracy theory that holds that Donald Trump has been leading a secret counter-conspiracy to outwit and defeat the cannibal-paedophiles," relates Thompson. A strain of the theory attracted tens of millions of views by young people around the world on Tik Tok.

What is to be done about such conspiracy theorists? Thompson believes they have to be shown up and called out and politicians who refuse to condemn them have to be shamed. Although Donald Trump may have been within his First Amendment rights when he recklessly whipped up his supporters at the Capitol, the digital platforms are also within their rights to decide his messages are dangerous and ban him for life.

It's probably impossible to expunge racist conspiracy theories completely but: "Pushing them out of the sunlight and into the shadowy margins of digital space is still eminently worthwhile," he says.

Thompson believes professional peer review, input from civil society and reputational pressure, above all, in deciding what not to print, is more effective than either law or regulation. In the end though the internet left the Garden of Eden a long time ago and the fundamental difficulty is not that human nature does not change as rapidly as technology but that it doesn't change at all, Mark Thompson believes.

January 6 and the challenge to American television journalism

> **America's partisan media landscape and abandonment of traditional newsgathering in favour of studio-based bias confirmation was the background to the violence of January 6, says ITV News US correspondent Robert Moore, the only TV journalist who was embedded with the mob as it stormed the Capitol on that fateful day**

During a few tumultuous hours on the afternoon of January 6, 2021, it appeared American democracy was facing an existential challenge. For the first time since the British stormed the Capitol in 1814, the perimeter of Congress was breached by insurrectionist forces. A mob of pro-Trump supporters, mobilised by the President's incendiary comments a few minutes earlier, caused mayhem in the citadel. Members of Congress were forced to flee to safety and shelter behind locked doors. The certification of the 2020 presidential election was suspended for nine hours. America's claim to be the world's pre-eminent and mature political system was in jeopardy. For decades the US Government has lectured other countries on good governance only to discover deep-seated flaws much closer to home.

Five people died as a result of the violence, some in disputed circumstances, among them a conspiracy theorist protester who was shot dead by a security agent defending the House of Representatives. The FBI launched its biggest investigation since 9/11, arresting at least 400 people, and a number of Congressional probes are seeking to understand what happened, and why.

Questions raised for TV news

While the law enforcement investigation has dominated the headlines, the events at the Capitol should also prompt serious self-reflection by American journalists. In particular January 6 raises questions for cable television news, not only in respect of the coverage of that day but also the more consequential issue of whether the extreme partisanship which has dominated so much of the television, radio and online conversation during the Trump years was a factor in nurturing the extremism which led to the crisis.

Conventional wisdom – certainly if you listen to Biden administration figures and Department of Justice lawyers – is that the blame for January 6 can be evenly divided between the far-right rioters and Donald Trump. According to that assessment, the combination of political rage by Trump's supporters and the President's own incendiary language was the perfect storm. Along with poor policing and a lamentable intelligence failure, all the forces coalesced at that one moment in time to permit political chaos to engulf Washington.

But that is too easy, too comfortable a narrative. It deflects responsibility away from segments of the media which should, at a minimum, examine their coverage and ask some difficult questions of themselves, and not only those on the conspiratorial right. If journalists are to cover the phenomenon of populism which is coursing through the Western democratic world then it is also time for all of us to look in the mirror and assess whether we are rising to the challenge of reporting on the fault lines which lie beneath our societies. Indeed, are we listening sufficiently to voices outside the corridors of power and to those in the heartland? Brexit asked that question of the UK media. The Trump presidency posed a similar question in the US. But here there is a further question: Is the free-wheeling nature of primetime cable news in America amplifying the very divisions journalists are reporting on?

Evolution of today's TV journalism environment

The US has a unique media ecosystem for a liberal democracy. The highly opinionated shows on cable TV, especially in the evening hours, have developed in the aftermath of the abandonment of the legal requirement to present news in a 'fair and balanced' way. The Fairness Doctrine, as it's been called, was in place from 1949 until 1987, and technically only applied to the free-to-air public broadcasters, not to cable, satellite and internet platforms. Nevertheless, once the Federal Communications Commission no longer enforced the rule amid the Reagan era slashing of regulations, the national broadcasting climate changed significantly.

Irrespective of the fact Fox News and other cable networks would not have fallen under the Fairness Doctrine, we are left living with the results of that disastrous 1980s regulatory roll-back. For in the years since, along with right-wing talk radio, we are now witnesses to a bewilderingly raucous and wildly partisan TV landscape. One cable station has been a cheerleader for Trump. Another has no hesitation in branding those who entered the Capitol on January 6 as domestic terrorists, no matter that there were no firearms on display and many of the protesters were naïve conspiracy theorists, not determined seditionists. Critically, what has been lost on both sides of the national debate is not just fairness and balance, but nuance.

Fuelled not just by this loss of balance but also by the toxicity of many social media posts and the algorithms which drive content, the crisis going forward is clear. Polling suggests a third of all Americans, 33 per cent, do not believe Joe Biden was legitimately elected president and 70 per cent of Republicans believe he won the presidency through fraud. According to the 2021 Edelman Trust Barometer, 59 per cent of Americans believe journalists are purposefully trying to mislead the public by saying things they know are false. In fact, the problem is most clearly seen with voters who lean to the right. A Gallup poll conducted for the Media Insight Project shows in 2000 47 per cent of Republicans trusted the media but two decades later it was a mere ten per cent. In contrast, voters who identify as Democrats show an *increased* trust in the media, from 53 per cent to 73 per cent. One side is feeling unheard, and by extension betrayed.

How networks fuel misinformation

As analysts have noted, the scale of the problem in raw numbers is immense. Between 50 and 55 million Americans believe the most recent presidential election was stolen. They are also the very Republican voters who are most likely to vote in the primary elections of 2022 and 2024, and who will therefore choose the next tranche of GOP congressional candidates and the next presidential nominee. So it is more, not less likely that conspiracy theorists gain a stronger foothold among Republican elected officials. In the aftermath of the disputed 2020 election, fringe sites are going mainstream. Threatening Fox News' dominance as the news provider of choice to conservatives are conspiracy-embracing outlets like One America News Network, and Steve Bannon's podcast 'War Room'.

The signs of what media partisanship is doing to the country's political health have been visible for some time. Polling by Navigator Research revealed Fox News viewers overwhelmingly supported Trump's 2019 declaration of a national emergency on the southern border. But while 84 per cent of the Fox News audience backed the declaration, only 21 per cent of Americans who did not watch Fox News thought the same. Even if Fox News attracts an inherently more conservative audience, viewers' perspectives on immigration and the value of the border wall was likely shaped by which channel they watched. That is hardly surprising given the drumbeat of alarmist and xenophobic content Fox News was broadcasting but it underlines the role of journalism and the importance of content selection in shaping the national conversation and the conspiracy theories which have taken root within it.

Ever since the early Obama years, Americans have been living in dual – and duelling – media echo chambers, often reflecting the agendas of the cable TV networks. The Trump presidency simply super-charged that media partisanship and it reached a climax on January 6. After all, if you deeply, fervently believed the presidential election had been stolen and a monumental political fraud had been committed why *wouldn't* you storm the Capitol in frustration? January 6 wasn't an aberration, it was the natural conclusion of a presidency which saw political value in igniting culture wars and elements within cable TV news that poured fuel on the fire.

The need for self-examination

To be fair, some platforms are beginning a process of self-examination after the Capitol riots, although the rigour and outcome of the reviews remain uncertain. Notably, on May 5, 2021, Facebook's Oversight Board, which is funded by the tech giant but presents itself as an independent body, did implicitly acknowledge the company's design and policy choices had fuelled the January 6 chaos. Significantly, in a judgement which maintained Donald Trump's ban from Facebook, the Board also wrote: "We urged Facebook to conduct a review into its contribution to the narrative of electoral fraud and political tensions that led to the events of January 6." This is a powerful rebuke and could be applied to a number of other media organisations. Cable networks on both sides of the political divide should follow Facebook's Oversight Board and review their coverage of the Trump era. Humility is needed if trust is to be regained.

The parallel question is whether there is a market for more balanced, nuanced, and less opinionated news programming. It is clear the template of deeply partisan news coverage by cable networks has been, in commercial terms, a success. Fierce partisanship in US politics and the media is not new, of course. It is as old as the Republic. But the Trump years, with the President's use of social media and populist rallies, drove it beyond anything we have seen for a generation.

In television terms, Donald Trump was ratings gold. The Fox News audience averaged 2.8 million in primetime in January 2017, the first month of his presidency, up 17 per cent on the previous year. Fox anchors such as Bill O'Reilly and Tucker Carlson saw viewing figures soar as they harnessed their high-octane, inflammatory programmes to Trump's anti-establishment and conspiratorial rhetoric. CNN and MSNBC also saw rising ratings on the other side of the divide as they took advantage of the sense of shock felt by liberal Americans. The White House was also a beneficiary. By lambasting the media paraded in front of him, infamously calling it the 'enemy of the people' and 'fake news,' Donald Trump had a perfect foil to keep his base of supporters in a state of permanent outrage with the left. For all the mutual disdain on display between the liberal press and the Trump White House it was a startlingly symbiotic relationship. They fed off each other, sustained each other and reaped the rewards. It is not clear the outcome of the Trump years is that American journalism will become more balanced. Conspiracies sell, moderation doesn't. That is the editorial and commercial challenge going forward for all media platforms, and not just America's cable TV channels.

The studio panel - time to rediscover newsgathering

Clearly, there was some extraordinarily powerful and impressive newspaper journalism during the Trump years, particularly at the *New York Times* and the *Washington Post*. With multiple scoops and strong sources – helped by a dysfunctional administration furiously leaking to a small cadre of reporters – and driven by their own fierce rivalry, the two newspapers succeeded in shining a light on the nepotism and nativism at the heart of the Trump presidency. Television news had a significantly less successful time holding Donald Trump to account. Indeed, White House news conferences became a notable circus as TV correspondents and Trump played to their respective audiences. There was a great deal of heat, very little light.

The American cable TV news industry has embraced one broadcasting format in particular which has proved detrimental to the national political conversation – the studio panel. There are some extraordinarily talented individuals on these discussion programmes, a brains trust for the TV shows which can be impressive and helpful for viewers. But the format has become over-used and fallen prey to partisanship. For almost the entire 24-hour cable news cycle, coverage is based on anchors and guests – often paid contributors – confirming each other's perspectives. Once primetime arrives there is a great deal of shouting about the political or cultural controversy of the day and almost no newsgathering outside the studio. The anchors start preaching and viewers are left to face a mind-numbing barrage of angry opinion, shaped by the agenda of the network. It is a constant, real-time example of confirmation bias. Viewers tune into Fox News to hear validation of their pro-Trump, anti-establishment agenda. Similarly, liberals watch CNN or MSNBC to hear an echo of their disgust at Republicans' conduct. Anchors like Tucker Carlson and Rachel Maddow have become the networks' star performers and there is no dividend for them to dial back their deeply partisan content. There is nothing wrong with an animated studio debate if alternative views are tested against each other. But irrespective of the selection of studio guests the 'panelisation' of news cannot replace newsgathering. If it does, there is a heavy journalistic price to pay. On January 6, I witnessed that myself.

Inside the mob on January 6

While cable news stations had assembled their panels that day, with a dozen contributors in position and ready to echo each other's views, almost no reporters and crews were actually covering the demonstration. Everyone was talking *about* the protesters and no-one was listening *to* the protesters. At noon on January 6, I was on the Ellipse, an area on the National Mall to the south of the White House, interviewing Trump loyalists. It was crystal clear there would be an attack of some kind on the Capitol within hours, although whether it would be successful or not was impossible to know. At 2pm, having clearly heard the warnings, an ITV News television crew was poised on the west side of Congress, filming the protesters' attempt to outflank the police and invade the Capitol. And here is the extraordinary fact: In the city with the highest concentration of TV journalists in the world, we were alone. For all the significance of the protest in those perilous final days of a wild presidency the networks' coverage was almost exclusively studio-based. US TV reporters were positioned at various pre-designated places within Congress but they were in front of a fixed camera with constant commitments to do live analysis and no remit to roam. At this defining moment, the very core of journalism – newsgathering – had been sacrificed by the networks. TV executives had chosen self-affirming discussion panels over in-the-field reporting, even though the dramatic events were playing out within sight and earshot of their studios.

This wasn't just the case on January 6. For much of the Trump presidency there was a lack of newsgathering outside of Washington and therefore multiple missed opportunities to focus on what was happening within the country. This is not without irony, for many of the US networks' foreign correspondents have done important and courageous work overseas, reporting on some of the most dangerous conflicts in the world. But at home, where conflict was brewing in plain sight, it's been a distinct weakness and a constant frustration for many of my US colleagues.

I saw the exact same flaw in American television reporting a few months earlier. In Louisville, Kentucky, on September 5, 2020, ITV News reported on the mobilisation of far-right militias onto the streets of the city, an attempt by heavily-armed groups to claim back the downtown area from Black Lives Matter demonstrators. This deployment of weapon-toting far-right vigilantes was clearly a major development as the militias flexed their muscles after a summer of protest by black activists. It also dramatically foreshadowed what would happen four months later at the Capitol. To our surprise, we were the only network television crew in Louisville, although there were some enterprising freelance camera operators and livestream video-bloggers at the scene.

ITV News had seen the signs of the rumbling volcano of white supremacist sentiment in America because we were looking, listening and newsgathering, and not studio-based. American TV news networks are the big beasts in the jungle and the best resourced news organisations in the world. They spend large sums of money on 'talent' – mostly on studio-based anchors and analysts. The issue is whether they can now recalibrate and demonstrate a similar commitment to newsgathering and field reporting. That is even more essential in a media landscape where local and regional newspapers are either closing or being hollowed out.

Perhaps the most alarming, grimmest statistic in all US journalism is that 2,100 local and regional newspapers have closed down in the last 15 years, creating in swathes of rural America what has been called a 'news desert'. Half of America's 3,142 counties have only one newspaper, over 200 counties have no local newspaper at all. Television news has an opportunity to step into the void. It's not just about coverage of politics and the White House, it's about reporting on homelessness, racial equity, the wealth gap, the further dislocation of America's white working class amid huge technology shifts derived from AI and robotics, health care, policing reform, holding the social media companies to account and the impact of climate change. The canvas is vast, the opportunities for television news are significant and few of these stories are best told from a Washington or New York studio.

Back to first principles of journalism
The growth of conspiracy theories, ricocheting around social media and taking ever-deeper root during the pandemic and enforced social isolation, is the other great challenge for American journalism. One central question remains unresolved: Is it better to ignore conspiracy theories to avoid giving them a broader platform or to attempt to debunk such views? Again, January 6 wasn't the peak of this dark world of wild, irrational, deeply-held beliefs, it just put them on clearer display than ever before. Many of those who surrounded me on the steps of the Capitol and who stormed into the building were clearly under the influence of conspiratorial media platforms and online chat rooms. Indeed, beyond the false narrative of election theft that was motivating the rioters, it was also possible to watch the birth of a whole new conspiracy theory, the dimensions of which we are only beginning to grasp.

As we all know, the events of the insurrection at the Capitol were born out of the false claim, perpetuated by Donald Trump, that the election of Joe Biden was based on a fraud. No evidence of a significant shift of votes, or of systematic malpractice, has been found, let alone on a scale that would have tipped states like Pennsylvania and Wisconsin into Trump's Electoral College column. But notably, and still under-reported, is that large numbers of Americans – a shockingly high number – believe the attack on the Capitol was orchestrated by *left-wing* forces seeking to discredit conservatives. That might seem like a fringe theory, given the eye-witness accounts by journalists, including myself, who saw events unfold in real-time. But a survey conducted in March 2021 by Reuters/Ipsos showed that a *majority* of Republican voters, 55 per cent, believe the attack on Congress was a false-flag operation. Such conspiracy theories are extremely durable and difficult to overcome. It is the same with Q-Anon views, the bizarrely entrenched belief that a super-hero within the US Government is battling to save the nation against evil and corrupt forces.

As American journalism takes stock in the aftermath of the insurrection and the Trump maelstrom, there needs to be a meaningful discussion between the media and tech platforms about how to take on and deconstruct these dark and fast-spreading obsessions. Facebook has begun that process but that debate should be taking place in every newsroom in America. Facing a crisis of trust in an era of populism, television news organisations need to revert to first principles, showcasing editorial balance and listening to people with diverse perspectives far beyond the studio, voices which may sometimes be the softest-spoken. Above all, we must remember we are newsgatherers or we are nothing but noise.

About the contributor

Robert Moore is the award-winning Washington-based correspondent for ITV News, who reported from America throughout the Trump presidency. He was the only TV correspondent in the world who accompanied the insurrectionist mob as it stormed Congress on January 6, 2021. He has previously reported from Moscow, the Middle East and Africa. His book on the Kursk submarine disaster was an international best seller.

Ego uber alles: Will the Trump brand play on?

Matt Frei of Channel Four News recalls his history with Donald J Trump. He spotted the narcissism from outset. That took 'The Donald' into and out of the White House, but what is his legacy and what will he do with it?

The first and last time I met Donald Trump was in the sweltering New York summer of 2013. He was busy dipping his toes into politics and mulling a possible presidential run. The rest of us were still busy laughing at him and his wannabe hair. Entering Trump Tower on Fifth Avenue was a bit like stepping into a theme park with only one ride, one circus and one purpose: to celebrate the man after whom the building was named. The shops in the marble and chrome lobby sold a dizzying array of products from books, written by one author – you guessed him – ties, tee-shirts, sweaters, babygrows, portraits, pens, tie pins, cufflinks, aftershave, mineral water and even steaks… all of them items which could brandish his name. Their qualification was they had a surface to display the name and they could be sold. Anything qualified. The Trump babygrow would have set me back 45 dollars. It was an orgy of single-minded branding and it felt like being water boarded by a name. It was thus something of a relief to be ushered into the golden elevator by one of the supersized ushers – more heavyweight boxer than lift attendant. In that capsule of gold, the name was nowhere to be seen. There was just a large mirror to remind the passenger that he or she wasn't Donald Trump.

Meeting the man in the flesh

The lift opened its doors with a whisper on the 56th floor, the one just below Trump's Versailles-imitation penthouse duplex. I was surprised to find his office also strangely devoid of his name. I guess by the time you reached the 56th floor the point ought to have sunk in. There was one secretary and his beloved daughter Ivanka was levitating with diaphanous detachment in the background. The atmosphere was more small family law firm than sweat shop of ego. The conditioned air was arctic and humming with understated efficiency. The man himself entered the boardroom where the interview was to take place quietly without the usual bombast and fanfare we later came to expect.

He was tall. His gait was lumbering, as if gravity was an issue, and his bright red tie hung like a sporran. He greeted me and the crew politely and, unusually for a CEO with a global image to nurture, he was unaccompanied by minders, PR masseurs or bag carriers. 'The Donald' has always done his own press, even as The President. He insisted on looking through the camera's viewfinder to inspect the shot and he demonstratively placed on the glass table a small tape recorder which he informed us was already switched on.

To be honest the whole interview, which lasted longer than an hour was conducted by me in a misguided spirit of disbelieving jocularity. I had been slightly reluctant to make the trip to New York to spend the day with a man I knew had an opinion on everything under the sun but whose opinion, I thought, was not necessarily worth seeking. My bad.

The Trump Weltanschauung

Buried inside our meandering conversation about everything from Scottish independence – not a fan – to Edward Snowden – should be executed for treason – to China, yes CHINA – 'they are eating our lunch and must be stopped' – was an intriguing admission that has become increasingly relevant as America and the world wonders if Donald Trump, the past master of reinvention has a second political act in him.

Trump, as you may remember and as his ardent believers have never forgotten, was at the time engaged in an outrageous campaign to disbar President Obama from the presidency by questioning whether America's first black president was actually born in the USA. He was. In Hawaii. And while almost all the media and much of the country thought the question was pungent with implied racism, the Commander-in-Chief eventually felt it necessary to produce his birth certificate. The clamour died down. And while almost everybody was busy laughing at 'The Donald' almost everybody had also missed the point, that was to become one of the hallmarks of Trumpian populism: in the seedbed of bitterness, resentment and phantasy even the most absurd lie can become a reality for enough people to rearrange the political furniture. After all Donald Trump's presidential career started with the 'birther' lie and ended with the biggest lie of them all, the one that led to the storming of the Capitol on January 6, the one that almost ended America's 200 year-long experiment with democracy – that the 2020 election had been stolen, that Biden was illegitimate, that Trump was the rightful President. That lie was supported by more than 140 Republican lawmakers on the night of January 7, 2021, as the debris was still being cleared from a shattered Congress. They voted to overturn the election result despite everything that had happened. According to opinion polls they were supported by 80 percent of Republican voters.

No such thing as bad publicity for DJT, incontinent with ego

But I digress. In our conversation high above Fifth Avenue, I put it to Trump he had become a laughing stock over the 'Birther thing'. I mentioned the 2012 White House Correspondents' dinner, an annual soiree where the sitting president is guest of honour and required to make a speech sending himself up. The guests are hundreds of journalists who get to invite Hollywood stars or corporate titans who need impressing. Or Donald Trump. The reality TV mogul and his wife Melania were guests on the *Newsweek* table and we were all watching closely as Obama laid into The Donald with the kind of belittling derision Trump really hated. To paraphrase, the President said: "Now that we have laid the questions over my birth to rest, The Donald can get back to the stuff that really matters… like who faked the moon landings." The crowd roared with laughter. 'The Donald' look down at his rubber chicken. The wife looked embarrassed.

I reminded him of the scene. "You must have felt terrible?" I asked.

"Wrong!" he said. "Soo wrong. I loved it. Loved it. Because this was supposed to be Obama's night… and all anyone could talk about… was me." Except of course it wasn't. There were plenty of other conversations swirling around the petit fours and cheap wine. But Trump, who sees the entire universe through the prism of his ego, only had eyes and ears for himself. Blame his mother, his father, or the wiring in his brain or whatever but for Donald everything since the beginning of time has always been about Donald. He is incontinent with ego. And in desperate need of money to pay off some 900 million dollars of reported debts.

Life after the White House

So I think it is almost inevitable that in retirement Mr Trump will focus less on a Presidential library – there would only be room for one author anyway – and continue to brandish his brand, raise funds and cause trouble. However distorted his narcissistic view of the universe may be it is a fact he has received more votes than any other candidate in US history –74 million. Apart from the guy who beat him, Joe Biden. But five million more people put their name against Trump's name than against Obama's during his first historic election in 2008. That fact should make jaws drop. Whether you like it or not Trump has filled his political accounts with capital and can spend the next few years figuring out how to spend it while working on his golf swing. He is flirting or perhaps planning to set up his own social media platform after he was sent into *Twitter* and *Facebook* exile but he won't even need to set up his own political party should he want to run again, because no other Republican will be able to emerge from under the slab of Trump. He still has the power to make or break candidates. The number of Republican Congressmen and Congresswomen or Senators who are prepared to defy him openly can be measured on the fingers of two very small hands. The Grand Old Party can't live without him but nor can they live with him. He is the parasite that has taken over the host.

What is Trump's populist appeal?
None of this is to suggest Trump will run again for president or even win. When it comes to the White House, he could tell himself: Been there. Done that. The majority of voters who don't want to repeat that kind of trauma will probably make a return to 1600 Pennsylvania Avenue unlikely. But for American democracy to function it needs the two political parties to be credible, stable and serious. And one of them is still high on Trump crack. Understanding the addiction is to grasp the essence of Trump's American populism.

Watching Trump descend on the freezing flats of Iowa during the 2016 Caucuses I used to wonder why hog farmers who could barely pay the mortgage on their land would wait in the Arctic cold for a New York billionaire who so disdained any part of America outside the Upper East Side and Palm Beach and he would insist on flying back to his own bed every night on the campaign trail. Trump never ever practises the kind of beer swilling, glad handing, back slapping, baby cheek squeezing retail politics that are de rigeur in American politics. For starters he is teetotal. And that old cliché of presidential politics – would you have a beer or even a Diet Coke with the candidate – never applied to Trump. You wouldn't ask. He would never say yes. And that wasn't the point.

Trump says the unsayable, shame means nothing.
Trump with all his rage and vitriol, despising immigrants, making fun of the physically and mentally challenged, treating the travelling press at his rallies like Christians in the Roman Coliseum was adored by his supporters precisely because he had the balls to mouth the prejudices every other politician didn't even dare to whisper. Trump is blissfully unencumbered by shame. He is also very good at being bad. And he turned his badness into a mark of authenticity. After decades of slick, spit polished politics, bulging with focus group approved promises and low on results, authenticity became perhaps most valued ingredient in campaign politics. Voters preferred a candidate who was authentically offensive rather than inauthentically groomed. And the more the liberal, metropolitan media became outraged, the more his crowd lapped it up. The trouble with Trump's populism is that it works less well in a time of national crisis. Covid was Trump's undoing. With his cavalier attitude to the virus he made Americans feel unsafe. He looked unhinged. The man who was notoriously paranoid about germs – he admitted as much in our interview – killed his own presidential career by not taking the pandemic seriously. And yet, he still managed to get four million more votes than during his winning election in 2016.

Look back in anger?
Trump has weaponised the swelling tide against political correctness and woke culture. Anger and resentment are the true currency of his populism. A return to

normality and prosperity are its greatest threat. Boring Biden is the rehab America has deserved after four years of tumultuous Trump. In the end Donald Trump's wealth and all its glittering prizes are not aspirational to his supporters. By now most Americans know the system is rigged against them, the dream is a sham and they will never get to the 56th Floor in a golden elevator. They just love the fact a guy who has all the money to belong to all the clubs behaves like someone who doesn't give a shit about ever being a member of any of them.

About the contributor
Matt Frei is the Emmy Award-winning presenter of Channel Four News and LBC. He is author of *Italy: The Unfinished Revolution* and *Only in America*. Previously he was a long-time foreign correspondent for BBC News.

Politics, pandemics and the race that Trumped all others

The BBC's North America Editor Jon Sopel spent two years on the US presidential election road, from elation in Florida to the farce at Four Seasons Total Landscaping in Philadelphia. The final day, he recalls, was both tumultuous and astonishing

Setting the scene – Washington, December 1, 2020
It is now nearly a month since the election was over and the President is yet to concede. He may never. He won't do so willingly or with a happy heart, even though the result is clear. But why would you expect this race to conclude with neatly creased wrapping paper, a pretty ribbon and a bow? Why should the manner of his departure be any different from his arrival – or the period when he was in office, for that matter? There was Thanksgiving 2020. The President answered reporters' questions for the first time since the election in the Diplomatic Reception Room in the White House.

It was a perfect visual metaphor. Power shifts fast in Washington, and there was Donald Trump sitting behind a desk that was way too small, in a chair he could barely fit his behind into. For a man who cares so deeply about image, becoming the butt of endless jokes and memes must be agony. And the abject failure of any of the court cases to gain traction even worse. Throughout this, Joe Biden has stubbornly refused to engage in any kind of Twitter war. He's just ignored Donald Trump (something else that has probably irritated the incumbent) and gone about appointing the people who will fill the key roles in his administration.

In the beginning
June 18, 2019, Orlando, Florida. 503 days until polling.

Yes, it is more than 500 days out from the 2020 election, but this is where Donald Trump's bid for a second term begins. His campaign launch is at the Amway

Center and it's no accident he's chosen Florida. Thousands – literally thousands – are queuing to get in. Excited, dressed up, indefatigable, enthusiastic. Forget the storms, they're here to see Donald. The faithful are really faithful. Devoted.

I ask one man – on camera – what he likes about the President and he tells me he is Jesus-like. He has been sent here to do God's work. I have thought of Donald Trump in many ways in the past three years that I have been reporting on his doings on a daily basis, but I struggle to see this particular similarity. Anyway, I smile benignly, thinking this bit of *vox pop* is definitely going to be on the news. One woman I speak to has travelled the breadth of America to be at the rally. She's come from California. The crowd, when they become listless after waiting in line for hours to get through layer upon layer of security, start chanting 'Four more years', then 'Lock her up' – one of the unexpected hits of the 2016 campaign – and 'Build the wall', still a firm favourite. One man, six feet six inches tall, is a dead ringer for Abraham Lincoln and dressed like him. We all want our photo next to him.

MAGA (Make America Great Again) hats are selling like hot cakes. People have improvised their own Donald Trump costumes. During the arduous 2016 campaign I never saw once this level of enthusiasm, adoration even, for Hillary Clinton. Two and a half years into his presidency Trump still has a big section of the American public eating out of the palm of his hand.

Donald and Melania come out to whoops and hollering like a boy band might get from an audience of adolescent girls – and while this audience is decidedly older, the decibels aren't any lower. The speech, full of unfinished sentences, is a meandering, scattergun rehash of all the things he said in 2016 – with some big boasts (fair enough) about the state of the economy. On this performance, that is going to need some working on. It has to be more than Robert Mueller and the witch hunt, and the Speaker of the House, Nancy Pelosi, and the do-nothing Democrats. That feels a bit anaemic.

What I had forgotten, though, having not been to many Trump rallies since the last election, is how well he feeds off the audience. At one point he has been reading off autocue for 15 minutes – and it is dull. Lists of things we've done, lists of crimes committed by the Democrats. The audience is quiet and fidgety, so he starts riffing on whether Make America Great Again was the greatest political campaign slogan of all time. Spoiler alert – he thinks it was. And he gets the audience involved. Hands up if you think this, hands up if you think that. And then he starts road-testing the slogan for 2020: Keep America Great. Yes, the audience cries. Yes, Donald Trump cries. No-one does politics as entertainment better. And so it shall be. MAGA is out. KAG is in.

Momentarily I feel sorry for all the traders out on the street with their stalls full of MAGA merchandise. But it's a passing concern. KAG hats are a whole new marketing and merchandising opportunity…

In the end, the decisive day, November 7, 2020

What a day. Tumultuous and astonishing don't begin to describe it. It is a day that unfolds in multiple locations at different times. So, forgive me if I borrow from the TV drama, *24*, and go all Kiefer Sutherland, with split screens as events unfold in different places, before going full screen as we concentrate on one part of it.

08.00 Georgetown

Sleep, it is good to be re-acquainted with you. We've been apart too long. It is the most beautiful autumn morning, cool, crisp, not a cloud in the sky. I go out for a long walk along the canal. It is beautiful out.

09.30 The White House

Donald Trump is off to play golf, by the sound of things, but he has tweeted that his crack legal team, led by Rudy Giuliani, will be holding a news conference at the Four Seasons in Philadelphia. I wonder what evidence they've turned up. It will take place at 11.30am. But not long after this tweet comes another, but this time from the Four Seasons Hotel itself, in what looks like an epic piece of trolling of the President by the luxury hotel chain. It is one for the ages: 'To clarify, President Trump's press conference will NOT be held at Four Seasons Hotel Philadelphia. It will be held at Four Seasons Total Landscaping – no relation with the hotel.' To say that Four Seasons Total Landscaping is not the same as the Four Seasons Hotel is the understatement of the century. It is like saying the Taj Mahal curry house on the Bayswater Road is not the same as the Taj Mahal in Agra.

11.00 Georgetown

Biden's lead is creeping up in Pennsylvania, and we've had a tip that when the Democratic challenger's margin goes above 30,000, it's possible the networks will call it for him – and once they do, the 20 electoral college votes from PA will put him over the 270 mark which ensures victory.

11.15 CNN studios, Washington

John King is reporting a new 'vote dump' is imminent and the latest batch of ballots have now been counted. King, a handsome silver fox CNN veteran, has become crack cocaine. You get one fix of him, but it quickly wears off and you need another. Back to John King's big board – and Biden has moved beyond a 30,000 lead over Trump, and then with much whooshing and whizzbangery the BIG announcement is made: Wolf Blitzer (their version of David Dimbleby) makes the historic statement that Joseph R. Biden Jr is the President-elect of the United States. They really do 'the moment' well. Other networks follow suit. Van Jones, a black commentator, author and lawyer who is in the studio as the result is declared, provides the viral moment of the day with his emotional and heartfelt reaction to the result. "It's easier to be a dad, it's easier to tell your kids character matters – it matters," he said. "This is vindication for a lot of people who have really suffered. 'I can't breathe' – that wasn't just George Floyd. A lot of people felt like they couldn't breathe," he said, choking back the tears, and wiping his eyes with a handkerchief. "This is a big deal for us, just to get some peace and have a chance for a reset. The character of the country matters. Being a good man matters. I just want my sons to look at this, look at this, it's easy to do it the cheap way and get away with stuff."

11.30 Four Seasons Total Landscaping, Philadelphia
The news conference venue is in the car park of a run-down shopping centre in a slightly crumbly neighbourhood. And Four Seasons Total Landscaping is next to Fantasy Island Adult Books and Novelties, and just across the street from the Delaware Valley Cremation Center. The company, which is more used to providing mulching, weed control, shrub pruning and leaf removal – among other services – is now letting out its parking lot at the back for the most bizarre news conference ever. Trump/Pence posters are plastered to the small garage door and a lectern is put up in front. This is where the counter-revolution shall begin. Let history record that the story which began with Donald Trump descending the gold elevator in his ritzy Manhattan apartment block on 5th Avenue to launch his presidential bid, ends here in a scruffy suburb of Philly, five years later. And with social media almost wetting itself laughing. It's as though we're watching a particularly ridiculous episode of *Veep* that has never been screened before because the writers thought it was too far-fetched. So much of what Donald Trump did with the endless procession of rallies was slick. But the fact they could book a garden centre by mistake speaks to the utter unprepared shambles of these final moments of the Trump campaign, whose confidence from Wednesday has become angry incredulity today.

Rudy Giuliani, whose credibility just seems to diminish every time he opens his mouth, snorts derisively at the news the networks have called Pennsylvania. "The networks," he screeches, "the networks!" he says again, his voice rising in an untenable crescendo, the intention being to ladle on the sarcasm. They don't decide elections, he tells reporters – the courts do. You just wonder whether at this moment a little 'oh shit, what have I just said' alarm might have been triggered in his head. It doesn't seem to have done. No, Rudy, it's not the courts who decide, it's the people who decide – a notion he probably thinks is hopelessly naïve and innocent. All anyone remembers are the jokes: "The press conference that the White House announced would be held at the Ritz, will actually take place next to the Ritz Crackers endcap-display in the snack food aisle of the Wawa at 7912 Roosevelt Boulevard," one person tweets. And then there are the garden centre jokes. Make America Rake Again. Lawn and Order.

11.30 Trump National Golf Course, Sterling, Virginia

The pool report has it that the President left the White House at just after ten, the on-duty pooler noting: "The President left the White House residence and walked alone to his vehicle. He wore a black windbreaker, dark pants and a white MAGA hat. It is a lovely day with blue skies and only a light breeze, but he leaned forward as he made his way towards the vehicle, as if he were heading into a stiff wind." A stiff wind indeed. Trump must be on the third or fourth hole of his round by the time the networks call it. You just wonder whether any official has dared interrupt the round to tell him the news. Or whether they get to the 18th and someone says: "I know what, Mr President, why don't we play 36 holes… such a lovely day."

No word comes from the golf course. We get one shot fed back to us of him playing. He is on the green, with a long putt to the pin. He strikes the ball firmly, but it comes up four feet short of the hole. What a glorious picture to write to in television terms: the President just coming up short.

11.30 My Georgetown apartment

From this moment my quiet Saturday morning goes helter-skeltering out of control. I cycle to the White House to be live at the top of the news. There is a slightly festive atmosphere in Georgetown – there are car horns honking and a few people waving. It is much the same as I lock up my bike on the corner of 17th Street and Pennsylvania Avenue – as close as my bike can get to the White House. In the live bit I do from inside the White House grounds I say Donald Trump is off playing golf – something I point out he will soon have a lot more time for.

12.45 The area around the White House

In the half-hour I have been inside the White House grounds the world has changed outside. Now it is not just the odd car horn honking. It is a traffic jam of cars, all converging on the blocks surrounding the White House, the occupants waving flags and shouting. Now, instead of one or two people wandering around, it is thousands of Americans homing in on the people's house. Washington is a liberal, Democrat voting city. And it is the most perfect autumn day. The Biden victory is producing its own soundtrack – car horns, whistles, maracas (who knew so many Washingtonians had maracas?) and bells. And human whoops of delight. Great big, unrestrained dollops of human delight. This is not just around the White House, it is across Washington. And it is not just across Washington, it is across the big cities of America.

There is something visceral. In 2008, when Barack Obama was elected, I was in the US. I had been reporting from Culpeper, Virginia, a town which the BBC had adopted for the campaign. As I drove back into DC in the small hours of that Wednesday morning, every traffic light you stopped at, people would get out and hug each other and weep. There was a fuzzy feeling of warmth that after America's long, painful history – from slavery, through Jim Crow, through segregation, through the civil rights struggle – it had taken the giant leap and elected this charismatic young African-American as its 44th president. The emotion that night was such a positive one for Obama.

The sentiment in DC now is, yes, of course pleasure Biden has won, but it is also of hatred and loathing and detestation of Donald Trump. And among those who felt marginalised by Donald Trump there is relief that the man who they see as having poked them in the eye, is now getting a taste of his own medicine. There are people holding rainbow flags. There are immigrant groups. There are people with strong political affiliations and people with none. They are dancing on the streets of Pennsylvania and 17th – but the real pleasure is they think they are also dancing on Donald Trump's political grave. And across Lafayette Park on 16th Street – now Black Lives Matter Plaza – it is a wild party.

12.45 Trump Campaign HQ, Rosslyn, Virginia

The President may be out playing golf, but the machine is whirring. A statement is released: We all know why Joe Biden is rushing to falsely pose as the winner and why his media allies are trying so hard to help him: they don't want the truth to be exposed. The simple fact is this election is far from over. Joe Biden has not been certified as the winner of any states, let alone any of the highly contested states headed for mandatory recounts, or states where our campaign has valid and legitimate legal challenges that could determine the ultimate victor.

14.30 Presidential motorcade from Trump National, Sterling, Virginia

It is just after 2.30pm when the President gets into 'the Beast' for the journey back into DC. As he drives out of the gates, large crowds have gathered. Some are cheering him on, others booing and jeering. One holds up a placard saying 'You're fired'. Another reads 'Pack your shit and go'. Some cars are driving up and down with Trump flags.

Though Democrats might wish it were so, this is not a repudiation of Trump and Trumpism, 2016 was not an aberration. It wasn't just a crazy, misguided holiday romance they have now thought better of. Tens of millions of Americans watched what he did over the four years he was president and were happy to renew the contract for another term. And that has another big knock-on for politics in Washington. Republican lawmakers will know Trump is still wearing the sheriff's badge and this will make them decidedly queasy about telling him he needs to accept defeat when millions of his supporters don't and won't. He may be on the cusp of losing power, but you'd better believe he is still powerful.

17.00 The White House

I have come back to do my report for the main evening news. Just alongside our live position is the chief political correspondent for *Fox News*, John Roberts, who is supremely well-connected to this administration – and a Trump favourite – and he is reporting that for all the outward defiance, some advisors, and maybe even Donald Trump himself, are beginning to accept the President has no legal avenue, that it is done – and they need to find a way to manage this. If Donald Trump were to open his bedroom window he would be all too aware of what is happening outside. Now even inside the White House grounds the sounds of the car horns and the celebrations can be heard clearly coming from 17th Street, H Street and Black Lives Matter Plaza. The ring of steel that's been erected around a wider than normal perimeter will keep the party goers out – but their noise and joy is infiltrating the most secure building on earth.

20.00 Wilmington, Delaware

Have the eyes of the whole world ever been on Wilmington, Delaware, before? They are tonight. Joe Biden and Kamala Harris are addressing the nation as President-elect and Vice-President-elect. And after a presidency of continuous turmoil, upheaval and division this is a clear resetting of the compass. With Joe Biden at the helm, the ship of state will be steered into calmer waters. Even the setting for the speech – a car park in Wilmington, Delaware – seems to speak to the change of direction for the country. Kamala Harris – the first woman to be VP, the first person of colour to hold the position – gives a brilliantly pitched speech. "While I may be the first woman in this office, I will not be the last – because every little girl watching tonight sees that this is a country of possibilities." And she continues to address the next generation: "... to the children of our country, regardless of your gender, our country has sent you a clear message: Dream with ambition, lead with conviction and see yourself in a way that others might not see you, simply because they've never seen it before. And we will applaud you every step of the way."

The President-elect, a practising Catholic, peppered his speech with biblical references. There was a time to build, a time to reap and a time to sow – but now was a time to heal, he told his audience – who honked their car horns appreciatively. Unity, coming together, putting aside differences, co-operation, no more demonisation, were the themes of this speech; will be the themes of his presidency. His only mention of Donald Trump is to say how disappointed his supporters must feel, and that he would be a president for all Americans.

But much of the speech is an implied rebuke to the current occupant of the White House. His most immediate priority would be to form a working party to deal with the coronavirus pandemic that would be driven by the science. He would fight racial injustice. Tackle climate change. He would be inclusive. Whether he'll succeed or not is another question. But there's no mistaking he wants to chart a very different course for the – still – most powerful country in the world. There is a spectacular fireworks display at the conclusion, even eclipsing the Trump pyrotechnics at the end of the Republican Convention. The excitement is palpable among the crowd, and it's clear to see on the faces of Kamala Harris and Joe Biden. He may be old, he may make the odd verbal slip, he may not have been the most inspiring candidate, this might have been his third attempt to win the presidency, after the best part of half a century in public life, but as I watch the scene unfold I am left with one powerful thought: whatever his shortcomings, could anyone else have beaten Donald Trump? Almost certainly not. Barack Obama argues that in politics you don't choose the moment, the moment chooses you. This is Joe Biden's moment. As Tony Blair said in 1997: "It is a new dawn, is it not?"

23.00 Johns Hopkins University, Baltimore
Some of the contours of this new dawn look just the same. At this famous academic institution, just an hour down the road from Wilmington, they've been compiling the most reliable coronavirus statistics for America; for the rest of the world. On November 7 more than 120,000 Americans tested positive, a new and grim record. 2020 hasn't been a normal election. 2020 hasn't been a normal year.

About the contributor
Jon Sopel has been the BBC's North America Editor since 2014. Previously he was chief political correspondent of BBC News. He has presented many of the BBC's news, current affairs and political programmes. This chapter is an edited extract from Jon Sopel's book *UnPresidented: Politics, pandemics and the race that Trumped all others* published by BBC Books/Penguin in January 2021. It is reproduced with permission of the author. Previously he had published two books on US politics and one of the first biographies of Tony Blair.

How close Donald Trump came to victory in 2020 – and what it means

Donald Trump definitely lost the presidential election to Joe Biden – but not by much. David Cowling analyses the numbers that show populism in the US is here to stay

In the immediate aftermath of the 2016 US presidential election many people asked: "How rubbish did Hillary Clinton have to be to lose to Donald Trump?" Four years later, we were entitled to ask: "How rubbish did Joe Biden have to be to nearly lose to Donald Trump?" The national popular vote swing in 2020's presidential election, compared with 2016, was 1.2 per cent from Republican to Democrat.

How is that possible? The challenges to Donald Trump's legitimacy as President began before he was even inaugurated, not least the view that his victory was only secured after Russian interference with the election. Impeachment followed and he was hunted throughout his four years of office with unprecedented ferocity. It seems the 45th President was so uniquely evil that the actions of all his 44 predecessors paled into insignificance by comparison.

It is certainly undeniable Donald Trump was not 'politics as normal'. He became President by defeating not only the Democrat establishment but the Republican establishment too. The Washington DC establishment 'swamp' as he described it, hated him with an all-consuming passion they were never reluctant to share. And if Washington flagged, there was always an endless succession of Hollywood stars and musicians on call to take up the slack: no film, no album, no single, could be launched upon the world without an expression of despair about the fascist apocalypse Donald Trump was visiting upon the US. He was the Mussolini of Middle America's Main Streets, and he had to be defeated in 2020 or else democracy itself would perish.

Let the figures speak for themselves

Of course, all of this could have been true and if it were then the American people would rise up in their millions to defeat him and save the nation from being crushed under his jackboot, his support would plummet and the Democrats would sweep the board in the House, the Senate and a whole raft of State elections held on the same day. If the relentlessly devastating critique of Donald Trump was correct how could there be any other outcome? Well, as the saying goes, let the figures speak for themselves.

Total votes cast in Presidential elections 2000-20

	Democrat	%	Republican	%	Others	%
2000	50,999,897	48.4	50,456,002	47.9	3,949,201	3.7
2004	59,028,444	48.3	62,040,610	50.7	1,226,291	1.0
2008	69,498,516	52.9	59,948,323	45.7	1,866,981	1.4
2012	65,915,795	51.1	60,933,504	47.2	2,236,111	1.7
2016	65,853,514	48.2	62,984,828	46.1	7,830,934	5.7
2020	81,281,502	51.3	74,222,593	46.9	2,890,510	1.8

Sources: US Federal Election Commission for 2000-16 results. 2020 figures taken from certified results reported on the Cook Political Report website.

The relentless four-year crusade against Donald Trump resulted in a 3.1 per cent increase in the Democrat vote and an 0.8 per cent increase in his vote. There was an astonishing increase of 21.7 million voters (+15.9 per cent) compared to 2016 – resulting in by far the biggest percentage turnout since the universal franchise was introduced in 1920. Given the widespread portrayal of the politics pursued by Donald Trump over the previous four years, surely the overwhelming majority of those extra votes should have gone to Joe Biden – after all, wasn't that why the Republicans were engaged in desperate attempts at voter suppression? However, in the event, 58 per cent of those additional votes went to Joe Biden and the other 42 per cent went to Donald Trump.

Far from being hurled down into the political equivalent of Dante's Inferno, in 31 States (plus Washington DC) Trump's vote share increased, compared with 2016. In 16 States his share decreased (but by less than one per cent in ten of these) and there was no change in his 2016 share in three states. The US Cook Political Report created a category of '15 Key Battlegrounds' in their analysis of the 2020 election, comprising the 13 most marginal states, plus two marginal Congressional Districts. Whereas Biden led Trump by 4.4 per cent in the national popular vote, in the combined popular vote in those key battlegrounds, Trump led Biden by 1.7 per cent.

The table below records the three most marginal states that took Mr Trump to his 2016 total of 304 Electoral College votes and the three which similarly took Mr Biden to his total of 306 in 2020 (remembering there were nearly 22 million extra votes in 2020). It appears Mr Biden's knife-edge victory in 2020 was fractionally sharper than Mr Trump's in 2016. Without Lady Gaga's pivotal endorsement of Mr Biden, who knows what the result might have been?

Most marginal States delivering victory in 2016 and 2020

2016	Vote majority	% majority	Electoral college votes
Michigan	10,704	0.2	16
Pennsylvania	44,292	0.7	20
Wisconsin	22,748	0.7	10

2020	Vote majority	% majority	Electoral college votes
Arizona	10,457	0.3	11
Georgia	12,670	0.3	16
Wisconsin	20,682	0.6	10

The next table sets out the increases in votes for the two parties, compared with 2016 and the overall change in percentage share of support within each state. The final column records the percentage swing from Republican to Democrat between 2016-2020. I was not surprised by the increase in Democrat votes, that was the direction of travel everyone expected. What I was not prepared for was the substantial increase in Republican votes that burst the Democrat balloon, seeing off claims they would sweep the nation on polling day at all levels of Federal and State elections.

	Increase in votes 2016-20		Change in % share 2016-20		Swing 2016-20
	Democrat	Republican	Dem	Rep	To Dem
			%	%	%
Alabama	120,077	122,915	+2.2	-0.1	1.2
Alaska	37,324	26,564	+6.2	+1.5	2.4
Arizona	510,976	409,285	+4.3	+0.4	2.0
Arkansas	43,438	75,775	+1.1	+1.8	-0.4
California	2,356,458	1,522,615	+1.8	+2.7	-0.5
Colorado	465,482	162,123	+7.2	-1.4	4.3
Connecticut	183,108	42,076	+4.6	-1.7	3.2
Delaware	60,665	15,476	+5.6	-1.9	3.8
Dist. Columbia	34,493	5,863	+1.2	+1.3	-0.1
Florida	792,070	1,050,845	+0.1	+2.2	-1.1
Georgia	596,544	372,733	+3.9	-1.5	2.7
Hawaii	99,239	68,017	+1.5	+4.3	-1.8
Idaho	97,256	145,064	+5.6	+4.6	0.5
Illinois	381,186	300,876	+1.7	+1.8	-0.1
Indiana	209,287	172,230	+3.2	+0.1	1.6
Iowa	105,392	96,689	+3.2	+1.9	0.7
Kansas	143,318	100,388	+5.5	-0.5	3.0
Kentucky	143,620	123,675	+3.5	-0.4	2.0
Louisiana	75,880	47,138	+1.4	+0.4	0.5
Maine	77,337	25,144	+5.3	-0.9	3.1
Maryland	307,095	33,245	+5.1	-1.7	3.4
Massachusetts	387,006	76,309	+5.6	-0.7	3.2
Michigan	535,201	370,309	+3.3	+0.3	1.5
Minnesota	349,333	161,097	+6.0	+0.4	2.7

Mississippi	54,377	56,075	+1.0	-0.3	0.7
Missouri	181,946	124,225	+3.3	0.0	1.7
Montana	67,077	64,362	+4.7	+0.7	2.0
Nebraska	90,089	60,885	+5.7	-0.3	3.0
Nevada	164,226	157,832	+2.2	+2.2	0.0
New Hampshire	76,395	19,864	+5.9	-1.1	3.5
New Jersey	460,057	281,341	+1.8	0.0	0.9
New Mexico	116,380	82,227	+6.0	+3.5	1.8
New York	674,867	425,265	+1.9	+1.3	0.3
North Carolina	494,976	396,144	+2.4	+0.1	1.2
North Dakota	21,144	18,801	+4.6	+2.1	2.3
Ohio	285,001	313,829	+1.6	+1.6	0.0
Oklahoma	83,515	71,144	+3.4	+0.1	1.7
Oregon	338,277	176,045	+6.4	+1.3	2.6
Pennsylvania	531,788	406,941	+2.5	+0.6	1.0
Rhode Island	54,961	19,379	+5.0	-0.3	2.7
South Carolina	236,168	229,714	+2.7	+0.2	1.3
South Dakota	33,013	33,322	+3.9	+0.3	1.8
Tennessee	143,318	329,550	+2.8	0.0	1.4
Texas	1,381,258	1,205,300	+3.3	-0.1	1.7
Utah	249,606	349,909	+9.9	+12.6	-1.4
Vermont	64,247	17,335	+9.4	+0.4	4.5
Virginia	432,095	192,987	+4.4	-0.4	2.4
Washington	626,894	362,904	+5.5	+2.0	1.8
West Virginia	47,190	56,011	+3.3	+0.1	1.6
Wisconsin	248,330	204,900	+2.8	+1.6	0.6
Wyoming	17,518	19,140	+4.7	+1.7	1.5

The final column registering swings to Joe Biden, compared with the Clinton/Trump contest in 2016, is also quite extraordinary. In six states plus the District of Columbia, there were swings to Donald Trump. In two other states there was no swing at all. The remaining 42 states showed swings to Mr Biden but in 25 of them these were two per cent or less. And what of the two great Democrat bastions of California and New York, both of which stood so proudly against President Trump and all his shameful machinations? California – the home of Hollywood and so much else besides – registered a small swing to Donald Trump and New York recorded the smallest swing of any State (0.3 per cent) to Mr Biden.

We have to stretch back three-quarters of a century, to the 1944 presidential election, before we can find a swing between the two main parties as low as the one in 2020. And yet the US electorate has certainly not held back from punishing parties and candidates when they disapprove of them. In 1952 they delivered a 7.5 per cent swing from Democrat to Republican and in 1964 a swing of 11.2 per cent from Republican to Democrat. In 1976 a swing of 12.6 per cent from Republican to Democrat and in 1980 a swing of 5.9 per cent from Democrat to Republican. Yet, in 2020, Mr Trump marginally increased his share of the vote over 2016, performed most competitively in the key marginal states, attracted an extra 11.2 million votes and sustained a swing against him of just 1.2 per cent.

Did the voters not notice?
We have a problem with the 2020 US Presidential election outcome – either the detailed election figures with their small shifts between the two candidates recorded above simply reflect average voter behaviour in most presidential contests, or else the four years of the Trump presidency were as utterly extraordinary as so many claimed. We cannot have it both ways. If the former, how does that sit with the fierce and relentlessly negative characterisation of Donald Trump's presidency over the previous four years? Did millions of voters simply not notice, or did they just not believe the picture presented to them? If the latter, then how can 2020 conceivably have resulted in such a close contest? And how could the House Democrats who were President Trump's fiercest and most determined critics, lose around ten seats to the Republicans on the same day?

In democracies, politics is the process by which people negotiate their way through differences and contradictory ideas. It was never designed to arbitrate between people who despise each other, that type of division, as history attests, drags us down a much darker road. Donald Trump has been characterised as an arrogant, brash, vulgar person, whose pre-2016 'fame' was based on a controversial business career and the tacky glamour of reality TV. However, for all that, some 74.2 million US citizens (some 46.9 per cent of all who voted in 2020) preferred him to Joe Biden. And after four highly controversial years in office, an additional 11.2 million people came out to support his bid for a second term (in the process reducing the swing against him to the lowest of any presidential election in 76 years).

'In your guts you know he's nuts'
If he had been buried electorally, as Barry 'In your guts you know he's nuts' Goldwater was in 1964, then his opponents might be excused for sneering and moving on. But he wasn't. And if they don't want to see him, or his like, elected ever again then they need to understand why so many millions voted for him in 2020, including increased numbers of Black, Latino and Asian voters – the very people we were told would not, and could not, support what he stood for.

Donald Trump won his first term as president, and very nearly won a second, by representing tens of millions of Americans who felt disenfranchised by a Democrat/ Republican establishment that is drenched with corporate cash and seemingly indifferent to the problems they face. The more Mr Trump's opponents ignore or disparage the reasons for his rise, the more difficult they will find it is to engage with those who voted for him, and they need to do that. Of course, there is the alternative of repeating our own roaring success in uniting the UK following the 2016 Brexit referendum, with its winning formula of characterising Leavers as ill-educated, misinformed, small-minded, racist bigots. But I would not recommend it. Mr Biden and his colleagues need to listen, not lecture, because if they don't then the many millions they narrowly defeated in November 2020 are likely to smoulder in isolation until the next time they win.

Early indications suggest a considerable amount of healing needs to take place. As his administration rolls out the Covid vaccines purchased by President Trump and as every US adult prepares to receive $1,400 under recent Covid Relief legislation, Mr Biden's approval ratings are positive. In March 2021 a Pew Research poll found 54 per cent approval for his performance. However, that figure comprised 86 per cent of Democrats but only 16 per cent of Republicans: a partisan divide as extreme as found in early polls that tested President Trump's approval ratings four years earlier. And a raft of other polls reveal similar chasms between supporters of the two parties. Republican states are pushing back against President Biden's initial flurry of executive orders, the Democrats are pushing forward on promoting reforms of the Supreme Court and challenging the filibuster rules in the Senate. None of this, so far, suggests anyone has even paused for breath before launching back into behaviour that dominated the previous four years, namely, politics as a substitute for civil war. The United States faces as many challenges at home as it does enemies abroad. How it deals with both while its politics remains simply two warring, irreconcilable tribes will be a wonder to behold.

About the contributor
David Cowling is a visiting senior research fellow at the policy institute at King's College, London. He has been involved in the analysis of the polls in every UK general election since 1987, first as ITN's political analyst and then as the BBC's Editor of Political Research.

Navigating the Trump storm

American journalism has survived an unprecedented onslaught from a populist president – but Bill Dunlop shows how it didn't manage it without taking sides

"Time will decide whether Wednesday's assault on the Capitol was a riot, an insurrection, a last gasp of a renegade president or an early skirmish in a civil war organized on far-right social media." So wrote the *Washington Post* on Saturday, January 9, 2021, as breathless coverage of the historic attack on the US Capitol transformed into considered reflection on what had taken place. A few weeks later, it became clear the answer wasn't one of the above: it was all four. How did America, the world's self-styled beacon of freedom and democracy, come to this? To what extent were the media – mainstream and social – responsible? And if it really was an early skirmish in a civil war, how should the media deal with that going forward?

The Capitol riot was the culmination of a five-year period in which a populist demagogue had sown mistrust in traditionally reputable sources of information, had hi-jacked a major social media platform with no pushback, and had spread, according to a *Washington Post* count, more than 30,000 lies and misleading statements to a cult audience of national proportions.[1] The traditional media – newspapers and major TV and radio networks – were admirably resilient in the face of powerful verbal abuse from Donald Trump, which often translated into physical abuse from his supporters. Protected by the free speech provisions of the US Constitution's First Amendment, the media could not be silenced, as they might have been in other countries; so instead they were relentlessly discredited.

Abandoning the centre ground

The Trump era forced US journalism into a split which was reflective of American society as a whole. Newspapers such as the *Washington Post* and *New York Times*, as well as broadcast outlets such as CNN, have traditionally claimed to occupy the centre ground, dispassionately reporting the facts and confining opinion strictly to its place, at the back of the publication. But it's very difficult for these outlets to claim today that they are in the centre. The division which is tearing America apart has seen the traditional media come down predominantly on the liberal side. It's evident in the way newspapers cover politics, in how they select, frame and headline stories, and in their choices over what makes it to the front page. On CNN, meanwhile, primetime news presenters now start their programmes with 'their take', ten minutes or more of an illustrated monologue decrying Trump and the Republicans' latest antics, liberally sprinkled with head-shaking and silent looks to camera.

Broadcasters used to have an obligation in the US, as in other countries, to cover stories in a balanced way. For four decades, the so-called 'Fairness Doctrine' required them to air issues of public interest using contrasting voices to represent different points of view. But in 1987, during the Reagan era's crusade against big government and over-regulation, the Federal Communications Commission eliminated the fairness doctrine, leading to the media free-for-all that exists today. That's not to say there are not still genuine editorial dilemmas for responsible broadcast outlets. In the months leading up to the presidential election, for example, a decision had to be made about how to cover Trump's speeches. The words were being spoken by the President – and therefore were inherently newsworthy. But the words contained abuse, exaggeration and a string of falsehoods, primarily about Trump's opponent Joe Biden. Did broadcasters have an obligation to air the speeches anyway? They mostly decided not; instead they recorded them and replayed only the clips they judged to be actually newsworthy.

Inevitably decisions like this led to complaints of censorship from the right. And it wasn't just the TV networks who were in the firing line. There was an outcry when, in the summer of 2020, the *New York Times* published a column by the right-wing Senator Tom Cotton headlined 'Send in the Troops' and calling for an 'overwhelming show of force' against the Black Lives Matter protests which had followed the death of George Floyd.[2] Staff at the paper protested vociferously about the inclusion of the column, even though it was written by an elected US senator and placed on an opinion page. Having initially defended the piece as 'part of a range of opinions, even those we may disagree with', within three days the *New York Times* publisher AG Sulzberger had reversed his position, stating: "Last week we saw a significant breakdown in our editing processes." The same day, the opinion page editor who had been responsible for publishing the column tendered his resignation.

It was just one of a series of occasions in which the *New York Times*, America's traditional paper of record, found itself uncomfortably squeezed between its historic mission to be a platform for all points of view, and a staff and readership that wanted the paper firmly in the liberal camp during the excesses of the Trump era.

Fox loses Trump

As decisions like these at TV networks and newspapers bolstered Trump supporters' view that the mainstream media was their enemy, they turned in two directions; firstly, to an increasingly rabid range of right-wing news channels, and secondly to the unregulated free-for-all that is social media. Surprisingly, perhaps, the erstwhile unassailable Fox News Channel found itself just as caught up in the Trump maelstrom as its more left-of-centre rivals. Trump's relationship with Fox News had become somewhat equivocal in the final year of his presidency. He would spend up to an hour on the phone with the obsequious hosts of the morning show *Fox and Friends* – to the point where they were clearly wondering how to politely get him off the line. But he hated that Fox also broadcast coverage of Joe Biden, his presidential rival – and he was particularly incensed when Rupert Murdoch reportedly told associates that he expected Trump to lose his re-election bid.[3]

The simmering resentment exploded on election night on November 3, 2020, when, to near-universal surprise, Fox's decision desk, tasked with calculating when it was safe to declare each state for one candidate or the other, made an early call that the swing state of Arizona would be won by Biden. All hell broke loose behind the scenes, including an angry phone call from the Trump camp to Rupert Murdoch himself, demanding that the declaration be reversed.[4] Murdoch refused – and the Trump love affair with Fox was definitively over. From that moment on, the President began to promote two upstart alternatives to the Fox News Channel: Newsmax and One America News Network.

The larger of the two, Newsmax, was owned by Chris Ruddy, a Trump buddy and frequent visitor to the President's estate at Mar-a-Lago. Ruddy is a smart man who actually understands journalistic principles; but he saw his chance to turn his network from a fringe outlet into a serious Fox rival. Using unashamed promotion of Trump's election fraud conspiracy theories, often anchored by defectors from Fox, Newsmax grew its ratings from just 58,000 before election day to 1.1 million as the momentous events of January unfolded.[5] One America News was smaller but also enjoyed an audience boost. The former Republican pollster Frank Luntz summed up the developments: Trump and his supporters, he said: "Want their news to affirm them, rather than inform them."[6]

What was Fox to do? The scale of what they were up against was clear from a glance at the Nielsen audience ratings. After the weeks of election fraud allegations culminated in the Capitol riot, it wasn't just Newsmax that was basking in renewed popularity. CNN's audience for January 2021 rose by 151 per cent over the previous year, and MSNBC's was up 65 per cent; but Fox News's audience was down 20 per cent.[7] Just five days after the attempted insurrection, Rupert Murdoch and his son Lachlan had made their decision: there was to be no drawing of breath or sense of shame over what had happened. The Murdochs were looking at a highly profitable empire which was being squeezed between liberal-leaning journalism on one side and right-wing fiction on the other – and they chose to double down and compete with the fiction.

And so, the hours of 'opinion' programming as opposed to 'news' programming were extended. Primetime stars like Sean Hannity and Laura Ingraham hardened their already uncompromising stance over both Biden and the electoral process. Worst of all, Tucker Carlson, the youngest Fox star and a man who attracts speculation that he himself might run for President, abandoned his last modicum of responsibility and started defending believers in the conspiracy theory that had taken hold among Trump supporters: QAnon. "No democratic government can ever tell you what to think," Carlson told his audience, cloaking his promotion of outright fantasy in the First Amendment. "Your mind belongs to you. It is yours and yours alone."[8] There was one man to whom that did not apply, though: Chris Stirewalt, the Fox political editor who had accurately called Arizona for Biden on election night, was fired.[9]

Social media and QAnon

That QAnon had taken such a grip on the American heartland wasn't primarily due to Fox: it was very much a product of social media. As conspiracy theories go, it's in a league of its own: Satanism, child sex trafficking and cannibalism are all in there, elements, it is said, of a global plot to bring down Donald Trump. According to a Reuters report, there were Russian-backed Twitter accounts mentioning QAnon as far back as November 2017.[10] From those roots it grew thanks to a conservative video blogger who promoted the conspiracy on YouTube.

However it wasn't until the Covid-19 crisis of 2020 that QAnon came into its own. Heartland Americans, fired up by Trump's Covid scepticism, were already convinced the whole pandemic was a conspiracy to take away their freedom. It was a short hop to integrating the anti-Covid conspiracy theory with that of QAnon. Everything was a good-versus-evil plot to bring down Trump, take away people's liberties and control their minds using vaccines and, for added value, new 5G phone technology. Between March and June 2020, the first four months of global awareness of Covid, QAnon-related posts grew by nearly 175 per cent on Facebook, 77 percent on Instagram and 63 percent on Twitter.[11] As on many previous occasions, algorithms based on people's interactions, such as comments, likes and shares, propelled the growth, and as had also become habitual, Twitter and Facebook management sat back and let it happen.

But that was about to change. Finally, after years of claiming to be nothing more than neutral platforms for other people's content, the combination of mass deaths from a global pandemic and growing fears over the threat to America's democratic process spurred senior executives at the social media giants to act. In July 2020, Twitter banned thousands of QAnon-related accounts, and changed its algorithms to stem the spread of others. Facebook's own analysis in August revealed it was hosting millions of followers across thousands of QAnon groups and pages. Management stepped in to restrict the activity, then announced in October, less than a month before the presidential election, that the conspiracy theory would be banned from Facebook's platforms altogether.[12]

As history would reveal, it was too little, too late. Trump himself remained on the platforms and his election fraud allegations were widely spread there. It wasn't until after the January 6 Capitol riot that he was finally banned from Twitter, Facebook and most other social media outlets. His expulsion was said by Twitter to be due to a breach of its policy against glorifying violence. Facebook took a similar position and subsequently referred its decision to a recently self-created Oversight Board. Both platforms were facing a serious reckoning over how their *laissez-faire* approach had contributed to such a disastrous moment for American democracy.

How the Trump era shakes down for the social media giants has yet to be determined, but with the left appalled at what was allowed to grow there, and the right howling about censorship, they'll be lucky to escape unscathed. In creating an Oversight Board, Facebook was tacitly nodding to its greatest fear; that its days of unregulated near-monopoly power could be coming to an end. Talk is growing in the United States and other countries of bolstering and enforcing anti-trust laws designed to stop companies like Facebook, Twitter and Alphabet, which owns Google, having the vast power over society that they wield today. On Wednesday January 27, 2021, Mark Zuckerberg made possibly the least surprising statement ever on a Facebook investors' call: "One of the top pieces of feedback that we're hearing from our community right now is that people don't want politics and fighting to take over their experience on our services." After years of raking in billions of dollars by allowing exactly that, Facebook was going to 'turn down the temperature and discourage divisive conversations' by presenting less political content on users' news feeds.[13] How long would that last? It's too early to say; but just five weeks later on March 2, Facebook lifted a ban it had imposed on political advertisements. Clearly there's a balance to be struck between saving civil society and stoking the bottom line.

The future under Biden

As America recovers from the shockwaves of the Trump era, a cooling of the rhetoric would seem like a good idea. Bringing people together to work things out is a trademark of Joe Biden; but with half the country believing he's not legitimately elected, and media magnates happy to cash in on perpetuating that view, it's not clear how much the temperature is going to come down. It is surely a missed opportunity that the Murdochs did not jump the other way after January 6. Fox News will reassert itself against the newer networks whatever happens: it has both the universal distribution and the financial muscle to do so. If only Rupert and Lachlan had reflected on what they had contributed to and decided to moderate their position for the Biden era, the whole landscape of American journalism might have become less polarised, to the benefit of the country as a whole.

But it was not to be. The once centrist press will remain in the liberal camp for the foreseeable future, the battle for viewers and listeners on the right will grow ever more intense and the social media platforms will lick their wounds, fiercely lobby politicians and hope the storm over their outsized power will quietly dissipate. In the final weeks of the Trump presidency there was an oft-stated view that after January 20, 2021, the day of Joe Biden's inauguration, the media should impose a self-denying ordinance on coverage of Trump. He would disappear to Florida, his words would no longer be relevant and there would be a new president with a new agenda to discuss. Months after Trump left the White House, how was that going?

During President Biden's first press conference on March 25 the correspondents couldn't help themselves. They didn't ask a single question about the Covid pandemic, but they did ask Biden if he would run for re-election in 2024 – almost four years later – and if he expected Trump to be his opponent. Yes, he said, he did expect to run again. As to Trump, he joked: "My predecessor? Oh God, I miss him!" Biden didn't have to look far to find him. In the same month, Trump was on a media blitz, giving interviews to a variety of right-wing networks to ensure his successor was not allowed to bask in the achievement of passing a pandemic relief bill and to twist the knife over a growing immigration crisis on the Mexican border. Also prominent in Trump's diatribes – repetition of the 'big lie' about how he'd only lost because of electoral fraud.

When a charismatic populist leader keeps a hold on his millions of followers and continues to disrupt societal norms from exile, journalism is stuck with it. Everything from the legislative agenda to security in the streets to voter suppression measures intended to restrict a fundamental right of all Americans are still influenced by him. These are matters which cannot be ignored.

Like it or not, the media are still talking about Donald Trump today – and they will be for years to come.

Notes

[1] *Washington Post*: "Trump's false or misleading claims total 30,573 over 4 years", January 24, 2021

[2] *New York Times*, June 3, 2020

[3] *Daily Beast*: "Rupert Murdoch Predicts a Landslide Win for Biden", October 15, 2020

[4] Vanity Fair Hive rolling election coverage, November 4, 2020

[5] *New York Times*: "Newsmax, Once a Right-Wing Also-Ran, Is Rising, and Trump Approves", November 22, 2020

[6] *Washington Post*: "Sean Hannity is the face of the post-Trump identity crisis at Fox News", February 2, 2021

[7] Nielsen ratings quoted by Associated Press, February 3, 2021

[8] *The Guardian*, February 5, 2021, quoting FOX News, January 25, 2021

[9] *Los Angeles Times*: "Fox News political editor Chris Stirewalt out in company restructuring", January 19, 2021

[10] Reuters: "QAnon received earlier boost from Russian accounts on Twitter, archives show", November 2, 2020

[11] AFP quoting Institute for Strategic Dialogue analysis, October 6, 2020

[12] BBC: "Facebook bans QAnon conspiracy theory accounts across all platforms", October 6, 2020

[13] CNN: "After building a radicalization engine, Mark Zuckerberg aims to 'turn down the temperature'", January 28, 2021

About the contributor

Bill Dunlop is a former Senior Programme Editor at Channel 4 News, Editorial Director of the pan-European channel Euronews and President and CEO of Eurovision Americas, Inc., the US arm of the European Broadcasting Union. He lives in Washington DC. He has served as a judge at both the Royal Television Society Journalism Awards in London and the International Emmy Awards in New York. Publications include *Perfect Storm: the multiple challenges facing public service news, and why tackling them is vital for democracy* for the EBU, and chapters for the Abramis publications *Brexit, Trump and the Media* and *Anti-Social Media*.

How Trump's abuse of the media has changed America forever

Donald Trump has known and used the power of media throughout his career, but his unprecedented abuse of the previously accepted information channels has changed forever the nature of US politics, society and democracy, argues long-term presidential watcher Professor Philip John Davies

In a response to the January 6 attack by Trump supporters on the US Capitol, the Screen Actors' Guild-American Federation of Television and Radio Artists referred Donald Trump, one of the union's members, to its disciplinary committee. The US President was accused of 'sustaining a reckless campaign of misinformation aimed at discrediting and ultimately threatening the safety of journalists, many of whom are SAG-AFTRA members.' Pre-empting his likely expulsion, Trump wrote to union president Gabrielle Carteris, resigning with the words 'regarding the so-called disciplinary committee hearing aimed at revoking my union membership. Who cares!'

It has not been often Donald Trump appeared so dismissive about his access to media outlets. His television, film, video and advertisement appearances stretch back over four decades. His 14 seasons anchoring *The Apprentice* were preceded and paralleled by numerous film and TV cameos. In 2020 Trump's financial disclosures indicated he received almost $100,000 in pensions from work covered by his SAG-AFTRA membership.

His brief appearance in the very successful movie *Home Alone 2: Lost in New York* proved one of the most memorable, for all its brevity. In a seven second appearance Trump directs the film's star, Macaulay Culkin to the lobby of the New York Plaza hotel. According to the film's director Chris Columbus, Trump's scene was a condition of being allowed to film at the Trump-owned property, 'he did bully his way into the movie'. In January 2021 Culkin tweeted his support for calls to remove the Trump sequences from the movie.

Undermining public trust in recognised media

As his media career grew Trump was increasingly invited to provide social and political commentary and opinion, as well as entertainment, on popular radio shows, on TV talk shows, and most notably from 2011 until his 2015 presidential election campaign on the morning news show *Fox and Friends*. Trump's media experience, his enthusiastic embrace of any available media outlets to deliver bold and often transgressive messages designed to publicise himself and to attack his critics transferred successfully into his campaign for the presidency. His style did not moderate once he had taken office. He challenged the authority, legitimacy and veracity of traditional journalistic sources and their staff in a calculated effort to undermine public trust in the fourth estate.

The fact President Trump took repeated opportunities to attack and undermine those elements in the media whom he perceived as his critics signified he understood well the import of his own symbiotic relationship with media outlets. As Ezra Klein points out in his book *Why We're Polarized*: "If it outrages, it leads." Donald Trump had a knack for attracting coverage that confirmed his critics in their outrage, while bolstering his supporters' belief that he was an indefatigable speaker of truth besieged by a babble of naysaying journalists.

He valued the reach of his media pronouncements and repeatedly spoke of his TV ratings, whether it was to criticise Arnold Schwarzenegger's hosting of *The Apprentice*, or to congratulate himself on the audience for his covid-19 briefings. During his administration's attempt to manage the coronavirus pandemic his tweets referred to his high TV ratings four times more than he mentioned the issue of mask-wearing to reduce life-threatening cross-infection.

Abusing the bully pulpit

President Theodore Roosevelt referred to the special privilege afforded to any president in occupying a 'bully pulpit', by which he meant it was a superb location from which to advocate a positive agenda for the nation. Uniquely among modern presidents Trump used this media centrality to attack by name scores of media outlets and journalists who attracted his ire, calling them 'nasty', 'clueless', 'disgusting', 'fake' and 'the enemy of the people'. Trump's audiences responded to his lead. During the January 6 riot in Washington Trump's supporters in the crowd harassed journalists, accused them of being controlled by China, damaged their equipment, and left graffiti on a door in the Capitol building urging 'Murder the Media'.

It has regularly been reported that Donald Trump's relationship with the media might extend to taking a significant ownership share in the sector. In 2016, when there were doubts that Trump would win the presidency, it was reported Jared Kushner was investigating the alternative of raising funds for a Trump TV network to add to the family business portfolio. Similarly, in 2020 *Forbes* reported Trump's post-election rift with Fox News could be the precursor to the creation of a Trump media company. In February 2021, the US House of Representatives Committee on Oversight and Reform followed up rumours that a proposal raising legal concerns had been made 'to provide President Donald Trump with an ownership stake in Parler', a social networking platform popular with conservative internet users and used extensively by participants in the January 6 Washington riot. While a media channel led by former President Trump showed no signs of emerging soon after his exit from the White House, he did suffer the loss of the outlet that became his major media 'channel': Twitter.

The legitimation of alternative sources of information

Twitter suspended the President's account on January 8, 2021, 'due to the risk of further incitement of violence', confirming a month later this was a permanent sanction. Until that time the platform had been a key element in Trump's media armoury. Many of Trump's Twitter-reported 88 million followers were not in the USA, and it is impossible to calculate how many of the follower accounts were fake. The President reached an audience of millions of American voters this way, but most Americans will have become aware of Trump's tweeted opinions and declarations second hand, when a tweet became the fodder for repeating and reporting on the myriad of television, cable, print, social media and other outlets that have emerged in recent years.

The President made very active use of Twitter, of press briefings, of other unregulated opportunities like the mass rallies the Trump administration continued throughout his four years in office and in the pandemic to generate media coverage. This strategy took the opportunity presented by an apparently ever-expanding number of different media outlets to keep Trump front and centre in American media coverage. The Pew Research Center found newspaper newsrooms lost 36,000 positions, or 51 per cent of their staff, in the 11 years to 2019. Digital newsrooms grew in the same period, but the overall loss of professional journalists amounted to 23 per cent.

Meanwhile the number of cable and internet delivered TV stations increased, with longer established stations like Fox and MSNBC being joined by others such as Newsmax, OANN and Right Side Broadcasting. Facebook and Twitter are social media platforms which provide the opportunity for many groups and opinion leaders to deliver opinion, analysis and news. In addition to these well-known providers there are others such as Parler, Gab, 8kun and Telegram. These media distributors are generally subjected to little regulation and have been seized on as a useful location especially by conservative opinion leaders and groups. An examination by the digital activist organisation ACRONYM found even on the relatively long-established platform Facebook, right-wing political groups dominated political activity. Another study by New York University's Center for

Cybersecurity found far-right content on Facebook attracting more engagement than other political posts. Together these developments have built an alternative body of media outlets to that offered by the mainstream media that Donald Trump has expended so much energy undermining.

Further research from Pew's Journalism and Media group on 'How Americans Navigated the News in 2020' found evidence that during election year around 50 per cent of the American public turned only to 'echo chambers' of media that reflected their pre-existing political beliefs. Less than a quarter of those surveyed used the traditional media of network television, print and radio as their major sources for political news, while almost as many (18 per cent) relied mainly on social media. Nearly half of those preferring social media were in the youngest age group, under 30 years-old. The fact those who took their news mainly from social media were less informed about current events may in part reflect the greater seniority of the other groups in addition to any correlation with choice of media source.

Influencing Republicans

A specific Trump impact was noted in the Pew research. Among Republican-leaning respondents around 30 per cent of respondents reported they relied mostly on Donald Trump, the Trump campaign and the Trump White House as a major source of election and coronavirus news. This section of the electorate was measurably more likely even than other Republicans in the electorate to believe the pandemic was being exaggerated and the administration's responses were adequate. They were also more likely to be concerned about the threat to the election posed by voter fraud and voting by mail – unsupported allegations that the President was promoting as part of his campaign to undermine public faith in any election result that did not go in his favour. This group additionally had little faith in the traditional media reporting on these topics.

The contemporary media landscape, with its multiple points of access and its echo chambers, has expanded the opportunity for key social media figures to influence the news agenda. An examination of social media activity in the last five months of 2020 conducted by the Election Integrity Partnership found that a small number of account holders, including Donald Trump and other members of his family, generated most of the disinformation contributing to the 'Big Lie' that the presidential election was stolen. This narrative, spread, repeated and amplified by sympathetic media sources large and small, helped to motivate the deadly January 6 attack on the US Capitol and to prompt threats to the safety of the nation's legislature and to US Vice-President Pence.

After the economic crash that ended the George W Bush years, growth steadily returned and was sustained through the Obama administration and into the Trump presidency. The recovery was not evenly spread, leaving some communities in economic sloth and stagnation, as well as feeling threatened by other social and political changes. Trade policy and globalisation, immigration, health care, taxation and similar topics are regular undercurrents in US politics and the debate on these and similar topics becomes more heated in times of economic and social tension. In such times the nation is likely to benefit from leadership with an open and uniting message.

Donald Trump embraced neither openness nor unity during his time in the White House. *The Washington Post* tallied over 30,000 false and misleading statements made by President Trump during his term of office. While some of this mass of misinformation appeared to recognise the feelings of population groups who felt threatened by some social and political changes of recent decades this manipulative rhetoric offered many distractions, fanned the flames of mistrust and pinpointed enemies rather than offering solutions.

Links to January 6

The power of modern media influencers, media echo chambers and media bubbles was evidenced in some of those who took part in the January 6 violence. Jenna Ryan, a real estate agent from Texas, who considered herself 'leaning Republican' and a lukewarm Trump supporter, became a reader of right-wing websites Epoch Times and Gateway Pundit, and a viewer of Alex Jones' *Infowars* and Stephen Bannon's *War Room: Pandemic*, and communicated with like-minded friends on Facebook. It was her Facebook posts from the US Capitol that brought the FBI to arrest her. 'I was down there based on what my president said', she told *The Washington Post*.

Michigan Republicans Meshawn Maddock and Ryan Kelley pinned the blame for instigating violence on Democrats, '[they] have got antifa; they have got BLM'. Maddock and Kelley helped organise 19 coaches of Michiganders to the US Capitol demonstrations. According to *The New York Times* the range of media they used in this effort included Twitter, Fox News, the Bridge Michigan news organisation, MLive.com, Parler, Stop the Steal news conferences, *The Detroit News*, Facebook, and *The Lansing State Journal*. By February 2021 Maddock had been elected co-chair of the Michigan Republican Party and Kelley declared his interest in running for the state governorship.

Rachel Powell, from Pennsylvania, became known as 'the Pink Hat Lady' from the images of her circulated by the FBI. According to *The New Yorker* the covid crisis led her to engage with conspiracy theories about both the coronavirus and the presidential election. Like Ryan, she was influenced by Alex Jones' *Infowars*, and had accepted Donald Trump and his personal attorney Rudy Giuliani as significant sources of information.

Long-term impact

Donald Trump is not currently a Twitter presence. President Joe Biden shows little of his predecessor's determination to dominate the media by any means. The atmosphere in the US political media world seems calmer, but the elements which fed five years of turmoil are still present.

The Republican Party regularly attracts only a minority of the national vote at presidential and senatorial level. The GOP's recent successes in capturing the White House and the US Senate have depended on the country's use of an Electoral College to select the president, and electing two senators per state, regardless of population size. Both practices currently operate to magnify the input of Republican states and of the smaller number of Republican voters nationwide. In some Republican states the party also gerrymanders constituency boundaries to increase its representation in the US House of Representatives and in state legislatures. The party's leadership has also resisted bipartisanship and deployed voter suppression techniques to protect its power. The US electorate is becoming more diverse over time, and some research suggests if this demographic shift follows historic patterns, it will increase the proportion of Democratic voters. Alternative projections posit that emerging and expanding voting groups may not be so predictable and may be open to Republican persuasion.

With margins so tight, and the future to play for, the link between politics and media becomes increasingly important. A media structure which has almost no regulatory requirements for balance and fairness and provides powerful echo chambers which can destabilise traditional media while amplifying partisanship currently works to the advantage of the Republicans. Quite apart from the possibility former President Trump may choose to run again for the White House, there are potential leaders of that party emerging who clearly take the Donald Trump style as their model.

Media proliferation is likely to continue and the engagement of politicians with those media and their search for new media is likely to deepen and extend. According to a Pew Research report 2019/20 saw the median Twitter and Facebook output of a Member of the US House of Representatives at more than 3,000 posts, with two-thirds of these posts being tweets. These aggregate 2.2 million messages were an increase of 50 per cent over the previous Congressional term. Follower numbers had almost trebled in four years and the Representatives' output had received two billion favourites and reactions. These numbers suggest the search for clicks and for other media connections centred on an influencer will remain a strong factor in contemporary US politics.

About the contributor
Philip John Davies is Emeritus Professor of American Studies at De Montfort University in Leicester and Distinguished Fellow at Oxford University's Rothermere American Institute. He was also Director of the Eccles Centre for American Studies at the British Library. He is an internationally recognised expert on US politics, having observed every US election since 1968, and has written extensively on American politics, elections and presidents.

Donald Trump: Populist victim of partisan impeachment?

Electing a self-proclaimed 'Disrupter-in-Chief' provided America with a tumultuous four-years of populist-style leadership, says Clodagh Harrington. A presidential term laden with unpredictable developments culminated in a finale involving the Commander-in-Chief of the United States facing an impeachment charge of 'incitement to insurrection'

For an individual who prides himself on deal making and norm-busting, Donald Trump may have surpassed his own expectations by becoming the first and only American president to have been doubly impeached. By any measure, this was a stunning development, not least because it resulted in him being twice acquitted. These are measures of the toxic political environment in which he presided, as both processes were as divisive as the circumstances in which they took place. So what can we deduce from the repeated utilisation of this emergency measure, supposedly drawn on for only the highest of crimes and misdemeanours? To what extent were these impeachment proceedings little more than an opportunity for opposition to weaponise the process, or were they genuinely cases where Watergate-levels of political artillery were required?

A moment of context may help. As anyone with an interest in US history will know, the 1970s was a time when the potential for partisan feuding was a strong as it ever was, and it is clear Richard Nixon would have gone to prison if the process had been allowed to run its course. Even those who remained loyal to Tricky Dicky were mindful by his final days in office that the bell was tolling. The president resigned before inevitable impeachment proceedings could begin against him. Broadly, the conclusions drawn from the Watergate crisis were that the system worked, but it very nearly didn't. The nation heaved a sigh of relief as Andrew Johnson retained the title of the only US president to face impeachment.

'Loud threats and bitter menaces'?

Fast forward to the Trump era, and the president was accused of impeachment charges arguably more serious than any Nixon potentially faced. The environment, inevitably partisan, was not comparable to that of Watergate, or even the more recent examples of Iran Contra or the Clinton scandals. If parallels were to be drawn, they were more in line with the impeachment articles drawn up against Andrew Johnson in 1868. Among the many accusations made against the seventeenth president, Item Ten accused him being regularly inclined to 'make and declare, with a loud voice, certain intemperate, inflammatory and scandalous harangues, and therein utter loud threats and bitter menaces…' (US Senate: 1868).

Such charges may not have differed significantly between the seventeenth and forty-fifth presidents, as populist rabble-rousing remained a durable vote-winner. Accusing the incumbent of bringing 'the high office of the President of the United States into contempt, ridicule and disgrace, to the great scandal of all good citizens' was a rather timeless charge, fitting both a nineteenth and twenty-first century populist leader (US Senate: 1868).

There was, however, one incomparable aspect. This was the platform from which the nation's leader could attract attention via the mainstreaming of new, specifically social, media in the twenty-first century. As a result of the upsurge in technologies that even a generation earlier were unthinkable, citizens everywhere had unprecedented access to information, mis-information and dis-information. Amongst the enormous positives that came with such developments, the potentially catastrophic downside for society was an undermining of objective truths. There may have been diametrically opposing political opinions, populist rhetoric and partisan mud-slinging in 1868 but generally speaking, as with the Watergate era, the truth remained an objective entity.

Hail to the Disrupter-in-Chief

By 2017, Americans were living in an era of 'alternative facts.' The term coined by White House spokesperson Kellyanne Conway sent a clear message that there was no need to engage with a truth that did not suit one's purpose (Conway: 2017). Other truths were available, to such an extent that former President Obama declared that as a result, the country had evolved to a state of 'epistemological crisis' (Obama: 2020). Had it merely been a case of members of the public finding their own 'facts' on notoriously unreliable information platforms, this would have come with its own set of problems. However, when the Commander-in-Chief of the world's most powerful nation engaged in falsehoods and conspiracy promotion, the potential political impact was seismic.

Candidate Trump's style of populism was on display from the early days of the 2016 campaign trail and evolved when he took office to the 'Disrupter-in-Chief', a role that delighted his supporters (Feldmann: 2018). Perhaps then it was not overly surprising to find impeachment rumblings had begun only months after Trump had settled in the Oval Office. In 2017, Congressman Al Green (D-TX) formally accused the president of 'obstruction of justice' arguing that the president had 'sown discord among the people of the United States' (House Resolution 646: 2017).

Among the allegations by Green and his colleagues that year were Trump's handling of the far-right marches in Charlottesville and his responses to NFL footballers kneeling in solidarity with the Black Lives Matters movement. Unsurprisingly, the Democrat initiative did not get the required votes, but this did not prevent him from repeatedly making efforts to have the president impeached. As it turned out, the challenges that did stick against President Trump involved allegations of possible electoral interference and impropriety. In the first Senate impeachment trial, it was the role of a hostile foreign power that was under examination.

Impeachment – Round One

In March 2019, Robert Mueller's two-year investigation drew to a close, culminating with a report which fell short of overtly concluding there had been direct collusion between the Trump campaign and the Russian state (Mueller: 2019). Beyond this reprieve, trouble continued to brew for the president. Nine months later the House Judiciary Committee announced it would be proceeding with two articles of impeachment against the president. These were 'abuse of power' and 'obstruction of Congress' in relation to the president's dealings with Ukraine, with specific accusations of 'betrayed the nation by abusing his high office to enlist a foreign power in corrupting democratic elections' (House Res. 660: 2019).

Unsurprisingly, the Senate voted in February 2020 along party lines to acquit the president. Mitt Romney was the notable Republican exception who voted in favour of conviction, later stating that it was the hardest decision of his life (Romney: 2020). The BBC's Nick Bryant commented that Romney's tearful speech sounded almost like 'a requiem for moderate Republicanism' (Bryant: 2021, 305). The president, buoyed by victory and the fierce loyalty of his fans, once again lived to fight another day. A televised victory rally was held in the East Room of the White House the morning after his acquittal, where invited guests applauded as the president lambasted the investigation as 'evil' and 'corrupt' (ABC News: 2020).

Public opinion fell along partisan lines, further fractured by the media sources they chose to obtain their news from. Those who only engaged with right-wing news outlets tended to view the president's motivation in a different light to those who chose to follow liberal media sources. This remained true beyond simple party identity, hence individuals adhering to the same political party may have different views, depending on their range of their media consumption. The narrower the diet, the more entrenched the views (Jurkowitz & Mitchell: 2020).

Delivering the 2020 State of the Union address on the eve of his acquittal, the president refused to shake hands with Nancy Pelosi who in turn ripped up her copy of his speech. This visual exchange of hostilities demonstrated in stark terms the level of mutual vitriol, compounded by the president's decision to award the Presidential Medal of Freedom to radio host Rush Limbaugh. In bestowing the nation's highest civilian honour on a right-wing shock jock who took aim at everyone from the first black president to female college students, the nation was left in no doubt as to Donald Trump's allegiance. (Walsh: 2021)

Impeachment – Round Two

Continuing in the vein of being a president like no other, by January 2021 Donald Trump faced a second impeachment. This time was more shocking for many in that it came as a result of the storming of the Capitol on January 6. Footage of an angry mob forcing their way into the chambers and offices of Congressional representatives was viewed around the world with disbelief. In the aftermath, with five known deaths including a police officer on duty, the president faced a number of options. Resignation would have allowed the Vice-President to step up. The House of Representatives passed a resolution which requested that Mike Pence invoke the 25th amendment to the constitution. Unsurprisingly, the VP was not inclined to claim his boss was unfit to serve and so wrote a letter to House Speaker Pelosi outlining his reasons for declining. He did not deem the move to be constitutional (Pence: 2021).

Instead, Trump was faced with a single article of impeachment. By any measure, 'incitement of insurrection' was a dramatic charge, not least as video footage was released of the security breach and just how close the mob came to the vice president, house speaker and others. The noose and gallows which appeared on the West Front of the US Capitol were not considered tongue in cheek props and the images taken on the day were verified as genuine by credible media sources including the Associated Press (AP: 2021).

With only the briefest of hindsight, it became clear those who had dismissed the 2016 Trump presidential campaign as at best a publicity stunt, at worst a bad joke had seriously underestimated both his campaign prowess and voter appeal. It was the former reality television star and brand mogul who continued to have many last laughs. Those who covered the 2016 campaign stated that only by being present at his rallies could the appeal really be understood (Stanley: 2016). The mutual exchange of love between the man and his crowd was palpable. Everything that drove the mainstream media and its adherents insane with liberal rage worked in clear reverse with his followers. They prized everything from his Make America Great Again hat to his liberating disregard for political correctness or, indeed, facts.

Beyond the rallies, Twitter was the realm where Trump could be his populist self as bluntly as in person, without the inconvenience of media gatekeeping or filter. A public adherent to the maxim of 'all publicity is good publicity,' the fact that a notable proportion of his Twitter followers were appalled by his tweets was doubtless a boon. Soon his opponents were hanging on his every tweet as much as his supporters were. This is not to suggest Trump was uninterested in utilising conventional media for political gain. He did, however, demonstrate that he knew by churning out controversial messages at opportune times, sure as night follows day, his tweets would show up on the cable news shows allowing him to repeatedly dominate the news cycle.

His mistrust of the mainstream media was not without grounding. In 2016, the MSM had talked down the chances of his victory (somewhat accurately, as he lost the popular vote) and when it was clear he would be the president, the coverage remained negative and disparaging. As his years in office progressed, there were few positive moments in his relationship with the MSM. Twitter remained his preferred platform and he successfully rallied the vast number of supporters that made up many, if not all, of his 80+ million followers.

Denying 2020 presidential election defeat

Perhaps his most dangerous use of the social media platform was his continuous refusal to accept the outcome of the 2020 presidential election. At first, his claims seemed absurd, but as time went on, and the conspiracy theory around the stolen election gathered pace and energy, the seriousness of the situation was clear. By January 2021, two-thirds of Republicans polled stated they still believed the election had not been free or fair (Laughlin & Shelburn: 2021).

As crowds descended on Washington DC to vent their frustration, Trump did what he does best. He rallied the crowd both online and offline and in doing so engaged in what Congress termed 'incitement to insurrection' (House Res. 24: 2021). The outcome involved a body count of five. Later that day, Trump tweeted messages of love to those at the Capitol and another (later removed) stating 'we will remember this day forever' (Trump: 2021). The statement holds true, although hardly in the way that the president meant. The populism of Trump came at a high price, not only in lives lost that day, but in the undermining of public trust in the democratic process and a fracturing of political norms. And that is too high a price for any nation to bear.

References

Bryant, Nick (2021) When America Stopped Being Great: A History of the President, London: Bloomsbury.
Comey, James (2018) A Higher Loyalty: Truth, Lies and Leadership, London: Macmillan.
Conley, Richard (2020) Donald Trump and American Populism, Edinburgh: Edinburgh University Press.

Conway, Kellyanne, Meet the Press (2017) NBC News January 22. Available at https://www.nbcnes.com/meet-the-press/video/conway-press-secretary-gave-alternative-facts-860142147643 Date accessed 31 March 2021.

Coppins, McKay, How Mitt Romney Decided Trump is Guilty, The Atlantic. Available at https://www.theatlantic.com/politics/archive/2020/02/romney-impeach-trump/606127/ Date accessed 31 March 2021.

Feldmann, Linda (2018) Disrupter in Chief: How Donald Trump is Changing the Presidency, Christian Science Monitor, January 4. Available at https://www.csmonitor.com/USA/Politics/2018/0104/Disrupter-in-chief-How-Donald-Trump-is-changing-the-presidency Date accessed 31 March 2021.

Goldberg, Jeffrey (2020), Why Obama Fears for our Democracy, The Atlantic, November 16. Available at https://www.theatlantic.com/ideas/archive/2020/11/why-obama-fears-for-our-democracy/617087/ Date accessed 31 March 2021.

Green, Al (2020) Washington Journal, C-Span, December 6. Available at https://www.c-span.org/video/?438169-3/washington-journal-representative-al-green-d-tx-discusses-call-impeach-president-trump Date accessed 31 March 2021.

H.Res.24 - Impeaching Donald John Trump, President of the United States, for High Crimes and Misdemeanors (2021) Available at https://www.congress.gov/bill/117th-congress/house-resolution/24/text Date accessed 31 March 2021.

H.Res.646 - Impeaching Donald John Trump, President of the United States, of High Misdemeanors (2017) Available at https://www.congress.gov/bill/115th-congress/house-resolution/646/text Date accessed 31 March 2021.

Harrington, Clodagh and Waddan, Alex (2020) 'Obama V Trump: The Politics of Presidential Legacy and Rollback, Edinburgh: Edinburgh University Press.

House Committee on the Judiciary, The Impeachment of Donald John Trump Evidentiary Record from the House of Representatives (116th) Available at https://judiciary.house.gov/the-impeachment-of-donald-john-trump/ Date accessed 31 March 2021.

Johnson, Andrew (1868) The Impeachment of the President of the United States. Available at https://www.senate.gov/artandhistory/history/common/briefing/Impeachment_Johnson.htm Date accessed 31 March 2021.

Jurkowitz, Mark and Mitchell, Amy (2020) Views About Ukraine: Impeachment Story Connect Closely with where Americans Get Their News, January 24. Available at https://www.journalism.org/2020/01/24/views-about-ukraine-impeachment-story-connect-closely-with-where-americans-get-their-news/ Date accessed 31 March 2021.

Laughlin, Nick et al (2021) How Voters' Trust in Elections Shifted in Response to Biden's Victory, Morning Consult, January 27. Available at https://morningconsult.com/form/tracking-voter-trust-in-elections/ Date accessed 31 March 2021.

Mueller, Robert (2019) Report on the Investigation in the 2016 Presidential Election, Washington DC. Available at https://www.justice.gov/archives/sco/file/1373816/download Date accessed 31 March 2021.

Pence, Mike (2021) Letter to Speaker Nancy Pelosi, January 12. Available at https://trumpwhitehouse.archives.gov/briefings-statements/letter-speaker-nancy-pelosi-25th-amendment-resolution/ Date accessed 31 March 2021.

Reeves, Jay et al, Capitol Assault a More Sinister Attack Than First Appeared, Associated Press, January 11. Available at https://apnews.com/article/donald-trump-ap-top-news-michael-pence-nancy-pelosi-capitol-siege-14c73ee280c256ab4ec193ac0f49ad54 Date accessed 31 March 2021.

Sonmez, Felicia et al (2019) Democrats Accuse Trump of Criminal Bribery, Wire Fraud in Report that Explains Articles of Impeachment, Washington Post, December 17. Available at https://www.washingtonpost.com/politics/trump-impeachment-live-updates/2019/12/16/3529da74-1ff1-11ea-bed5-880264cc91a9_story.html Date accessed 31 March 2021.

Tim Stanley (2016) The 2016 Presidential Election, University College London, November 17. (Live event)

Trump, Donald J. (2021) Twitter, January 6, 11:01pm. Available at https://twitter.com/jonkarl/status/1359212589453049873 Date accessed 31 March 2021.

Walsh, Joe (2021) Rush Limbuagh's Biggest – and Most Controversial – Moments, Forbes, February 17. Available at https://www.forbes.com/sites/joewalsh/2021/02/17/rush-limbaughs-biggest---and-most-controversial---moments/?sh=c02bcc227d6a Date accessed 31 March 2021.

About the contributor

Clodagh Harrington is Associate Professor of American Politics at De Montfort University, Leicester. Her main research area is the US Presidency and domestic policy. In 2020, EUP published *Obama V Trump: The Politics of Presidential Legacy and Rollback*, co-authored with Alex Waddan (University of Leicester). She is currently working on a subsequent project which will track the Biden administration's efforts to undermine the Trump legacy. Dr Harrington is a member of the PSA, BAAS and APG and is a regular contributor to UK and international media.

The lie in the machine: Truth, big tech and the limits of free speech

Mark Thompson looks at the long-standing history of rumour-that-becomes-fact – and wonders where is it all going

In the summer of the year 1255 the remains of a nine-year-old English boy were found at the bottom of a well. The boy had gone missing a few weeks earlier. A rumour soon started spreading that he'd been kidnapped, tortured and then crucified by members of the local Jewish community.

None of that was true. But some 90 Jews were arrested and 19 executed before the madness abated and the killing stopped. The false story gained currency in part because it had powerful backers, the Bishop of Lincoln, where the boy lived, and King Henry III among them.

We don't know if either believed the story, but both certainly benefited from it. The bishop acquired a new child martyr and a monetisable shrine. The king leapt on it as an excuse to confiscate the wealth of the Jews of England.

This was not the first instance of the so-called blood libel in England. A century earlier the death of another boy, William of Norwich, had also been blamed on the Jews. News of that death inspired copy-cat rumours that became rarer in the modern era but persisted through the 19th and 20th centuries, and spread from Europe to the Middle East and other parts of the world.

But to spell out what is already obvious, the ghost of little St Hugh is still far from exorcised. The conspiracy theory at the heart of QAnon is essentially the false legend of William and Hugh.

It was to free imaginary child victims just like them that Edgar Welch burst into the Comet Ping Pong pizza restaurant in Washington DC in December 2016 armed with an AR-15 and a revolver. The fantasy that Welch had discovered on Instagram was more elaborate than the rumour of little St Hugh, but the family resemblance is clear: children are being kidnapped, trafficked and murdered both for the purposes of paedophilia and also so that their blood can be drunk or extracted for a substance – adrenochrome – which, according to a cod-scientific claim derived from popular culture, offers a psychedelic high and eternal youth to those who imbibe it.

Modern myths

In the Pizzagate version of this modern version of the myth, many of the children were being held and tortured by the paedophiles in secret tunnels under the basement of Comet Ping Pong.

Which is why, when Welch turned up at the restaurant to save them, he asked to be directed to the basement. But there isn't one. No basement. No tunnels. No children – or at least no trafficked children, just real, healthy, free children eating pizza with their parents, children whom Edgar Welch then scared out of their wits by discharging his AR-15 into the ceiling.

It's hard to imagine a more thorough or widely publicised debunking of a conspiracy theory than this hapless one-man assault on Comet Ping Pong. But it's central to the QAnon conspiracy theory that holds that Donald Trump has been leading a secret counter-conspiracy to outwit and defeat the cannibal-paedophiles.

But Pizzagate has had other after-lives. A less overtly racist and ideological strain of it became one of 2020's bigger hits on Tik Tok, attracting many tens of millions of views by young people around the world. This resistance to refutation is one of the most important features of this kind of all-encompassing conspiracy theory.

The theory is plastic, endlessly extensible and doesn't strive for consistency or conventional believability anyway. Anyone who questions the truth of the conspiracy – or presents evidence which debunks it – can readily be incorporated into it as new villains. Awkward events like January 2021's assault on the US Capitol can be explained away as 'false flag' operations mounted by the bad guys, or 'fake news' produced by an establishment media which is of course itself a co-conspirator. In this way, evidence which debunks the conspiracy can serve to thicken the plot and even reinforce belief among the faithful.

Five deaths, two subsequent suicides and dozens of serious injuries after the assault on Capitol. Around a third of US voters claiming to believe that Donald Trump definitely or probably won the 2020 presidential election, something you can only believe if you buy into a covert exercise in electoral fraud so vast and involving so many Republican as well as Democratic officials – perhaps including Vice-president Pence and Senate minority leader Mitch McConnell? – that it's only conceivable in the context of a conspiracy of QAnon proportions.

But it's not just the election. QAnon supporters have also been active in fomenting opposition to Covid lockdowns in many countries, and seeding doubt over the safety of Covid and other vaccines.

Anthony Warner, who blew himself up in January 2021 along with a fair bit of downtown Nashville, was apparently a devotee of the adjacent Lizard people or Reptilian conspiracy theory which holds that many of the world's movers and shakers – including Her Majesty the Queen, the Bush family and the Rothschilds – are in fact alien reptiles.

This theory has been championed in recent decades by the British conspiracist – and former BBC colleague of mine – David Icke. You'd have thought its origins must lie in mid-20th century comic books and science fiction, but this myth dates at least back to late Victorian times, Theosophy and visceral fears of mass immigration and the insidious infiltration of society by 'others' who may not be quite as human as we are. It's always had an anti-Semitic flavour. Certainly many present-day advocates of the theory seem to regard the terms 'lizard' and 'Jew' as cognate.

The lizards in politics

Some 4 per cent of the sample – equivalent to 12m Americans – told one set of pollsters back in 2013 that they believed that 'lizard people control politics'. Multiple US polls have found that around a quarter of respondents, equivalent to over 80m people, claim to give credence to at least part of the broader QAnon system of beliefs – though in this context words like 'credence' and 'belief' deserve closer examination and we'll return to them.

As President, Donald Trump steadfastly refused to condemn QAnon, noting that its followers 'like me very much'. Particularly towards the end of the campaign he seemed to dog-whistle to them with pledges like the commitment to end the 'scourge of human trafficking' in America.

In a survey of 2,000 people in the UK in September 2020, again around a quarter of respondents agreed with the statements that 'elites in Hollywood, politics, the media and other powerful positions' are secretly engaged in extensive child trafficking and abuse, and that there is 'a single group of people who secretly control events and rule the world together.' Among younger respondents, claimed belief was higher.

QAnon is also gaining traction in France – the French minister for citizenship, Marlène Schiappa recently called its rise there 'very worrying' – as well in Germany and many other countries.

But what exactly are we dealing with? Sometimes it presents as a political protest movement but if so, it's a pretty strange one.

A September 2020 poll of QAnon fans found that, though most were supporters of Donald Trump, 28 per cent planned to vote for Joe Biden, while a 2018 Vox analysis of the QAnon subreddit found overlaps not just with conservative subreddits but with Way of the Bern, a subreddit for Bernie Sanders followers. If QAnon was a political party, in other words, its make-up might actually be to the left of today's Republican party.

So should we see it less as an ideological movement than a popular one – perhaps a last despairing revolt by America's white left-behinds, those whom automation and globalization and other broad social and economic changes have, at least in their own eyes, relegated to the bottom of the heap?

That doesn't quite fit either. QAnon supporters seem to be drawn from a wide spectrum of economic and social backgrounds and include veterans, law enforcement officials, lawyers and many other professionals.

What they do seem to be is predominantly white. Among Christian religious groups, in a post-election survey by the American Enterprise Institute, 27 per cent of white evangelicals said they believed the central QAnon assertion that President Trump has been secretly battling a ring of powerful paedophiles, compared to 15 per cent among white mainline protestants, 11 per cent of Latino Catholics and 7 per cent of Black protestants.

QAnon certainly triggers straightforward instances of 'fake news' – in other words false statements of fact presented as if accurate reportage – but the myth itself bears a closer resemblance to fictional storytelling than it does to conventional political discourse or journalism. And, to borrow a term from TV, it's radically cross-genre with features drawn from comic-books, movies, television series, and video-games.

Where racism is absent
In popular entertainment the racism is usually absent and the message may even be anti-racist – in V for Vendetta Jews are among the victims not the perpetrators, in Watchmen, black heroes turn the tables on white racists – but alas it's all too easy to take the now popularised narrative shapes and re-insert the older, uglier meanings.

And that's what QAnon does. There's no attempt at originality or coherence. There's no one author. It's a crowd-sourced mash-up, a greatest hits of all the old conspiracy-theories, and I suspect that much of its audience – including many of those who claim to pollsters that they believe the lot – are not really 'supporters' or 'true believers' in any real sense – but just that: an audience on the lookout for escapism and pleasingly spiteful answers to difficult questions.

Like radicalisation inspired by religious extremism, of those who consume the noxious material only a tiny percentage may turn to real-world action. But if only a fraction of one percent of the quarter or third of Americans who feel some level of affinity with QAnon are radicalised to the point of violence, that still represents many thousands of potential domestic terrorists.

There's one more puzzle to consider: which is that odd asymmetry of scepticism by which a believer can embrace QAnon with childlike credulity yet dismiss every rebuttal of it with the distrustfulness of a seasoned cynic.

Certainly since the Kennedy assassination and Watergate, the public have been coached by popular fiction, any number of politicians and more or less every conspiracy-theory going to believe that, whether it's UFOs or Covid masks, the government and elites lie about everything.

If everything is a lie, why not choose to believe the nuttiest, most entertaining lie out there? And if you suspect that your belief, or half-belief, in it will freak out the establishment, well so much the better.

This is why conventional anti fake news tactics are unlikely to do much to diminish support for QAnon and the false claims about the real world – like the stolen election – that it has spawned.

Nor should we hope for too much from political repudiation. It's very easy for politicians to dismiss the theory as such – as Republican leaders in both the Senate and the House have done – and yet to continue to give house room to the false real-world claims which have flowed from it.

Rather than just focus on the counter-factuality of these conspiracies and the false claims that flow from them, my instinct is that labels and health-warnings should emphasise the racist essence of QAnon and fables like it.

Just like the legend of little St Hugh, QAnon is essentially a supremacist fantasy about a white population rising up to take on and expose, expel or destroy hated ethnic minorities and other despised groups – and the most dangerous thing about it is not that it is fantastical nonsense, which it certainly is, but that it is hateful, divisive and liable to prompt violence among some of its followers.

Even racists understand that explicit anti-Jewish, anti-black, anti-Latino racism no longer plays well in public. QAnon and theories like it dress the prejudice up and disguise it with laser beams and lizard men, or throw in extraneous targets – Tom Hanks, the Queen – to muddy the water.

So show them up. Call them out. Shame those who spread these poisonous lies and those politicians who, like the Bishop of Lincoln three quarters of a millennium ago, put their own advantage above the public good by refusing to condemn them.

First Amendment limits

US courts have always accepted some limits to the exercise of the First Amendment. For instance, 'fighting talk' – speech which is intended to incite and lead to immediate violence – is not protected by the amendment. Nor is defamation, nor child pornography. Other countries also exclude hate speech defined in various ways. In the UK, for example, earlier legislation on incitement to racial hatred were expanded to include religious hatred in a 2006 act.

Now at least in principle, it might be argued that Donald Trump's riling up of his own supporters in the run-up to and aftermath of the January 6 Capitol attack was the kind of incitement excluded under the 'fighting talk' doctrine and so not protected by the First Amendment.

But the Supreme Court has – correctly in my view – set very tight conditions for the kind of 'incitement' that would lose its protection under the amendment and, although Trump's live remarks his supporters at the Ellipse just before the assault, and his other messaging around it, have not yet and may never come before the courts, it seems likely that they would be deemed to be protected by the amendment.

But – a big but – there's another central principle of free speech that's often forgotten. Free expression also implies an absolute right not to publish. Under the First Amendment, the government cannot compel speech – it cannot prevent you from publishing but it also can't force you to publish anything. In a repressive society, publishers often have no choice but to reproduce whatever lies the government wishes to promulgate. In free societies, the publishers make up their own minds what to include or not.

This is a live issue in many countries. In the US, for instance, over the years there have been a number of attempts by conservatives in different states to enforce a right of reply whereby politicians who are accused, say, of malfeasance in a newspaper would get a guaranteed right of reply. All have been thrown out by the courts because they constitute an attempt by the state to compel speech.

More recently Trump and a number of congressional Republicans have talked up the possibility of removing the extensive immunity digital companies enjoy from legal action over the content they distribute unless those companies also agree to give equal prominence to right-wing voices. This too seems to constitute a proposal to compel speech and would probably founder in the courts in the unlikely event it made it into law.

And, to state the obvious, no platform or publication has any legal or moral obligation to disseminate hateful lies like the ones contained in QAnon – indeed it's deeply regrettable that the major platforms waited so long to begin the arduous work of rooting it out. It's probably impossible to expunge the racist conspiracy theories completely but pushing them out of the sunlight and into the shadowy margins of digital space is still eminently worthwhile.

'A bad precedent'

So what should we make of Jack Dorsey's thoughtful remark that his own decision to ban Donald Trump from Twitter was a 'bad precedent'? As you've heard, I don't believe it was in terms of freedom of expression. But there's another consideration – which is about the extraordinary concentration of power that lies in his hands and those of a handful of other leaders in tech.

Because one can believe that the major platforms behaved responsibly in this instance and still worry about what would happen if one of them had taken the opposite view, or ejected a president or political party for purely personal reasons, or indeed fallen themselves under the spell of QAnon.

Is it really acceptable that half a dozen companies – perhaps in the end half a dozen individuals – should wield so much influence over, if not the totality of content available on the internet, then that portion which most people consume most of the time? What protections are there against the purely arbitrary exercise of this great power?

The internet left the Garden of Eden a long time ago now. The web magnifies and accelerates everything, the bad as well as the good, and it turns out not just that human nature doesn't change as rapidly as technology, but that it doesn't change much at all.

QAnon and other similar dark products of the human id adapt and mutate and ebb and flow, but they don't go away. Like background viruses, we're probably going to be living with them forever.

But no publisher or platform on earth has any legal or moral obligation to spread them or indeed to distribute any form of prejudice or hate. So eject them from your platform if you can, and ban their authors for life.

There will be hard cases – for instance when racist conspiracies get tangled up with electoral politics and the lines are hard to draw – but, as least to me, this January proved that not just venerable news organisations but relatively young digital companies can figure their way through them.

But those digital companies will only remain free from regulatory control if they move quickly to establish secure checks and balances to ensure that the unprecedented power they have over what the world sees and hears cannot be abused. And all of this is urgent. The world moves a lot faster now than it did in 13th century England.

This chapter is abridged from the Philip Geddes Memorial Lecture presented on March 5, 2021 at St Edmund Hall, Oxford.

About the contributor

Mark Thompson is former CEO of The New York Times Company and former Director-General of the BBC.

Section two
UK politics and the media
***

Reporting the populist wave

Richard Tait

In December 2015, Ipsos MORI asked the British public what was the most crucial issue facing the country. One per cent said Europe. In just five years, the UK's politics have been transformed. Britain has left the EU and elected a populist government with a big majority, an agenda of economic redistribution and cultural conservatism, and facing a fractured opposition. The chapters in this section analyse this transformation and how journalism has tried to keep up with changes it often failed to anticipate and still does not fully understand.

Through the electoral and political dramas which began with the 2016 EU Referendum, Sir John Curtice, professor of politics at the University of Strathclyde, has been one of the public's most trusted guides, as the BBC's psephologist, interpreting opinion polls and delivering astonishingly accurate election night predictions. His masterly analysis of public opinion since the 2019 General Election shows how complex British politics has become.

On Brexit, despite both Conservative and Labour parties claiming Brexit was 'done' and it was time to 'move on', the country remains evenly divided. Voters are far more attached to their side of this debate than to the political parties. Labour has failed to win back its former supporters who are happy to stay with the Tories. Most Scots still resent being taken out of the EU. Attitudes to the pandemic are more volatile, but the success of the vaccine programme came at the right time for Johnson and for the governing parties in Scotland and Wales. Sir John's analysis explains the May 6 election results which left Labour in power in Wales, the SNP in the driving seat in Scotland, and the Conservatives triumphant in England.

For the media, the challenge was keeping up. Gary Gibbon, political editor of Channel 4 News, the most analytical of news programmes, reports the period since the election and the Brexit deal as a roller-coaster. The Government, in full populist mode, looked to celebrate its victories by threatening to 'whack' journalists who did not play ball. It then found the pandemic meant it needed public service broadcasting and its credibility to get vital public messages across. This should have demonstrated beyond any doubt the value of 'shared truth' in an advanced democracy. But the jury is out on whether populism, which he thinks, 'appears to be an era not a moment', will resume its hostility to the broadcasters.

One of the challenges is trying to deal with a Government information operation which seems to prefer anonymous tips to on-the-record briefings or interviews. David Smith and Julian Mathews, Media lecturers at the University of Leicester, have analysed the Twitter timelines of three broadcast political editors – Laura Kuenssberg of the BBC, Robert Peston of ITV News and Beth Rigby of Sky News – to see how much of their journalism on social media came from anonymous sources. The short answer is quite a lot, and an 'incumbency bonus' with less attention given to the opposition.

One leading political journalist who has been very critical of this development is Peter Oborne. Raymond Snoddy, former media editor of *The Times,* and co-editor of this book, casts his expert eye over Oborne's transformation from a formidable conservative voice on right wing papers like the *Daily Mail* and the *Daily Telegraph* to a ferocious critic of what he calls populism's 'new moral barbarism'.

For Peter York, one of the country's sharpest cultural commentators, most populists are 'fakes'. Their claim to be 'of the people' does not stand up to much scrutiny. But if they are fakes, they are effective ones. The secret of their success is exploiting social media, allowing 'mad and formerly marginal conspiracy theories to go mainstream' and the support of the UK right wing press – with a special mention for The *Daily Mail* as 'a populist poster child'.

Faced with this populist media firepower and an ineffective approach to Brexit, Labour has been gleefully written off by its opponents as a hopeless case. Tor Clark, a former newspaper editor, now associate professor in journalism at the University of Leicester and co-editor of this book, takes a less apocalyptic view. After reporting on eight general elections he is unconvinced populism has destroyed the electoral cycle for good. The shifts in society and media may move Labour's way, as they have in the US with Joe Biden's narrow victory.

If Peter York thinks most populists are fakes, Dorothy Byrne thinks they are liars, too. For 17 years the respected head of news and current affairs at Channel 4, she famously called Boris Johnson 'a known liar' at the 2019 Edinburgh Television Festival. Now about to take up the headship of a Cambridge college, her parting shot to those still in the trenches is to be much bolder and call out untruths.

Whether her fellow television editors heed her advice, the fact that five years on from the EU Referendum there seems still to be no agreed way for broadcasters to deal effectively with misleading or downright untrue claims by politicians is a measure of the crisis the UK media faces with populism. For the sake of democracy as well as journalism it is a challenge which urgently requires solutions.

Public reactions to Brexit and Covid-19

Professor Sir John Curtice finds the completion of Brexit has had relatively little impact on public attitudes, leaving the country evenly divided on the subject. In contrast, perceptions of the Government's handling of the Covid-19 pandemic – and thus its popularity – have fluctuated considerably

The United Kingdom has faced two major policy challenges since the December 2019 General Election. First, the Government has had to deliver the principal policy on which it was elected – to 'get Brexit done'. This involved not only securing the new Parliament's approval for the terms of the withdrawal treaty that had been agreed by the UK and the EU the previous autumn, but also to negotiate a new long-term relationship with the EU by the end of 2020. In the event that negotiation was completed on Christmas Eve 2020, just days before the UK left the EU single market and customs union. At the same time, the Government has had to deal with a wholly unexpected development – the onset of the worst public health crisis for a century in the form of the Covid-19 pandemic. That crisis soon came to dominate the attention of both politicians and the public, as the country's social and economic life was put into a deep freeze from which it has proven more difficult to emerge than many had originally anticipated and which is likely to leave its mark for years to come.

In this chapter, we examine the impact these two developments have had on Britain's political landscape. First, we ask whether there are signs the completion of Brexit has been accompanied by a reduction in the intensity of the once fierce debate between 'Remainers' and 'Leavers'. In particular, are there signs that those who wanted to remain in the European Union are coming to accommodate themselves to the fact that Brexit has happened and is unlikely to be reversed any time soon? If so, does this also mean the disruptive impact of Brexit on the pattern of support for the political parties, whereby pro-Brexit (but often working class) voters swung to the Conservatives and anti-Brexit (often middle class) voters backed Labour and the Liberal Democrats (Cutts et al., 2020; Curtice, 2020a) has now begun to unwind? Does it also mean support for independence for Scotland, which had previously appeared to have risen on the back of a change of heart among some of those who had voted Remain (Curtice and Montagu, 2020, Curtice, 2020b), is now in decline?

Second, we assess how the public have reacted politically to a pandemic which presented the Conservatives with two distinct challenges. The first – and more obvious – was to convince voters it was dealing competently with the public health crisis, taking steps that were necessary and proportionate to minimising the loss of life. The second – more subtle but no less important – was to secure voters' consent to a dramatic increase in the role of the state in economic life, including paying the wages of many of those unable to work and borrowing money on a scale not seen since the Second World War. This policy response cut across the traditional Conservative preference for a rather less active state and thus might be thought to represent a potential risk to its electoral fortunes. At the same time the pandemic significantly increased the visibility of devolution, as outside England it was the devolved governments which were responsible for managing much of the public health response to the pandemic, including setting the rules on what people could and could not do in their everyday lives. The perceived relative performance of the UK's various governments in handling so crucial an issue might well feed into voters' views about how the different parts of the UK should be governed in future – including not least in Scotland.

Attitudes to Brexit

When Britain left the EU at the end of January 2020, the polls at that time suggested – as they had for some time – there was a narrow majority in favour of remaining in the EU (Curtice, 2021). That estimate was also reflected in the distribution of the vote – if not the parliamentary outcome – of the 2019 general election in which 52 per cent of the votes cast in Great Britain were for parties which voted in favour of the EU, while 47 per cent were given to parties which were backing the immediate implementation of Brexit. However, withdrawal from the EU in January 2020 together with the onset of the pandemic a few weeks later meant not only was there much less polling of people's attitudes towards Brexit but also there was debate to be had about which questions about the issue should now be asked. Asking people whether they supported 'Remain' versus 'Leave' might no longer be regarded as appropriate – perhaps the question that should be posed now was whether people would vote to rejoin or stay out?

In practice, both approaches have been adopted. Table 1 summarises how people have answered when asked how they would vote in response to the proposition on the 2016 EU Referendum ballot paper and how they would vote if faced with a proposal (somewhat variously worded) to rejoin or stay out of the EU. The pattern of response to the choice between remaining versus leaving the EU suggests the implementation of Brexit has done little to change the balance of opinion on the principle of EU membership. After support for Remain dipped slightly in the months immediately after January 2020 (four polls conducted between February and April 2020 on average put support for Remain at 51 per cent and Leave on 49 per cent), the figures subsequently nudged back up again to Remain 52 per cent, Leave 48 per cent. There is relatively little sign here of Remain voters accommodating themselves to the reality of Brexit.

Table 1 Polling on Attitudes towards EU membership February 2020-March 2021

	Remain vs Leave			Rejoin/Stay Out		
	Remain	Leave	N	Rejoin	Stay Out	N
Feb-Aug 2020	52	48	11	48	52	6
Sept 2020-Mar 2021	52	48	9	49	51	9

Among the polls included under Rejoin/Stay Out some asked whether people would vote to (re-)join or stay out, others whether they would vote for or against (re-)joining.

Source: Average of polls conducted by BMG, Deltapoll, Kantar, Number Cruncher Politics, Savanta ComRes and YouGov.

That said, the picture is a little different when voters have been asked whether they would vote to rejoin or stay out of the EU. The pattern of answers to this question have suggested that now Brexit has happened there is a small majority in favour of staying out of the EU. This picture was confirmed when both types of question were asked of the same respondents on the NatCen mixed mode random probability panel in July 2020 (Curtice, 2020c). This suggested support for rejoining the EU was five points lower than for remaining in the institution. The principal explanation for the difference was that whereas 87 per cent of those who voted Remain in 2016 said they would vote Remain again, only 80 per cent indicated they would vote to rejoin. Here then is evidence that some of those who would still prefer to be part of the EU are not sure the decision made to leave should necessarily be reversed. Even so, this does little to alter the picture of a country which still appears to be almost equally divided on the issue of EU membership.

Still, much might be thought to rest on voters' reaction to the conclusion of the negotiations between the UK and the EU over their long-term relationship – and the country's exit from the EU single market and customs union. Perhaps that represented a watershed moment when Remain voters began to accept the issue was done and dusted? But, equally, perhaps a settlement widely regarded as representing a 'hard Brexit' simply reinforced the existing division between Remainers and Leavers?

Three published polls asked people what they thought of Mr Johnson's Christmas Eve deal shortly after it had been concluded. All suggested that while many had not come to a firm view, among those who had opinion was divided. Deltapoll found 38 per cent thought the deal was good for the UK, while 30 per cent reckoned it was bad – the remainder did not know. YouGov estimated just 17 per cent thought it was a good deal for Britain, but equally only 21 per cent reckoned it was bad. As many as 31 per cent said neither while another 31 per cent did not know. Meanwhile, Opinium reported while 30 per cent thought the agreement was better than being in the EU, 38 per cent took the opposite view. One in three either said neither (15 per cent) or they did not know (18 per cent).

All three polls also suggested that those Remain voters and Leave supporters who had formed a view had come to very different conclusions. According to YouGov just 9 per cent of Remain voters felt the deal was a good one, while 36 per cent expressed the opposite view. In contrast, the equivalent figures among Leave supporters were 27 per cent and 10 per cent respectively. Deltapoll reported more than twice as many Remain voters reckoned the deal was bad (53 per cent) than felt it was good (24 per cent), while more than three times as many Leave supporters believed it was good (57 per cent) than stated that it was bad (14 per cent). The two camps were even more divided in their response to Opinium's question. Just 15 per cent of Remain voters thought the new agreement was better than being in the EU, while 60 per cent felt it was worse. Conversely, 53 per cent of Leave supporters believed it was better than being in the EU while only 11 per cent felt it was worse.

In short, in so far as voters did form a view about the deal it appears they were inclined to regard it through the prism of their prior views about Brexit. It thus perhaps should not come as a surprise that there was little sign of any marked change in people's attitudes towards the principle of EU membership following the conclusion of the deal. Six polls conducted between January and March 2020 on average found 49 per cent were in favour of rejoining while 51 per cent wanted to stay out – exactly the same as in the equivalent polls over the previous four months.

Still, it may be one thing to express a view, another to feel the issue at stake matters. Hitherto many voters had appeared to have a strong commitment to one side or the other in the Brexit debate. Most were willing to acknowledge being a 'Remainer' or a 'Leaver', while many said they identified 'very strongly' with one of those labels (Curtice and Montagu, 2019; Hobolt et al., 2020). Perhaps these identities are no longer felt as intently?

Table 2 Strength of Brexit Identity, June 2018 – January 2021

Strength of Brexit identity	June 18	Feb 19	Mar 19	Sept 19	Nov/Dec. 19	Feb 20	July 20	Jan 21
	%	%	%	%	%	%	%	%
Very strong	44	46	46	46	42	42	39	37
Fairly strong	33	34	33	33	33	34	32	37
Not very strong	12	11	11	12	12	15	15	15
None	11	9	9	9	12	10	14	11

Source: NatCen Mixed Mode Random Probability Panel

There is some evidence to support this proposition. According to NatCen's random probability panel, during 2019 – when the debate over Brexit in Parliament was at its most intense – as many as 46 per cent said they were a 'very strong' Remainer or a 'very strong' Leaver. Less than one in ten denied they were a Remainer or a Leaver at all. However, by the time the UK had left the EU the proportion with a very strong attachment had slipped to 42 per cent (although the drop was already in evidence during the 2019 election campaign) and then it fell further to just 37 per cent after the country's exit from the single market. That said, nearly three-quarters (74 per cent) of voters still feel either 'very' or 'fairly' strongly attached to one side or the other in the Brexit debate, a figure which still far outstrips the proportion who feel the same way about a political party (44 per cent in January 2021). Moreover, there is little sign of the decline being the preserve of Remainers (45 per cent), who continue to be more likely than Leavers (37 per cent) to say their Brexit identity is 'very strong'.

Perhaps the relative decline in the intensity of people's feelings about Brexit means their attitudes towards the EU are no longer influencing which political party they support to the extent they did in December 2019 – and some of the disruption of the traditional patterns of support for the parties witnessed at that election has started to be reversed. After all, Labour and the Liberal Democrats, who had both been advocating a second referendum on the Brexit decision, dropped their opposition to Brexit in the wake of the outcome of the 2019 election, while Labour actually voted in favour of the Christmas Eve deal when it was brought before the House of Commons. Although the Conservative Government has continued to extol the merits of its Brexit deal, Remain voters have received little encouragement from the opposition parties to continue to support them as a way of expressing their continuing antipathy to Brexit.

Not least of the reasons for this lack of encouragement was an apparent determination by the Labour Party to try to recapture the support the party had lost among Leave voters in 2017 and 2019, a decline that came to be symbolised by the party's loss of its so-called 'Red Wall' parliamentary constituencies – traditionally safe but Leave-inclined constituencies to the north of Birmingham (Mattinson, 2020). Moreover, the party appeared to be making some progress towards reviving its electoral fortunes when by the early autumn of 2020 it drew neck-and-neck with the Conservatives in the polls. But was this a sign the gulf between the voting preferences of Remain and Leave supporters had narrowed at all?

Table 3: Party Support by 2016 EU Referendum Vote, 2019 Election – March 2021

Remain Voters	2019 Election	July 2020	October 2020	March 2021
	%	%	%	%
Conservative	20	22	21	24
Labour	48	52	54	50
Liberal Democrat	21	11	11	11
Greens	4	5	5	6
Brexit/UKIP/Reform	0	0	0	0
Leave Voters	2019 Election	July 2020	October 2020	March 2021
	%	%	%	%
Conservative	74	68	64	65
Labour	15	17	20	18
Liberal Democrat	3	3	2	3
Greens	2	2	3	2
Brexit/UKIP/Reform	4	4	7	6

Sources: 2019: Average of post-election polls by YouGov and Lord Ashcroft. July 2020-March 2021: Average of polls conducted closest to the end of the month by BMG, Deltapoll, Kantar, Number Cruncher Politics, Opinium, Savanta ComRes, YouGov. Not all companies published in each of these months.

Table 3 compares the pattern of support for the parties among Remain and Leave voters at the time of the December 2019 election with the position at three time points during the course of the ensuing 15 months. These time points are July 2020, when after having had nearly a 20-point lead in the initial weeks of the pandemic, the Conservatives were still six points ahead of Labour in the polls, October 2020, when the two parties were neck-and-neck, and March 2021, when the Conservatives were once again six points ahead (but still well short of the 12-point lead registered at the election). The Liberal Democrats, meanwhile, were running at 7 per cent in each of these months, after having recorded 12 per cent in 2019.

Three points stand out. First, Brexit continues to be an important dividing line. Around two-thirds of Leave voters still support the Conservatives, whereas the party has only been registering between a fifth and a quarter of the vote among those who backed Remain. Meanwhile, the combined tally for Labour and the Liberal Democrats has been close to the mirror image of that pattern. Second, however, the level of support for the Conservatives among Remain voters has proven relatively stable – indeed it has been showing signs of nudging up a little on the position in 2019. In contrast, support for the party has eased somewhat as compared with 2019 among Leave voters (with some, perhaps, now backing the Brexit/Reform Party). Nevertheless (and third), there has not been any sign of Labour having any success in narrowing the gap between its support among Remain voters and that among Leave supporters. At 32 points the difference in March 2021 was almost exactly the same as the 33-point gap in evidence in 2019. The link between Leave voters and Conservative support may have weakened a little, but there is no sign of the Brexit divide loosening its grip on the character of support for Labour (or indeed the Liberal Democrats), despite the party's attempt to reconnect with Leave voters.

But what of the political division in Scotland, where not only did voters vote in favour of staying in the EU by nearly two to one but also one of the legacies of the EU Referendum was to see some Remain voters swing in favour of independence while some Leave supporters switched in the opposite direction, creating a gap between the two groups in their attitude towards Scotland's constitutional question not previously been in evidence (Curtice, 2020b)? By the time of the 2019 election not only was support for independence running on average in the polls at 49 per cent, four points up on the Yes vote at the time of the 2014 independence referendum, but no less than 55 per cent of Remain voters were now in favour of independence, while just 30 per cent of Leave supporters took the same view. Equally, according to the British Election Study, 52 per cent of Remain voters backed the SNP at the December 2019 election, compared with just 27 per cent of Leave supporters.

These gaps have not shown any sign of diminishing. Although, as discussed further below, the level of support for independence has fluctuated since 2019, the difference between Remain and Leave voters has persisted. In eight polls conducted in March 2021, support for independence averaged 54 per cent among Remain voters and 32 per cent among Leave supporters, a 22-point gap that almost matched the 25-point gap at the time of the 2019 election. Similarly, there was still a 24-point difference in the propensity of the two groups to vote for the SNP. There was little sign north of the border of any diminution in the role Brexit was playing in shaping voters' political preferences.

The politics of the pandemic

Brexit is an issue of principle where voters disagree about the objective of public policy. In the case of Covid-19 in contrast there was no dispute that the aim was minimise its impact on both the nation's health and its economy. Although there might be debate about how that objective might be best achieved, the immediate issue of concern for most voters was the Government's ability to handle competently what was evidently a significant public health crisis. Thus, it was perhaps little surprising that, despite the draconian nature of the public health measures announced by the UK Government (together with the devolved administrations) on March 23, 2020 – and despite criticism they had been introduced too late – the early weeks of the coronavirus pandemic were greeted with high levels of public approval of the Government's actions and, as we have already noted, high levels of support for the Conservatives (see Table 4).

Table 4 Perceptions of UK Government's handling of coronavirus and party support, March 2020-March 2021

	% govt handling coronavirus 'very' or 'somewhat' well	Vote Intentions	
		% Conservative	% Labour
2020			
March/Apr	63	50	31
May/June	44	43	37
July/Aug	42	42	37
Sept/Oct	32	40	40
2020/1			
Nov/Dec/Jan	35	40	38
2021			
Feb/Mar	45	42	36

Sources: Government handling of coronavirus: YouGov COVID-19 tracker; Vote intentions: Average of polls conducted closest to the end of the last month of the period by BMG, Deltapoll, Ipsos MORI, Kantar, Number Cruncher Politics, Opinium, Redfield & Wilton, Savanta ComRes, YouGov. Not all companies published in each of these months.

However, this mood did not last long. In the early summer, the public rapidly became more critical of how the pandemic was being handled, following an adverse public reaction to the decision of Dominic Cummings, a special adviser to the Prime Minister, to travel from London to Durham after he and his wife suspected that they had contracted the disease rather than (as advised) staying at home in the capital (Fancourt et al., 2020). Evaluations – and support for the Government – then fell further in the early autumn as it became apparent, after a lull in the summer, that the prevalence of the disease was increasing once again and, in the face of opposition criticism, the Government found itself having to re-introduce restrictions. However, after a further serious wave of cases in early 2021, evaluations, and the Government's popularity, began to improve markedly in February and March 2021 as it became apparent the UK had become one of the first countries in the world to embark successfully on a mass Covid-19 vaccination programme.

The impact of perceptions of the Government's handling of coronavirus on people's willingness to support the Conservatives can be discerned more directly in Table 5. The first two columns show the percentage who thought the Government was handling the pandemic well and the proportion who thought it was doing so badly broken down by how people said they would vote now. Conservative and Labour supporters have consistently regarded the Government's actions very differently. However, much of this pattern will reflect that the fact many existing Conservative supporters were inclined to think the Government was doing well (and Labour supporters badly) – rather than that voters were backing the Government because they thought it was performing well.

Table 5: Evaluations of how well Government handling coronavirus by party support July 2020-March 2021

% well-%badly	Vote Intention		2019 Vote		2019 Conservatives who voted	
	Con	Lab	Con	Lab	Remain	Leave
July 2020	70-13	13-74	60-2	15-72	61-22	61-22
Sept/Oct 2020	65-17	10-79	52-31	31-78	59-24	52-32
Feb/Mar 2021	78-11	17-72	65-21	17-71	71-16	62-22

Source: Average of polls by Opinium. Figures for Conservatives who voted Remain and Leave in 2016 not available for Mar. 2021; figures quoted are for Feb. 2021 only.

Nevertheless, we can secure some indication of the extent to which the Conservatives' standing in the polls was being affected by voters' perceptions of the handling of the coronavirus by comparing the figures in the first two columns of Table 5 with those in the third and fourth columns. These latter columns show how people viewed the Government's handling of Brexit according to how they voted in the 2019 General Election. It is apparent at each of the three time periods covered by the table those who voted Conservative in 2019 were less likely to say the Government was handling things well (and more likely to state they were doing so badly) than were those who were indicating that they would currently support the Conservatives – implying that among those who backed the Conservatives in 2019 but were now no longer doing so, there were many who felt the Government was dealing badly with the pandemic. We can also see, latterly at least, those 2019 Conservatives who had voted Leave in 2016 were less likely than those who had voted Remain to feel the pandemic was being handled well, a pattern which might well help explain why, as we saw earlier at Table 3, support for the Conservatives has held up less well among Leave supporters than it has among Remain voters.

But how do Conservative voters feel about the substantial expansion of the role of the state occasioned by the pandemic? After all, we would expect Conservative supporters to be less keen than their Labour counterparts on increasing taxes and spending more on public services. The 2017 British Social Attitudes survey, for example, found while 67 per cent of Labour supporters were in favour of increasing taxes and spending more on health, education and social services, a lower proportion, 53 per cent, of Conservative identifiers did so. Even so, the gap between the two groups of voters is perhaps not as large as might be anticipated from the political rhetoric often to be heard on this issue. Moreover, perhaps we need to bear in mind attitudes to taxation and spending may be influenced both by the purpose of public expenditure and who has incurred it.

In any event, polling by Savanta ComRes on how the cost of paying for the support given to people and businesses during the pandemic suggests Conservative supporters are not averse to increasing taxes in order to pay for the extra spending. For example, the company found in three polls it conducted between January and March 2021 that on average 47 per cent of those who voted for the party in 2019 supported a one per cent increase in income tax to help pay the costs of the pandemic, while only 31 per cent were opposed. In contrast, only 39 per cent of Labour supporters backed the idea while 35 per cent were opposed. It may, of course, be the case Labour supporters are more likely to think someone other than the general taxpayer should pay – such as businesses – or that they are less likely to be convinced the debt needs to be paid back at all. However, it seems increasing taxes to pay for some of the costs of the pandemic may not put as much strain on the Conservatives' electoral coalition as might have been anticipated.

Still, the adverse perceptions many voters had of the Government's handling of the pandemic did cost it support for much of the first year. Meanwhile, in the devolved nations voters were in a position to compare the relative performance of their devolved administration with that of the UK Government – a comparison which might be thought to have implications for voters' attitudes towards the future governance of the UK. If voters came to the conclusion that their devolved government had handled the pandemic worse than the UK government, that might be felt to bolster the case for remaining part of the UK. On the other hand, if the devolved administration was thought to have performed better, perhaps some voters might ask whether it should become a more powerful body.

In Scotland (and indeed Wales) it was the latter perception which prevailed. For example, according to YouGov by August 2020 nearly four in five (79 per cent) felt the Scottish Government was handling the pandemic well, and only a little under one in five (18 per cent) believed it was doing so badly. In contrast, the equivalent figures for the UK Government were 23 per cent and 73 per cent respectively.

Moreover, this was not simply a case of voters viewing developments through a partisan lens. Even among those who had voted No to Scottish independence in 2014, 72 per cent believed the Scottish Government was doing a good job of responding to the crisis while only 35 per cent said the same of the UK Government.

This gulf in perceived performance appears to have had an impact on some people's views about how Scotland should be governed. Between June 2020 and January 2021 the polls consistently suggested a narrow majority at least would now vote Yes to independence in any rerun of the 2014 independence referendum. On average 19 polls conducted during this period put Yes on 54 per cent of the vote No on 46 per cent, the first time the polls had ever consistently suggested there was majority support for leaving the UK. Meanwhile, two polls conducted at this time, one by YouGov and one by Panelbase, found whereas just 4 per cent of those who had voted Yes in 2014 felt Scotland would have handled the pandemic worse as an independent country, as many as 20 per cent of those who had backed No believed the public health crisis would have been handled better. Here was strong circumstantial evidence at least that perceptions of the competence of the two governments on this crucial public policy issue were feeding into people's views about Scotland's constitutional status.

However, there were already signs at the turn of the year that this boost to support for independence was waning – by this stage support for Yes was running at 52 per cent, and this was clearly confirmed in polls conducted in February and March 2021, in 14 of which support for Yes and No averaged 50 per cent apiece, that is, back at the level at which it had been after Brexit had been concluded but before the onset of the pandemic. Meanwhile, although the polls still suggested the Scottish Government's handling of the pandemic was rated more highly than that of the UK Government, albeit not by as large a margin as earlier, two polls conducted in March, one by YouGov and one by Opinium, reported now 9 per cent of 2014 Yes voters felt an independent Scotland might have handled the pandemic worse, while the proportion of No supporters who felt it might have been handled better had slipped to 16 per cent. Although voters were seemingly as likely to credit the Scottish Government as they were the UK Government for the success of the vaccine rollout, the fact perceptions of the UK Government's handling of the pandemic had improved somewhat may have played a role in reversing the earlier apparent impact of the pandemic on attitudes towards how Scotland should be governed.

Conclusion

Since the 2019 General Election political life in Britain has been dominated by one issue – the pandemic. Unsurprisingly, the perceived competence of the Government in handling the issue has brought about fluctuations in the political parties' short-term electoral fortunes, and may for a while at least have had some impact on levels of support for Scottish independence. Yet, although it would be wrong to believe this is a subject on which voters necessarily put their partisan loyalties to one side, it is apparent perceptions of the Government's competence are potentially volatile, and that there have been some marked changes in the balance of public opinion – in both directions – during the course of the first year of the public health crisis. Although in the longer-term the pandemic will undoubtedly frame some of the policy choices facing the country in its post-pandemic future, it has not so far proven to be an issue that has fundamentally changed the political landscape.

The same is not true of Brexit. Brexit may have been done and largely been missing from the headlines, yet few have changed their minds, leaving the country more or less evenly divided on the principle of whether it should be in or out of the EU. Commitment to being a Remainer or a Leaver may not be as strong as it was, but it is still far stronger than commitment to a party. Party support is still heavily shaped by where people stand on the issue and in particular Labour's acceptance of Brexit appears so far to have done little to reconnect it with its former Leave supporters. Meanwhile, the issue is still undermining support for the Union north of the border. Far from being a debate that is over, the question of Britain's relationship with the EU still has the potential to be re-ignited once more – as perhaps it might when Britain does get around to debating its post-pandemic future.

References

Curtice, J. (2020a), *Was the 2019 Election A Success?*, London: NatCen Social Research. Available at https://whatukthinks.org/eu/analysis/was-the-2019-general-election-a-success/

Curtice, J. (2020b), 'High noon for the Union?', *IPPR Progressive Review*, 27 (3): 223-34.

Curtice, J. (2020c), *Has Brexit gone off the boil? Or are the embers of Brexit still glowing?*, London: NatCen Social Research. Available at https://whatukthinks.org/eu/analysis/has-brexit-gone-off-the-boil-or-are-the-embers-of-brexit-still-glowing/

Curtice, J. (2021), 'The legacy of Brexit', in Menon, A. (ed.), *Brexit and Beyond*, London: UK in a Changing Europe. Available at https://ukandeu.ac.uk/research-papers/brexit-and-beyond/

Curtice, J. and Montagu, I. (2019), 'The EU debate: Has Brexit polarised Britain?', in Curtice, J., Clery, E., Perry, J., Phillips, M. and Rahim, N. (eds), *British Social Attitudes 36*, London: NatCen Social Research. Available at https://www.bsa.natcen.ac.uk/latest-report/british-social-attitudes-36/the-eu-debate.aspx

Curtice, J. and Montagu, I. (2020), *Is Brexit Fuelling Support for Independence?*, Edinburgh: ScotCen Social Research. Available at https://whatscotlandthinks.org/wp-content/uploads/2020/11/SSA-2019-Scotland-paper-v5.pdf

Cutts, D., Goodwin, M., Heath, O., and Surridge, P. (2020), 'Brexit, the 2019 election, and the realignment of British politics', *Political Quarterly*, 91 (1): 7-23.

Fancourt, D., Steptoe, A., and Wright, L. (2020), 'The Cummings effect: politics, trust and behaviours during the COVID19 pandemic', *The Lancet*, 396 (10249): 464-5.

Hobolt, S., Leeper, T., and Tilley, J. (2020), 'Divided by the vote: affective polarization in the wakeof the Brexit referendum', *British Journal of Political Science,* First View. Available at https://doi.org/10.1017/S0007123420000125

Mattinson, D. (2020), *Beyond the Red Wall: Why Labour Lost,. How the Conservatives Won, and What Happens Next?*, London: Biteback.

About the contributor

Professor Sir John Curtice is Professor of Politics at the University of Strathclyde and Senior Research Fellow at NatCen Social Research and the ESRC's 'The UK in a Changing Europe' initiative. He has written extensively about voting behaviour in elections and referendums in the UK, as well as on British political and social attitudes more generally. He is also a regular contributor to British and international media coverage of UK politics, including as commentator and analyst on the BBC's election night programmes.

When news broadcasters became critical workers

As Covid spread, public service broadcasting helped to inform and to bind the nation. Has an institution under threat earned the right to a reprieve? Gary Gibbon thinks we should give it serious thought

In January 2020, politicians and political journalists let out a giant collective sigh like a punctured airship. Even the losing combatants in the Brexit wars acknowledged some relief that the fighting was over. An all-consuming protracted political street brawl had ended. A majority government had been elected just before Christmas. The political agenda was about to break out of the straight jacket of Brexit. Something like the normal rhythms of political life might be returning. And then came Covid.

At that very moment, broadcasters were still cowering, awaiting the details of how Dominic Cummings intended to 'whack' the broadcasting establishment.[1] He felt that we collectively had neglected or rejected the sentiments and instincts which his Vote Leave campaign tapped into. Even though our exit from the EU had now been decided, the culture wars which were simmering in our politics and which were brought to the boil by the Brexit referendum were still very much with us.

The public health emergency crashed in on Dominic Cummings' world and everyone else's too. Public service broadcasters were suddenly as relevant to the dissemination of vital information as they had been in the 1940s. You could, Downing Street discovered, appropriate a section of the media day with a live press conference from No 10 at 5pm. That could help you shape the news agenda.[2] But you still needed the rest of the public broadcasting apparatus to get complicated and fast-changing messages across to the population and to make compelling and accessible what government graphics alone could not.

Special access news programme filming from overwhelmed NHS intensive care units was seen in government as a central component in the plan to frighten the population into comprehending the risk to the health service and the need to obey draconian restrictions on our way of life.

The Government's leading officials did their best to convey the risks and metrics of Covid in their press conference appearances. The news bulletins, whose viewing figures soared[3] as people were first locked indoors and straining to understand why and for how long, often hammered home the message, deployed more professional communication tools and played a vital role in getting public adherence to unprecedented constraints.

Enter the lockdown sceptics

Did the broadcasters lay too much of their art and wizardry at the feet of the Government? A section of Tory MPs felt so and, by the autumn of 2020, they seemed to have the Prime Minister in their thrall as he became the key voice holding back on a second lockdown.[4] Boris Johnson's defence will be that the variants detected that autumn altered all the numbers and couldn't have been predicted. Plenty of senior officials in government working around him believe the projections in September modelled pretty accurately what befell the UK in the second surge.

But the Covid Recovery Group of Tory MPs, the Great Barrington Declaration and other lockdown sceptics did not capture the bulk of public opinion.[5] Public service broadcasting unquestionably contributed to an agreed national understanding of the fundamental risks of Covid.

An extraordinary and challenging phenomenon was explained each day with professional, calm clarity. Expert views were distilled, harnessed. The fact that most of the population were largely drinking from the same well of unpolluted news helped to create a coming together of the nation.

Those who challenged the lockdown response got air time on mainstream broadcasts. But the bogus science which could reign in pockets of the online world and, for instance, on some US news programmes, was challenged on mainstream UK bulletins. There were agreed facts across the nation and that helped the country on the journey through Covid.

In the US, without that broadcasting structure, facts were disputed, feeding division, ignorance and sickness. There was 'shared truth' at the heart of the UK's experience of the Covid challenge and it's worth pondering how precious that was.

As a political journalist, the focus of work changed utterly. Downing Street press conferences with government experts began to dominate the news cycle.

At 5pm we were told the data about the threat to health which would continue to restrict our freedom. Some in No 10 revelled at the control over the news agenda this gave them and hoped to carry on the experiment into peace time with an expensive new studio in 9 Downing Street. Those plans have been abandoned as the penny dropped that the questions might get trickier and more persistent post-Covid.[6]

A delighted Downing Street aide told me a few months into the Covid press conferences that the public were baffled and offended by the carping tone of journalists questioning the Prime Minister and others. Many of these viewers, the aide said, had never watched a press conference in their lives and, focus groups suggested, they thought the journalists were being rude and unpatriotic.

One day, historians may be pondering whether the replication of these press conferences by the devolved governments contributed decisively to a greater sense of separateness. Scottish government aides believed it was boosting Nicola Sturgeon's standing and allowed their voters a direct comparison with her style and Boris Johnson's, which hugely benefitted Sturgeon.

Scottish government aides told me that for some Scots these press conferences replaced their normal television bulletin watching. They'd got what they needed to know at lunchtime and little else in the news would affect them.

For Downing Street, the format gave them an appearance of accountability without too much persistent challenge. Questioners were not only chosen by No 10 but could be muted by it after one question. In face-to-face press conferences it's much harder to avoid a supplementary question. Another reason why the £2.6m studio in 9 Downing Street won't be used the way it was originally planned.

The new golden sources

Suddenly for political journalists the cast list of necessary contacts changed dramatically. Epidemiologists and mathematical modellers I'd never heard of before became the golden sources everyone wanted to talk to. Many were generous with their time and patient with their explanations. The Science Media Centre came into many journalists' lives for the first time. It's a wonderful creation that promotes the clearer understanding of what science has discovered.[7] Could statisticians and data experts mount a similar permanent operation in the future?

On the main news bulletins, public service broadcasting looked like it was doing what it is supposed to do: acknowledging complexity and explaining it. This is of course the exact opposite of what populist politicians and biased TV networks in unregulated jurisdictions do. Their main purpose is to simplify and divide, to drive people into sheep pens as far apart from the opposing sheep as possible.[8]

But as we emerge blinking from the restrictions and deprivations of Covid, threats to public service broadcasting are all around us. Culture Secretary Oliver Dowden said the rise of Netflix, Amazon Prime and others had 'lobbed a grenade' into our system of broadcasting. A review is underway.[9] But this is still about politics, not just new technologies. What kind of country do we want to live in?

Soon after Boris Johnson parted company with Dominic Cummings, No 10 aides briefed that the war on public service broadcasting had softened. It had, we were told, got out of hand.

The establishment side of Boris Johnson's fluid political personality yearned to be seen in the same gilt frame as Angela Merkel and Emmanuel Macron, aides said. He hated being spoken of in the same breath as Donald Trump and was embarrassed by the praise heaped on him by Trump. But Trump saw Boris Johnson's Brexit project as a trailblazer for his own electoral success and pioneering an assault on cherished post-war institutions he longed to take further. Johnson's team would continue for some time to demonise sections of news broadcasting and tried to rewrite the way politics is covered in the UK.

In his pomp, Dominic Cummings decreed that chatting to journalists was off limits for just about everyone in government.[10] I remember meetings with ministers and special advisers at this time that were extraordinary cloak and dagger affairs. One senior No 10 aide circled a cafe to check no-one was watching them, looked nervously out the window throughout our meeting to make sure they weren't spotted. One minister chose a windowless basement cafe for our meeting and then insisted he leave a couple of minutes before me in case we were seen at the door.

No 10 in 'whack' mode

In February 2020, even as Covid lapped at our shores, No 10 was trying to divide up journalists into acceptable and unacceptable camps.

A select few political reporters were summoned to a briefing at No 10 with David Frost, the EU negotiator. Given he is a public servant and the communications team are all paid for out of public money, the convention is that all the media that can be fitted in the room are entitled to the same briefing.

But No 10 was still in what Dominic Cummings had coined as 'whack' mode. On this occasion, Downing Street wanted to punish newspapers whose coverage it didn't like and establish a new, more Trumpian approach to media relations. All newspapers and broadcasters turned up at No 10 for the briefing but an official, on instruction from Boris Johnson's team, tried to separate the desirables from the undesirables and send the latter out the famous front door. We all decided to leave.[11]

All this comes as the truth is getting strained even more than usual in other, non-health aspects of our politics. The Government breaks the terms of an international agreement and says it isn't doing that.[12] The Prime Minister is accused of trying to get party donors to do up his flat on the quiet and repeatedly dodges questions on whether that is what he was up to.[13] Our political leaders have often told us black is white but even Tory MPs who supported Boris Johnson's leadership campaign in 2019 tell you they are embarrassed how far their leader takes this.

High handed tactics and populist instincts have not disappeared. Populism throughout the West would appear to be an era not a moment. Different countries have different defences. We may develop new ones here. But for now, public service broadcasting is one of the bulwarks or guardrails of our open society.[14]

As social media threatens to polarise our national discourse and lure us into one-sided conversations that don't just reflect our views but harden them, we have to ask what tools we have to maintain civilised and informed discourse?

And now for the future

Education can help enormously, instilling a sense of the complexity of choices and a proper regard for the other side of an argument. Most importantly, our schools need to train young people to interrogate the evidence, to audit their own information sources better, to understand who is trying to manipulate and polarise them and how. Maybe our legislators need to reflect more on whether public service broadcasting is a good and whether its place in our national life and its prominence on the channel menu are worth preserving.

The driving mission of some in government remains some sort of re-wilding of the media landscape. Do we really want our population to lose the purified water wells of regulated broadcasting? Can we honestly look at America's experience over the last four decades and say: "Seems to do the trick. Can we have some of that?"

Public service broadcasting is far from perfect. It sometimes cowers too much. It can still make the mistake of thinking that balance is about giving equal airtime rather than subjecting arguments to equal rigour. It has sometimes listened to its own narrow recruitment seam too exclusively.

Go back over bulletin running orders at the beginning of 2020 and the TV and radio bulletins weren't always quicker than the government or its advisers to spot the health emergency that was coming towards us. Peacocking journalists asking the same question as each other at a government press conferences so they can prioritise 'reporter involvement' was a grim spectacle we could do without.

But Covid has surely brought into focus some of the benefits of the public service broadcasting apparatus which Dominic Cummings, back in 2019 as he came into government, wanted to put into intensive care.

In March 2020, as lockdown restrictions came into force, those who worked in public service broadcasting news were designated 'critical workers', free to travel to work when so many others were required by law to stay at home. There was something acknowledged in that law and that moment: the importance of shared truth in an advanced democracy. You see little sign of our politicians scrabbling to make sure it has permanence.

Notes

[1] *Independent* February 20, 2020

[2] www.statista.com January 12, 2021

[3] www.ofcom.org.uk August 13, 2020

[4] *Daily Mail* April 26, 2021; www.dominiccummings.com April 23, 2021

[5] www.ipsos.com

[6] www.politicshome.com April 20, 2021

[7] www.sciencemediacentre.org

[8] www.digitalnewsreport.org "The Rise of Populism and the Consequences for News and Media Use" (2019), Richard Fletcher, Reuters Institute

[9] *Daily Telegraph* November 10, 2020

[10] *The Times* February 2, 2020

[11] *PR Week* February 4, 2020

[12] *Financial Times* September 6, 2020

[13] *The Times* April 28, 2021

[14] '*How Democracies Die*' (2018) Levitsky and Ziblatt pp. 97-117

About the contributor

Gary Gibbon has been political editor of *Channel 4 News* since 2005. Before that he was the programme's political correspondent. He won the RTS Specialist Journalist Award in 2011 and was nominated for the same award in 2016 and 2021 and for RTS Interview of the Year in 2017. In 2006, with Jon Snow and Robert Hamilton, he won the 2005 RTS Home News Award for revealing the Attorney General's legal opinion on the War in Iraq, a report also nominated for a 2006 Bafta.

Johnson and Oborne: Parallel lives, diverging views

Prime Minister Boris Johnson and political journalist Peter Oborne have trod the same ground for four decades. Now the latter is following a different path. Raymond Snoddy looks at how it happened

There are few people better qualified to hold Prime Minister Boris Johnson to account, or explain the curious phenomenon of his rise to power than Peter Oborne. And Oborne does so with gusto in his latest book – *The Assault on Truth: Boris Johnson, Donald Trump and the Emergence of a New Barbarism.*

The opening paragraph gives the flavour of what Oborne has in store:

> *"You're looking to hire a new member of staff. A candidate presents himself. He is charming, intelligent, amusing, well connected, with glowing references. But a check throws up uncomfortable facts. He was sacked from his first job after university for lying. He was sacked again, after a similar episode later on in his career. Close inspection reveals that he has a history of deception, misrepresentation, false statements and serial fabrications. You'd probably be more likely to call the police than hire this individual."*

Yet on December 12, 2019 the British people chose Boris Johnson as their Prime Minister.

Oborne has an endless selection of Johnson lies and misrepresentations to choose from but one stands out among the others, more egregious and troubling in its political implications – Johnson on Northern Ireland.

The Prime Minister repeatedly stated on visits to Northern Ireland, on television and in the House of Commons, that there would be no custom checks or controls on goods moving from Great Britain to Northern Ireland or from Northern Ireland to Great Britain.

In fact, such controls became inevitable after Johnson signed his revised deal with Europe in October 2019, and as Oborne notes, he must have known this because he personally signed off the deal. The very next day, on October 22, Johnson insisted in Parliament there would be no border checks between Great Britain and Northern Ireland.

"This bare-faced lie in all its moral squalor remains on the Commons order paper," says Oborne who noted that the false claim was then made repeatedly during the following general election campaign.

Apart from limiting trade between Britain and Northern Ireland there are increasing fears that the new border controls could undermine the Good Friday Agreement. It could also increase the danger of a resumption of violence on the island of Ireland as the resentment of Unionists grows at what some see as a betrayal. And that is indeed what happened with outbreaks of rioting in some parts of Belfast and in a number of other Northern Ireland towns.

They go back a long way

Oborne is perfectly placed to judge the Johnson record for many reasons. He has been a political journalist for more than 40 years and has earned a high degree of moral authority for resigning as the highly paid chief political commentator for the *Daily Telegraph* on a matter of principle. He left because he believed that the Telegraph's coverage, or more precisely lack of coverage of the affairs of HSBC, one of the paper's prominent advertisers, amounted to a "fraud on its readers."

His 40 years' experience of political reporting enables him to compare and contrast Johnson's predecessors in Number 10.

Tony Blair gave an early flavour of what was to come, in a far more extreme form, with Boris Johnson. Blair believed, as many on the Left do, Oborne argues, that they are exempt from the constraints of truth-telling in pursuit of a greater good. This belief led directly to 'calamity' when New Labour peddled lies about Saddam Hussein's weapons of mass destruction to make the case for war against Iraq in 2003.

As for Blair's immediate successors Gordon Brown, David Cameron and Theresa May, they were all too capable of being devious. But they were not habitual liars and all "were driven by a sense of public duty and integrity." According to Oborne standards of truth telling collapsed at the precise moment Boris Johnson and his associates entered 10 Downing Street in the early afternoon of 24 July 2019.

The central reason why Oborne is particularly suitable for unravelling the Johnson mystery is that he worked happily with the Prime Minister, who hired him as a political correspondent at *The Spectator* in 2001 where he was the editor. He was therefore well placed to see, and try to explain, the metamorphosis from talented weekly magazine editor to someone accused of being a serial liar.

"He (Johnson) was a joy to work with, a fine editor and a loyal colleague with the quickest mind I have ever encountered. Nothing needed explaining twice," says Oborne, who finds it difficult to reconcile such two different people, or different versions of the same person. The 'good Boris' stood up for British institutions, which the 'bad Boris' remorselessly attacks, and once believed in the honest politics he now subverts.

Boris, the editor, accused Tony Blair of treating Parliament and the public with contempt. "He might have been looking ahead to his own premiership. Johnson wanted Blair to be impeached," Oborne added.

So how did the transformation from Johnson of *The Spectator* to today's Prime Minister occur? Oborne says he can only offer "informed speculation."

The process began when Johnson was elected, and then re-elected Mayor of London in 2008 and 2012 despite the capital being a Labour stronghold. Johnson ran London as he had run *The Spectator*, with frequent absences and leaving the detail to capable deputies. His electoral success in London stimulated his ambition to new heights and many Tories began to see him as someone who could win seats.

"Like Donald Trump after the 2016 presidential election, Johnson's electoral Midas touch encouraged his own party thereafter to give him a pass to lie and cheat," Oborne observes.

On balance Johnson probably agreed with Remain rather than Leave but his career was the only thing that mattered. "Johnson made a bargain. The Vote Leave campaign would propel him to Downing Street, and he would be their figurehead," says Oborne.

Johnson the actor needed a scriptwriter and he found that person in Dominic Cummings. Together the two mounted a 'reverse takeover' of the Tory party, Oborne believes. In such an analysis, in both the US and the UK, truth was transferred from public into private hands almost like the privatisation of the water and electricity companies.

"Truth falls into the hands of a new and unaccountable set of owners. It can be bought and sold by shareholders, poisoned and polluted and turned into an instrument of state and private power," Oborne argues. In this case, the takeover of the Conservatives has been accomplished by Brexit supporters on the right-wing of the party.

Since the Brexiteers' victory in the June 2016 Referendum, Johnson has often behaved as if that victory gave him a political legitimacy "to trash British institutions like Parliament, the Supreme Court and the BBC."

What does he believe?

Oborne also makes a serious attempt to get to the heart of the political philosophy underlying the behaviour of both President Trump and Prime Minister Johnson.

For Oborne it is mesmerising to think that Johnson and Trump, though leaders of the Tory and Republican parties, embody progressive, rather than conservative insights about human nature.

"They are with Rousseau and the French revolution rather than Montesquieu and the American constitution. They think the end justifies the means," Oborne argues. As a result, they wage permanent war on institutions, despise due process, and feel entitled to fabricate and twist the truth.

Above all Trump and Johnson, according to Oborne, reject the Burkeian wisdom that you need to support institutions to protect society from human weaknesses. As Lenin asked in another context: "What is to be done?"

Oborne believes the threat goes far beyond the personalities of Trump and Johnson. The UK is faced by something much more serious, a structural fascination with "the short term, the transient and destructive" and it's time to start the fight back.

Oborne believes there are a number of actions individuals can take to fight against intolerable levels of deceit. He has sent his excellent little book to the Speaker of the House of Commons, Sir Lindsay Hoyle, arguing that in future any lies or misinformation should be corrected on the public record within seven days. And just in case Mr Speaker has not managed to read *The Assault on Truth*, Oborne has helpfully sent him a selection of lies or misleading statements uttered by the Prime Minister in the House of Commons.

They obviously include: "There will be no checks between NI and GB." And the other false claims are many and various. They include:

- "We brought in the lockdown in care homes ahead of the general lockdown." They didn't.

- "The economy, under this Conservative government has grown by 73 per cent." It didn't. Under Conservative led-governments since 2010 the economy grew by 20 per cent. The economy grew by 73 per cent between 1990 and 2017 but that included 13 years of Labour government. And so it goes on.

Oborne also wants citizens represented by Conservative MPs to write to them demanding retractions every time they hear a lie or misleading statement from Johnson or his ministers.

He also suggests that those attacked in a government statement from ministerial sources should sue. Serving a writ for defamation on a minister, especially Boris Johnson, in a public place would be a valuable demonstration that ministers should take responsibility for what they or their underlings say and do.

Despite his willingness to lead a fight-back against the falsehoods of Boris Johnson, Peter Oborne is not optimistic about the chances of success. But he concludes: "It is time to stand and fight for decency, tolerance, truth and the freedom which comes with it. Serious times of suffering, tragedy and hardship now lie ahead."

The Assault on Truth: Boris Johnson, Donald Trump and the emergence of a new moral barbarism. Simon & Schuster, £12.99

About the contributor
Raymond Snoddy is a media journalist and co-editor of this book. He reported on media for the *Financial Times* and *The Times*. He presented *NewsWatch* on the BBC 2004-2012 and Channel 4's award-winning series *Hard News*. He is the author of a biography of media tycoon Michael Green and of *The Good, the Bad and the Ugly*, which looked at the UK national press in the 1990s. He was awarded an OBE for services to journalism in 2000.

Johnson and journalism: Anonymous sources in senior journalists' social media feeds

Does evidence of increased use of non-attributable sources by top journalists at times of political drama reveal an abuse of the long-established practice and purpose of anonymous briefings, ask David Smith and Julian Matthews

The Johnson premiership will always remain indelibly linked with the Covid-19 pandemic. But, for a time, it also threatened to remain similarly tied in its long-term legacy to Johnson's employment of the divisive and, for some, Machiavellian figure of Dominic Cummings as his chief special advisor. Cummings was brought in alongside several others in similar roles after Boris Johnson's successful bid to become Prime Minister in the summer of 2019, in what several suggested amounted to a 'Vote Leave' government (eg Freedland, 2019). Cummings was only in the role for 16 months before his resignation in November 2020, amidst much briefing and counter-briefing between various senior Government figures. But this was long enough to become a mainstay of opposition ire and of news headlines alike. Indeed, Cummings' role in Government seemed at once to be cast both as influential and as controversial as that of his predecessor Alastair Campbell, advisor to Tony Blair in the 90s and 00s, while his tendency to 'become the story' was similarly reminiscent of the Andy Coulson era in the 2010s.

Part of the wider controversy behind Cummings' influence at the head of government concerns the energy with which he and others were alleged to anonymously brief senior journalists at the BBC and ITV, particularly Laura Kuenssberg and Robert Peston. Kuenssberg and Peston can rightly pride themselves on their access to senior political figures and the speed with which they are able to use such access to inform the 24-hour breaking news cycle. But with such access and speed came scrutiny about whether this can be abused by various powerful sources, like Cummings, to retain anonymity while conducting nakedly partisan political work. The rise of the special advisor and the heightened attention placed on their role, particularly those who support media-facing functions, has come alongside concerns about their alleged role in concentrating power in the hands of the Prime Minister, taking Westminster politics away from the 'real world' and generating tensions between and amongst ministers and civil servants, all of which has raised questions concerning whose interests they serve: Government, ministers or themselves (Yong and Hazell, 2014)?

While now an essential part of the Government machinery, their role as 'temporary civil servants' who nonetheless carry out political tasks has thereby resulted in the designation of a Code of Conduct for Special Advisors in 2016, part of which states: 'Special advisers... are able to represent Ministers' views on Government policy to the media with a degree of political commitment that would not be possible for other civil servants. However, briefing on purely party political matters must be handled by the party machine' (Cabinet Office, 2016). But, as the journalist Nick Cohen has noted, 'as long as journalists are the eager conduits for unattributed spin, the code is unenforceable' (2019).

Goodbye to the truth?

The greatest journalistic scrutiny of the relationship between such powerful-but-anonymous sources and senior journalists has, however, come from Peter Oborne, whose excoriating comments on Laura Kuenssberg and Robert Peston were published on openDemocracy.net on October 22, 2019, following a series of scoops that both journalists had tweeted concerning Government plans to elude possible parliamentary constrictions on leaving the European Union without a deal (Oborne, 2019). Oborne wrote: 'Political editors are so pleased to be given 'insider' or 'exclusive' information that they report it without challenge or question,' alleging this happened by the Johnson Government '[making] its views known to friendly political editors, who push them without much inspection or analysis out into the public domain'. He added: "This client journalism allows Downing Street to frame the story as it wants. Some allow themselves to be used as tools to smear the Government's opponents. They say goodbye to the truth. Social media has provided new ways of breaking the boundaries of decent, honest journalism."

This last part of Oborne's criticism attracts attention in particular. Have the logics of doing journalism on social media resulted in a change in the journalist-source dynamic in the way Oborne claims? Is the principle of anonymity – used in some circumstances to protect whistle-blowing and to hold power to account – used in *these* circumstances simply to exploit journalists' need for speed on social media in order to abuse power and remain unaccountable: to leak, to attack opponents, to fly political kites? Furthermore, is it only Government spin doctors who utilise this mechanism (to the extent that it exists), or do other political actors filter similarly partisan, confidential views through the Twitter accounts of senior journalists in this way too?

To investigate this, we conducted a content analysis of the Twitter timelines of three of the most prominent broadcast political journalists in the UK, Laura Kuenssberg, Robert Peston and Beth Rigby, working for the BBC, ITV and Sky News respectively. We searched their timelines for the period when Dominic Cummings was chief special advisor to the Prime Minister: 24 July 2019 to 13 November 2020, using a search query containing the terms: Source OR Official OR MP OR minister OR insider OR strategist OR aide OR advisor OR adviser OR understood OR believed OR learnt OR learned OR told OR tells OR apparently. After filtering for false positives, we were left with 128 (LK), 138 (RP) and 216 (BR) tweets, a total of 482 tweets. We manually coded these tweets to examine the frequency by which anonymous briefing occurred, which political actors were attributed as providing anonymous briefings and on what they briefed journalists.

Findings: How much, what and who?

Figure 1 shows the frequency of appearances of anonymous sources for each journalist across the time period sampled, while Table 1 demonstrates to which news topics these tweets are oriented. As Figure 1 shows, there were periods of considerable levels of anonymous briefing alongside other more fallow periods during the 17 months. The peaks in each journalist's use of anonymous sources appear in September and October 2019 in each case, while the journalists' timelines in the summer months of 2020 were much less likely to feature such sourcing practices. The period of September and October 2019 is indicative of the fractious debate surrounding the Brexit negotiations and the Government's domestic difficulties in this area – in other words, around the time of Peter Oborne's criticism of this practice. The period which immediately followed was notably marked by a dramatic abeyance in the use of such sources, as the general election neared, and Boris Johnson fulfilled his mission to secure a majority and 'Get Brexit Done'. Thereafter there was something of a revival in anonymous briefings during the spring of 2020, as the Covid-19 pandemic emerged and was met with the Government's 'lockdown' strategy in late March. After a summer lull, the use of anonymous sources re-surfaced in the autumn, marking the resurgence of the pandemic and the various briefings that underscored Dominic Cummings' unexpected and acrimonious departure from Downing Street.

Overall, it seems clear from this data that patterns in anonymous sourcing are driven by the shifting fabric of news events. As Table 1 shows, Brexit has been a dominant feature (at around a third of topics in tweets featuring anonymous sources), with Covid-19 and the election also significant. 'Other' events include general policy discussions but also Labour Party leadership developments, at 11 per cent of all such coverage. Meanwhile, more personal briefings which named (and sometimes explicitly attacked) other political actors amounted to almost one third of these tweets – a considerable and concerning deployment of this device among sources. With some relatively minor differences, the three journalists were often similar in both the frequency and the distribution of topics covered by these tweets, which we would tentatively suggest implies that much of this activity is source-driven, rather than journalist-driven. The most substantial differences here lie in the relatively higher number of anonymous briefings which emerge in the tweet timeline of Beth Rigby, the higher quantity of personality-oriented briefing which occurs in Rigby's timeline and a more even distribution of tweets across the sample period in Laura Kuenssberg's tweets.

Figure 1: Frequency of Anonymous Sources in Journalists' Tweets

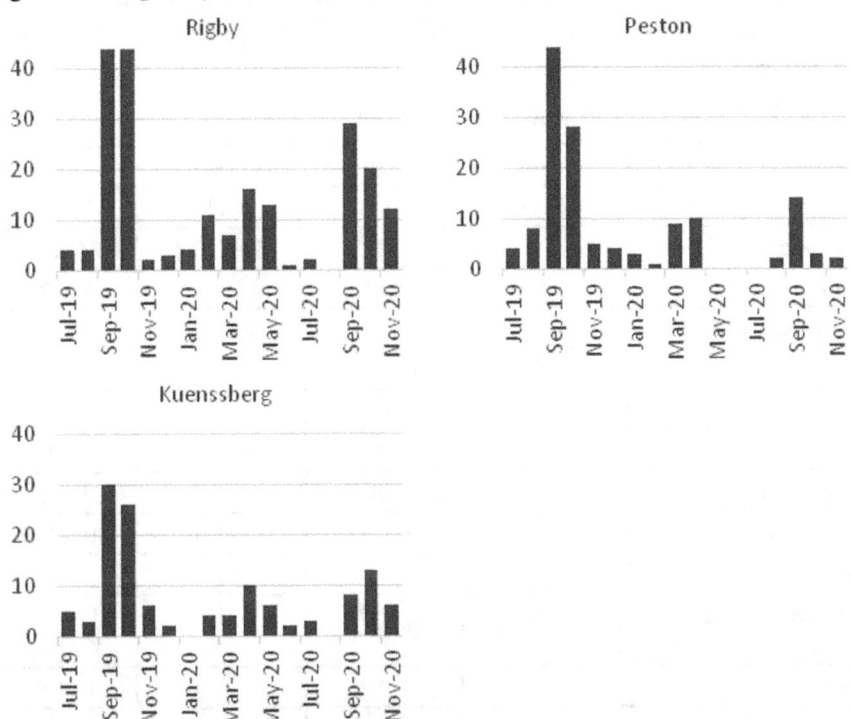

Table 1: Topics of Tweets Featuring Anonymous Sources

Topic	Rigby	Peston	Kuenssberg	Total
	N (%)	N (%)	N (%)	N (%)
Brexit	76 (35.2)	42 (30.4)	39 (30.5)	157 (32.6)
Covid-19	33 (15.3)	28 (20.3)	23 (18.0)	84 (17.4)
Election 2019	19 (8.8)	21 (15.2)	18 (14.1)	58 (12.0)
Other	19 (8.8)	17 (12.3)	17 (13.3)	53 (11.0)
Personalities	69 (31.9)	30 (21.7)	31 (24.2)	130 (27.0)
Total	216	138	128	482

Table 2 displays the attribution of sources in anonymous briefings within tweets in the dataset. Comments from unnamed sources (e.g. 'a source', 'I'm told that', etc) are cited most often of all at 28 per cent of all such sources. Significant opportunities to appear anonymously are provided to both Government and ministerial/cabinet voices, at 13 per cent and 12 per cent respectively, pointing to journalists' attention towards backstage comments concerning the business of government as much as the visibility craved by (and machinations of) certain politicians. The voice of No.10, as distinct from the Government, is also significant at 10 per cent. This speaks to the presence and actions of the special advisor as an increasingly important operator in modern political communication and the potential opportunities for partisan attacks on political opponents that this form of sourcing offers.

Table 2: The Sources of Anonymous Briefings

Source	Rigby	Peston	Kuenssberg	Total
	N (%)	N (%)	N (%)	N (%)
Unnamed	64 (29.6)	38 (25.7)	34 (26.6)	136 (28.2)
Government	35 (16.2)	17 (12.3)	12 (9.4)	64 (13.3)
Ministers/Cabinet	17 (7.9)	16 (11.6)	26 (20.3)	59 (12.2)
No.10	14 (6.5)	18 (13)	17 (13.3)	49 (10.2)
MP	17 (7.9)	0	7 (5.5)	24 (5)
Conservative Party	23 (10.6)	12 (8.7)	10 (7.8)	45 (9.3)
Labour Party	9 (4.2)	12 (8.7)	9 (7)	30 (6.2)
Other parties	2 (0.9)	6 (4.3)	2 (1.6)	10 (2.1)
EU	18 (8.3)	4 (2.9)	2 (1.6)	24 (5)
Whitehall/Civil service	5 (2.3)	4 (2.9)	2 (1.6)	11 (2.3)
Advisors	7 (3.2)	1 (0.7)	1 (0.8)	9 (1.9)
Local Government	0	0	3 (2.3)	3 (0.6)
Medical	2 (0.9)	5 (3.6)	0	7 (1.5)
Political Organisations	2 (0.9)	2 (1.4)	2 (1.6)	6 (1.2)
International Politician	0	1 (0.7)	0	1 (0.2)
Independent Organisations	0	1 (0.7)	0	1 (0.2)
Media	0	1 (0.7)	0	1 (0.2)
Other	1 (0.5)	0	1 (0.8)	2 (0.4)
Total	216	138	128	482

In terms of parties, we see more attention is given to Conservative Party voices than Labour Party voices, while significantly less attention is given to other parties. As such, we can observe that an incumbency bonus seems to appear here as in news coverage more generally (Green-Pedersen et al., 2017), and this is even more acute when the above-named levers of government are taken into consideration. As players in particular policy discussions, the voices of EU and local government also feature, with EU sources the most significant of these, particularly around Brexit discussions. Whitehall/civil service sources also appear on a few occasions. The presence of 'advisors' is low, but it seems unlikely that such sources would go on the record in an identifiable way, and it cannot be discounted that these and other actors are highly likely to be represented among the 'unnamed' (ie completely anonymous) category among others.

There are a number of similarities in the number and types of comments the journalists included. Still, viewed in relative terms, Rigby stands out as including the greater number of anonymous sources (at 29.6 per cent), in addition to the greater number of voices of Government (at 16.2 per cent), and those from the Conservative Party (at 10.6 per cent). It remains an open question as to whether this reflects a form of practice different to those followed by the other journalists.

Drawing back the veil

The patterns above indicate a variety of senior political actors use anonymity to provide information to journalists at opportune moments in the political events cycle. In many cases, whether through negotiation or due to routine journalistic practice, there are no identifying attributes provided when such sourcing practices are used. Where general indications of identity are given, it is clear anonymity is deployed by those in positions of power – in this case, the Government, the Conservative Party and EU sources – most of all. Journalists reproduce the claims made by these sources in their social media feeds in what we might refer to as the '*first edition* of the first draft of history', raising questions about the overall political impact of such sourcing practices and whether (and how) these sources appear correspondingly in later broadcast TV news bulletins. This evidence also adds something to our understanding of how journalists use social media to carry out their work in the hybrid media system (Chadwick, 2017).

In response to Peter Oborne's criticisms, Robert Peston (2019) claimed his job is to 'draw back the veil' on those in power, in what amounts to a distinctly different view about the appropriate relations between journalists and power to that which Oborne offered. For Peston, 'drawing back the veil' means relaying to the public the ideas, claims and policies advanced by those in power. Essentially, this position invokes the public's *right to know* about decisions taken which may affect them. Oborne's position, on the other hand, seems to be that this indicates a naivety about the possible abuses of the anonymity principle, a principle reserved in its highest ethical form for those telling truth to power. As the old saying goes: "Journalism is printing what someone else does not want printed; everything else is public relations."

References

Cabinet Office (2016) Code of Conduct for Special Advisers. Available from: https://assets.publishing.service.gov.uk/government/uploads/system/uploads/attachment_data/file/832599/201612_Code_of_Conduct_for_Special_Advisers.pdf.

Chadwick, A. (2017) *The Hybrid Media System: Politics and Power*. Second Edition. Oxford University Press.

Cohen, N. (2019, 22 October) Meet Dominic Slack-Oxley: The Biggest Source of Fake News in Britain. *The Spectator*. Available from: https://www.spectator.co.uk/article/meet-dominic-slack-oxley-the-biggest-source-of-fake-news-in-britain.

Freedland, J. (2019, 24 July) This is a Vote Leave government now. There will be no one else to blame. *The Guardian*. Available from: https://www.theguardian.com/commentisfree/2019/jul/24/boris-johnson-brexiters-government-no-one-else-to-blame.

Green-Pedersen, C., Mortensen, P., & Thesen, G. (2017). The Incumbency Bonus Revisited: Causes and Consequences of Media Dominance. *British Journal of Political Science*, 47(1), 131-148. doi:10.1017/S0007123415000022.

Oborne, P. (2019, 22 October) British journalists have become part of Johnson's fake news machine. *openDemocracy*. Available from: https://www.opendemocracy.net/en/opendemocracyuk/british-journalists-have-become-part-of-johnsons-fake-news-machine/.

Peston, R. (2019, 22 October) "My Job Is to Draw Back the Veil": Robert Peston Responds to Peter Oborne. *openDemocracy*. Available from: https://www.opendemocracy.net/en/opendemocracyuk/my-job-draw-back-veil-robert-peston-responds-peter-oborne/.

Yong, B., & Hazell, R. (2016). *Special Advisors: Who They Are, What They Do and Why They Matter*. Hart Publishing.

About the contributors

Dr David Smith is Lecturer in Media and Communication in the School of Media, Communication and Sociology at the University of Leicester and Visiting Fellow of the School of Social Sciences and Humanities at Loughborough University. His research interests lie in the field of political communication, the reporting of election campaigns and the mediation of migration issues. He has been involved in the Loughborough University studies of UK election and referendum campaigns since 2015, and his work has been published in *Journalism* and the *European Journal of Communication*. He is Managing Editor of the International Journal of Press/Politics.

Dr Julian Matthews lectures in the School of Media, Communication and Sociology at the University of Leicester, UK. His research interests focus on journalism, news making and the reporting of social problems. He is the author of Producing Serious News for Citizen Children: A Study of the BBC's Children's Programme, Newsround (Edwin Mellen Press, 2010) and the co-editor of The Cultural Intermediaries Reader (Sage, 2014). He writes frequently about the reporting of immigration, terrorism and environmental issues while also convening the British Sociological Association Media Study Group and editing the international journal, Sociology Compass.

(Most) populists aren't what they seem...

Peter York, cultural commentator extraordinaire, looks to the roots of populism among Kansas folk in the 19th century and compares them to the elite populist leaders of today

'All music is folk music. I ain't never heard no horse sing a song.'
– Louis Armstrong

What exactly does it take to be one of 'the people?' (Are you? How do you know?) This matters for any political grouping that claims to be 'of' – never mind 'by, with, or from' – the people. And what does it take to be part of the 'establishment' or 'elite' – whether 'liberal metropolitan', 'global' or 'deep-state'? This too matters for anyone claiming to be '*anti*-elite' or '*anti*-Establishment'..

Populist parties – all the rage now in many countries – constantly say they're 'for' the people and 'against' the elites. *All the time.* Just check, say, Marine Le Pen or our very own Nigel Farage. Clearly, these are people who need people – *real* people, *decent* people, the salt of the earth. But what sort of people are, say, the Ukip leaders themselves?

Ukip – certainly not *of* the people

Ukip, originally the Anti-Federalist League, was founded in 1991 by Alan Sked, a Glasgow University-educated history professor, with a politics DPhil from Merton College, Oxford, supervised by AJP Taylor. He went on to teach at the LSE before entering politics. History and A-list universities are distinctly 'elite' in populist terms. Sked left Ukip in 1997 after falling out with Farage – saying in an interview, "Don't blame me for Farage."

That year, the party got a lucky break with the death of Sir James Goldsmith, the Old Etonian billionaire entrepreneur – father of Zac and Jemima Goldsmith with his third wife, née Lady Annabel Vane-Tempest Stewart; daughter of the 8th

Marquess of Londonderry and the inspiration of Annabel's in Berkeley Square. Goldsmith set up the populist anti-EU Referendum Party in 1994. It was well-funded and well-run, easily outgunning Ukip for Eurosceptic votes. But when he died in 1997, it disbanded and Ukip inherited most of its followers.

Just who are Nigel Farage and his fellow 'Kippers'?

Nigel Farage, who's currently selling some sort of wealth management scheme,[1] is part of the privately-educated seven per cent of the nation. He wears those covert coats with velvet collars. His father was a stockbroker and he worked as a City metals trader before going into politics. He's never been elected as a Westminster MP but for 20 years, until 2020, he was an MEP – better paid, and with much more generous expenses, than an MP[2] – working in the institution he urged British voters to despise and desert. In his 'year out' in 2017, after the UK referendum victory, Leave EU's Aaron Banks supported him with £450,000 worth of Chelsea house rentals, travel, entertainment expenses and the rest.[3]

Another former Ukip leader (2009-10) is the Eton-educated Lord Pearson of Rannoch. He was a Conservative life peer from 1990, but left the Conservatives (with the 21st Baron Willoughby de Broke, an hereditary peer) in 2007 to join Ukip. He has a large Scottish estate and is active in the pro-hunting Countryside Alliance. And yet another recruit to Ukip in 2011 was the colourful hereditary peer and former Conservative minister, Alexander Hesketh, the third Baron Hesketh.

Now political parties can be broad churches – the Conservative Party used to be one. But all this privilege doesn't sit well with Ukip's anti-establishment rhetoric. Its policies may or may not be *for* the people. But what it certainly isn't, in terms of its origins and leadership, is *of* the people. The same goes for the leadership of the Brexit Party (which, formally, wasn't a political party at all, but a limited company).

Ukip's leaders may be surprisingly un-proletarian but its rank-and-file members and supporters aren't. Its core base – as all the demographic analyses have shown – is *older, white working-class men* with few qualifications of any kind. They include many who feel themselves left behind by social and occupational change and let down by careerist politicians who, so they believe, just won't talk about their concerns, particularly immigration.[4]

And who is Donald J Trump?

Trump is yet another example of the long history of parties of the Right borrowing the language of the Left and using it to great effect. *It works!* Look at the Trump supporters, struggling to cope but perfectly comfortable with a self-proclaimed billionaire ('I'm really rich') who talks contemptuously about 'losers', ardently believing his claims to have done everything possible to support them.

Trump was born to real wealth – though, if he'd simply invested in a tracker fund what he inherited from his father, he'd be significantly richer than he is now (even before the impact of the potential civil court cases and criminal investigations that are under way), despite the money he's earned on *The Apprentice*.[5] But, notwithstanding a military school-education followed by Wharton Business School, Trump was never 'establishment' – in Upper East Side Manhattan social terms – rather he was a 'bridge and tunnel' rich boy from suburban Queens. So he dedicated his early business years to courting smart Manhattanites and lobbying *Forbes* to rank him higher in its Rich List than he warranted. The populism and calling out Wall Street, Silicon Valley and the Washington 'swamp' came much later.

Many of the founders and leaders of today's populist parties now just aren't like their followers. The followers either don't know – there are plenty of vox pops where Magas (Make American Great Agains) still describe Trump as a *self-made man* – or don't care: all this fussing about class origins and elite linkages is just what bitter, twisted liberals do. *Like fact-checking.* It doesn't make the slightest difference because populists say what their followers want to hear – they pick the right victimhood stories – and are usually *much* more entertaining than mainstream politicians.

The roots of real populism…are on the Left

The roots of the populist 'us-and-them' stance are American, late 19th century, left-wing and *real*. It's all described in the American political and cultural commentator Thomas Frank's 2020 book *The People – No*. Franks shows how the US political and financial establishment fought back against left-wing populism for more than a century, often by stealing its clothes and its language.

The original People's Party, a coalition of small farmers, labour unions and greenbank parties, pitted against the Gilded Age plutocrats of Wall Street who foreclosed on farm mortgages and drove down pay rates, emerged in Frank's native Kansas in 1892.

The People's Party, which also supported other new causes like women's and black rights, was genuine grassroots, as opposed to Astroturf (that wonderful American word for fake grassroots movements like the Tea Party, organised for the rich and powerful by well-paid lobbyists and PRs in Washington's K-Street). But the right-wing populists making the running this century are, according to the British political commentator Mehdi Hasan (now in the US working for Al Jazeera)…fake.[6]

What characterises all populist parties is a simple us and them, good and evil proposition, virtuous plain folk against the corrupt elite. What's changed is how they are established, by whom and with whose money. And the increasing creativity in definitions of the people and the elites.

Then and now: the Kansas roots and the plants today
The plain people of 1890s Kansas were who they said they were. Everyone knew where they lived. They weren't aliases on the internet, let alone foreign trolls or bots. And their causes were clear and collective. They didn't have Washington lobbyists to write their scripts. And the Wall St grandees really did bear down on those small farmers and industrial workers. The elites weren't today's straw men, from Hollywood celebrities and Washington bureaucrats to public intellectuals and the mainstream media. People knew where they stood. Follow the money.

The *new* right-wing populists – the 'whataboutists' are constantly trying to create a false equivalence with left-wing parties who use some of the old populists' language but have grown-up policies and consistent agendas – know that the world is vastly more complex now. Because of the internet, it's much easier to create a computer game-show of imaginary villains no one's really met. People like the illuminati (who are they when they're at home?) – or the globalists? Conspiracy theories grow and interbreed on their platforms.

Who are the elite?
In a post-industrial online world where it's perfectly possibly not to know who your employer really is – who owns what through a secret Panama Papers hidden web network – you can do that. In the industrial age the business owner was the man with his name over the door, the man in the Roller who lived in the big house just outside the mill town. But globalisation and the internet have enabled the post-truth[7] approach that characterises modern populist parties. Like Humpty Dumpty in Lewis Carroll's 1871 *Through the Looking Glass* ("When I use a word, it means just what I choose it to mean — neither more nor less.") the new populists have alternative facts.[8]

Populist parties in the 21st century operate quite differently from the old political parties, with their definable origins, obvious vested interests, manifestos and meeting rooms. Populism is about an operational style, the 'political technology'[9] of creating the brand, the charismatic leader, the stance and the rhetoric, the feeling and the momentum. It's about achieving power rather than what you'll do when you actually have it – all that tedious crunching and compromising to get anything done. Boring.

Populists assume people don't want to hear that and they're often right.

Do as I say, not as I do
When populists are in office things change. So Donald Trump bad-mouthed Wall Street in early speeches but, once in office, installed two former Goldman Sachs men to run the economy – three if you count Steve Bannon. Trump attacked the 'swamp' of government bureaucracy.

He replaced as many of the judiciary as he could with his sympathisers and put regulators like the Environmental Protection Agency under people explicitly opposed to the principle of regulation.

Populism is what political scientists call a thin ideology, short on actual policies. It has to team up with something settled and familiar to give it ballast. That's usually nationalism – anti-immigration, anti-multiculturalism. Build that wall. Ban those Muslims (but not the rich ones!).

Let's stay with nationalism for a moment (as opposed, in George Orwell's distinction[10], to true patriotism), the nationalism of ministers with flags in their front rooms, of media fuss as about patriotic songs, of 'Make Britain great again' and all that.

Populist nationalism is the second strand of their strategy. For a set of nationalist groups fighting against all the international post-war structures like the EU, UN and Nato, the populists are extraordinarily well networked amongst themselves and, with big money, across the world.

Think of Steve Bannon encouraging Victor Orban (and Tommy Robinson). Think of Nigel Farage in Donald Trump's golden Trump Tower lift after his 2016 US election victory. Think of the Russians lending money to Marine Le Pen. It's difficult for anyone over 50 to imagine the curious complicity of right-wing Americans populists and Putin's Russia, but they clearly have common enemies.

GB News, the new Fox-lite UK broadcaster wears a big British flag, and its supporters constantly accuse the BBC – the British Broadcasting Corporation, banned by law from raising outside funds – of being out of touch with ordinary Brits. But follow the money. GB News' money is coming overwhelmingly from overseas, with some from the Legatum Group, based in Dubai and other funding from Discovery, a US media conglomerate, amongst others. By coincidence the Legatum Institute thinktank, also supported in part by the Legatum Group, has just taken on Professor Matthew Goodwin – who has made a highly successful career by being one of the first academics to observe and report sympathetically on national populism and right-wing voters in the UK – as Director of its Centre for UK Prosperity.

Who is Boris Johnson?

The Eton- and Oxford-educated Boris Johnson became a populist both by being entertaining and performative and because, to become 'world king', he needed to be elected by the Conservative party members who, by 2019, were overwhelmingly Europhobic. His involvement in the Leave campaign came from a calculation of personal advantage rather than any deep conviction: as recently as 2013, he'd written persuasively that Britain's problems were her own fault rather than the EU's.[11]

But once installed as the friendly face of Vote Leave, he took on, with a will, the populist us- and-them stances and the post-truth slogans supplied by Leave's inspired campaign director Dominic Cummings. He became, operationally, a populist. And, in the view of his former *Spectator* colleague Peter Oborne in *The Assault on Truth*,[12] he became a changed man, constantly lying, like his friend Donald Trump. (According to *The Washington Post* fact-checkers, Trump told 30,573 demonstrable lies and misleading statements from 2018 to 2021).[13]

Steve Bannon, Trump's one-time strategy director and the would-be inspiration and co-ordinator of right-wing populist parties around Europe, claims he helped Johnson write the 2018 resignation speech that served as his application for Prime Minister (King).[14] The PM is very unkeen on this story, as he is now on all stories that twin him and Trump as examples of unprincipled blonde ambition.

Tories dress right...

Once in office as PM, Johnson successfully culled the broad-church centre-rightists and Remainers of the more liberal one-nation wing of the party – while still presenting himself as a one-nation' Tory, through his style. If he sounded like, say, Harold Macmillan, he could persuade himself and others that he shared Macmillan's world-view, while still employing Dominic Cummings to dream up and sell policies, backed by a group of bright-eyed young Vote Leave online campaigners hidden in the wings. Some said they, rather than the not very memorable cabinet ministers sitting round that table, were really running the show!

Is it all down to the internet?

Why are populists so...popular? The internet and social media are absolutely central to it. Social media allow people to fake it till they make it.

Populists love to spread conspiracy theories, make sweeping assertions and emotive, evidence-free claims – often under the cover of anonymity. New media have cut out the gatekeepers, the editors and fact-checkers; the named byline professional journalists; and the regulators – you don't even need to pretend to be impartial or balanced online. The internet creates places for people like you, no holds barred. Places where, say, American white supremacists can get together and swap tips without having to convene visible public meetings in pointy hats.

The internet enables mad and formerly marginal ideas to go mainstream. Reliable research[15] shows that 31 per cent of Leave voters believe the replacement conspiracy theory that posits that there's a hidden plan to replace white voters with Muslims and impose Sharia Law in the UK. (Only 6 per cent of Remain voters believe it). In the US about 40 per cent of Trump 2016 voters believe it too. This would've been impossible without the internet, which allows fake news to spread round the world unchallenged.

Populists love social media and they're much better at using them than traditional politicians. This gives them two great advantages. The first is the 'go with the flow' impression that their views are far more widely held than they really are. Determined pro-posters, bots and trolls – what Trump called '400lb boys in their rooms', Macedonian teenagers making money by making things up, plus Putin's Russian St Petersburg Internet Research Agency – create a swelling stage army. You don't need many real people online.

When Donald Trump came down the Trump Tower elevator to announce his presidential candidacy in 2015, many of the rapturous audience had allegedly been recruited from an extras agency called Extra Mile at $50 an hour, according to the *Daily Mail*.[16] The internet also allows trolls to look like mobs at the door, intimidating a whole range of victims. Trolls can say things they'd never say in 'mainstream media' under their own names. Populists can tell lies with impunity online.

Mainstream legacy media have to be more careful – and public service broadcasters are strictly regulated. But Britain's tabloid national newspapers – the least trusted in Europe according to Pew research[17] – have had a hundred years to practise and perfect populist dog-whistle language just this side of the law. Even with plummeting print sales they remain influential and agenda-setting because the Westminster village still reads newspapers, their key stories and columnists turn up on TV and radio, and their content is constantly Googled.

The *Mail* sets the agenda

The *Daily Mail*, the UK's second biggest selling national newspaper (but arguably its most influential), is a populist poster child. Consider its notorious front page of November 4, 2016 with 'Enemies of the people' headlined over the faces of the three judges who'd (correctly) ruled that the Conservative government needed Parliament's consent to trigger Article 50 and leave the EU. It used one of Stalin's favourite phrases, the cue for those enemies to be arrested, executed and 'disappeared'.

So how 'peoply' is the *Mail* itself? Its controlling shareholder is the Eton-educated, billionaire the 4th Viscount Rothermere. Its current editor is the Eton-educated Geordie Greig, former editor of the society magazine *Tatler*, established in 1709. Its former editor (July 1992 to November 2018) – including when that 'Enemies' front page was published – was Paul Dacre. The son of a journalist, privately educated (but not at Eton!) and part of the 4 per cent of his contemporaries who went to university (Leeds). When he left the editorship Dacre was earning almost £2.7m a year, had a house in Belgravia, an estate in Sussex, and another with 17,000 acres in Scotland, and had sent his sons to…Eton. He deserved it all – he'd done a brilliant job as editor, driving the *Mail* to topdog sales status, but you wonder when exactly he'd been alongside the people.

How to speak 'Mailspeak'

There's a whole language that papers like the *Mail* use to display their sympathies for the salt of the earth. The *Mail*'s particular genius lies in constantly redefining the people and the elites to fit the particular subject it is banging on about. The people almost always excludes union members and Labour Party supporters. Equally, the *Mail*'s elite usually excludes the real top 0.1 per cent of major wealth owners – plutocrats, big corporations, toffs, whoever – in favour of what Rod Liddle calls the 'bien pensant' – as if, say, high-minded celebrities, *Guardian* journalists, BBC producers, judges and senior civil servants had all the money and all the power in the country.

At the heart of this narrative is the implication of hypocrisy – the notion that anyone remotely successful and well paid who supports any socially liberal cause must be virtue signalling (actually a *Spectator* invention).

There's been *Mail*-speak about this forever. It used to call this group do-gooders – as if doing good was bad and intrusive…meddling. It updated this recently with the attack on 'wokeness', something which every right-wing medium across the Western world has simultaneously mainstreamed from the anglosphere's right-wing 'Talking Point Central' (it's probably in Delaware!).

In a time of worldwide pandemic, global recession and desperate political divides like the current American situation, the *Mail* appears to think that the greatest challenge facing Britain is 'wokeness' threatening. It's our freedom they say – there's a 'politically correct cancel culture' and it's suppressing all those shy people who daren't say what they really feel – except that they're all shouting it from the rooftops daily in the *Sun*, *Mail*, *Express* and *Telegraph* (Smet for short).

Populists and their media allies bang on about un-British activities on the left. They never acknowledge their own doubly fake origins, neither really of 'the people' nor of the country.

Notes

[1] https://www.theneweuropean.co.uk/brexit-news/nigel-farage-launches-financial-advice-newsletter-freedom-fortune-3849058

[2] https://www.euronews.com/2019/04/04/what-are-the-perks-of-being-an-mep-euronews-answers

[3] https://www.theguardian.com/politics/2019/may/16/arron-banks-allegedly-gave-450000-funding-to-nigel-farage-after-brexit-vote

[4] Goodwin and Ford in Revolt on the Right, March 18, 2014 https://www.routledge.com/Revolt-on-the-Right-Explaining-Support-for-the-Radical-Right-in-Britain/Ford-Goodwin/p/book/9780415661508

[5] https://www.bbc.co.uk/news/business-35836623

[6] The Rise of Fake Populism https://www.youtube.com/watch?v=_bvd4uxhJ3o

[7] https://www.amazon.co.uk/Post-Truth-New-Truth-Fight-Back/dp/1785036874 Post Truth: The New War on Truth and How to Fight Back, Matt d'Ancona, May 11, 2017)

[8] https://edition.cnn.com/2017/01/22/politics/kellyanne-conway-alternative-facts/index.html Kellyanne Conway, Meet the Press Interview, January 22, 2017

[9] https://journals.sagepub.com/doi/full/10.1177/1940161218790035

[10] George Orwell's 'Notes on Nationalism' was first published in Polemic, in October 1945. It's also at https://www.orwellfoundation.com/ the-orwell-foundation/orwell/essays-and-other-works/notes-on-nationalism/

[11] https://www.telegraph.co.uk/news/politics/10052646/Quitting-the-EU-wont-solve-our-problems-says-Boris-Johnson.html

[12] https://www.amazon.co.uk/Assault-Truth-Johnson-Emergence-Barbarism/dp/139850100X

[13] *Washington Post* January 24, 2021

[14] https://www.theguardian.com/politics/2019/jun/22/boris-johnson-steve-bannon-texts-foreign-secretary-resignation-speech

[15] https://www.theguardian.com/commentisfree/2018/nov/25/populism-and-the-internet-a-toxic-mix-shaping-the-age-of-conspiracy-theories

[16] https://www.dailymail.co.uk/news/article-3128230/Did-Donald-Trump-hire-PAID-ACTORS-presidential-campaign-launch-Claims-professionals-extras-brought-pose-supporters.html

[17] https://www.pewresearch.org/global/wp-content/uploads/sites/2/2018/05/PJ_2018.05.17_Media-Politics-Western-Europe_Fact-Sheet_UK.pdf

About the contributor

Peter York is a capitalist tool by background, as a market researcher and management consultant. In parallel he is a social commentator, journalist, occasional TV presenter and author of 11 books, ranging from the best-selling *Official Sloane Ranger Handbook* to *Authenticity is a Con*, an attack on the cult of authenticity, and, most recently, *The War Against the BBC* (Penguin, November 2020), co-authored with Patrick Barwise..

Must Labour lose?

Four general election defeats, failure to land blows on a dysfunctional Prime Minister and mid-term election reverses to an incumbent government has led some to suggest we are seeing the breakdown of the Labour Party's traditional coalition of support and to wonder if the mountain the party must climb to ever govern again is too high. Tor Clark looks at long-term and recent political history to try to answer this crucial question

Must Labour lose? This was the title of academic and journalistic enquiries into the state of the Labour Party in the early 1990s. It seemed that question was categorically dealt with by New Labour's landslide election victory in 1997, followed by two more large wins against an enfeebled Conservative opposition.

By mid-1992 Labour had lost four elections in a row. The Conservative Party and its leaders were often viewed as deeply unpopular in parts of the country but continued to win general elections – with the support of a right-leaning national press.

In 2021 Labour has lost four general elections in a row. The Conservative Party and its leaders – particularly Prime Minister Boris Johnson, Home Secretary Priti Patel and Education Secretary Gavin Williamson – are often viewed as incompetent and deeply unpopular in parts of the country but they were the leaders of a party which won a huge Commons majority at the December 2019 General Election then ousted the Labour Party from Hartlepool, a constituency it had held since its creation, in the May 2021 byelection.

Despite Labour having a competent and electable new leader in Keir Starmer and facing a government which many people – its own supporters included – would acknowledge had made a major hash of the opening phase of the coronavirus pandemic in early 2020, the Labour Party has failed to cut through electorally and without its traditional support in Scotland, many do wonder if it could ever form a majority UK government again. So, must Labour lose? A look at political and media history may help understand the issue and see how it might play out.

A little political history

The Labour Party at the time of writing is only 115 years old. Before it adopted its current name in 1906, it was the Labour Representation Committee, a name which reveals its original intention under its first leader, another Keir, this one Hardie. The party grew out of the trade union movement with the aim of improving the lives of working – labouring – people. That's what the trades unions wanted – better wages, better housing, better education, better healthcare.

In the 19th century Marx and Engels had offered socialism as a way to improve the lives of working people, and in the Victorian and Edwardian eras, when poverty, sickness and inequality were endemic, the ideas of socialism appeared very attractive as an intellectual vehicle to achieve these goals and brought middle class intellectuals into the Labour 'movement'.

The earliest Labour governments often gave cabinet seats to trade union leaders such as JH Thomas and Ernest Bevin, but by the time of the first majority Labour government in 1945, middle class intellectuals such as Attlee, Cripps and Dalton were running the party and the leadership of this group has persisted to the present day.

Labour was essentially a coalition between working class voters, who largely wanted their own living conditions improved, and middle class intellectuals, who largely wanted a more equal society generally. This was an electoral coalition which held together through leaderships from Attlee to Miliband. The Labour Party was seen as being largely in favour of improving the lives of working people.

To some extent the success of Harold Wilson from 1964 and Tony Blair from 1997 was in portraying the Labour Party as being largely in favour of improving the lives of both working class and middle class people. The delivery of socialism, or more accurately social democracy, was seen by both working people and the middle classes as desirable and in their interests.

The Labour Party was always a coalition of these two interest groups, held together by the mutual desirability of its central intellectual aim. But the two groups were quite different in many areas. Much of the working class was socially conservative but voted Labour because they felt no connection with the Conservative Party. Much of Labour's middle-class intellectual supporters had little to no connection or knowledge with the lives and views of their working class counterparts.

So these groups could be viewed as quite different in outlook despite sharing the same political vehicle and, if they could be separated, the Labour Party would have a much narrower support base. So when Scottish independence and Brexit arose at a similar time, the two issues challenged this traditional coalition and presented Labour with a truly existential crisis.

Listen to the views of the two sides of Labour's electoral coalition on immigration for example and watch the intellectuals shudder at the views of the traditional voters. There is nothing at all in common with their approach to this crucial issue.

The 2016 EU Referendum gave these voters a chance to vote differently to their leadership and perhaps demonstrate they thought they were being ignored. When that didn't work they moved their domestic cross from Labour to the Brexit Party. Eventually, when the Brexit Party disappeared, they just went the whole way and voted Tory, something perhaps they couldn't have imagined they might have done even ten years earlier. But Labour didn't listen to them on Brexit or immigration – indeed Labour told them they were wrong and either refused to hear their views or belittled them for even holding those views. This was their revenge.

A little media history
The 'free' press the UK enjoys is rooted in the radical press of the late 18th and early 19th centuries, which successfully challenged the domination of the dull and middle class establishment press of the time, campaigned for wholesale political and social reform and ushered in a long period of free-thinking and cheap journalism for the masses.

Mass literacy and cheap journalism encouraged a printed mass media in succession to the radical press and these newer and more commercial newspapers took up a range of political views.

In the 20th century the working class was served by pro-Labour *Daily Herald* and *Daily Mirror*. The middle class had their interests championed overtly by the *Daily Express, Daily Mail, Daily Telegraph* and less explicitly by the most establishment of the papers *The Times*, which had always enjoyed a small but influential circulation. In the centre sat *The Guardian*, whose own constitution set it up as a left-Liberal publication.

But perhaps most instructive in all this was the position of the newspaper which became the biggest seller from about 1978, *The Sun*. From 1979 political parties believed they needed the support of *The Sun* in order to sway the outcome of general elections with the votes of the paper's millions of readers – and shape political views between elections.

The Sun had previously been the *Daily Herald*, champion of the working classes since 1912, but always struggling to make a profit. Eventually, it was bought and revamped by the owners of the *Daily Mirror*, which understandably wanted to separate it from its working class-orientated, Labour Party-supporting flagship paper. Eventually, in 1969 the Mirror group unwisely sold it to Australian newspaper entrepreneur Rupert Murdoch.

Murdoch rapidly grew its circulation, largely by taking staff and content ideas from the *Mirror*, and toyed through the 1970s with its political allegiance, before the arrival of a new and somewhat populist leader of the Conservative Party in 1975 persuaded him to take the counter-intuitive gamble of aligning a solidly working class audience newspaper with the Conservative Party in time for the 1979 General Election, which the Tories, now led by Margaret Thatcher, won.

The Sun's support for the Tories continued through the 1980s and became emblematic for many of the social and political attitudes of the time – from Gotcha to white van man. But the success of *The Sun* also demonstrated how a conservative outlook and ideas could prove popular with a working class audience, especially if they were centred around forms of patriotism. Thatcherite *Sun*-readers were a warning from history which the left failed to heed.

The Sun switched allegiance for the three Blair-inspired Labour victories in 1997, 2001 and 2005, before returning to what it surely saw as more comfortable territory of Tory support from 2010 onwards. *The Sun*'s political support is centred on two aspects: firstly not necessarily being right at general elections, but being on the winning side, and secondly, Rupert Murdoch's political interests. This explains the switch to Blair's New Labour and another interesting policy direction which became apparent in the late 80s and grew through the next 25 years – anti-Europeanism.

Given Europe really wasn't a major domestic issue in the 1980s, that it had 66 per cent support when last tested in the 1975 Common Market referendum and anti-Europeanism attracted the support of extremely few leading mainstream politicians, the anti-Europeanism of *The Sun* and eventually other newspapers on the right of UK politics may well have proven crucial to the eventual success of Brexit. It should also be remembered that the Scottish version of *The Sun* adopted independence as a policy at the same time as Scottish nationalism rose to electoral prominence.

So, it can be argued that the subliminal and constant pushing of certain agendas by the popular press, over time will have an impact on the political views and voting intentions of ordinary people, particularly those who might normally be expected to vote Labour. To some extent *The Sun* set the political tone of the 80s and 90s, the period when the mature voters of today received their political socialisation.

The current media environment

Readers of *The Guardian* and listeners to broadcast news, especially BBC News, must never cease to wonder how Boris Johnson's Conservative Party retains so much support. But if the rest of the media landscape is surveyed, a different picture emerges. Much of the UK national press remains right wing in consistent political approach. *The Sun, Express, Mail and Telegraph* between them account for the vast majority of UK newspaper circulation.

At the same time much political discussion has moved rather unsatisfactorily to digital and social media, where much of it is unmediated by journalists and populism runs rife.

Vested interests shout at each other when they are not simply enforcing their own prejudices on social media and populism encourages the divergence and hardening of easy answers to complex political problems.

While *The Guardian* and BBC News raise questions about the Johnson government's handling of the pandemic, the right wing papers simply trumpet the resolution or success of 'Boris' – note 'Boris' rather than 'Johnson' – often at the expense of the EU and always at the expense of Labour.

'Take Back Control' and 'Get Brexit Done' were great slogans and headlines which hid the interminable complexity (and potential impossibility) of what those actions would actually involve. The opposite side was unable to produce any form of words to directly and simply challenge either slogan, so the simplistic slogans won their respective polls.

The challenge for Labour

New Labour ran out of steam in the 2010 General Election. Cameron's Conservatives strengthened their grip on power by cannibalising the vote of their erstwhile coalition partners, the Liberal Democrats, at the 2015 general election, as Labour was sensationally almost wiped out by the SNP in its previous stronghold of Scotland.

A seeming fightback by Jeremy Corbyn's Labour against a badly organised Conservative government under Theresa May in 2017 gave the party brief hope, but the reality of the leadership of Jeremy Corbyn's hard-left cabal was exposed in the catastrophic defeat it led its party to in 2019.

From the 1960s, apart from the short-lived loony-left interregnum of the mid-80s, Labour was largely led by middle-class social democrats with a very pro-European outlook. These politicians continued to be elected by their traditional areas of working class support but it could be argued had less and less in common with these voters.

Jeremy Corbyn's ideological socialist politics after his election as leader in 2015 appealed to intellectual, middle-class and often metropolitan voters, but could be seen as irrelevant by its traditional supporters, who particularly did not appreciate his seeming lack of patriotism. He was relentlessly portrayed as a loony lefty by the right-wing press, especially *The Sun*.

One of the ironies of the current Labour position is Corbyn himself had been consistently anti-EU before becoming party leader and campaigned very half-heartedly for Remain in the 2016 EU Referendum when forced to adopt the party's official stance. He was then forced by the middle-class intellectuals in his party to support a second referendum in the 2019 general election, both positions which alienated much traditional Labour supporters – and eventually forced them into the arms of the Conservative Party.

So in April 2020 Corbyn bequeathed an electorally defeated party, which had lost much of its traditional support in the north of England and Scotland, to new leader Keir Starmer, named after the first leader of the Labour movement when it was setting up the Labour Representation Committee – Keir Hardie. What are his chances?

Must Labour lose?

The Labour Party in May 2021 had the smallest parliamentary representation it has had since 1935, a decade before it established itself as a governing party – 202 House of Commons seats. It had just lost the once rock solid seat of Hartlepool and looked on course to also lose the Batley and Spen byelection, due to be held in the summer of 2021. Its relatively recently-elected leader Keir Starmer had taken Prime Minister Boris Johnson apart at Prime Minister's Questions in spring 2020, before lockdown restrictions made that weekly parliamentary sparring impractical and his advantage was lost.

Though the Covid pandemic was a national crisis which could be expected to create a little national unity and support for the government of the day, that government faced so many problems it might have been expected the opposition might have won praise for its critique and its promotion of viable alternative strategies.

But the success of the Covid vaccine roll-out programme in the spring of 2021 and the entrenched political divisions caused by Brexit in England (as described compellingly in chapter 9 of this book by Professor Sir John Curtice) and the strength of the SNP in Scotland have made it hard for a revamped Labour Party to make any kind of electoral progress against the Conservatives.

So the easy answer to this question, seemingly, is 'Yes' but that is too simplistic and there are a handful of political circumstances which could transform Labour's electoral prospects.

Firstly, though voters' opinions on Brexit have transformed Britain's electoral map, Brexit will recede into the background as the years go by and Brexit supporters will get older as Remain-supporting better educated younger voters become more dominant. As Brexit recedes as an issue, and if the Johnson government fails to deliver its levelling-up improvements to its new supporters in northern former Labour 'Red Wall' constituencies, that change could happen even sooner. Traditional Labour voters in Red Wall seats may be socially conservative, but they are unlikely to be economically Conservative and they are most likely to be the first to be negatively impacted if Brexit turns out not to be the success the Tories have promised. So the Tories' love affair with the Red Wall constituencies may be short-lived and they may return to Labour relatively soon.

The waning of the partisan political press may also play a part in Labour being able to overcome obstacles, as younger and often more educated voters are no longer swayed by the dwindling sales of traditional right-wing newspapers, though this may be counteracted by the even more partisan influence of social media, which because of its lack of adherence to the most basic notions of professional accuracy, may pose a more distorting and polarising effect on political opinion-forming.

If Starmer learns from the success of the Blair era, rather than the failure of the Corbyn era, he may conclude that offering prosperity to the many not the few, both working class and middle class voters might be a way forward, a way of reuniting his currently divided electoral coalition behind a common goal.

To do this he must continue to challenge Johnson's government but also advance bright, new popular policies of his own, policies which voters of all backgrounds can support and seek to also recapture the more middle class and southern seats won by Blair's New Labour between 1997 and 2005.

Indeed if we are witnessing a fundamental shift in socio-economic groups' political loyalties, which is temporarily benefiting the Conservatives, in the longer-term there will be more middle-class voters – or more who aspire to be middle class – and this is the more promising group for Labour to target. We have seen this shift in America and it worked well for Joe Biden and the Democrats in 2020.

Nor is this kind of voter realignment so unusual. In the late 19th and early 20th centuries this was precisely the alignment of British politics, with the Conservative and Unionist Party of Disraeli and Salisbury winning support from working men and the most privileged in society while the Liberals won strong support from the middle class. The decline of the Liberals forced the middle class into Tory arms as the enfranchisement of all the working class and women after the First World War boosted support for Labour.

Ultimately a Labour Party trumpeting social justice and prosperity may have a wider electoral appeal than a Conservative Party espousing isolationist nationalism and neo-liberal economics.

Finally, there is the inevitability of electoral cycles. Voters always eventually become weary of one particular political party or political ideology. The Conservatives were ejected in 1964 after 13 years in office; the Tories electorally destroyed in 1997 after 18 years in power; New Labour defeated in 2010 after 13 years; and in 2024, the end of the Johnson government maximum five-year term, his government will have been in power for 13 years. The power of simple voter fatigue cannot be underestimated.

To succeed, Starmer's Labour must actively challenge a government which has made many mistakes. Starmer himself must pit himself winningly against the charismatic, but often inept Johnson, who does not do detail, makes questionable promises and is easily bested by the former barrister's rapier-like deployment of detailed argument.

Most importantly the party must develop policies which win support from a broad section of society, including new middle-class voters in England and, if possible, regain its former traditional supporters in Scotland and northern England.

Of course the 2021 vaccine bounce may turn into a post-pandemic boom and the Conservative Party may conclude Johnson has served his purpose and replace him with his popular Chancellor, Rishi Sunak, which would offer Starmer a whole new battle to fight. But even though the future is not clear for Keir Starmer's Labour Party, history offers compelling evidence it is not doomed to permanent failure and indeed is likely to be successful again.

About the contributor

Tor Clark is Associate Professor in Journalism, BA Journalism programme director and Deputy Head of the School of Media, Communication and Sociology at the University of Leicester. Previously he was the editor of UK regional newspapers. He has been a political journalist since 1988 and has covered eight UK general elections, the last four for BBC Leicester. He is co-editor of this book.

The pursuit of truth – or not

The response by Boris Johnson and his government to Covid-19 has been incompetent, says Dorothy Byrne, Many journalists also think it's been dishonest, but broadcast journalists won't say that. They should, she says

When a man lies often enough, every now and then something he says will turn out to be true. And so it happened with Boris Johnson. He said our country would be 'record-breaking' in this pandemic and it has been, twice over. At one point the UK had achieved the highest rate of Covid-19 deaths per capita in the whole world (though it had fallen down the list at the time of writing) and we also suffered the worst fall in GDP in Europe. But how did Boris Johnson and his cabinet fare when it came to telling the truth intentionally about the greatest disaster in our country since the Second World War?

Privately, radio and television journalists will reel off what they think are the most outrageous lies of this government's Covid-19 catastrophe; how they made out it was just 'following the science', or 'protecting the NHS and care homes', or awarding PPE contracts sensibly.

"I think this government lies more than any government we have ever known. They lie habitually. You wouldn't bother to ring some of the normal channels, you can't trust them or rather, you can trust them to lie," one told me. Another said, "It's like facts don't exist."

A third was furious when a major exclusive they had obtained was denied by government press officers. "They put up a big rebuttal even although we were right. Sometimes they were flailing about but over PPE and care homes, they were deeply dishonest." You won't hear these journalists speak like that in public. It's not the done thing for broadcast journalists to tell the truth about political lies.

Calling out Boris

Back in autumn 2019, I condemned Boris Johnson as a known liar in the annual MacTaggart Lecture at the Edinburgh Television Festival. A number of my colleagues in broadcasting disapproved strongly. They did not dispute the accuracy of my statement. That Boris Johnson is a notorious liar is accepted among UK journalists across the political spectrum.

He was sacked by *The Times* early on in his career for an untruthful front-page story which he misattributed to his own godfather. As the *Daily Telegraph's* Brussels' correspondent between 1989 and 1994, he regularly disseminated 'Euromyths'. He was sacked in 2004 as party vice chairman and shadow arts minister for dishonestly assuring the then leader Michael Howard that reports he had had an affair with a columnist were an "inverted pyramid of piffle." Yet almost all broadcast journalists believe they should not use the 'L' word about Johnson.

Firstly, it's rude and we're British. And secondly, they fear the public could thereby think we have lost our impartiality. Well, that's a risk we have to take. I am indeed not impartial between truth and lies. The public doesn't have the wherewithal to research the facts about politicians' statements and therefore judge accurately whether they are telling the truth. They rely on us for that.

At Channel Four[1] we gave 1,700 people three stories we knew were true and three which were lies. Only 4 per cent of respondents identified them correctly. We, as journalists, are their guides to truth because we have the time and the research expertise to check the facts. We are failing them if we don't speak out when we know politicians are lying.

In the 2016 Brexit Referendum campaign, UK broadcast journalists reported dishonest statements without declaring that they knew these statements to be untrue; thus giving credence to lies. But since then, Donald Trump has polluted our politics further. "He changed the culture. He demolished the principle that politicians should speak the truth honestly," a journalist for another UK broadcaster told me.

In the United States, journalists knew Donald Trump was lying when he said he was cheated of his 'rightful election victory'. But a significant number reported what Trump said right up to the January 6 moment of the attack on the Capitol in Washington, as if it were normal political discourse. People died and the most powerful democracy on earth was put at threat partly because journalists and influential social media commentators disseminated lies rather than calling them out.

Many say it's misleading and unhelpful to liken Boris Johnson to Donald Trump. However, Trump realised that if he spoke a lie often enough, he could get a significant proportion of voters to believe it.

I think we have seen that in the UK in this pandemic. Ministers have made untrue statements over and over again and it has worked for them. A significant proportion of the population has accepted these statements. Partly this is because they sympathised with a government dealing with a plague without precedent for which it could not be blamed. But partly this is because broadcast journalists have not said that we have been lied to in significant ways.

Back in 2019, I was complaining about Johnson's lies concerning EU rules on condoms and kippers. What halcyon days they were pre-pandemic when a politician lying about fish seemed like a big deal. Now he and his cabinet lie about life and death. Back then, his lies were specific. Now the lies are so vast in their ambition that they create a parallel universe.

In one universe, the NHS coped in the first wave of the pandemic and we all clapped them each week for doing so. I stopped the clapping after a bit. I felt I was being used as an enabler.

In the other (real) universe, my consultant doctor friends told me of being instructed to refuse intensive care to anyone aged 65 or over because their hospitals were overwhelmed. Other older friends were not allowed admission to hospital despite being critically ill.

They were told they didn't need hospital treatment but that was a lie. In fact, there were insufficient facilities for everyone who needed medical help. The Covid-19 Bereaved Families for Justice group believes hundreds of their relatives died because they were told wrongly to stay at home.

I decided that if I got Covid, I would create a fake identity as a woman of 59 with no medical problems. I think lying in order to save your life is acceptable. Here's what Boris Johnson should have said at those daily press conferences: "If you are old and get Covid, we might just have to let you die."

'Following the science' or something else?

The Government stated from early on it was 'following the science', when in fact it had rejected scientists' advice to lock down. As a journalist for another broadcaster put it: "It was horseshit that they were being led by the science. They waited a week to lock down and the infection rates doubled." Of course, that journalist has never told viewers the Government was talking horseshit.

The Government similarly rejected advice to impose a two week 'circuit breaker' in September 2020 and encouraged people to meet at Christmas. Some official statements contradicted the truth completely.

Matt Hancock claimed in May 2020 that the Government had "thrown a protective ring round our care homes," when in fact thousands of elderly people were discharged from hospital into care homes, care workers were denied PPE and even told they didn't need it, and care homes couldn't get their staff tested for months. Forty thousand people died in care homes.

In January this year, Johnson said: "What I can tell you is that we truly did everything we could, and continue to do everything that we can, to minimise loss of life…" That statement is manifestly untrue. Note how he used the word *'truly'*. Whenever someone uses that word, feel suspicious. Another of Johnson's favourite phrases is, 'in all candour'. Again, if he is really telling the truth, why does he have to keep telling me he isn't lying?

Every now and then statements have been so ludicrous that no sensible person could believe them. Nobody thought a man drives to Barnard Castle to check his eyesight and it was wrong that the BBC criticised Emily Maitlis for saying so. I have a piece of advice for Dominic Cummings: "Never try to have a secret affair. No wife would fall for your stories."

Similarly, when then Downing Street press secretary Allegra Stratton told us Boris Johnson was a 'feminist', I also thought she had over-reached herself. Who could believe this of a man who said: "Voting Tory will cause your wife to have bigger breasts," and referred to female volleyball players as "semi-naked women… 'glistening like wet otters."

I assume this statement was part of a wider strategy to reposition Johnson to female voters. "Hey sisters, this isn't just a man who lies about women," which is what bothered Michael Howard when he sacked Johnson for lying in 2004. This is a man who has lied habitually to the women in his life and that's what should bother us. Remember that when he's trying to convince you of his honesty.

Holding truth to Boris?

In the past, lying politicians were held to account on TV and radio. They were not named as liars, but their statements were analysed forensically in lengthy interviews. Not anymore. In this pandemic, we have not seen Boris Johnson putting himself up for the sort of grilling to which, for example, Margaret Thatcher subjected herself over the Falklands. Johnson and senior cabinet ministers have failed to appear on *Newsnight* or *Channel Four News*, the two programmes with the time to carry in-depth interviews.

A leading broadcast journalist told me: "They just don't believe in accountability. In one of the great crises of modern times, where is the major interview with the Prime Minister? I can't think of a time when a Prime Minister in a crisis has put himself up so little. There is no proper scrutiny. It's a complete contempt for accountability."

Another says: "Nobody has really challenged the Government in a ruthless and meticulous way that has struck home." A couple of Andrew Marr prime ministerial interviews do not suffice.

Regular press conferences should not be mistaken for accountability. Political journalists, who generally lacked any scientific background, were too often asking a series of disconnected questions. As one journalist put it: "At press conferences, they can deflect questions and the lack of follow-up completely neuters the ability to hold them to account."

The only relevant big hitter to appear regularly on the BBC *Today* programme has been Matt Hancock. Often the ministers sent along to *Today* were not those responsible for the key decisions on Covid and appeared to be reading out pre-prepared statements. As one broadcaster told me: "Their news training is all about tone. So long as they stay calm and seem reasonable, it makes the interviewer seem irritable and interrupting."

Learn from the Education Secretary
Gavin Williamson literally parrots the same response to any question. Asked in January by Piers Morgan on ITV if he would resign because he was so useless, he replied: 'My focus is making sure we deliver the very best for all children."

In March, when Andrew Marr questioned him on his U-turns in decision-making, guess what his response was? "My focus has been doing what is right for children." When Sophy Ridge of *Sky News* also tried to get him to respond to her questions on his failings, he replied: "My focus is always about trying to deliver the very best for children."

Indeed, just type into Google, 'Gavin Williamson .... my focus is' and you can waste hours of your life counting the ways in which this man refuses to answer questions. Gavin Williamson probably would go to an optician for an eye test, rather than take a drive, but the test would fail because his focus would always be in the wrong place.

Some broadcast journalists have felt the public would think it unfair to savage Johnson in interview. One said, in an off-the-record comment: "The media have pulled their punches. They have not felt it would look right morally to be holding the leader's feet to the fire in an emergency. The Government record on PPE and Test and Trace has been lamentable, the contracts stink, but the Government has been almost completely unaccountable."

In the absence of these grillings of old, broadcast journalists tell viewers the facts and then state the government point of view. "It's ludicrous. The Government denies it so we can't just say it's true. You can't report facts as you see them." As another put it: 'The reason for not lying it is that you are going to get caught out. But they don't get caught out.'

Across all platforms, disinformation and misinformation are rampant. We are living in an age of information anarchy. Much of political discourse is about matters of opinion but some is about matters of fact. Broadcast journalists were given a duty, laid down in regulation, to tell the truth. If fear of being perceived to be partial prevents us from telling viewers and listeners which statements by politicians are true and which false, then we fail in that duty.

All I am asking is that at least sometimes, when the Government makes an untrue statement, broadcast journalists say it's untrue. Our audiences deserve that.

Notes
[1] https://www.thedrum.com/news/2017/02/06/only-4-people-can-distinguish-fake-news-truth-channel-4-study-finds

About the contributor
Dorothy Byrne was Editor-at Large at Channel Four Television up to the end of April 2021. Prior to that she was Head of News and Current Affairs at Channel Four for 17 years during which time the channel's news and current affairs output won many Bafta, RTS, International Emmy and other awards. She has received awards from Bafta, the RTS, The Grierson Trust and Women in Film and Television for her major contributions to television journalism.

Section three
Covid, journalism and society
***

The vaccine may be working on the population, but what about the health of the media?

John Mair

Boosterism is the watch word for Prime Minister Johnson's policy on the pandemic. Boosterism tempered by some caution once he too became a (near fatal) victim of the virus.

Boosterism too, along with scepticism, have been the watch words of the British media. Television and radio have told it like it is however unpleasant the truth. The public have chosen them as their main information source. The printed press have been unable to slough off their political and Political pre-dispositions.

They cheered for Boris much of the time. Some have taken to continual sniping on restrictions to 'freedoms' such as lockdowns, the vaccination programme and the wearing of masks. They may well have pushed the public health envelope open too much and too soon with unintended consequences.

I have developed a sub-genre of pandemic studies editing and publishing four books in the last year (*The Virus and the Media, Pandemic – where did we go wrong?, Pandemic – where are we still going wrong?* and *Pandemic – a year of mistakes?*) – all published by Bite Sized Books. I would therefore claim some agency or expertise in the subject. It does seem to me that, until recently and the vaccine bounce, the Covid pandemic has not been the proudest moment for the media or for the populist government of Boris Johnson.

Juliet Rix is an award-winning freelance journalist. In *When the politics of science met the science of politics* she turns the spotlight on the sheer scientific illiteracy

The vaccine may be working on the population, but what about the health of the media?

of much of the British press. She has been among the scientists to find out their perspective.

In her words: "In a pandemic of a previously unknown disease, science is obviously central to an effective response. The Government appeared to acknowledge this from the start, with Boris Johnson's soon-familiar mantra, 'We are following the science'. But science is not a flag at the front of a parade. Especially in relation to a novel virus about which we are constantly learning, 'the science' is a complex, shape-shifting beast. Populism doesn't do complex, slogans do not come with caveats, and neither, on the whole, do headlines."

Alan Rusbridger is one of the greats of British journalism. He edited *The Guardian* through a purple patch of 20 years. That ended with a Pulitzer Prize for the Edward Snowden revelations on the US's National Security Agency. Now he chairs the Reuters Institute for the Study of Journalism at Oxford University where he is head of house at Lady Margaret Hall.

In *The Virus and journalism: Telling truth to the hacks?* Alan muses on how journalism has reported the pandemic. He draws a rather instructive parallel with journalism and climate change: "In four months (of the pandemic) you had a compressed version of how climate change has been playing out in the media over four decades. Ignore; deny; underplay; ghetto-ise; marginalise; question; disparage; balance; shrug; pay attention; pivot; reassess; jump."

He goes on to call for some self-reflection: "I do think journalists need to look into the mirror a bit more and try to see themselves as others see them. The best of journalism will thrive. Maybe it needed a pandemic to wake us up to its importance."

To a different and much more intimate essay in *The view from the hospital frontline*, a report from the wards of Leicester Royal Infirmary by Julian Barwell.

In April 2020, Professor Barwell, a clinical geneticist, decided it was time to don his white coat and stethoscope again and go back onto the wards. This is his first-hand story of what he found inside the hospital and how it changed his perception of what was happening in the outside world. It is a cracking and moving read.

On a personal level: "My lasting memory will be holding my phone to patients' ears, if they didn't have their own, so they could speak to their families, perhaps for the last time. So intimate and personal, it felt like an intrusion and was something I had never witnessed in 30 years. It moved me deeply and is something I will hold with me forever." And on a professional level: "Research is the answer to the pandemic and everything else is mere stalling."

From the frontline in the ICUs to the frontline in the newsrooms. Television, especially the BBC, has had a good Covid war. Mark Easton is the Home Affairs Editor of BBC News and has broken some of its scoops, including the discovery of a secret morgue for victims in the glades of Surrey.

Finding it took persistence, filming it patience, transmitting it was courageous. In *Covering Covid reveals uncomfortable truths* he explores some of the ethical dilemmas he faced with that story, and journalism more generally, with reporting the pandemic.

"The virus has proved to be one of those rare events that directly changes the lives of every single person on the planet ...The Covid pandemic is more than a story. It is a matter of life and death. We may not wish to hear that. We may prefer things were not as they are. We may yearn for a different reality. But when the stakes are this high, the media has a responsibility to destroy illusions. The truth is uncomfortable," he says.

For a more academic treatment of the reporting of the pandemic, Professor Rob Dover of Hull University offers it in *Populism, anti-system politics and the media: A spotlight on Covid-19*. He explores what he calls anti-system populist politicians and media who have developed tropes on intolerance since the Brexit debate. "When it comes to Brexit those experts are dismissed as 'remoaners'. During the pandemic, virologists and epidemiologists have been denigrated with personal attacks in the legacy media (e.g. 'Dr Doom') or in terms of having psychological needs to continue the lockdowns."

Dover continues: "Those advancing the agenda of disruption (be it through Brexit, Maga, and no Covid restrictions) see the established order as one of managed decline, and they see themselves as being on a historical mission to break free of this historical inevitability and to deliver a form of 19th century laissez-faire on the world."

The pandemic exposed the fissures in British society in terms of class, age, geography and race. In *Now you see 'race', now you don't: The hyper-visibility and hyper-invisibility of race and Covid-19 in political and public health discourse* Dr Paul Ian Campbell of the University of Leicester places the high death rate among black and brown communities in a theoretical context. He says the media have been generalised and unhelpful and have missed the more important point about inequality in 21st century Britain.

As he puts it: "The higher Covid-19 infection and mortality rates among people from these communities have frequently been framed as the result of either a cultural or physiological dysfunction within particular minority-ethnic communities. The logical progression of this viewpoint is that Britain's extraordinarily high Covid-19 infection and mortality rate, which has resulted in 127,000 deaths, is only in part the consequence of ineffective policy or inaction. It is instead viewed as a seemingly 'obvious' and inevitable consequence of Britain as a multiracial society which is home to people of colour who, unlike the white population, are simply more prone to contract and spread the virus."

Finally, by way of summary, my fellow editor and doyen of the media corps Raymond Snoddy, late of *The Times* and *Financial Times*, poses the need for a full

The vaccine may be working on the population, but what about the health of the media?

inquiry in *Messengers as well as messages in the spotlight* – written long before that announced by Boris Johnson on May 10 2021.

Johnson was vague (deliberately?) on timing and scope of his inquiry. Snoddy lays down some lines to follow on government action and inaction, but calls the remit to widen to include the media.

The press have not come out of Covid smelling of roses. "It is not just the Government that needs to learn the lessons from the often-egregious mistakes made," he says. "A number of national newspaper editors also face a steep learning curve not just to cope with the current pandemic, which has not gone away, but for the inevitable, further pandemics to come."

The Covid pandemic was quite simply the biggest public health crisis, the biggest fiscal crisis and a civic/societal one too that the UK has faced since the end of the Second World War. It may, but only may, be ending well thanks to the superb work of scientists in Britain and elsewhere and the herculean work of the National Health Service in saving lives and inoculating millions against the virus.

The British media may not come out with such a clean bill of health.

When the politics of science met the science of politics

'Following the science' emerged as one of the mantras of the pandemic. But was it merely a slogan that politicians trotted out and an umbrella under which many actions were justified? Juliet Rix analyses what happened

In a pandemic of a previously unknown disease, science is obviously central to an effective response. The UK Government appeared to acknowledge this from the start, with Boris Johnson's soon-familiar mantra 'We are following the science'.

But science is not a flag at the front of a parade. Especially in relation to a novel virus about which we are constantly learning, 'the science' is a complex, shape-shifting beast. Populism doesn't do complex, slogans do not come with caveats, and neither, on the whole, do headlines.

So how has the media done at presenting the scientific evidence behind populist pronouncements? And how has it been for the scientists trying to keep the media informed?

Positive, but with reservations
"Our experience has been mostly positive," says Fiona Fox, Director of the Science Media Centre, the excellent service that provides journalists with scientific briefings and introductions to scientists willing to be interviewed.

There has, though, been a problem with politics. "Some scientists have definitely not enjoyed being pressured to answer questions about policy," she says. "I have had emails saying, 'I don't want to [talk to the press] anymore because I'm supposed to be speaking about the science, and then I am asked if Boris is wrong about Christmas'."

It has been tricky, agrees David Leon, Professor of Epidemiology at the London School of Hygiene and Tropical Medicine. "Journalists ask questions like, 'What will happen when schools re-open?' They are good questions, but we're being asked to peer into crystal balls, and 'we don't know' doesn't make good copy."

"The media has used scientists to criticise government policy," Fox continues, "some are happy to be used in that way; others are not." And there's a danger, she says, that the public will assume that rather than presenting their own opinion, the scientist is expressing a scientific consensus.

Equally, it may be clear that they are not, says Dr Jeremy Rossman of the School of Biosciences at the University of Kent, and such fragmentation can be just as damaging to scientific credibility. A media polarised by populism, "can then pick a scientist for any angle." But Rossman doesn't see silence as an option: "When governments are not acting on the science and are pushing their countries in directions that, as a virologist in the middle of a pandemic, I see as incredibly dangerous, I feel compelled to comment."

Seen but not heard

Sometimes there *is* a consensus, says behavioural scientist Professor Susan Michie, a member of both the UK Government's Scientific Advisory Group for Emergencies (Sage) and Independent Sage. If government isn't listening, she says, the only way scientists can make themselves heard is through the media.

"Last summer [2020] was really difficult," she continues, "the Government was promoting an unrealistically positive message (at the time of Eat Out to Help Out). It made people feel good, but the scientists knew it would only lead one way. The same happened at Christmas. The politicians were telling people what they wanted to hear and scientists like myself who were having to counter that in the media, were labelled doom merchants."

It's happening again with vaccines, Michie adds. The government narrative – backed by sectors of the press – is all about "British success, and the vaccine roll-out as the answer to everything."

Witness, she says, the slick promotional video, *A Beacon of Hope,* the Prime Minister pinned to his Twitter account on March 10. "This is dangerous," and it's been left to scientists, speaking to the media, to try to provide the crucial caveats: "Vaccines do not provide 100 per cent protection, we don't know how effective they are against transmission, there are variants of concern…Once more, we are the ones making the bad news stories, so we are seen as the problem."

The media hasn't always helped. As the roll-out began, a range of publications and broadcasters quoted and vox-popped emotional recipients of early jabs joyfully proclaiming that they could now hug their grandchildren – failing to point out that significant protection takes two to three weeks to kick in.

Such public health messages are perhaps primarily the responsibility of government, but if those in power are failing to provide them, the press surely still has a role. Provision of key facts is a basic tenet of good reporting and most media outlets would say they want to help their audience stay safe – which may not have happened in this case.

"Both Israeli and Public Health England data show," Michie points out, "that in the nine days after vaccination the rates of infection have gone up. The most likely explanation is that people are dropping their guard".

A deficit of data

There have been some basic scientific errors in press coverage, such as the oft-repeated reassurance as vaccine rollout began, that the Pfizer trial had "already put the jab into more than 40,000 arms." No it hadn't. The trial involved more than 40,000 people, but only half of them received the vaccine. The other half were, as in any good trial, the control group. This wasn't wilful misrepresentation, just lack of understanding and attention to detail.

"I've found many of the journalists I've spoken to be highly scientifically literate," says Rossman, "but there is a deficit in understanding data, knowing what numbers mean – our education system does not teach this well. An efficacy of 75 per cent, for example, is often not properly explained…I've never seen an article that differentiates between efficacy and effectiveness [efficacy comes from trial data, effectiveness is real world] and there is rarely any mention of effectiveness at what – preventing death? Hospitalisation? Mild to moderate symptomatic disease? Transmission? These are all different."

A leading newspaper actually wrote in an explainer on understanding vaccine data that 93 per cent efficacy meant that in the trial this percentage of vaccinated people did not get Covid-19. It doesn't, of course, it means that of the trial participants who got Covid-19, 93 per cent were in the unvaccinated group, only 7 per cent among the vaccinated.

To be fair this glaring error was quickly corrected, and that has been one of the better features of the pandemic press, says Fox: "Newsrooms have become more responsive and it's been much easier to get inaccuracies put right."

More frequent than a lack of truth is a lack of the whole truth. Key scientific study results, especially where commercial and governmental interests are involved as with drugs and vaccines, have often been first reported by press release. News outlets dutifully repeat the top lines without digging down into the data.

Was the efficacy of the Oxford AstraZeneca vaccine in its first set of trials the 70 per cent that appeared in many headlines? Only if you included a small group given a different dosage from that being provided to the public. The relevant figure was 62 per cent. And what about that fact that there were no hospitalisations or deaths in the South African trial of the same vaccine. Perfectly true, but there weren't any in the vaccinated or unvaccinated group, so that tells us precisely nothing about the vaccine.

Hanging in the balance

It's hard for scientists to ensure they are not misused by the media, and for the media to understand that it is not balance to give equal weight to evidenced science and un-evidenced ideology (something the BBC has apologised for doing in relation to climate change).

Michie describes a bad experience with a prominent UK radio programme. It was at the time of the anti-lockdown, pro-natural herd immunity 'Great Barrington Declaration' (declared, in more or less (un)repeatable terms, by every scientist I have spoken to, to be absolute rubbish). Michie agreed to go on the show on condition she was not put head to head as equals with "this fringe minority saying something incredibly dangerous." She received full assurances but, in the end, that is exactly what happened "and their views, for which there was no supporting evidence, got the first and last word."

Things get particularly difficult when political reporters cover science-based stories, says Fox, and with the Government wanting to claim credit for scientific successes and to use science to justify its actions, this inevitably happens.

"We had a briefing on a new health study lined up for a Monday with the four clinical researchers who had all the details," Fox says, "but when we switched on the *Andrew Marr Show* on Sunday they were reporting it. It wasn't wrong but it wasn't science and it was a lost opportunity to understand it properly. By Monday the story was old and nobody was interested".

Worse is when scientific data is co-opted out of context. "Take the graph that was used to justify going from tiers to lockdown," says Fox. "The BBC's Political Editor Laura Kuenssberg was given the graph (showing up to 4000 deaths a day if no action was taken) by No 10. The Government used it to imply there was new evidence, but Sage had been warning for quite some time that the tiers were not working. That graph was just part of a series modelling what might happen, and the scientists who created it were very unhappy about how it was used.

"Sharing 'new' data was convenient for the Government who didn't want to admit they had been ignoring scientific advice. Anti-lockdown papers like the *Telegraph* and the *Mail* then pulled the graph apart for days, undermining public trust in scientific evidence."

Sometimes there genuinely is new evidence and populist governments, looking over their shoulders at the popular press, find it difficult to pivot. "Political reporters are after 'scalps'…there's a 'gotcha' style," says Fox. These are perfectly legitimate political stories, and the Government has invited them by setting distracting numerical targets (around testing for example), but "this does not help public understanding of science or encourage people to admit when they get something wrong."

This has been difficult for scientists, agrees Rossman, "At the beginning many of us were saying masks were not the answer for the general public, then we realised how high community transmission was and we started saying everyone should wear masks. I still get reporters saying, 'but you said before…'. Yes, I did, and I was wrong. We know more now; the evidence has changed. That's how science works."

Evidence, evidence, evidence
"There has been so much attention given to hand washing and surfaces that we have lost the fact that most transmission is airborne," Rossmann continues. The messaging and coverage have not changed with the evidence, and many people still don't understand that the virus can be passed not only in droplets emitted directly by infected people, but also in much smaller aerosols that can hang in the air, especially indoors.

Important truths are drowned out too by the populist obsession with keeping things simple. "Science by headline can be dangerous," Rossman says. "Self-isolate for ten days, stay six feet apart – infection can last longer, the virus can spread further. Science rarely produces a single number – the reality is a range."

Michie would like to see the press go beyond reacting and be more proactive in drawing attention to the bigger picture. "Independent Sage has been pushing for months and months for a zero Covid strategy. The media have made it impossible and we've now had to switch to calling it 'maximum suppression'. Every time we said 'zero Covid' they characterised it as unrealistic to get to zero; they wouldn't engage with what it actually meant and that it is the strategy of the most successful countries, those that have done best both in terms of health and their economies. Why are we not learning from other countries?"

It would certainly have been easier for the press if the Government had been more open, says Fox, "If I had been running their media strategy, I'd have told them to say, 'This is a new situation, we're going to try this, but we might get it wrong'."

Its failure to do so, and the overlay of 'British exceptionalism', says Michie, has distorted the coverage away from the science. And crucially, adds Rossman, "'The science' isn't one expert's view or the results of one study, "'The science' should mean every bit of evidence we have to date," – and it will keep changing.

This is challenging for any media organisation, as well as for the scientists who continue to brief them, but Michie concludes: "When large numbers of avoidable deaths and people's livelihoods are at stake, and the whole of society needs to get out of these restrictions, it is surely in everybody's interests to have an accurate portrayal of the situation."

This hasn't always happened and "there have been days when we've been tearing our hair out," admits Fox. "But I try to be positive. This pandemic has raised the status of science and health journalists and that can only be good for the future."

About the contributor

Juliet Rix is a freelance journalist working for *The Guardian*, the *Telegraph*, *The Times*, the BBC and others. She studied natural sciences at Cambridge and has an ongoing interest in health journalism. Juliet worked in BBC television science features and current affairs before moving into radio reporting and then going freelance.

The virus and journalism: Telling truth to the hacks?

Alan Rusbridger, former editor of The Guardian and chair of the Reuters Institute for the Study of Journalism, muses on how his craft comes out of the Covid pandemic

In some ways the Covid-19 crisis in 2020 was a dress rehearsal for climate change. It began as a faraway problem of uncertain severity. A few people affected on the other side of the world. The story failed on almost every count. There was no newsroom metric in existence which would convince a busy news editor – under pressure to drive clicks, or subscriptions, or dwell-time – this was worth paying much attention to.

Add this: many papers have had to cut back on science or health specialists and foreign correspondents. So, there was no-one internally to raise the alarm. For the first month, from around the start of December 2019, the story barely merited a mention, it was a discussion circulating among scientists. About five weeks in, the first risk assessments in the West began to appear – but not very much in the media. By eight weeks in, the mainstream medical press had begun to take serious notice. And then, as the effects of the disease began to show up in Europe and America, the mainstream media began to prick up their ears. It was not easy to catch up. The experts disagreed – and very few newsrooms had the scientific authority to choose between them. The predominant message was there wasn't too much to be alarmed about. This was no worse than the flu. Some news outlets were in full denial mode or parroted the dripping scepticism coming out of the White House and elsewhere. Few newsrooms were skilled at communicating risk. The average reader had no clear direction through most of February, just mixed messages.

Alarm replaces complacency

It was early March 2020, fully three months into the crisis, that alarm replaced complacency. A story that had hitherto been in the hands of science and medical writers now swamped everything. Within a short time this was now an emergency that overwhelmed everyone. It was no longer just about health, it was about business, transport, jobs, security, the economy, immigration, communications, defence, food, banking, sport. It was too late. In four months you had a compressed version of how climate change has been playing out in the media over four decades. Ignore; deny; underplay; ghetto-ise; marginalise; question; disparage; balance; shrug; pay attention; pivot; reassess; jump.

The greatest long-term crisis of our time is, naturally, the greatest challenge for the news. How can it be reported accurately? What attitude should a newsroom take? What proportion of the news should be dedicated to it? How do you make a business model out of gritty, detailed reporting on a subject that frightens us?

Who do we trust with the news?

Covid-19 could not have announced itself at a worse time in terms of the question about who to believe. Survey after survey showed unprecedented confusion about where to place trust. Nearly two thirds of adults polled by Edelman in 2018 said they could no longer tell a responsible source of news from the opposite. This was not how it was supposed to be.

The official script for journalism was once people woke up to the ocean of rubbish and lies all around them they'd come back to the safe harbour of professionally-produced news. You couldn't leave this stuff to amateurs or give it away for free. Sooner or later people would flood back to the haven of proper journalism. It's not that this official narrative was completely wrong, but nor was it right in the way the hopers hoped it would be. There was a surge of eyeballs to mainstream media sites, but it was too soon to judge if the increased traffic would remotely compensate for the drastic loss of revenues as copy sales plummeted and advertising disappeared. It normally didn't.

Just as the UK Government recognised journalists as essential workers during the Covid crisis, the industry looked more fragile than ever. Surveys of trust showed the public, especially the older public, relying on journalists but not trusting them. Another Edelman special report in early March found journalists at the bottom of the trust pile with 43 per cent of the view that you could believe them 'to tell the truth about the virus'. That compared with 63 per cent for 'a person like yourself'.

As the pandemic wore on, so trust in both UK politicians and news organisations slumped. Between April and May 2020, according to Reuters Institute for the Study of Journalism [RISJ], trust in the Government plunged a full 19 points, partly, it was thought, as a result of newspaper investigations which appeared to show double standards between what the Government was saying and what its top advisers were actually doing. But if reporters expected gratitude for their efforts they were disappointed, the same period saw an 11 point fall in trust in news organisations.

I am a recovering journalist…

I spent most of my working life in journalism; I would like people to believe the best of it. I like the company of journalists and, as an editor, was frequently lost in admiration for colleagues, on *The Guardian* and beyond, who were clever, brave, resourceful, quick, honest, perceptive, knowledgeable and humane. But it was impossible to be blind to so much journalism that was none of those things, journalism that was stupid, corrupt, ignorant, aggressive, bullying, lazy and malign. But it all sailed under the flag of something we called 'journalism'. Somehow, we expected the public to be able to distinguish the good from the bad and to recognise it's not all the same, even if we give it the same name.

But making a general defence of journalism was hardly helped by those who wanted to drag the response to Covid into the dreaded culture wars. Seriously, why publish James Delingpole, who, at the height of the Covid-19 crisis, took to retweeting the claims of quack doctors who claimed to be able to cure coronavirus patients? Or, if you're trying to make the case of journalism as a reliable system of knowledge, why commission Toby Young to spread misinformation on herd immunity? Remember his June 2020 pronouncement in the *Telegraph* that the virus had 'all but disappeared'?

Over there, the Fox and its coop

Of course, the worst 'mainstream' offender was *Fox News*. The pattern of Fox reflecting or assisting the Trump candidacy and administration had persisted over years. Most recently, look at the almost perfect correlation of the news channel's coverage of coronavirus in late February/early March 2020 to see how numerous *Fox* hosts mirrored the White House line, a journey from outright scepticism to belated acknowledgment of the gravity of the pandemic. By April 2020 the channel's coverage of Covid-19 was sufficiently misleading that a group of 74 professors of journalism and journalists wrote an open letter condemning the coverage as 'a danger to public health… Indeed, it is not an overstatement to say that your misreporting endangers your own viewers and not only them, for in a pandemic, individual behaviour affects significant numbers of other people as well."

Ben Smith in the *New York Times* pointed out the channel was notionally run by Murdoch's son, Lachlan, and questioned why Rupert Murdoch himself hadn't got a grip. Maybe, at 89, he was simply no longer up to it. Maybe he no longer cared? Maybe it was more important to Murdoch to stick with the President than insist on rigorous editorial standards. Or was he now so ideologically aligned with elements of the populist right he no longer knew science from slant? Whatever the reason, the channel waited until the 11th hour to dump Trump – but at what cost to its own reputation and the general attempt by decent journalists to make the case their craft stands apart, and above, from the information chaos all around.

'Truth to power? Or more reflection?
The official story paints journalists as people who tell 'the truth to power'. But 'truth' is a big word and we seldom like to reflect on our own power. I do think journalists need to look into the mirror a bit more and try to see themselves as others see them. The best of journalism will thrive. Maybe it needed a pandemic to wake us up to its importance.

This chapter is adapted from News and How to Use it by Alan Rusbridger, published by Canongate, in November 2020.

About the contributor
Alan Rusbridger is Principal of Lady Margaret Hall at Oxford University. From 1995 to 2015 he was editor-in chief of *The Guardian*. He is now chair of the Reuters Institute for the Study of Journalism and a member of the Facebook Oversight Board.

The view from the hospital frontline

When the first wave of the Covid-19 pandemic started to bite in April 2020 and his hospital began to fill up with coronavirus patients for the first time, Professor Julian Barwell, a clinical geneticist, decided it was time to don his white coat and stethoscope again and go back onto the wards of his hospital. This is his first-hand story of what he found inside the hospital and how it changed his perception of what was happening in the outside world

At the start of April 2020, as the Covid-19 pandemic took hold on the country and patients began arriving in my hospital, I decided it was time to return to the acute medical wards after 19 years away. It turned into an inspiring period in my professional life and changed my perspective on life inside and outside the hospital.

Normally I am a clinical geneticist with a specialist interest in familial cancer which means I look after people with a personal or strong family history of cancer to understand the cause of the disease in the family and go on to try to reduce the burden of the disease of the family through lifestyle, medication, preventative surgery or screening.

We have discussed this more broadly in the media describing the impact of decisions by celebrities on healthcare behaviour by the general population, such as the Angelina Jolie effect on genetic testing and preventative breast surgery. We have also highlighted the use of new technologies and partnerships in identifying the cause of disease in families through the 100,000 Genome Project and finding genetic weaknesses in tumours we can target, treating disease for what it is, rather than what it looks like: Thinking beyond the scope.

I entered clinical genetics from acute medicine in 2001 and as the Covid pandemic first took hold in the spring of 2020 in the UK, I volunteered to return to the ward. I chose medical oncology where cancer patients were being treated with acute emergencies such as chest infections, blood clots, spinal cord compression, severe constipation or pain. Although this was not a nominated Covid ward, there was always the possibility a patient might have Covid, whilst waiting for their swab result to come back, or the patient might be developing Covid. I was worried about the impact of Covid in cancer patients and thought it would be important to help, although I often felt torn between this and the needs of my own patients in clinical genetics.

It is easy to forget how little we knew about Covid at this time. Stories of overrun hospitals from the Far East had been in the popular press and, at times, it certainly felt like a feeding frenzy of fear. There were a number of concerns about fake news but I was personally struck by three things; how we reconnected with nature during a stunning spring, the desire for people to step up and help, and how many of the rushed moments of our lives involving after-school clubs and hobbies suddenly stopped, giving time for reflection. I remember asking my outstanding junior doctor if she was worried and she replied: "I was born for this moment." It captured the mood and many colleagues with prior experience in other specialities volunteered to help on the wards, palliative care and the intensive care units. It was time to finally sort out a will, take a deep breath and sort out some extra online training in the days before starting.

Friends and family were incredibly supportive as there were a huge number of changes to come to terms with in a short period of time. A new job, new colleagues, the potential of catching Covid, but in a strange way one of the most difficult was coming to terms with new computer systems. The human body, patients and diseases hadn't changed but what I could do in a digital age had altered. This took some time to fully get up to speed with and was frustrating. Whilst explaining to a nurse it had been 19 years since I had worked on a ward, my pride was slightly dented when asked if I had come out of retirement, which was a bit disconcerting at the age of 47!

The junior doctors, however, were now a generation below me and had been brought up in the internet, mobile phone and social media age. I noted their confidence in reading and assimilating information from screens rather than written notes. No longer did we have prescription charts or observations such as blood pressure and temperature charts by the patients' bed but an online warning system that meant we could be called at any time by a monitoring alert team.

It is important to remember the importance of human interactions in the digital age. Emotionally, it was nice to work with patients in an acute setting and have the immediacy of care-giving which is not always there in a speciality that tends to guide patients through concepts of risk and endeavour to drive forward technological and social thinking change.

I would pay tribute to the families and patients I communicated with throughout this difficult time. For me the secret of communication in healthcare is treat everybody like your best friend's mother, father, sister or child. If you do this with respect, passion, compassion and humour then it is nearly always well-received. Asking somebody the name of their dog when they say who is usually at home with them or their golf handicap when they say they first felt the pain of cancer after swinging a club makes all the difference to the bond we make with our patients. It was particularly tough to see people I knew either personally or my own patients from clinical genetics on the wards but it was a constant reminder that regardless of background, finances, job or education, we are all on the same journey through life and no one is immune from illness or suffering.

Personally, due to family circumstances, I was extremely worried about passing on the virus to my wife and children and so I stayed alone in my bedroom for six weeks when not working and my wife slept downstairs. Food was brought to the door of the bedroom and I was the only person allowed to use the toilet downstairs. So after working from 7.15am to 5pm I would come home, strip in the hallway so my clothes could be washed, head straight to the shower and then to the bedroom. As someone not used to being alone, this was difficult and in the background there was the thought of catching the disease and having to face it alone.

Over time, eulogies for fellow healthcare workers from within my Trust have come in and the psychological battle was as immense as the clinical one. I wrote a worry list as I went back to the ward with 29 entries. I was able to rationalise 28 of them but the one which stood out that was difficult to reconcile, was how to show compassion to dying patients without their relatives by their side.

The Hospital Trust did everything it could to help with communications, food and well-being support. They were incredibly supportive throughout. As the number of admissions and people dying increased, I captured a sense within many of my friends in medicine, concern about the speed of decision-making around the use of masks, lockdowns, establishing testing at pace and scale, the ramping up of ordering PPE and shielding the vulnerable (particularly those in care homes). Perhaps we would have done things differently if we were blessed with the best medical time travelling machine, the retrospectoscope! Sadly, I worry that many healthcare professionals will be deeply affected for a long time to come by what they have seen and coped with over the past year.

Of course, the coordination of research and developing of a vaccine was a great success. Research is the answer to the pandemic and everything else is mere stalling. The use of links with industry and the pre-established coordinated and integrated Clinical Research Network meant we were able to develop and deliver studies at pace and scale. Although this impacted on current open research projects, the pace of establishing these projects and then delivering them was truly mind-blowing in terms of staff/patient engagement and logistics. I was pleased to see this played out responsibility and accurately in the media as word about the value of steroids, vaccines and viral genome mapping emerged.

At the same time all of this was happening, I was reflecting on concerns raised in the media and popular press on the impingement on personal freedoms of lockdowns and suggestions that alternative approaches such as full shielding of the elderly/vulnerable and carrying on as usual were being discussed. No one knew the right answer and, of course, we were mindful on how the 'protect the NHS' message would have dire consequences on those working in other industries.

I was inspired by the general good humour, resilience and steely determination of patients, relatives and staff. I was proud to be working for the NHS, which seemed to almost become a new religion with rainbow symbols and weekly doorstep rituals through appreciation and applause.

In my room every evening, I wrote my story in a Covid diary blog. I found writing about current affairs, personal reflections and scientific explanation mixture cathartic. Being able to share my thoughts with friends felt like a positive new form of journalism. Like medicine, our media is being more personalised. Covid has magnified many of the social and digital disparity issues which were already brewing under the surface and I sense the 21st century has now truly arrived.

My lasting memory will be holding my phone to patients' ears, if they didn't have their own, so they could speak to their families, perhaps for the last time. So intimate and personal, it felt like an intrusion and was something I had never witnessed in 30 years. It moved me deeply and is something I will hold with me forever. For all the years of exams, qualifications, academic papers and media work, nothing can compete with caring for a dying patient you have built a relationship with whilst maintaining their dignity and supporting their family. There is no greater honour.

Although ward work was very rewarding, it was comforting to return to clinical genetics and look after the patients I had spent decades training for. Further on through the pandemic, I helped call family members of intensive care patients too sick to speak to their relatives. Visitors were understandably not allowed in to see their relatives in the unit and I helped out on weekends. This was emotionally very draining but was hugely appreciated by the clinical team working so hard and by family desperately waiting for positive news. They were often struggling themselves with Covid at home alone and self-isolating. It felt so strange building relationships with people I had never met and probably never would. Over the year I had learnt so much about the wider hospital and had a much clearer view on where clinical genetics fits into the bigger picture. I felt humbled but also proud that I have helped. So much, including me, has changed.

About the contributor

Julian Barwell FRCP (UK) PhD is Clinical Geneticist and Honorary Professor in Genomic Medicine at the University Hospitals of Leicester NHS Trust, Academic Champion in Clinical Genetics at the University of Leicester and Clinical Lead for Division 3 for the Clinical Research Network in the East Midlands. During the first wave of the coronavirus pandemic he returned to the wards at Leicester Royal Infirmary where he normally works as a cancer genetics consultant to help out treating the influx of Covid-19 patients. He lives with his wife and children in Rutland and away from work enjoys writing and performing in musical theatre. His covid diary blog is available at https://www.facebook.com/pages/category/Doctor/Dr-Julian-Barwell-115373416770182/

Covering covid reveals uncomfortable truths

BBC News home editor Mark Easton found a hidden morgue for covid victims in the Surrey countryside. Finding it took persistence, filming it patience, transmitting it on BBC network news courage. Here he looks at the ethical and practical dilemmas of his scoop

The philosopher Friedrich Nietzsche complained: "Sometimes people don't want to hear the truth because they don't want their illusions destroyed." It is a frustration shared with many news reporters, especially in an era when social media has turned shooting the messenger into a global sport. Journalists routinely wade through a stream of online abuse and fury if their stories challenge the prejudices or sensibilities of their audience.

What exactly is news?

News is a strange commodity. People may say they consume it because they want to get closer to objective truth, but consumption habits suggest a different interpretation of the phrase 'news you can use'. Often its purpose is to give people a sense of righteousness, to bolster their world view, to reflect their values, to improve their mood.

Publishers know consumers are often looking for a quick hit, to touch the outside world, confirm their biases, extract emotional value and move on. Some may denigrate 'clickbait', but all news organisations tailor their output to appeal to different audiences.

For example, broadcast news editors look closely at which headlines are getting the most interest online and adjust their television output accordingly. Deciding which story should lead the evening bulletin is not a neutral act. There is no pure science behind the running order. It is a subjective decision about perceptions of relevance, looking to chime with the current disposition and preoccupations of the potential audience. How we report the world is related to how the audience wants us to report the world, reflecting people's hopes and fears. Editors may even actively seek to adjust the news agenda to change how people are feeling.

At the height of the pandemic, an unremitting digest of distress and death was unpalatable for some. 'The news is just too gloomy', people complained. 'Lift me up', they said. 'Make me smile'. 'Give me hope'. Reporters were encouraged to find positive stories to lighten the mood and encourage fortitude in the face of profound social challenges.

Accentuate the positive?

There is a danger in news disproportionately reporting the negative, a focus on conflict and failure. It can misrepresent people's lived experience and paint a dishonest picture of the world. But the search for more uplifting stories during lockdown reveals that the purpose of news is not just to inform but to stimulate. It has an emotional dimension and, I would argue, responsibility.

The Black Lives Matter protests in the summer of 2020 prompted broadcasters to reflect upon the accusation that news output too rarely viewed society through the eyes of ethnic minorities. The BBC, among others, sought to adjust its editorial processes better to reflect the experience of what it termed 'hard to reach audiences'.

The truth? The tone

News media, therefore, are not striving to impart some pure objective truth, but rather to hold a mirror up to the world, reflecting the stories and events that are of concern to the consumers they are seeking to attract. The news is more than a list of facts delivered in a neutral monotone. We want people to engage or what is the point? Telling stories well means getting the audience to invest emotionally, to feel something about what you are telling them, to react to the information being imparted. The tone of a story is as important as the words. I have been accused on social media of being the BBC's 'doom and gloom correspondent', a criticism I reject but one which suggests my reports are not delivered in the way some people want to hear them or, perhaps, that they don't want to hear them at all.

The news market and the bubble

News providers, including the BBC, are in competition with each other for eyes and ears and clicks. News is a commodity and consumers have never had such a choice of suppliers. They can pick the news that appeals most, surround themselves with a take on the world that reflects their values and beliefs. The phenomenon of the social media bubble is well-documented, an environment that reinforces prejudices and avoids uncomfortable truths. People engage only with the news they want to hear, avoiding the challenge of what may be a complicated and difficult reality. This can encourage some newspaper editors, for example, to 'photoshop' the news, to put it through a particular filter, erasing and accentuating to achieve a result more acceptable to their readers.

The need to inform

But the arrival of covid-19 reminded us of the importance of clear and unvarnished information, particularly when people's lives may depend upon it. Focus groups suggested audiences wanted it warts and all. The virus has proved to be one of those rare events that directly changes the lives of every single person on the planet. The details often make depressing and sobering reading. The consequences are challenging and distressing. Yet news audiences grew dramatically as the pandemic raged. A few cocooned themselves with their conspiracies, preferring to see out the pandemic in a bubble of reassuring deception. The vast majority, however, wanted to arm themselves with the facts, however painful.

That said, the humanity of the coverage still mattered to people. The statistical dashboard of the pandemic, the emotionless numbers appearing on our TV screens every night counting the dead and the dying, the dry graphs illustrating the rises and falls in infection and mortality, the raw data told a story, but it did not reflect the emotional experience of the health emergency.

Facts AND feelings

Truth cannot be reduced to a number on a spreadsheet. Audiences want facts but they also want feelings. The tears of exhausted nurses, the grief of bereaved families, the anger of desperate shopkeepers, the fear of shielding pensioners, the frustration of incarcerated youngsters – understanding the personal and psychological effects of the pandemic is a crucial part of the story.

A graphic showing that UK deaths from coronavirus have exceeded 100,000 is likely to be less affecting than a single interview with a husband mourning the loss of his wife. A chart illustrating excess deaths cannot match the image of a gravedigger grimly preparing another plot for another covid victim. One side effect of coronavirus is to heighten our emotional state. Fear, grief, lockdown and uncertainty have left many people raw and vulnerable. The daily news can be psychologically challenging. Even journalists, normally the most dispassionate of news consumers, have confided to me that tears have rolled down their cheeks as they watched a particularly powerful report on a TV bulletin. We all have our covid experience and so coverage of the pandemic is personal in a way that most news is not. Each tragedy speaks to us directly and, with defences battered, the litany of suffering affects people deeply.

The ethics of covering covid

This presents some ethical questions about how we should cover this story. At the BBC, news presenters routinely advise if an upcoming report contains scenes 'which some viewers may find upsetting'. The warning implies broadcasters bear a responsibility to protect the feelings of the audience. It is not just the BBC of course. In every newsroom, editors will discuss whether some details are 'too much' to publish, or even if the emotional impact of a particular news item crosses the line of good taste. In the middle of a pandemic, those conversations are more common and, I would say, more important.

The (temporary) covid morgue

In early January 2021, at the height of the second wave of the pandemic, I was given access to a temporary morgue put up in the Surrey countryside to deal with the county's excess deaths. With hospital mortuaries overflowing, a succession of unmarked vehicles reversed up to the curtained door of the storage facility to unload body bags. Around half were marked 'Covid+'.

The people in charge of the facility allowed us to film because they wanted to demonstrate the seriousness of the pandemic. But they also asked us not to show the bodies on television. They said it would be upsetting for relatives. Here was the ethical dilemma. The fridges in the Surrey woods, piled high with the victims of Covid, illustrated a shocking reality of the health crisis that had not been seen previously. If I agreed to the request, would my report be sanitising the truth, airbrushing the dead from the story and diminishing its power? Recent coverage suggested we had fewer qualms about showing body bags in other countries.

To show or not show the body bags?

On the other hand, the body bags did not contain the remains of an unknown victim in some far-away clime. They were local people, mums and dads, grandparents and children. It was probable grieving relatives of the dead would be watching. There was a direct emotional connection between the bodies in the morgue and some in our audience.

I decided to agree to the request not to show the body bags. It was too close to home. Even though they were zipped inside white plastic cocoons, Surrey's covid victims deserved dignity and their families deserved respect. The essential power and truth of the report could be retained, I felt, by showing without showing.

There were inevitable complaints about the report. I was accused of being 'insensitive', 'ghoulish' and 'overdramatic'. The film was described as 'inappropriate', 'distasteful' and 'upsetting'. To protect the bereaved from distress, viewers protested, we should have simply reported the fact of a shortage of mortuary capacity and avoided the need for 'disgusting and unnecessary footage' illustrating the implications.

No-one wrote to complain we should have shown the body bags. The critics were united in believing it was wrong to show the emergency morgue at all. I suspect their outrage was at being presented with an uncomfortable truth. One can only imagine the likely response if we had broadcast in full what I saw in that tent in Surrey.

News stories and emotions

The incident, however, has made me think about shock value in news. We talk about news 'stories', and story-telling is about emotional connections. "Make 'em laugh, make 'em cry, make 'em wait", as the novelist Charles Reade put it. If you want to grab someone's attention, inflame their passions. Surprise them. Outrage them. Intrigue them. That's true of the best journalism and the worst clickbait.

It has been suggested news editors have been too concerned about upsetting their consumers during the health emergency, that by dialling down on the true horror of the pandemic they have created space for conspiracy and fake news. If 120,000 people have really died after contracting covid, Twitter trolls ask, where are the bodies? Not showing the stacked bags of human remains stored in a Surrey wood on the nightly news, it may be argued, is to be complicit in undermining the truth.

In textbook BBC fashion, I would contend the truth lies somewhere in the middle. A balance must be struck. There is little value in so exciting the passions of your audience that perspective is washed away in a flood of outrage or tears. But equally, true understanding is impossible if you minimise the emotional reality of a situation. The covid pandemic is more than a story. It is a matter of life and death. We may not wish to hear that. We may prefer things were not as they are. We may yearn for a different reality. But when the stakes are this high, the media has a responsibility to destroy illusions. The truth is uncomfortable.

About the contributor

Mark Easton has been the BBC's home editor since 2004. Before that he was home and social affairs editor at Channel 4 News and political editor at Five News.

Populism, anti-system politics and the media: A spotlight on Covid-19

Anti-system politicians in positions of power and influence and a compliant legacy and digital media have created a climate of disinformation and uncertainty for ordinary citizens during the Covid-19 pandemic, argues Professor Robert Dover

Early in the first term of David Cameron's coalition government, the radicals within the Conservative side of the government were described as having Maoist tendencies: this term was used to describe their ambition to rip down established institutions and processes. The usually sober *Financial Times* ran a recurring item assessing Conservative policy initiatives on a Mao-meter (The *Financial Times* 2010). The jollity of the *Financial Times*' pastiche was replaced with clearer critiques around the radical policies that starkly reduced the size of the state between 2010 and 2020. The radical redrawing of the state and the stretching of political norms and conventions set the stage for the pandemic. Despite having a world class virology research base (within universities, industry and defence), and strong doctrine around epidemics the health of the public had been allowed to become very poor (ensuring poorer outcomes from Covid than was experienced by countries with healthier populations), the health service was precariously positioned with reduced capacity, and the long established local public health and track and trace capabilities had been abolished during the ten years of austerity. It was a perfect (viral) storm.

These contemporary anti-system neo-Maoists believe in breaking down established political and social orders to create a chaos that results in the strongest being able to innovate and flourish (Hopkin 2020) (A. Davis 2021). They believe the societal and political order will correct itself in the face of existential crises, but assert this from within political brands that are established, safe and well-considered. They have been ably supported by a broadcast, and paper and internet based legacy media. These anti-system politicians, that won their Brexit and mishandled the pandemic, are unified by the following beliefs: 1) the existing system is broken, 2) the existing system will see 'us' continue to lose influence and power in the global system; 3) there is an identifiable cause of the dysfunction in the system, and this can be labelled as the establishment in various forms and outsiders who undermining the nation; 4) those establishment interests (be they political, media, academic, economic), and outsiders, who represent the cause of the dysfunction should be subject to an immune system response from the new political order; 5) nearly all means justify these ends; 6) only a 'strong' government can place the nation back to the position it should have always been in. The economic logic underpinning this vision is starkly neo-liberal, whilst appealing to working class voters who are the most likely to be negatively impacted by it. Ironically, these voters have also been the most likely to suffer negative outcomes in the pandemic.

Within the new economic model, the preferred solution is for the government to be an outsourcing broker. The size of the state is therefore reduced whilst – in the exceptional moment of the pandemic – the size of its financial draw is exponentially increased. The UK's experiment with such a model, enacted at a large scale because of Covid, is one tainted by accusations of corruption as party doners and friends of ministers have been accused of being given contracts they were not well qualified to win. Similarly, former high ranking government officials have been accused of seeking to enrich themselves through their privileged connections. Interestingly, and echoing the sense of British exceptionalism that marked the Brexit referendum and exit negotiations, the legacy media has stuck with describing these contractual situations as 'croynism', whilst describing similar accusations abroad as corruption; a far more damaging linguistic tick. The reproduction of British exceptionalism is a key theme from the pandemic thus far, with far wider resonances.

This ideology of anti-system has a close relationship with technological disruptions, particularly in the society-changing innovations in communication, in travel and of data collection. This ideology is closely related to the radical libertarian spirit that fuelled the emergence of the dot.com era in technology and these technologists find themselves in unhappy concert with those forcefully pushing largely illiberal political disruption.

The disruptive technologists who have underpinned the infrastructure of modern societies had the vision of a form of participant capitalism, of sharing, of looser ties, and social liberalism but in which – paradoxically – they have become kleptocrats. These paradoxes exist in the political realm too. Experts and those who maintain the status quo order are enemies of this disruption, because they actively work to avoid the chaos that the neo-Maoists believe is the route to a better form of politics and social order. When it comes to Brexit those experts are dismissed as 'remoaners'. During the pandemic virologists and epidemiologists have been denigrated with personal attacks in the legacy media (e.g. 'Dr Doom') or in terms of needing the lockdown to continue for their psychological needs.

Those advancing the agenda of disruption (be it through Brexit, MAGA and Covid derestriction) see the established order as one of managed decline, and themselves as being on a historical mission to break free of this historical inevitability and to deliver a form of 19th century laissez-faire on the world. So, rather than cooperating with the World Health Organisation or the European Union on the pandemic the US and the UK initially preferred to act unilaterally. By luck, rather than judgement, UK public money had been long helping Oxford University establish the research platform on which vaccines could be quickly repurposed for Covid-19 (Safi 2021). This is precisely the sort of research investment that Boris Johnson's government has sought to undermine since winning re-election in the winter of 2019.

Anti-system politics has taken the forms of questioning and undermining certified expertise, undermining government expertise, questioning the motivation for official and government action, and pushing myths, disinformation and seeking to undermine and change the settled post-war social compact. The surprising turn has been that anti-system politicians have not remained at the fringes of mainstream politics, but in many cases across Europe and North America taken up occupancy in positions of government. The anti-system campaigners have become the establishment, whilst maintaining their narrative that they remain outsiders seeking to bend the establishment into serving the will of the people. This notion of subversion coming from within the state apparatus is relatively novel. It has – in the cases of the UK and America – also caused intelligence agencies to be in the invidious position of directly and indirectly investigating those they are responsible to. Even worse, anti-system politicians, who have achieved office, have been poor keepers of secrets and have tried to involve themselves in investigations (Atkinson, et al. 2020) (Hellinger 2019). In this era of digitally driven populism, the core functions of government have become politicised by all sides in an unprecedented way: legacy and new media outlets have become the key battlegrounds in this contest.

The attempt to politicise government science, public health, and analytical functions is important for us to note and understand. Surprise at these attempts springs from a particular understanding of government functions being apolitical. But the functions of government are not apolitical, because government agencies and officials seek to both protect and advance the state and its interests. This, in and of itself, is a choice that represents identifiable forms of political choice, with political, social and economic consequences. Government departments and civil servants are not party political, but they are political. To understand this provides an angle through which to see why government offices became legitimate targets for anti-system political actors: public authorities represent a hindrance to their transformation of society. For those tasked with protecting the Crown and the continuation of Parliamentary democracy, the fierce debate around the proroguing of Parliament demonstrated the extent to which anti-system politicians would go to secure their preferred outcomes: almost nothing was off-limits to their higher ideals, something that should concern those who seek to protect the constitutional balance (Schleiter and Fleming 2020) (White 2019).

In the case of Brexit, covered elsewhere in this book, the consequences are mostly political and economic: things likely to be electorally forgiven over time. The UK's fitful exit from the *European Exchange Rate Mechanism* and resulting economic damage was largely forgiven by 2005, and replaced by the critique of Labour's handling of the economic crisis of 2008 (Aykens 2002) (Green and Jennings 2017). The onset of the Covid-19 pandemic added loss of life, and impairment of life opportunities to the list of consequences, which are far less likely to be forgiven. The early stages of the pandemic (in January-February 2020) was refracted through anti-system lenses in both the UK and US, leading to catastrophic public health outcomes. The virus was downplayed in terms of its lethality, as part of anti-Chinese sentiment, and in terms of the exceptionalism of the UK to face the virus down without locking down, closing the borders or implementing functioning track and trace systems. The right-leaning legacy media played a full role in (re)producing and supporting these narratives.

One of the lessons that we need to learn from the Covid-19 disinformation and populist politics is that the amplification of misleading narratives is only partly done via platforms and outlets that are open to academic researchers and other interested parties such as journalists and third sector organisations. Legacy media outlets have continued to play a highly politicised role: the editorials of *The Sun* newspaper have heavily emphasised the economic need of lifting lockdowns quickly, of reopening schools (vilifying teachers and teaching unions as anti-education in the process), and to downplay the risks of Covid (Liddle 2021). When the UK went into its second full lockdown in November 2020, *The Sun* published an editorial supporting the government's move: it has fore-run government policies on many issues since 2015. Academics and journalists find easy headlines in reporting and analysing inflammatory material posted on *Twitter* and *Facebook*, largely because it is simple to find, and relatively straightforward to collect and analyse. The assessment of online harms is therefore skewed by the constraints inherent in research budgets and the design of studies, rather than being a true reflection of the information contest. This is important, because these hidden communication pathologies help to shape the public policy response, and result in a misdirection of resourcing to countering dangerous or subversive narratives.

The large social media companies have been slow to arrive at the position that they could and should remove posts inciting violence and hatred, or which facilitate wilfully poor public health outcomes (Facebook 2020). Since the summer of 2020 this has now become commonplace. In the US, this platform centred censorship was triggered by the possible commercial fallout from allowing the then

President Trump to push disinformation in the pursuit of re-election in November 2020 (Ashokkumar, et al. 2020). But it also helpfully coalesced with governmental pressure to clamp down upon disinformation concerning the pandemic, which had gained considerable traction.

As John Downey, David Smith and I found in our research on crisis communications, disinformation often originates on the so-called 'Dark Web', where it is pre-refined and amplified prior to making its way on to the indexed web and open social media platforms (UK Defence Select Committee 2019). This mechanism allows state actors to acquire plausible deniability and more difficult for researchers to locate the 'patient zero' of disinformation campaigns. The first mover advantage into the information space also provides disinformation with greater longevity: we found that the initial speculation around security incidents published before the first official tweet, were still circulating 30 days after the incident. These insights suggest changes to official communications doctrine, particularly in seeing a foreshortening of the time to make the first communication, establishing an authoritative voice, a single point of reference, and clear and consistent messages. The British government's communication of public health advice during the early phases of the pandemic was inconsistent and confusing. A year into the pandemic the British government's official communications finally reflect the reality that Covid-19 is an airborne illness, although it maintains the confusing fiction that schools do not require significant mitigations for this airborne illness. The point here is that having public health messages in tension undermines the public's confidence in the communications themselves but also the underpinning competence: something that comes through in the public opinion surveying.

Focusing on the impact of social media on shaping the public's understanding of and attitude towards Covid-19 obscures an important element in modern communications technology. Much as the August 2011 riots in the UK were organised and escalated by encrypted Blackberry Messenger messages, disinformation about Covid-19 has circulated freely on popular private messaging services such as WhatsApp and Signal, and on deliberately less well-regulated social media sites such as 4Chan, which find their way indirectly onto mainstream platforms and onto legacy media platforms too. Ironically, the British government's difficulties with corruption allegations also stems from its use of WhatsApp as a means of communication (Cummings 2021). Disrupting the production and reproduction of disinformation on encrypted messaging platforms is a technologically sophisticated activity, and not something that has successfully scaled, even within government security circles. This – in part – informs the recent warning to Facebook from the UK Home Secretary, Priti Patel, not to encrypt its platform which – in her view – would facilitate the exploitation of children and other serious crimes (Molloy 2021).

While the Covid-19 pandemic persists, and mutations and vaccine escape look likely, the future communications challenges will continue to come from encrypted and discrete platforms, and from the rapid development and use of 'deep fake' technologies. These technologies have reached a level of maturation where convincing videos can be created (mis)using the face and voice of trusted figures to push disinformation or to maliciously edit videos to discredit a particular individual (Roth 2021). Even at the time of writing, the quality of deep fake videos is such that it requires significant computing power in enforcement agencies to identify them. By the time this is done a significant cleavage of an internet community – by accident or design – will be pushing or commenting upon the fake as if it were real. The much-discussed hybrid media system continues to act as a mechanism for amplifying sensationalist narratives: a combination of accessibility, profit driven motive and information contest. Whilst anti-system politicians continue to feature strongly in our democracies, and as demonstrated by the discourse around Covid the current media landscape offers little defence against those wishing to recast politics or to deceive ill-equipped publics.

Some of the material in this chapter is adapted from Hacker, Faker, Influencer, Spy by Robert Dover, which will be published by Hurst and Company in late 2021.

References

Anderson, J, and L Rainie. 2021. *Many tech experts say digital disruption will hurt democracy.* . Washington DC: Pew Research Center. Internet & Technology.

Ashokkumar, A, S Talaifar, W. T Fraser, R Landabur, M Buhrmester, Á Gómez, and W. B. Swann Jr. 2020. "Censoring political opposition online: Who does it and why." *Journal of experimental social psychology,* 104031.

Atkinson, JD, K Ingman, JPJ Pierandozzi, and P. Stump. 2020. "At the Intersection of Mainstream & Alternative Media: Spygate & the Hannity Rant." *Journal of Communication Inquiry* 1-18.

Aykens, P. 2002. "Conflicting authorities: states, currency markets and the ERM crisis of 1992-93." *Review of International Studies* 359-380.

Cummings, D. 2021. *Dominic Cummings Blog.* April 23. Accessed April 27, 2021. https://dominiccummings.com/2021/04/23/statement-regarding-no10-claims-today/.

Davis, A. 2021. *Reckless opportunists: Elites at the end of the establishment.* Manchester: Manchester University Press.

Facebook. 2020. *Keeping People Safe and Informed About the Coronavirus.* December 18. Accessed April 27, 2021. https://about.fb.com/news/2020/12/coronavirus/.

Green, J, and W Jennings. 2017. *Will Brexit be another Black Wednesday for the Conservatives? Lessons from the ERM crisis. LSE Brexit.* London: LSE: Brexit.

Hellinger, DC. 2019. "Trumpism, Fake News and the "New Normal"." In *Conspiracies and Conspiracy Theories in the Age of Trump,* by DC Hellinger, 79-103. Berlin: Springer.

Hopkin, Jonathan. 2020. *Anti-System Politics: The Crisis of Market Liberalism in Rich Democracies.* Oxford: Oxford University Press.

Liddle, R. 2021. *Teaching Unions Top the List of Covid Baddies.* February 24. Accessed February 26, 2021. https://www.thesun.co.uk/news/14154004/teaching-unions-top-list-covid-baddies/.

Molloy, D. 2021. *Priti Patel: Facebook encryption plan 'must not hamper child protection'.* April 19. Accessed April 27, 2021. https://www.bbc.co.uk/news/technology-56795852.

Muller, E. 2020. "Delimiting disruption: Why Uber is disruptive, but Airbnb is not." *International Journal of Research in Marketing* 43-55.

Roth, A. 2021. "European MPs targeted by deepfake video calls imitating Russian opposition." *The Guardian*, April 21.

Safi, M. 2021. "Oxford/AstraZeneca Covid vaccine research 'was 97% publicly funded'." *The Guardian*, April 15.

Schleiter, P, and TG Fleming. 2020. "Parliamentary Prorogation in Comparative Context." *The Political Quarterly* 641-648.

Si, S, and H. Chen. 2020. "A literature review of disruptive innovation: What it is, how it works and where it goes." *Journal of Engineering and Technology Management* 101568.

UK Defence Select Committee. 2019. "UK's vulnerability to hybrid threats examined." London, December 12.

White, J. 2019. *Performative prorogation: what Johnson, Cummings and Co are trying to teach the public.* British Policy and Politics: LSE Blog, London: LSE.

n.d. "Williamson, P. J., Wan, F., Eden, Y., & Linan, L. (2020). Is disruptive innovation in emerging economies different? Evidence from China. Journal of Engineering and Technology Management, 57, 101590."

About the contributor

Professor Robert Dover is Professor of Intelligence and National Security and Head of the Department of Criminology and Sociology at the University of Hull. Previously he was Associate Professor of Intelligence and International Security at the University of Leicester and Director of the Glendonbrook Institute for Enterprise Development at Loughborough University in London and Associate Dean for Enterprise at Loughborough University in London (LUiL).

Now you see 'race', now you don't: The hyper-visibility and hyper-invisibility of race and Covid-19 in political and public health discourse

The perceptions of the experience of Black, Asian and minority ethnic groups during the Covid-19 pandemic have been generalised and unhelpful and have missed the more important point about inequality in 21st century Britain, says Dr Paul Ian Campbell

'Race' and ethnicity were included as risk factors for experiencing severe Covid-19-related illness in UK Government modelling and public health policy for the first time in February 2021 - nearly a year after Britain officially recorded its first Covid-19 fatality. In an interview with ITV's *Good Morning Britain* a month earlier Home Secretary Priti Patel explained one of the causes in the UK's most recent coronavirus spike was because 'certain ethnicities... were more susceptible to coronavirus.' These two examples highlight the contrasting ways race was framed in Covid-19-related public health policy and interventions and in Covid-19-related political discourse during the first year of the pandemic in the UK. They show how race appeared to be both absent in relation to Covid-19-related policy and interventions and at the same time a core feature of Covid-19-related political discourse. This chapter attempts to illustrate and make sense of this seemingly paradoxical situation.

Race and Covid-19 in Britain 2020-2021 - the great 'amplifier'

Covid-19 infections and mortality rates rose sharply across Europe and Britain during the early months of 2020, prompting the UK Government to enact its first national lockdown on March 23. This included implementing a policy of social distancing as well as suspending all non-essential sectors of the economy including sport and leisure (Campbell 2020a and 2020b). The infection of Prime Minister Boris Johnson in March alongside other high-profile individuals led senior Tory cabinet minister Michael Gove to inform the British public the virus did 'not discriminate'. A new common sense began to circulate that Covid-19 was 'the great leveller'.

By April data from the US and UK indicated the infection and mortality rates of Covid-19 were disproportionately high within each nation's raced communities compared to each's respective aggregate White populations. It was evident that while the virus was unable to 'see' race, its severity was being experienced unevenly along colour lines in Britain. Of the 3,883 Covid-19 patients registered as critical in the UK on March 10, 2020, 34 per cent were from minority ethnic communities. This was despite people from these communities accounting for less than 15 per cent of the general population (Campbell 2020a). Although the chances of being infected and surviving Covid-19 varied across different minority ethnic communities (it was also further complicated by issues of gender and disability within these groups), in October the Progressive Policy Think Tank found if Britain's White populations had experienced similar 'risk and rate[s] of death' from Covid-19 as its aggregate Black, Asian and minority ethnic (BAME) communities the nation would have experienced around an extra 35,000 deaths at that point (Patel et al 19.10.20).

Some initial explanations speculated biological causes for the disparities, such as attributing lower Covid-19 survival rates to 'lower' levels of Vitamin D among people of colour (Minhas, et al 2020). These suppositions were quickly dismissed due to the miniscule biological variations between people from different raced backgrounds and by the fact the infection and mortality rates in the UK were not consistent with data from countries where people of colour were in the numerical majority. It was soon apparent that high Covid-19 mortality rates correlated with people who had underlying health conditions and who were living in socio-economically challenging situations. All of which were more likely to be experienced by Britons from minority ethnic communities. This is what race scholars mean by race is a proxy for certain conditions of social life. That is, if you are Black, South Asian, Gypsy Roma Traveller communities (and so on) in the UK, society is structured in such a way that you are more likely to encounter and experience certain conditions of social life that leave you more prone to contracting the virus and less likely to survive it. Put another way, instead of Covid-19 being the great leveller, it amplifies existing racial inequalities.

The absence of race in Covid-19 public health policy

Despite this reality the recognition of race as a risk factor appeared to be largely absent in Covid-19 public health responses and related policy between March 2020 and February 2021. Pertinently, many policy interventions served to exacerbate pre-existing social inequalities experienced by Britain's non-White communities. It also created *new* social and health-related inequalities between Britain's minority ethnic and White communities in all areas of social life, including employment, education and leisure. Since March 2020, varying degrees of social distancing have been the UK Government's official policy with the population directed to work from home where possible. But people from Britain's minority ethnic communities were, and still are, more likely to be employed in low-skilled, manual-based and people-facing professions which cannot be done from home.

They were also overrepresented in half of the eight areas of work identified as essential to keeping society functioning during the first lockdown and forced to remain open – health and social care, (education and) childcare, food and other necessary goods, and transport. They also accounted for over 44.3 per cent of NHS staff (Campbell 2020a). British workers from these communities were overwhelmingly clustered in occupations which remained opened for face-to-face business. This placed them at a higher risk of exposure, infection and death. It was perhaps unsurprising, though tragic, that it was exactly these occupations which have comparatively witnessed some of the most severe Covid-19 infections and mortality rates for Britain's non-White workers. This included people from minority ethnic backgrounds accounting for six out of every ten caring staff and nine out of every ten doctors who had died by June 2020 (see *The Guardian* 25.5.20 and BBC.co.uk 16.06.20, respectively).

In March 2020, The Office of Qualifications and Examinations Regulation announced that year's formal GCSE and A level exams were to be replaced with a tri-based-formula for grading. This consisted of a pupil's predicted grade, a rank for how confident their teacher was of them achieving the predicted grade and the extent to which the predicted score correlated with the school's historic performance. Various scholars, journalists, Think Tanks, parliamentarians and the House of Commons Education Committee constituted a cacophony of voices which warned Education Secretary Gavin Williamson of the unfairness of this new model. They specifically warned of its potential to impact most negatively on children from BAME communities and other at-risk groups (see *The Guardian* 10.7.2020). The Runnymede Trust, for example, directed Whitehall to research which highlighted how educationalists could sometimes hold the same racial biases about people from certain BAME communities not being suited to academic pursuits which exist in wider society. These views often translated into lower expectations of and predicted grades for the BAME students they teach (their students frequently go on to outperform their predicted grade scores (Campbell 2020c). Moreover, a school's historical performance is intimately connected to a host of wider socio-economic and geographic factors which work in favour of schools located in affluent areas and against schools usually based in inner-urban and socio-economically challenged areas. These are also the areas typically home to many of Britain's BAME communities (Campbell 2020a). *The Guardian* (17.8.20) reported how this last factor led to 40 per cent of A level grades being downgraded, typically for pupils who attended schools in Britain's poorer and more diverse communities.

On September 12, the Football Association in England 'restarted' local football after a five month pause. Little consideration was given to the potential of local football to act as a conduit for the transmission of Covid-19 directly into the BAME communities they served. Safety considerations and interventions were directed almost entirely on the welfare of the players, who were deemed to be at low risk because of the relatively low-level risk of transmission when playing outdoors. This combined with the generally young age and healthy physical condition of most people who play regular sport suggests all players, including those from minority ethnic backgrounds, were not at an especially high risk of possessing the underlying conditions which lead to mortality from the coronavirus or to having a severe reaction if infected (Minhas, et al 2020).

But local football is a cultural activity which extends far beyond the 22 players on the pitch. Clubs and matches are often situated within the geographic and social heart of local communities. Consequently, they carry the potential to transmit the virus directly into the local communities that constitute them. Following a charity match at Burnside Working Men's Club in the north-east of England in August 2020, for example, 300 people in the local area had to self-isolate after 61 attendees tested positive for Covid-19 (BBC.co.uk 11.9.20).

BAME players and local clubs are similarly socially, culturally and geographically plugged into the communities where the impact of Covid-19 is much more lethal and who require the most protection. For example the Highfield Rangers football club's base in Leicester doubles as a multi-purpose community centre. It is a key site for sociability for retired members of Leicester's Black community. Likewise Punjab FC in Gravesend often operate out of their local Gurdwara. The cultural functions of BAME sport bring them directly into contact with the communities they serve and where a Covid-19 outbreak effecting hundreds of people, like that at Burnside, would have the most devasting consequences (see Campbell 2020b).

The presence of race in political media discourse

In comparison to the discussion above, race, and by extension, minority ethnic communities in Britain, have been a more present feature in Covid-19 public health and political-related media discourse. Here, however, this has almost entirely been in relation to race as a causal factor for the spread of Covid-19, for spikes in transmissions or for the UK's extraordinarily high death rate when compared to other wealthy nations.

During summer 2020 numerous journalists speculated how the 'black' Black Lives Matter protests which swept across various UK cities would act as a catalyst for an upward surge in infections. One BBC.co.uk article on June 9 was headlined *Coronavirus: Lockdown rules 'undermined by BLM protest policing'*. Likewise on June 30 and July 1 the *Daily Telegraph* and *Daily Mail* led with '*Exclusive: Black Lives Matter protest may have spread virus in Birmingham, says city's health chief*', and '*Black Lives Matter protest may have sparked new Covid spike among 20 to 30 year-olds in Birmingham as health chief calls for national investigation*', respectively.

Similar anxieties were expressed across various media platforms that summer over the potential for religious festivals predominantly celebrated by South Asian communities, such as Eid [and later Diwali], to also act as catalysts for the spread of the virus. The day after the *Daily Mail* warned its readers about BLM being linked to rising Covid-19 cases in Birmingham, it presaged that Eid was 'problematic' because celebrating people were likely to flaunt public health guidelines and swell the number of infections, especially in those 'locked down' areas, which had high concentrations of Muslim residents (*Daily Mail* 2.07.20). By comparison similar concerns appeared to be not as embroidered in the coverage given to the VE Day celebrations that spring or to the Government's initial plans to loosen lockdown restrictions during Christmas and New Year's Eve, which were planned to allow up to three households to mix during the holiday period. This was despite concerns among the scientific community of rising cases across the nation in November.

On July 4, the Conservative Government launched a three-tier lockdown system which immediately placed various cities with comparatively high infection rates under its most stringent lockdown measures. The above average infection rate in Leicester, which resulted in parts of the city being placed in Tier 3, was initially reported as being in part caused by its Bangladeshi community. According to these reports in the local and national press, this community's limited capacity to fully 'understand' English and follow Covid-19 regulations, the increased likelihood of them residing in in multi-generational households and living in congested inner urban areas in the city were common causal explanations proffered. This narrative was summarised by Criminologist Amy Clarke (13.07.20) who asserts:'[T]he spike in new Covid-19 case numbers [in Leicester] became racialised ... and the blame has been placed on the city's immigrant and ethnic minority population (see also TheOldhamTimes.co.uk 29.07.20).'

Britain's BAME communities were again 'the news of the day' during the early months of 2021. This time they appeared in stories about their apparent hesitancy to take the Covid-19 vaccine. Politicians and parliamentarians on both sides of the aisle quickly responded to and in turn legitimised and amplified these explicit and implicit narratives. In January Conservative Under-Secretary of State for Covid-19 Vaccines Nadhim Zahawi and London Mayor Sadiq Khan publicly asked that minority ethnic communities 'put aside' their historical distrust of the state and fully engage with the vaccination programme 'to save lives' (*The Guardian* 31.01.21). In what appeared to be an attempt to distance BAME resistances to the vaccination roll-out from the long history of persecution and state violence directed at BAME communities, Conservative Exchequer Secretary to the Treasury, Kemi Badenoch, explained to a select committee that Covid-19 hesitancy among BAME communities was linked to a cultural disposition within these groups. It was an inherent cultural antipathy to state and authority which they brought with them 'from the countries *they come from*" [author's italics] (White, 11.3.2012). The reframing of forms of Black resistance from political acts in response to wider historical, structural or systemic violence, to merely mindless and pathological acts is reminiscent of one of the tenets of Bonilla Silva's (2006) 'Colour-Blind Racism'. These kinds of constructions of minority groups often, but not exclusively, by politicians on the centre or right of politics is not new. Historian Stephen Caunce (1994) reminds us how the British (political) media and British state have a long history of framing minority ethnic groups as inherently and culturally problematic.

Hyper-visibility of hyper-invisibility of race in Covid-19 Britain and its consequences

The Black and minority ethnic experience in the UK, especially for people whose heritages derive from the old colonies, is contradictory (Campbell 2018). In the White political and cultural imagination, BAME communities and individuals simultaneously occupy the position of citizen and foreigner, 'us' and 'them' (and in some instances, cast as 'the enemy within', according to Baroness Warsi (21.06.18)). We have also seen examples of how they are what Solanke (2018) would describe as 'hyper-visible' and 'hyper-invisible'. This speaks to the contradictory tendencies for race and racialised individuals in the UK to be both the central focus of the White gaze and yet also cloaked from it. This paper has shone light on how this situation can sometimes happen even within the same area of public, political and social life. Solanke (2018, 52) asserts this situation is both 'problematic' and dangerous. Buchanan and Settles (2019) elucidate that the hyper-visibility of marginalised individuals often results in them being 'the focus of increased surveillance' from those in positions of power or the wider community.

On the other hand a simultaneous invisibility often denies the same groups and individuals 'recognition, power and a voice'. For example, in his independent review of race and the Criminal Justice System, MP David Lammy (2017) illustrated how at the level of law enforcement, the hyper-visibility of race has contributed to the stigmatisation of young Black men and racial bias among police officers. It also translates into overzealous use of racial profiling and heavy-handed policing tactics on particular minority-ethnic communities. Conversely there has been a historical inability to 'see' and address a distinct lack of racial diversity – that is a hyper-invisibility of race – among those within the CJS, who are the law makers and law enforcers.

The over-representation and under-representation of race in political Covid-19 media discourse and Covid-19 health policy respectively also lead to negative and real-world consequences for Britons of colour. We have seen, for example, how politicians, journalists and political commentators frequently espoused what Bonilla Silva (2006) might describe as 'colour-blind' accounts of race in relation to Covid-19 during the first year of the pandemic. These mediated narratives have not framed the higher rates of infections among Britain's raced communities in relation to systemic and structural systems of inequality in the UK, which means people from minority-ethnic backgrounds are more likely to reside in tightly packed urban areas or be employed within low skilled jobs. Instead, the higher Covid-19 infection and mortality rates among people from these communities have frequently been framed as the result of either a cultural or physiological dysfunction within particular minority-ethnic communities. The logical progression of this viewpoint is that Britain's extraordinarily high Covid-19 infection and mortality rate, which has resulted in 126,000 deaths at the time of writing, is only in part the consequence of ineffective policy or inaction. It is instead viewed as a seemingly 'obvious' and inevitable consequence of Britain as a multiracial society which is home to people of colour who, unlike the White population, are simply more prone to contract and spread the virus. This is a position neatly captured in Home Secretary Priti Patel's matter of fact response to the question, 'Why does the UK 'have currently the worst death rate in the world?': '[There are] a range of reasons as to why the numbers are so high… [including] certain ethnicities, as we know, are more susceptible to coronavirus', she reasoned. One consequence of 'playing the race-card' in this way is it stigmatises minority-ethnic communities, erodes cultural cohesion and fuels cross-racial and cross-community tensions at a time when racial tensions, hate-crimes and the demonisation of minority-ethnic communities in the UK are at their statistical highest since the turn of the century, according to the UK Government's own statistics (see Home Office 2019).

The limited meaningful consideration given to race in Covid-19 health policy for much of the past year has already translated into real-world consequences and existential threats for Britons of colour. Not only has this situation limited the ability of policies and interventions to mitigate the impact of Covid-19 on Britain's communities of colour, but we have seen how in some instances, the enacting of 'colour-blind' policies has exacerbated pre-existing inequities within and between communities and has manifested new ones.

This last point is pertinent. A recent report by the British Academy has found the 'social, economic and cultural effects of the pandemic' will continue to impact the UK for the next decade. The first 12 months of the pandemic has unequivocally illustrated how a failure to make race visible and thus a central consideration across *all* Covid-19 policy as we move forward, will mean the next ten years will be painful for all, but most painful and most protracted for British citizens who already experience multiple inequalities due to the colour of their skin.

References

BBC.co.uk (11.9.2020) 'Coronavirus: Further 33 Covid cases after charity match' https://www.bbc.co.uk/news/uk-england-tyne-54117729

BBC.co.uk (16.6.2020) 'Coronavirus: Report on BAME Covid-19 deaths sparks call for action' https://www.bbc.co.uk/news/uk-53065306

Bonilla-Silva, E. (2006) Racism without racists: Color-blind racism and the persistence of racial inequality in the United States, Rowman & Littlefield Publishers.

Buchanan N. T., and Settles I. H (2019) 'Managing (in)visibility and hypervisibility in the Workplace' Journal of Vocational Behavior Volume 113, August 2019, Pages 1-5

Campbell, P. I. (2018) Keynote Lecture: 'The African-Caribbean influence on British sport and social life and the influence of British sport and social life on African-Caribbean Communities' British Society of Sport History Conference Westminster University 7-8 September 2018

Campbell, P. I. (2020a) 'Coronavirus is hitting BAME communities hard on every front' The Conversation https://theconversation.com/coronavirus-is-hitting-bame-communities-hard-on-every-front-136327

Campbell, P. I. (2020b) Education training, retirement and career transition for ex-professional footballers: 'From being idolised to stacking shelves' Bingley: Emerald

Campbell. P. I. (2020c) 'Race Equality and Higher Education: Why have sociologists argued that UK universities should 'decolonise' the curriculum in all subjects for the benefit of all their students?' Sociological Review

Campbell, P. I. (2020d) 'COVID-19, BAME communities and local football: can local BAME football win against COVID-19?' Identities: Global Studies in Culture and Power https://www.identitiesjournal.com/blog-articles?fbclid=IwAR1p2fzefkH4A8cq5lxl89tgqkHB34dLcYWVU53dW-OLsbUD-PdW7JbyQZ8

Caunce, S. (1994) Oral History and the Local Historian London Longman

Clarke, A. (13.7.2020) 'Leicester lockdown: blame on minority communities needs to be challenged' The Conversation https://theconversation.com/profiles/amy-clarke-1134587

Daily Mail (1.7.2020) 'Black Lives Matter protest may have sparked new Covid spike among 20 to 30-year-olds in Birmingham as health chief calls for national investigation' https://www.dailymail.co.uk/news/article-8478133/Black-Lives-Matter-protest-sparked-new-Covid-spike-20-30-year-olds-Birmingham.html

Daily Mail (2.7.20200 'Ministers were warned of spike in cases in the North West three weeks ago and that Eid would be 'problematic' in locked down areas, SAGE files reveal' https://www.dailymail.co.uk/news/article-8580495/Ministers-warned-Eid-problematic-locked-areas-weeks-ago.html

Home Office (2019) Hate Crime, England and Wales, 2018/19 https://assets.publishing.service.gov.uk/government/uploads/system/uploads/attachment_data/file/839172/hate-crime-1819-hosb2419.pdf

Lammy, D. (2017) The Lammy Review: An Independent Review into the Treatment Of, and Outcomes For, Black, Asian and Minority Ethnic Individuals in the Criminal Justice System. UK government https://www.gov. uk/government/uploads/system/uploads/attachment_data/file/643001/lammyreview-final-report.pdf

Minhas, J.S., Martin, C.A., Campbell, P.I & Pareek, M. (August 16, 2020) 'Project Restart and COVID-19 – how do we reduce risk for ethnic minority athletes?' British Journal Of Sports Medicine https://blogs.bmj.com/bjsm/2020/08/16/project-restart-and-covid-19-how-do-we-reduce-risk-for-ethnic-minority-athletes/?s=07&fbclid=IwAR3_koutigqumL0VigbGZ2hvWTw85ovL9pWYb28Z9VnozfI4ZE4D42hq67o

Patel, P, Kapoor, A. and Treloar, N. (19.10.2020) 'Ethnic inequalities in Covid-19 are playing out again – how can we stop them?' The Progressive Policy Think Tank https://www.ippr.org/blog/ethnic-inequalities-in-covid-19-are-playing-out-again-how-can-we-stop-them

The Guardian (10.7.2020) 'MPs warn about bias in predicted results for pupils in England' https://www.theguardian.com/education/2020/jul/10/mps-warn-bias-predicted-results-pupils-england

https://www.theguardian.com/society/2015/oct/13/reported-hate-crimes-rise-by-almost-a-fifth

The Guardian (17.8.2020) 'What do the U-turns on exam results mean for the UK's students?' https://www.theguardian.com/education/2020/aug/17/what-does-the-uk-governments-u-turn-on-exam-results-mean

The Guardian (25.5.2020) 'Six in 10 UK health workers killed by Covid-19 are BAME' https://www.theguardian.com/world/2020/may/25/six-in-10-uk-health-workers-killed-by-covid-19-are-bame

The Guardian (31.1.2021) 'Tory minister and Labour mayor reassure groups resisting inoculation' https://www.theguardian.com/world/2021/jan/31/tory-minister-and-labour-mayor-reassure-groups-resisting-inoculation

Warsi, S (21.6.2018) 'The Enemy Within? A Tale of Muslim Britain' DICE School of Media, Communication and Sociology https://webcache.googleusercontent.com/search?q=cache:wR9WGKyh07MJ:https://www2.le.ac.uk/news/events/2018/june/uolevent.2018-06-01.5050709213+&cd=1&hl=en&ct=clnk&gl=uk

White, N. (11.3.2021) 'Vaccine hesitancy among ethnic minorities is due to 'attitudes in countries they come from,' says equalities minister' https://www.independent.co.uk/news/uk/politics/covid-vaccine-hesitancy-bame-b1815323.html

About the contributor

Dr Paul Ian Campbell is Lecturer in Sociology at the University of Leicester. He is an award winning academic in the areas of race, ethnicity and inclusion in sport and in education. His latest book *Education, Retirement and Career Transitions for 'Black' Ex-Professional Footballers*, published in October 2020, offers a case study of 16 Black British professional footballers' experiences of retirement and transition from careers as professional athletes to mainstream work. The author has written on these issues in *The Conversation* 'Coronavirus is hitting BAME communities hard on every front' (https://theconversation.com/coronavirus-is-hitting-bame-communities-hard-on-every-front-136327) and *Identities Global Studies in Culture* 'COVID-19, BAME communities and local football: can local BAME football win against COVID-19?' (https://www.identitiesjournal.com/blog-collection/covid-19-bame-communities-and-local-football-can-local-bame-football-win-against-covid-19)

Messengers as well as messages in the spotlight

The public inquiry into the UK's handling of the pandemic will take place in 2022. Raymond Snoddy wants media behaviour to be examined too

Prime Minister Boris Johnson will sanction an official inquiry into the UK's handling of the Covid-19 pandemic in Spring 2022 after what appeared to be a period of equivocation. The Johnson approach has always been that now is not the right time, or as he told the House of Commons in March 2021, it would be held, "as soon as it is right to do so, as soon as it wouldn't be an irresponsible diversion of the energies of the key officials involved."

For Labour, the Liberal Democrats and epidemiologists such as Professor Neil Ferguson of Imperial College London, there is an urgent need for an inquiry as soon as possible, so that lessons can be learned quickly to avoid the repetition of past mistakes. Given this government's record on openness, cynics might worry that it will not be 'the right time' before it would be too late to report its results this side of the next general election campaign.

The media, and the national press in particular, should be in the vanguard of calls for an inquiry as soon as possible, to achieve clarity rather than retribution – at this stage, although many will hope for both. After what appeared to be a period of equivocation Prime Minister Boris Johnson had indeed now did promised a full inquiry in 2022.

What are the questions?

In the meantime it is easy to list some of the questions that the official inquiry will have to address. They can however be rolled into one over-arching question.

How did it come to pass that the UK – a member of the G7 group of developed industrial nations with a long-established National Health Service, a sophisticated public-health system and a plethora of distinguished scientists – manage to have some of the highest death rates in the world until the joint effect of lockdowns and a very successful mass vaccination programme cut deaths rates sharply?

How did the UK in mid-May 2021 have above 127,000 deaths of those who died within 28 days of being diagnosed with Covid-19, a number that rises beyond 150,000 on the measure of excess deaths compared with the previous five-year average?

Just some of the questions this government will have to answer include:

- Did it fail to take the pandemic seriously enough at the outset?
- Why was personal protective equipment (PPE) in such short supply, a shortage followed by chaotic ordering and deliveries?
- Why were elderly patients discharged from hospitals to care homes without being tested for the virus?
- Why did it set up its own test and trace system at the cost of £37bn (over two years) when local authority health systems could, many argue, have provided a more effective, and certainly more cost-effective, service?
- Why were border controls and quarantines not introduced at airports when the scale of the pandemic threat became clear?
- Was it too slow in ordering the initial lockdown and too fast in lifting the restrictions and then repeating the same process a second time?
- Did it really, as it always claimed, 'follow the science' or were crucial scientific warnings simply overridden?

And there is a second over-arching question. How many of those deaths were unnecessary and resulted from the Government's handling, or mishandling, of the crisis?

It looks now that Johnson will indeed face such questions, and many others although whether an inquiry report will be published before the next general election remains open to question. Yet politicians should not be the only ones facing scrutiny on how they performed, albeit it in the most difficult of circumstances.

The UK media needs a mirror

Some sections of the media should also do some soul searching over whether they all rose adequately to the challenge of covering the biggest story since the Second World War and the most devastating pandemic since the global outbreak of influenza in 1918.

The biggest single question is whether the UK's right-wing tabloids may have put readers' lives at risk by railing against the lockdowns and routinely ridiculing the Government's scientific advisers as doom-mongers and trying to undermine their recommendations. To what extent did they influence, successfully from their point of view, flawed government policy?

Throughout the pandemic, newspapers such as *The Sun* and *the Daily Mail*, consistently gave greater priority to protecting the economy, including the hospitality sector, than saving lives by mobilising public support for lockdowns.

A flavour of the approach can be seen from the front pages on March 24, 2020 reporting the announcement of the UK's first lockdown the previous day.

'House arrest' was how the *Sun* put it, while the *Daily Telegraph* saw the announcement as the 'End of freedom'. The *Daily Mail* spluttered about the 'astonishing restrictions on daily life' in lockdown Britain implying that they were too severe.

As it happens the newspapers, which later sought to stiffen Prime Minister Johnson's resolve in standing up to the negativity of the scientists and open up the economy as soon as possible, were the same newspapers which enthusiastically supported Brexit.

The same wellspring is almost certainly a populist libertarianism, with an instinctive objection to being 'pushed around' by experts, particularly when, in the nature of science, there were often different scientific opinions to select. There is almost certainly also an inbuilt bias against scientific understanding on many newspapers because of a preponderance of arts graduates in their ranks.

It is not always clear that some of the popular tabloids fully grasped the devastating nature of the exponential spread of a lethal virus and how rapidly it can travel in developed, interconnected societies.

There was also marked enthusiasm for portraying the pandemic as a disease of the elderly, who are indeed the sector of society most at risk, but not exclusively so. The young can also spread Covid-19 and suffer greatly from its longer-term effects – Long Covid.

Giving dissident voices too much space?

Naturally papers such as the *Daily Mail* greeted the launch of the Great Barrington Declaration in October 2020 by three scientists – Sunetra Gupta, professor of theoretical epidemiology from Oxford; Martin Kulldorff, professor of medicine at Harvard; and Jay Bhattacharya, professor of medicine and economics at Stanford – with extensive coverage.

The essential argument was that only the vulnerable were at risk, so all you had to do was protect them and let the rest of the population, at low risk of death, go about their normal business, thereby creating 'herd immunity'. The damage caused to society, and in particular the economy and the mental health of individuals, would, as a result, be much less than the blunt tool of a universal lockdown.

By implication from the weight of mainly sympathetic coverage in the *Daily Mail* – though dissenting voices were reported – the paper obviously thought that the Great Barrington Declaration had merit. As it and other papers said, more than 12,000 scientists internationally had signed the declaration, although there was no attempt to reflect the fact that, according to Unesco, there are more than 8m scientists in the world.

The flaws in the declaration became apparent very quickly. Very large numbers of people could be described as 'vulnerable' and it is far from clear how they could all be protected if the virus was let rip in society to create herd immunity. The three had nothing to say about Long Covid, which was already emerging at the time, and affected more than the elderly cohorts with life-changing effects.

Perhaps the biggest flaw was the fact that creating a large pool of Covid-19 throughout society would mean greater opportunities for the emergence of variants, possibly even more lethal and infectious, which was exactly what happened.

On the whole the established media performed well in the pandemic, certainly in comparison to the conspiracy theories and falsehoods spread by social media, from the campaigns of the anti-vaxxers to spurious claims that Covid-19 has somehow been caused by 5G telecommunication masts or that Bill Gates was trying to use the vaccines to achieve world domination. Such conspiracy theories were given a degree of houseroom, complete with reader comments, on the websites of the tabloids.

How media life adapted

It was still a truly remarkable achievement for national, regional and local newspapers to continue publishing professional editions remotely during lockdowns without missing a beat or an edition.

Although drama production was interrupted, television news and current affairs programmes were produced from back bedrooms and attracted audiences larger than those seen for many years. Tim Davie, Director-General of the BBC summed the challenge up very well:

"It's hard to overstate the shock to the TV sector as the Covid-19 crisis took hold. Production was forced to a halt. Live events were postponed or cancelled. Collapsing ad revenues brought major challenges to the wider market," he said. "At the same time the way audiences responded as the BBC transformed its output almost overnight to meet the needs of the nation was incredible."

It was an experience that happened all across Europe as research for the European Broadcasting Union revealed. Public service broadcasters rediscovered their essential role-serving the public – and with it their morale and sense of purpose.

Audiences to main TV news bulletins grew by more than 20 per cent with the larger audiences recording high levels of trust. Unfortunately, that phenomenon tended to fade as Covid fatigue set in and, in the end, some viewers found the news too negative and switched off.

One accusation that can, however, be levelled at British broadcasters is that they failed to portray adequately the sheer enormity of the number of deaths and the grim scenes in hospital intensive care units and bodies stacked up in temporary mortuaries.

There were startling images of coffins in Bergamo in Italy and mass graves in Brazil aplenty – but not, initially, in Birmingham. As a result it was that little bit easier for people who had not experienced deaths in their immediate family to believe they were not at risk from the pandemic.

It was hardly the fault of the broadcasters alone. In the early months it was hard to persuade hospitals or local authorities to grant access. BBC *Newsnight* journalist Mark Urban told how he tried to make a film about temporary mortuaries but gave up after being blocked by local authorities.

Mark Easton, BBC News' Home Editor did eventually manage to do a moving story on bodies piling up in mortuaries but only after protracted negotiations. Even then it proved controversial with many viewers as he explains in chapter 19 of this book.

Gradually Covid hospital wards were opened up to broadcasters who demonstrated that such stories could be filmed without any breach of patient privacy. It was the perfect way to illustrate the challenge and danger faced by health workers while educating the general public about the seriousness of the pandemic threat.

Some newspapers got under the flannel, bluff and misleading statements that emerged routinely from the Government. *Sunday Times* Insight journalists revealed the sense of chaos in Downing Street at the outset in March 2020, and told how just as scientists were starting to warn that the country might be much further into the epidemic than previously thought, the go-ahead was given for 250,000 to attend the Cheltenham race festival.

The Times in March 2021 revealed how on September 18 the previous year the Government's most senior advisers – Dominic Cummings, Cabinet Secretary Simon Case, Sir Patrick Vallance and Professor Chris Whitty – had met with the Prime Minister. All the advisers were convinced of the need for an immediate 'circuit breaker' of at least two weeks in England because of the surge in cases, but not the Prime Minister.

"Dom said that we can't let the second wave crash, we can't repeat the mistakes we made during the first lockdown, but Boris said no," the paper reported a government source as saying. By the time Johnson implemented a new lockdown five days later, the number of cases had quadrupled.

Tabloids such as *The Sun* and *the Daily Mail* launched successful campaigns. *The Sun* mobilised its 'Jabs Army' to encourage thousands of volunteers to come forward to help with the vaccination programme. The *Daily Mail,* through its readers, raised millions of pounds to deliver missing PPE for NHS staff and later further millions to pay for laptops for children to learn at home during the lockdown.

Determined to open up

But the biggest media issues involved those same right-wing tabloids and their consistent determination to open up the economy and the schools, almost at any cost. It is possible to choose almost any edition of the *Daily Mail* to make the point, but that of February 23, 2021 serves as well as any.

It covered Prime Minister Johnson's announcement of his cautious roadmap to lifting the restrictions from the re-opening of schools on March 8 to the end of all curbs on meetings and events on June 21. The coverage in the *Mail* illustrates perfectly the paper's approach, and some of the inherent contradictions involved.

'The end in sight – but it's going to take months: What are we waiting for?' was the way the *Mail's* front page put it, followed by page after page in similar vein.

Right-wing Tory MPs were quoted as saying "this is a hammer blow" and commentator Henry Deedes argued that the Prime Minister was dogged by doubt and that "doom-monger Sages (the Government's scientific advisers) have got Boris on the run."

The fact that most pubs and restaurants would not be able to fully re-open until May was described as 'a death sentence for pubs' alongside Easter staycation hopes being dashed, while there would be no foreign travel before May 17 at the earliest. In its leader column the paper noted the huge success of the vaccination programme yet the Prime Minister's trademark optimism seemed to have deserted him.

"Instead of marching the high road to freedom Britain will mostly limp out of lockdown – piling more misery on frayed families and the beleaguered business community alike," the paper argued.

Time for a press inquiry?

Yet there in the midst of the 'Why are we waiting?' coverage there was a stark warning of the reason behind the scientific and political caution – the forecast that another 91,000 people would die if the rules were to be scrapped in April, as the *Daily Mail* had wanted. Naturally Sir Patrick Vallance and Chris Whitty were denounced as 'Sagenaysayers' for their professional expertise.

There is an urgent need for measured, comprehensive academic research into the performance of the national newspapers and how the right-wing tabloids in particular covered the Covid-19 crisis.

For now, there is a prima facie case to be answered that some newspapers and their websites reaching many millions of people misled their readers on where the difficult balance should be drawn between opening up the economy and 'freedom' and taking the measures necessary to at least contain the worst aspects of Covid-19.

It is not just the Government that needs to learn the lessons from the often-egregious mistakes made. A number of national newspaper editors also face a steep learning curve not just to cope with the current pandemic, which has not gone away, but for the inevitable, further pandemics to come.- in an interdependent world.

So far the *Daily Mail* seems to have learned very little. On March 30, 2021, celebrating the first modest lifting of restrictions the previous day, 'the first steps to freedom', the paper repeated the exact same splash headline that first appeared on February 23 – 'What are we waiting for?'

The paper wanted the relaxation dates to be brought forward in the light of improved data with not a single Covid death reported in half the country the previous Sunday. The data had changed and so should the dates for lifting remaining restrictions, said the *Mail*. Those who wanted a summer holiday abroad should be allowed to do so, according to 40 MPs, even though more than 36,000 new cases a day were being reported in France, most of them the more lethal Kent variant with the Indian variant yet to come.

"Fears of a third wave driven by rising infections in Europe and the threat of new variants able to resist inoculation are hypothetical," the *Mail* insisted.

Presumably it was hypothetical in the same way as the first and second waves were hypothetical.

It was almost as if now that the UK had left the European Union, the Continent didn't exist any more. Tell that to the Covid-19 virus.

About the contributor

Raymond Snoddy is a media journalist and co-editor of this book. He reported on media for the *Financial Times* and *The Times*. He presented *NewsWatch* on the BBC 2004-2012 and Channel 4's award-winning series *Hard News*. He is the author of a biography of media tycoon Michael Green and of *The Good, the Bad and the Ugly*, which looked at the UK national press in the 1990s. He was awarded an OBE for services to journalism in 2000.

Section four
Outside the metropolitan elite
***

The future of this United Kingdom is in the hands of those far detached from those who think they rule us

Neil Fowler

As much as many in London and some of the elite universities might forget, successful life does exist outside their environs and, in fact, it has been those living in these places who have broadly written the script on the direction of the United Kingdom in recent years, whether it has been devolution, Brexit or the 2019 General Election.

Cue much grinding of teeth from those metropolists who take pride in standing apart from the crowd, but it can be argued they are now the outliers and out of sync with the rest of the nation at large

So in our tour outside these capitals of right thinking we seek to examine how the un-metropolitan non-elites have been faring in these days of Covid and crisis.

First up is co-editor of this book, Tor Clark, Associate Professor in Journalism at the University of Leicester, who reviews how the provincial press has coped with the pandemic.

"The UK regional press, having survived years of decline, was just re-establishing itself as a successful publisher of news via digital and social media when the pandemic struck," he says. And he is hopeful. It's "still full of dedicated professionals working hard to provide reliable local news to their communities, an endeavour which had been dangerous over the past year and had become perhaps even more vital than it had ever been to its local communities."

The future of this United Kingdom is in the hands of those far detached from those who...

Gavin Esler, formerly of the BBC parish, examines the whole state of the UK nation in *How Britain ends*. He believes with or without Brexit, the damage is done and the UK is already broken up into its constituent nations.

"There are two possibilities for the future," he writes. "We could recognise the erosion of Britishness and begin a process of profound reform, or we can stumble along in what the writer Peter Geoghegan calls a 'Zombie union'. It's a failed marriage, but one in which no one wants the trouble and expense of having to leave, until something finally snaps."

We now travel to the constituent parts of this United Kingdom, firstly to Scotland, where Maurice Smith asks *Who was the godfather of the new populism? Archie Gemmill or Alex Salmond?* and draws a delightful parallel between 'Ally's Tartan Army' in Argentina in 1978 and 'Alex/Nicola's Tartan Army' in Scotland in 2021.

"There is a long way to go, but might all this force the collapse of the United Kingdom and the creation of a new Scotland? Or will this latest turn of events simply follow the fate of the 1978 World Cup, snatching defeat from the jaws of victory? Inevitably, as in sport, it remains too soon to tell," he writes.

Still in Scotland, John McLellan, former editor of *The Scotsman* and also director of communications for the Scottish Conservatives in 2012-13 looks at *Political reality and the issue of perception between Boris and Nicola*.

Commentators have said the Scottish parliamentary elections of 2021 were an outstanding success for the SNP, but he argues it was the Conservatives who gained the most remarkable results. So what happens now?

"Perception is political reality and under both Alex Salmond and Nicola Sturgeon the SNP has expertly created the perception that Scotland is being done down and held back by the United Kingdom. But if the SNP is seen to block the UK Government doing what it can to give the Scottish recovery the same boost as the vaccine programme just for the sake of political point-scoring, that perception will change," he argues.

Over the water, Gail Walker, former editor of the *Belfast Telegraph*, writes on *Upper and lower case unionism: Populism playing out on the streets in Northern Ireland*.

"The Good Friday Agreement seemed to have sorted the 'Northern Irish problem'," she says – "and then Brexit came along and produced a new border in the Irish Sea.

"The union message isn't exclusive to Northern Ireland of course. But this is where the impact of that message on people is greatest and where the implications of getting it wrong – whatever 'it' may turn out to be – carry the highest tariff. It remains to be seen what the new normal is to look like in Belfast, because very few want the old one back."

In Wales, Martin Shipton, political editor-at-large of the *Western Mail*, sees the Welsh nation still at some form of crossroads. Having persuaded the poorest UK nation, which had most to lose from leaving the EU to do just that, populists at both ends of the M4 have made scrapping the Welsh Parliament their next target, he says,

"For now," he writes, "Mark Drakeford's own version of the vaccine bounce may have seen him claim a renewed mandate for his 'nationalist-lite' agenda. But with the future of the UK in doubt, the choice for the people of Wales could within a few years lie between a leap into the unknown with independence or assimilation into a greater England. Neither outcome can be taken for granted."

Back in rural England David Banks, former editor of the *Daily Mirror*, and now publisher of a digital and very local news outlet, wonders *Is there life the other side of the red wall?* "Is populism in play in rural areas as it is the cities?" he asks.

"What failure of the democratic system projects the likes of Trump and Johnson – publicity-loving 'bad lads' from all corners of the world of entertainment – into the number one posts in politics? While the United States' public replaced an extraordinary one-term President Trump with a more traditional figure in Joe Biden – bringing to a close a disturbing but temporary aberration – the UK continues to labour under the weight of prime ministerial scandal and talk of celebrity entryism.

"Will it provoke another red wall revolution to reshape British politics? Currently, an electorate pummelled by pandemic and dazzled by its wished-for celebrity democracy shows no sign of returning government to business as usual."

And in the final chapter in this section, Professor Barnie Choudhury of the University of Buckingham asks *How did the media report Brexit and Covid when it came to South Asian communities?*

Mainstream journalists are missing out on important stories in these dramatic times by not looking at stories through a racially-diverse lens, he says. "Reporting superficially the story of the day is not good enough. What we must do is embrace the idea that the more different voices, from different walks of life, different experiences, can only enhance what we do. Unless we grasp that fundamental axiom, we will continue to fall into the trap of seeing our world through a white lens."

The pandemic and the provincial press

The UK regional press, having survived years of decline, was just re-establishing itself as a successful publisher of news via digital and social media when the pandemic struck. Former regional newspaper editor Tor Clark looks at how the coronavirus crisis impacted local newspapers

Local newspapers in the UK have a had a very good run. For around 130 years before the railways even made a national press possible and 200 years before anything like a mass readership for the nationals, the regional press was developing all across Britain.

Even when national newspapers enjoyed multi-million circulations, the good old local paper was able to keep selling vast numbers of copies to its local community. As recently as 30 years ago several UK evening newspapers, such as the *Manchester Evening News*, the Wolverhampton *Express and Star* or the *Birmingham Evening Mail* all sold close to a quarter of a million copies every evening.

Hard-copy sales have declined dramatically since then for reasons explored in several of this book's predecessors (see Mair et al 2012, 2013; Clark, 2016; Perch 2016 for example), but even in these circumstances the UK regional press was committed to migrating its audience online and, when digital readership is taken into account, local newspapers at the start of the 2020s still had huge readerships. Their digital access figures show actual readerships are in many cases as high as they were in the newspapers' heyday (Sharman, 2019). Most readers are not paying for their news and advertisers are not advertising online as they did in previous times, but the audience for local news is still actively consuming it.

The rise and dominance of digital news
Local newspapers developed their websites and created new audiences who would not have never purchased the print version of their papers. As social media developed with the rise of first Facebook and then Twitter after 2005, so regional newspapers

began to ensure their news made it onto those platforms, which operated by slightly different rules, especially the 'shareability' (Harcup and O'Neill, 2017) of the story being published, which actually altered the professional news values of reporters and news desks for the first time in decades.

A game-changing technological development, the switch from commonly accessing digital information via desktop computers to access via laptops and especially mobile phones only, accelerated the digital and social media news functionality of local newspapers. Further developments in social media such as Instagram were quickly seized on and used to gain more audience involvement. By 2019 many newspapers were lauding the value of Instagram to access hard to reach local communities with grassroots stories which may never have achieved any prominence in traditional print newspapers.

Together with the application of social media analytics, the enthusiastic embrace of digital and particularly social media platforms was transforming how local journalism was done by the 2010s. Reporters had to produce stories which would be read and shared on social media. The way stories were loaded onto social media was considered to generate maximum interest. When a particular kind of story generated interest, similar stories were provided or similar approaches were adopted to retain or grow the audiences generated by the original stories.

These tactics were a huge success. By June 2017 ABC figures revealed the *Birmingham Mail* had 409,000 unique users, 280,000 Facebook likes and 242,000 Twitter followers (Sharman, 2017) at the same time as its once huge print sales had declined to 18,000 per day (Better Retailing, 2017).

The UK regional press had grown huge digital and social media audiences by 2020 while retaining small circulation print titles and advertising revenue from both print and digital advertising. Some papers had experimented with paywalls and subscription models with varying success. But an essential problem remained that though large digital audiences existed, they did not want to pay for the journalism they consumed, so the squeezing of the physical resources and infrastructure of regional press continued, despite its growing audiences.

The Covid crisis strikes

So, there were some reasons to be cheerful for the UK regional press before the Covid-19 pandemic hit in early 2020, but despair soon set in afterwards. Firstly, lockdowns were commercially damaging. Closed businesses with furloughed staff did not advertise. 'Stay at home' instructions meant people did not go out and casually buy a newspaper. And unexpectedly, but damagingly, the algorithms which governed digital advertising led advertisers to request not to have their adverts associated with reports of the biggest news story of the decade – Covid-19. There was only one story, but the costly production of that news generated little advertising revenue to pay the news producers' costs.

The industry was already financially challenged but, with the pandemic robbing it of paying readers and advertisers ironically at the time of the greatest appetite for news, more change was inevitable. In July 2020 regional media giant Reach announced 550 redundancies, which it attributed to the impact of the Covid-19 pandemic (Sharman, 2020a). Amid the many changes made in that dramatic culling of staff was the merger of the editorships of *Leicester Mercury* and *Coventry Telegraph*.

The idea that these two former large evening newspapers, each serving communities of around 300,000 people would not have their own editors, would have been unimaginable just a few years earlier, let alone in their heyday. But now the staff of the once 180,000-selling Leicester Mercury were huddled together in one small ground floor room, with the editor no longer present in the corner; or rather they would have been, if they hadn't all been working from home because of the pandemic putting their city into permanent lockdown. Worse was to follow at Reach when in March 2021 the firm announced the closure of all bar 15 of its large number of regional newspaper offices, leaving neither the *Coventry Telegraph* nor the *Leicester Mercury* with offices in their own cities (Sharman, 2021b).

And there were closures, sometimes of loss-making editions, but also of long-established titles. In September 2020, with little acknowledgement, JPI, the successor company to Johnston Press, which had gone into administration and been taken over by its creditors in 2018, closed 14 titles, deemed to be no longer viable including the *Kenilworth Weekly News* and *Warwick Courier*, which were incorporated into the *Leamington Courier,* and the *Belper News, Ilkeston Advertiser* and *Ripley and Heanor News*, which were incorporated into the *Derbyshire Times*. These closures meant these communities lost newspapers which focused on them solely, and that kind of coverage, despite all the assurances of the publishers, could not be delivered by the titles into which they had been folded (Sharman, 2020c).

JPI Media, still the UK's third biggest local publisher, was only to be a temporary vehicle for Johnston Press's creditors and at the very end of 2020 it was sold to a new firm called National World led, once again, by former Local World and national newspaper executive David Montgomery, who pledged it had a bright future. A positive development following the arrival of National World was the re-installation of dedicated editors for individual titles, such as the *Blackpool Gazette*, in 2021.

The pandemic continued the devastating losses of paid-for sales of local newspapers. In February 2021, holdthefrontpage.co.uk reported that all 41 UK regional daily newspapers for which it could access reliable figures, had seen double digit sales decreases in July-December 2020 (Sharman 2021a). Year-on-year declines in sales ranged from -13 per cent at the *Oxford Mail* to -34 per cent at the Wolverhampton *Express and Star*, once the biggest-selling regional newspaper in the UK with sales of more than 250,000, and -37 per cent at *The Scotsman*.

All the declines followed even heavier losses of sales the previous year, though the irony of these seemingly disastrous figures was contrasted to the success of the papers' digital operations by reporter David Sharman, who noted: "Despite the fall in print sales during the pandemic, online readership has continued to grow over the same period with both Reach and Newsquest recently publishing record audience figures for their regional titles." (Sharman, 2021a).

The continuing reorganisation of the UK regional press left three huge multinational conglomerates (Reach, Newsquest and JPI) owning the largest number of newspapers, but other smaller groups, such as Tindle, Archant and the recently-arrived 21st century version of Iliffe, with significant ownerships, which offered a potential way forward if the largest groups could ever be persuaded to consider their own break-up.

Across the UK small bands of dedicated reporters soldiered on producing ever more copy for multiple print, digital and social media publication, often from remote or out-of-town offices, while their owners' revenues dramatically declined, locking many of those still working for the major conglomerates into a never-ending spiral of editorial cutbacks.

Where now for the UK regional press?
So as the UK looked like it was emerging from the Covid-19 crisis in the late spring of 2021 and the economy began to open up again, the regional press shook itself down and faced an uncertain future.

In the negative column hard copy circulation continued to plummet, traditional editorial jobs continued to be lost and in some places the experience of journalists working from home during the pandemic made publishers' decisions to close local offices easier – though the closure of newspaper offices all over the UK was a process which had started long before 2020.

All of this damaged the traditional places of local newspapers in their local communities. The serious plight of the regional press had been acknowledged in the Cairncross Report of 2019 (Cairncross, 2019), but little action had appeared to take place to safeguard the supply of reliable public information to local communities and several local newspapers had been closed as unviable, leaving their communities without a truly local paper.

In the positive column digital and social media readerships were very healthy and local news was reaching local audiences through these channels. The restoration of local editors to local papers begun by National World was reversing years of seemingly endless retreat by its predecessor, Johnston Press, and some news providers were actually recruiting new staff to develop their digital journalism services.

Meanwhile the BBC Local Democracy Reporters scheme was actually adding resources to local newsgathering teams to cover the serious civic and political news which had been in danger of being marginalised in ever-stretched newsrooms (Clark 2021).

At the same time huge international media companies such as Facebook and Google had pumped investment into local journalism in a belated attempt at compensating the grassroots journalism that had originated so much of its content over the past decade or so.

It is debatable whether a subscription route to provide long-term, sustainable funding for the UK regional press had really been properly attempted, so the sector limped on financially using a mixture of outdated funding formats. The essential dilemma remained that these news providers had swapped loyal readers, who paid for their local journalism year-in, year-out six nights a week, for an equally-sized or even bigger army of digital readers who accessed all the local news they wanted free of charge 24-hours a day.

The UK regional press emerged from Covid-19 battered, bruised, reduced, sometimes homeless and totally unsure of its long-term future, but still full of dedicated professionals working hard to provide reliable local news to their communities, an endeavour which had been dangerous over the past year and had become perhaps even more vital than it had ever been to its local communities.

References

Better Retailing (2018), ABC figures show circulation drop across all regional papers, https://www.betterretailing.com/rn-archives/abc-figures-show-circulation-drop-across-all-regional-papers/ September 3, 2018, accessed, March 4, 2021.

Cairncross, F., (2019) *The Cairncross Review: A Sustainable Future for Journalism*, available at https://www.gov.uk/government/publications/the-cairncross-review-a-sustainable-future-for-journalism accessed 19.02.2019

Clark, T, (2016) '300 Years in the History of the Regional Press' in Mair, J, Clark T, Fowler, N, Snoddy, R and Tait, R, *Last Words? How Can Journalism Survive the Decline of Print?* Bury St Edmunds: Abramis

Clark, T., (2021) 'From The Silent Watchdog to the Lost Watchdog: The Decline of the UK Regional Press' Coverage of Local Government over 40 Years' Media History: TandFonline.com

Harcup, T., and O'Neill, D., (2017), What is news? News values revisited (again) in Journalism Studies, Volume 8, Issue 12. Routledge.

Mair, J, Fowler, N and Reeves, I, (2012) *What Do We Mean By Local? Grass-Roots Journalism – Its Death and Rebirth*, Bury St Edmunds: Abramis

Mair, J, Keeble, RL, and Fowler, N, (2013) *What Do We Mean By Local? The Rise, Fall – and Possible Rise Again – of Local Journalism*, Bury St Edmunds: Abramis

Perch, K, (2016) 'The collapse of the business model of regional newspapers has been far greater than previously stated and is undermining public sphere journalism' in Mair, J, Clark T, Fowler, N, Snoddy, R and Tait, R, *Last Words? How Can Journalism Survive the Decline of Print?* Bury St Edmunds: Abramis.

Sharman, D., (2017) Daily Doubles Wed Audience year-on-year in latest ABCes, https://www.holdthefrontpage.co.uk/2017/news/abce-figures-reveal-daily-has-doubled-web-audience-since-last-june/ July 20, 2017, accessed March 4, 2021.

Sharman, D, (2019b) 'ABCs: Regional publisher records Facebook and Twitter top threes' https://www.holdthefrontpage.co.uk/2019/news/abcs-regional-publisher-records-facebook-and-twitter-top-threes/ February 28, 2019, accessed April 1, 2019.

Sharman, D., (2020a) Reach to axe 550 jobs after coronavirus hits business https://www.holdthefrontpage.co.uk/2020/news/reach-to-axe-550-jobs-after-coronavirus-hits-business/ July 7, 2020, accessed March 4, 2021.

Sharman, (2020c) Publisher ceases publication of 14 'no longer viable' titles https://www.holdthefrontpage.co.uk/2020/news/publisher-ceases-publication-of-14-no-longer-viable-titles September 21, 2020, accessed March 4, 2021.

Sharman, D., (2021a) 'Pandemic hits sales as all dailies record double-digit circulation drops' https://www.holdthefrontpage.co.uk/2021/news/abc-data-reveals-double-digit-circulation-drops-at-all-dailies/ February 24, 2021, accessed February 25, 2021.

Sharman, D., (2021b) 'Publisher to close all bar 15 offices…' Reach plc to close all bar 15 of its newspaper offices - Journalism News from HoldtheFrontPage March 19, 2021, accessed May 6, 2021.

About the contributor

Tor Clark is Associate Professor in Journalism, BA Journalism programme director and Deputy Head of the School of Media, Communication and Sociology at the University of Leicester. Previously he worked at all levels in UK local newspapers before becoming editor of two regional newspapers. He researches and has regularly published on the history and prospects of the UK regional press. He is co-editor of this book.

How Britain ends…

With or without Brexit, the damage is done and the UK is already broken up into its constituent nations, says former BBC Newsnight host Gavin Esler, who has recently published a book on the state of the nation

One of the United Kingdom's national newspapers recently commissioned an article based on my book *How Britain Ends*. The book's central idea – as the title suggests – is that the United Kingdom as currently constituted may have had its day. What many of us think of as 'national' – meaning British – has changed significantly, for 'national' newspapers and much else. *The Sun, Mail* and *Times*, for example, have Scottish editions. Many more of us now see ourselves primarily as English, Scottish, Welsh or Irish rather than British.

Ideas of what 'British' means are often vague and backward-looking, focused on the past and rarely a vision for the future, or coherent about the present. When the English politics professor Matthew Goodwin asked Twitter users for recommendations about an up-to-date book about Britishness he received numerous suggestions about England and Englishness, and nothing serious about Britishness in the 21st century. The Twitterati went for historian Linda Colley's excellent 1992 account *Britons*, but her narrative ends in 1837. They suggested an essay by George Orwell from 1941, Jeremy Paxman's *The English,* Roger Scruton's *England: An Elegy* and various jokey references to *The Beano* and *Viz*. In *Watching the English* the anthropologist Kate Fox writes: "Britishness seems to me a rather meaningless term; when people use it they nearly always really mean 'Englishness.'" She's right.

What is 'being British'?
Britishness, historically, was defined by Protestantism, empire and war. All three past pillars have crumbled. For the future the big question is whether 'being British' still has any coherent meaning beyond nostalgia for former glories. Can the United Kingdom be reinvented, and if so, how? Or is drifting apart inevitable?

Nostalgic pessimism dogs even our current battles. In 2016 the Conservative MP Jacob Rees-Mogg likened Brexit to ancient English battles, Crecy and Agincourt, noting: "We win all these things." By 'we' he could only mean England. Scotland was generally on the side of the French. Brexit we were told was to 'take back control' – again the sense something in the past had been lost and recovery demanded sacrifice, including references to 'the Blitz spirit'. Some Brexiters even saw the BBC Proms temporary refusal to sing *Rule, Britannia,* a song from 1740, as a betrayal of 'national' British resolve. Post-imperial, 21st century Brexit Britain frequently sounded like an echo of Shakespeare's John of Gaunt in *Richard II*, lamenting (in 1595 when the play was written) that the English of his day were not as good as former generations. John of Gaunt was, of course, a Belgian, Jean de Ghent.

The United Kingdom is a remarkable survivor. We reinvented the Union every century since 1603. Each reinvention – 1707, 1801 and 1922 – came as a result of conflict or crisis, and each presented new opportunities. Brexit, coronavirus and the resulting economic dislocation are our shared simultaneous crises of the 21st century. The opportunity is for a long overdue reinvention of the UK with some citing the success of the coronavirus vaccination programme as evidence of a successful union. It may be too late. The UK which survived Scottish, Welsh and even violent Irish nationalism, may not survive the consequences of the less studied phenomenon of English nationalism because England is the elephant in the bed, and the pachyderm is growing restless.

England accounts for 84 per cent of the UK population, and an even larger slice of the economy. The IPPR (Institute for Public Policy Research) noted that since Scottish and Welsh devolution in the 1990s more people in England identify primarily as 'English', fewer as 'British'. English flags are more in evidence in housing estates and on cars, in places way beyond England football matches. The IPPR argued that the 2016 Brexit referendum was itself motivated by resurgent feelings of English identity and exceptionalism, but if the key slogan was 'take back control' who was doing the taking? Not voters in Scotland and Northern Ireland, where majorities voted to remain in the EU. As a friend in Northern Ireland put it: "An Englishman, Irishman and Scotsman walk into a pub. The Englishman wants to go home, so everyone has to leave." But not everyone is willing.

Scotland. Brexit. No thank you!

Scotland's First Minister Nicola Sturgeon insists Boris Johnson may have a mandate to take England out of the EU, but has no mandate to do the same for Scotland. Scots voters seem to agree. In 2016, 62 per cent of Scots voted Remain, a Remain majority in every Scottish electoral district. From June 2020 to January 2021 there were 20 surveys of Scottish opinion, and every poll showed a majority of Scots in favour of independence. In Wales, support for independence has never been strong, yet by the end of 2020 it was the highest ever recorded at 33 per cent. The independence campaigners of *YesCymru* claim a surge in membership from 2,500 at the start of 2020 to more than 15,000 by the end of the year.

In Northern Ireland, after years of peace since the 1998 Good Friday Agreement, there were even bigger shocks. Boris Johnson complacently insisted the Irish border – a source of terrorist conflict for years and the only land border between the EU and UK – was somehow not an issue. Amid widespread ridicule in Ireland north and south, Johnson compared it to the 'border' between two London boroughs, Camden and Westminster. The laughter stopped in October 2019 when, in his brief encounter with the Irish prime minister Leo Varadkar, Johnson solved his 'Irish Question' through creating a notional customs border in the Irish Sea. To the dismay of Ulster Unionists he accepted new bureaucratic checks on goods moving between Great Britain and Northern Ireland, dividing the UK for the first time in 100 years.

In what was once the Conservative *and Unionist* Party Margaret Thatcher insisted Northern Ireland was 'as British as Finchley'. Boris Johnson stoked up Ulster's insecurities by ensuring this part of the UK, in customs terms, was as British as France. Leaving the European Union undermined that other union. Former Labour Prime Minister Gordon Brown concluded the UK risked becoming a 'failed state'. Former Conservative Chancellor of the Exchequer, George Osborne, suggested Northern Ireland was on the edge of leaving the Union and Scotland might follow, with Boris Johnson going down in history as the worst British Prime Minister ever for 'unleashing English nationalism'. Osborne suggested the only way to stop the break-up of the UK was for Johnson not to allow Scots the opportunity to vote on independence. Anti-democratic unionist defeatism is not an alarm bell; it's a death knell.

The pandemic – a common cause for a disunited kingdom?

A common struggle against a common enemy – the coronavirus – should, like a war, have pulled the UK together. Devolved administrations in Scotland, Wales and Northern Ireland were, alongside Westminster, fighting the same enemy with access to the same science in the worst health crisis in living memory, yet in 2020 different leaders often implemented different policies with different priorities at different times. The UK has a National Health Service but it is operationally devolved. There isn't one chief medical officer. There are four, one each for Scotland, Northern Ireland, Wales and England. The English CMO acts as Westminster government adviser. The NHS is a British institution, but answerable to different politicians in London, Edinburgh, Cardiff and Belfast. There is no British education system. Decisions at Westminster on the opening of schools or universities had no relevance in Scotland. Scots generally take different exams and have different term times. Northern Ireland and Wales have considerable educational autonomy. There is no British legal system. Northern Ireland formerly had no-jury courts and for years banned abortion, while buying a house or getting a divorce is very different in Scotland and England. There is no 'British' religion. The Church of England has the Queen at its head, and bishops in the House of Lords. The Church of Scotland sees the Queen as no more than a respected believer and attempts to impose bishops on Scotland led to war in the 17th century. There is no British police force. England and Wales enjoy or endure a hodgepodge of 43 forces. Scotland and Northern Ireland make do with one each. And so on. When coronavirus led the Westminster government to close shops and pubs (or fail to do so) there were bitter complaints from local politicians across England that they were not consulted, their voices unheard. The mayor of Greater Manchester Andy Burnham was a vocal critic, while local councils from Hartlepool to Liverpool, London's mayor Sadiq Khan and education authorities across England tried to defy or criticise Westminster guidance, (or lack thereof).

'One Nation'?

In all of this the Johnson Government claimed to speak for Britain when the Prime Minister insisted he was a 'One Nation Conservative', the retort from some in Scotland, Wales and Northern Ireland was that the 'One Nation' was England. While the great success of the UK vaccination programme was heralded in government as an example of the union working, others said it showed the NHS working, unlike the botched test and trace system or PPE procurement where friends and Tory cronies were involved and the death toll exceeded 120,000. UK Government ministers did pose for Zoom interviews in front of Union Jack flags, bizarrely even in their own homes, but beyond the PR window dressing, was this the only credible forward-looking narrative about Britishness?

'English-ness?'

English writers often see nationalism as a peculiar vice inflicting lesser people, including the Scots and Irish. Even the perceptive Kate Fox claims: "The English are not usually given to patriotic boasting." Even if we ignore Cecil Rhodes' claim that 99 per cent of the world would prefer to be English (not in Scotland, Cecil, mate) or the England football fans chanting 'Two World Wars and One World Cup' plus the fringe hooliganism of the 'English Defence League', Ms Fox' claim is a very English style of subtle patriotic boasting. It's a humble brag about the modesty of English exceptionalism.

The economist Sir Dennis Robertson noted: "The Englishman has long been used to living in a certain haze as to what his country is, whether England or England-and-Wales or Great Britain or the United Kingdom of Great Britain and Northern Ireland or the United Kingdom plus its dependent territories or that larger unit which he used to call the British Empire." Even George Orwell in his 1941 wartime essay *Notes on Nationalism* sees England as exceptional. He writes that preserving the independence of what was then called Eire, Scotland or 'even Wales' was a 'delusion' if it was 'unaided' by 'British protection'. By British he obviously means English.

In 2020 the historian David Edgerton noted with wry humour: "Nationalism in British parlance was the doctrine which encapsulated the dubious claims of natives, whether Indian, African, Irish, Scottish, Welsh." Miraculously the English consider themselves immune from such 'dubious claims' but Edgerton suggests that's just because they do not recognise their own nationalist streak. Everyone else does. The author Louis de Bernieres bluntly suggested in the *Financial Times* and a subsequent letter to *The Times* that if Scots and Irish people wanted to leave the UK that would be a great opportunity for England without recalcitrant Celts. At least de Bernieres avoids the 'certain haze' and his English nationalism joins the competing 'dubious claims' of the other 'natives'.

The foreign correspondent comes home…

In 2014, during the Scottish independence referendum, and in 2015 and 2016 in the General Election and Brexit campaigns, I reported for the BBC from Shetland to Cornwall, Belfast to Kent. As a foreign correspondent I have reported on every continent on Earth except Antarctica, but deepest Britain was a shock. I knew Brazil more than Bolton. I could navigate Berlin and Washington without maps but was lost in Birmingham and Wolverhampton. I would check into a hotel and catch the BBC national and international news at 10pm. Each night the affable presenter Huw Edwards would tell the audience, "That's all from us. Now it's time for the news where you are." This wasn't God speaking to Moses on the mountain-top, but it certainly was 'Us' broadcasting to 'Them'. In 2014 the Scottish writer James Robertson began performing a witty poem called *The News Where You Are*. (Watch on *YouTube* to get a strong sense of his humour.) Here's a flavour:

> "The news where *you* are comes after the news where *we* are.
>
> The news where we are *is* the news. It comes first.
>
> The news where you are is the news where *you* are. It comes *after*.
>
> *We* do not have the news where you are.
>
> The news where you are may be news to you but it is *not* news to us.
>
> The news may be international, national or regional. The news where we are may be international news. The news where you are is *never* international news. Where you are is not international."

The Palestinian-American writer Edward Said described language dividing people into us and them as 'othering'. On my travels I heard how strongly people in Scotland, Wales, Northern Ireland and England-outside-London often felt othered by Westminster and disconnected from 'national' news. Most of the important things in their lives were health, jobs, schools, and policing, generally devolved issues, but the big money and real power lay with the often distrusted parliamentarians in London.

If Westminster is the Mother of Parliaments its children have grown up to go different ways. No major European country has retained Westminster's archaic system to deliver landslides in terms of seats for parties with a minority of votes, in a parliament with an unelected upper chamber presided over by an unelected head of state. Boris Johnson in 2019 secured an 80 seat majority, while 56 per cent of British voters did not vote for him. Modern states usually also have written constitutions to decide with varying degrees of clarity who does what, yet the myth of effortless superiority continues. The historian Linda Colley notes British scholars, lawyers and administrators helped write constitutions for some 70 countries worldwide including Germany, Iraq, and a host of former British colonies.

Written constitutions are good enough for Johnny Foreigner, but 'we British' are above such fripperies with an uncodified set of rules, laws and precedents impossible for us ordinary folk to comprehend. British voters are treated like illiterate peasants confronted with the Latin Mass of pre-Reformation Europe and a few British illuminati from the constitutional priesthood interpret it for us. The peasants just have to have faith. But do we?

Trust in Britain?

Every year the New York PR company Edelman publishes extensive surveys of public trust in the four types of institutions that are most important in our lives, government, business, NGOs and the media. In the 2020 survey the UK came second to bottom, 27th out of 28 OECD countries, just ahead of Vladimir Putin's Russia. Yes, *Putin's Russia*. In their 2020 report Cambridge University's Centre for the Future of Democracy noted more than half of British voters were dissatisfied with democracy itself. In September 2019 an *ITN/Channel 5* poll found seven in ten (71 per cent) felt MPs were untrustworthy. The Ipsos Mori Veracity Index survey (November 2019) showed trust in British politicians fell by five percentage points in a year to a new low. During the 2019 General Election campaign, just 14 per cent of the British public said they trusted politicians to tell the truth. Boris Johnson's landslide was based on a minority of voters, the majority of whom didn't trust him or indeed any politician, in a country without an agreed and codified constitution in which increasing numbers of citizens felt the pull of competing nationalisms, and were sceptical about whether the news they read or heard accurately reflected their lives. Oxford University's Reuters Institute found that in the UK in 2020: "Trust in the news has fallen over 20 percentage points since 2015. Even the most trusted brands like the BBC are seen by many as pushing or suppressing agendas, especially over polarising issues like Brexit."

How long can it survive?

A crisis, as the American politician Rahm Emanuel famously noted, is too good to waste. The United Kingdom has a concatenation of crises compounded by a loss of public trust and unshakeable complacency among some politicians and media commentators that the UK is miraculously better than other nations. There are two possibilities for the future. We could recognise the erosion of Britishness and begin a process of profound reform, or we can stumble along in what the writer Peter Geoghegan calls a 'Zombie union'. It's a failed marriage, but one in which no one wants the trouble and expense of having to leave, until something finally snaps. Either way, nostalgia is not a strategy, but it is part of how Britain ends.

About the contributor

Gavin Esler is an award-winning television and radio broadcaster, novelist, journalist and Chancellor of the University of Kent. He is the author of five novels and four non-fiction books, most recently *How Britain Ends - English Nationalism and the Re-birth of Four Nations*. Previously he was a BBC journalist, serving as a well-travelled foreign correspondent and BBC chief North America correspondent for eight years before becoming host of BBC 2's nightly news programme *Newsnight* from 2003 to 2014. In 2019 he stood as a candidate for the pro-European Change UK party in the European Parliament elections. He left the BBC in 2018 and is now a freelance journalist and writer.

Who was the godfather of the new populism? Archie Gemmill or Alex Salmond?

Maurice Smith draws a parallel between 'Ally's Tartan Army' in Argentina in 1978 and 'Alex/Nicola's Tartan Army' in Scotland in 2021

One of Scotland's most celebrated collective moments of the last five decades is instantly recognisable, even to those who were not born when it actually happened on June 11, 1978.

Picture the scene: a small, prematurely balding footballer runs past several Dutch defenders and slots the ball into the net, to the incredulous roars of a few thousand supporters at Mendoza, Argentina, and many more back home. It was the 69th minute of a vital World Cup tie, and for a few moments Archie Gemmill had – improbably – secured his country's passage to the next round of a World Cup tournament that had proved to be ill-fated from the moment he and his teammates had arrived in the southern hemisphere.

Football aficionados will know that success proved elusive for Scotland that day. Four minutes after Gemmill's goal, Johnny Rep pulled one back for the Dutch. Even though Scotland won the game 3-2, they failed to qualify by a single goal. Two earlier dire performances had sealed their fate and an early flight home, having effectively stolen defeat from the jaws of victory.

Scotland has a long history of glorious, and sometimes not-so-glorious, failure.

Some political commentators of the day believed that the national side's ignominious exit from World Cup 1978 actually marked a watershed in its politics. Just as Scottish manager Ally McLeod was speculating that his team might even win the trophy, support for the Scottish National Party was ebbing.

The party had won 11 Westminster Parliamentary seats in 1974 on the back of massive excitement about North Sea oil and a renewed sense of national self-confidence. Post Argentina, Scotland stumbled headlong into bitter division.

A referendum, which would have ushered in a devolved parliament, failed, leading indirectly to the collapse of the Callaghan administration in 1979. SNP representation shrivelled to just two Westminster seats as Mrs Thatcher swept to power. The rest, as they say, is history.

Scottish bubbles and moot points

Whether the bursting of the Scottish bubble in Argentina had any direct impact on the deflation of the SNP remains a moot point. But what is germane is the fact that support for independence over the decades has been expressed often in emotional terms more than practical ones.

Scottish politics has had its share of demagogues over the years – a young Jim Sillars and a fiery Tommy Sheridan, for example – and certainly since devolution arrived after the UK Labour landslide of 1997, nationalism and populism have travelled hand in hand.

Devolution was expressed in terms of destiny during the heady days of cross-party support for a Scottish Parliament during the 1990s. The campaign – backed by Labour and Liberal Democrats – stemmed from 'The Claim of Right for Scotland', launched with a mix of piety and populism as Scotland in opposition claimed some kind of consensus.

The Claim of Right had no direct electoral fundament. It was a claim based on opposition party disgruntlement about the Conservatives' third successive election victory in 1987. By 1990, the self-appointed Scottish Constitutional Convention had published the Claim – on St Andrew's Day, of course – demanding a devolved Scottish Parliament and a fairer say in running Scottish affairs.

Despite its symbolism, and the fact it was demanding something, which by contemporary standards seemed radical (at least to the Tories), the Claim was wrapped in sombre tones. The Convention was chaired by an Episcopalian priest, Canon Kenyon Wright. It was supported by terribly serious chaps from the Labour and Liberal Democrat parties; Donald Dewar and David Steel were establishment figures rather than nationalist firebrands.

Devolution as a concept proved popular, rather than populist. Although the Tories won a fourth term in 1992, devolution seemed inevitable by the time of the New Labour landslide five years later.

The SNP, whose brand of populism has always been more explicit, joined the campaign for a yes vote to devolution in 1997, having shunned the Constitutional Convention for reasons almost too obscure to recall. That referendum was won easily, and by the time the Parliament was established two years later, Scottish politics had converged around a new consensus. Even the Conservatives, long opposed to devolution, realised that proportional representation offered them some way back north of the border, having lost virtually every Westminster seat by the end of John Major's dismal period of power.

Devolution settled into a cosy first eight years, with little sign of the populist storm to follow. Labour and the Liberal Democrats formed a joint administration, helped by the system of proportional representation that had been designed, supposedly, to ensure that no single party could achieve an absolute majority.

It is generally held that the single greatest legislative achievement of those two coalition administrations was the banning of tobacco smoking indoors (something that had been achieved earlier in several jurisdictions including the Irish Republic and New York City).

The SNP takes the crown

The arrival of Alex Salmond's Scottish National Party to power in 2007 was seismic. Recently appointed prime minister Gordon Brown – elected unopposed as Labour Party leader – refused at first to call Salmond with the customary congratulations. Without irony, Brown said his first move would be to remind the SNP that they did not enjoy majority support in Scotland, which Brown tended to regard as a personal fiefdom. Brown himself had just been installed at 10 Downing Street via a party selection that bordered on acclamation.

Those first four years of SNP rule were notable for a rather under-stated form of populism. The party's strategy was to demonstrate competence rather than revolutionary zeal. In minority, it even relied on back-door deals with the Tories to get budgets approved. Long-awaited infrastructure projects were finally given the go-ahead, a few overdue policies enacted. Salmond – and his deputy Nicola Sturgeon – were praised generally for sensible government.

The tactic was clever, and from the SNP's perspective it worked well. Labour's inability to respond to its 2007 defeat, topped by Brown's ousting from Downing Street three years later, helped the SNP – once dubbed 'the Tartan Tories' – to convince Labour voters that it was more left-of-centre and intent on pursuing progressive politics.

If 2007 created a few tremors, the bigger SNP victory four years later was a political earthquake. It emitted an early sign too that populism could succeed, especially in the period post the 2008 financial crisis. For more than a decade now electorates all over the West have used elections to kick back at the establishment. Suddenly right-wing parties in France, Germany and Spain have attracted bigger votes. Right-wing incumbent parties – the Tories here in the UK, Republicans in the US – have re-invented themselves as populists, or allowed themselves to be taken over by rampant populists like Boris Johnson and Donald Trump – two national leaders whose elevation to power would have seemed unlikely just a few years previously.

Could Scottish populism deliver independence?

Scotland, however, was the first place where modern populism actually brought significant electoral success. The SNP's 2011 victory led almost inevitably to an independence referendum in 2014. That was a campaign marked by emotional appeals to escape austerity and absentee rule by the simple means of creating a new country.

The lowering of the Scottish voting age to 16 in 2014 bolstered the youthful appeal of nationalism: why not vote for real change, the chance to re-invent Scotland, to kick back at the old parties and the austerity – fiscal and in terms of ideas – they represented?

Salmond and his team exuded a super-confident outlook about the prospects for an independent Scotland: a Scotland that would easily retain membership of the EU, floating on North Sea oil, confidently joining the top table just like other small, successful nations. The whole thing would cost little and take less than two years, according to the SNP.

Those 2007 and 2011 results in Scotland might have served as a warning to the UK established parties, and to others further abroad. The battle for hearts and minds has moved online. Liberal activists saw nothing wrong with the slick web-based operations that helped turn out a big vote for Barack Obama in 2008; the wielding of social media to support Trump, Le Pen, Vote Leave and – yes – Scottish independence was unforeseen by those on the left or right. Its impact has been to turn politics upside down.

Although the Yes side lost the 2014 referendum by 55 to 45 per cent, it is fair to say that the winners learned little or nothing from the experience. Defeat seemed to galvanise nationalist support – when Sturgeon replaced Salmond in the wake of the referendum defeat, party membership soared four-fold to more than 120,000, a huge figure for a country the size of Scotland.

There followed massive wins in three Westminster elections, and a third successive win for the SNP at Holyrood in 2016. Support for independence is highest among the under-50s, and Yes began to register a narrow overall lead in successive opinion polls during 2020.

No way to win a nation?
The 2014 No campaign – led by David Cameron and George Osborne at Downing Street level – had been intensely negative.

That campaign spawned the original Project Fear, supposedly a tongue-in-cheek soubriquet coined by staff of the Better Together campaign chaired by former Labour chancellor Alistair Darling. Osborne convinced himself and his prime minister that their dire warnings of what would happen if Alex Salmond won was the reason he lost.

A special unit in the Treasury, reporting to Osborne's permanent secretary Sir Nick (now Lord) McPherson, had lobbied dozens of Scottish companies to go public about the economic calamities to be endured by an independent Scotland. Osborne turned up in Edinburgh one morning to say that if an indy Scotland wanted to use the British pound, well, it just couldn't… and so on.

The Yes campaign's confident, more positive campaign convinced numerous voters to support independence. Many of them were first-time voters. Many more were previously Labour stalwarts. While it is true that numerous older voters were rattled by dire warnings about the fate of their pensions, the evidence that Project Fear worked is less clear. It could be argued that the tactic helped grow support for independence by 20 points during the lengthy campaign.

Undeterred, Osborne and Cameron played exactly the same tactic in the Euro referendum two years later. But they were up against a Leave campaign that started from a much higher base than had the SNP.

Arguably, Leave was led by a much more ruthless group, well-funded and willing to make any claim to support getting out of Europe. Where Salmond produced a bulky (if controversial) white paper, Leave used the side of a bus to make ridiculous promises about using EU money for the NHS. Campaigners claimed Turkey was poised to join the EU, with 12m Turks flooding in as a result. Populist Johnson and ultra-populist Farage may not have been formally allied, but they shared a common goal and a similarly vague adherence to the facts.

In the face of that, Project Fear mark two collapsed. A half-hearted and complacent Remain campaign lost to the populists. People wanted to kick 'the man', protest against globalisation and the loss of traditional jobs, against the banks getting bailed out, against foreigners moving in, against French and Spanish trawlers fishing 'our waters', and so on. The Leave campaign's attitude to campaigning scruples made the Scottish referendum seem like a Sunday school picnic. But there is little doubt that Leave learned tricks from observing the Scottish campaign.

Their success was not lost across the Atlantic. When Leave prevailed in June 2016, Donald Trump had just about tied up the Republican Party nomination. Populism was his theme too. But from that summer he and his supporters stepped up the rhetoric harshly. The Brits had shown that populism worked, and they were the first to do so successfully within all the major democracies.

For Turkey read Mexico and the Muslim countries: bogeymen everywhere. Brexit inspired the likes of Steve Bannon, Trump's campaign consigliore. 'America first!' was the cry, just as 'Britain first' was exclaimed by the killer of Labour MP Jo Cox. It led to Trump's bombastic, chilling inauguration speech in 2017, and four years of fake news, conspiracy theories and deepening social division as the United States fell into the well of paranoia, introspection and disengagement from the outside world.

There is no known link from the SNP campaigns of 2007 and 2011 and the depths of Trumpism or the shallowness of Boris Johnson. But the populist experiments of the SNP in Edinburgh – and especially the proclaimed anti-establishment positions of a party that offered a seductive opportunity to voters eager to express dismay at their circumstances – paved the way for the more successful campaigns in England and the US.

Sturgeon takes over the mantle

Since 2014 Salmond's erstwhile understudy has led the Scottish government against Brexit and through the pandemic. A populist by approach – who became used to addressing adoring fans in mass meetings that resembled evangelical events – Nicola Sturgeon has increasingly found herself under attack within the independence movement. Some believe she has been too cautious, hesitant about demanding another referendum, especially after Johnson's landslide general election win in December 2019.

In 2021 her former mentor Salmond – bruised by a lengthy judicial and parliamentary battle over allegations of improper behaviour, for which he was acquitted after a High Court trial – sought to put her under pressure by launching his own Alba Party. Sometimes populists come to believe their old parties just are not populist enough.

Salmond's old guard swamped social media with bold claims that hundreds of thousands of Scots would vote for Alba, effectively gaming the system to produce a claimed super-majority for independence. Come May 6, Salmond's party gathered just 1.7 per cent of the popular vote, and no seats.

His nemesis led her party to victory, and the SNP has formed the government at Holyrood for the fourth successive time. By the next election the SNP will have run Scotland for nearly 20 years. Yet it fell a single seat short of a majority and will rely on the independence-supporting Greens to remain in charge.

Will Westminster wilt in the face of a majority of Scottish MSPs backing a referendum? Or will it seek to face down the renewed demands from Edinburgh? Scottish voters often seem to hint at one thing but mean another. There may be a majority for a referendum, but is there a majority for independence itself? The Sturgeon SNP is a populist – and popular – party, commanding more support than its major Union-supporting rival parties combined.

There is a long way to go, but might all this force the collapse of the United Kingdom and the creation of a new Scotland? Or will this latest turn of events simply follow the fate of the 1978 World Cup, snatching defeat from the jaws of victory? Inevitably, as in sport, it remains too soon to tell.

About the contributor

Maurice Smith is a journalist, commentator and documentary producer based in Glasgow. He was previously business editor of BBC Scotland and a reporter with the *Glasgow Herald*.

Political reality and the issue of perception between Boris and Nicola

Commentators have said the Scottish parliamentary elections of 2021 were an outstanding success for the SNP, but John McLellan argues that it was the Conservatives who gained the most remarkable results. What happens now?

Night after night throughout the pandemic, the stooped, tousled figure of Prime Minister Boris Johnson dominated the news bulletins as he blustered his way through grim Covid-19 statistics, the latest health advice and whatever switch in the UK Government's tactics was being announced.

There was brief respite from the unremitting gloom in the summer of 2020 when Chancellor Rishi Sunak rolled up his sleeves to be pictured waiting on tables to promote the Eat Out to Help Out scheme, the most visible of his recovery measures. Only when it was too late did it emerge that what was a highly popular scheme to boost the hospitality trade was literally a fatal error which instead boosted the spread of the virus in readiness for the autumn's second wave of infection.

Meanwhile in Scotland, the miraculously coiffured First Minister Nicola Sturgeon was on the news bulletins even more frequently than the Prime Minister, only occasionally giving up her daily conferences to less able lieutenants.

And the more she appeared the more her popularity grew, and for the second half of 2020 her net approval ratings were higher than Boris Johnson's, not just in Scotland but across the whole UK; from April 2020 until the middle of March 2021, her UK net approval score in a succession of polls was never below zero, compared to Johnson whose highest scores were when he was recovering from his near-fatal brush with Covid-19 in April 2020 but, unlike his health, they went steadily downhill thereafter and were never out the red from September to January. Only by March and the undeniable success of the vaccine roll-out did his UK approval edge ahead of Sturgeon.

In Scotland the gap was a chasm, with an Opinium survey in January 2021 giving Sturgeon +57 compared to Johnson's -7 and, even after the exposure of her uncharacteristically forgetful handling of the Alex Salmond affair, her net positive score in an Ipsos/ Mori poll was still 32, which the other Scottish political leaders would have sacrificed a limb to achieve.

As media philosopher Marshall McLuhan famously put it, the medium is the message and in the pandemic the medium for the message was the voice and the personality of those called upon to communicate vital information on which the entire nation was hanging every single day. To them fell the job of persuading us to accept meekly that hitherto unthinkable withdrawals of basic liberties and the transformation of the nation into the closest thing to a police state anyone had ever experienced were necessary and proportionate.

Differences? What differences?
The SNP was often accused of deliberately deviating from UK policy simply to emphasise difference, most notably when not following the UK Government in dropping the 'Stay at Home' message in May 2020; introducing different tier systems; and naming of the pop-up hospital after Scottish First World War nurse Louisa Jordan instead of Florence Nightingale.

However, despite slight presentational and timing variances, the longer view shows the two governments were following essentially the same strategy. Even with health care fully devolved and the Scottish Government free to chart its own course if it wanted, there was similar hesitancy at the start, the same relaxation in summer, virtually identical clinical advice, the same infection rates, and the same death rate.

Give or take a week or two, Scotland has enjoyed the same fast vaccination programme as the rest of the UK, thanks to the tight contracts the UK Government signed last year after July's decision not to join the EU's vaccine procurement programme.

At the time it suited the SNP's narrative of a negative, isolationist UK acting against its citizens' best interests and senior figures didn't hold back:

- Constitution Secretary Mike Russell MSP: "This idiotic refusal is all about Brexit and nothing to do with the pandemic. It will cost lives."

- Shadow Brexit Secretary Dr Philippa Whitford MP: "The UK Government's short-sighted and increasingly isolationist approach does nothing but hinder the ability to tackle the virus effectively."

- Childcare Minister Maree Todd MSP: "Like watching a deliberate car crash in slow motion."

- Housing Minister Kevin Stewart MSP: "This lunacy shows how ideological, inept and irresponsible Brexiteer buffoons are."

Whether by design or accident, the First Minister did not join the apoplectic condemnation and so, when the success of the UK programme became clear at the same time as anger was boiling over within the EU at the glacial pace of its own programme, Sturgeon could dodge Conservative demands for a humble apology.

Despite the SNP condemnation of the UK vaccine strategy, and the UK Government sending in the Army to assist the Scottish roll-out, the Lord Ashcroft Polls survey of more than 2000 voters just before the May 6 election showed that 64 per cent believed Sturgeon had handled the pandemic well, compared to more than half who believed the Prime Minister's response had been poor.

Similarly, polls regularly showed her government being given the credit for protecting jobs when the vast majority were preserved by the UK Government's furlough and self-employment income support schemes. To borrow the words of the popular Irish philosopher Frank Carson, 'It's the way she tells 'em'.

Changed tactics

Survey after survey emphasised the First Minister's popularity, but also clearly showed that independence and a referendum were way down the list of priorities for all but committed Nationalists. As the election campaign began to heat up, the SNP changed tactics from challenging Westminster for the right to hold a referendum to selling Sturgeon's leadership qualities.

Having argued all the way through the pandemic that her daily Covid broadcasts were not political, the SNP's final election image was not of Sturgeon but a podium looking remarkably similar to the one used for her daily briefings, with the caption 'Every vote counts in deciding who will be First Minister'.

And it worked, as people who did not want a referendum any time soon voted for the SNP in their thousands because of her assured performance throughout the pandemic. But so too did thousands of English voters back Boris Johnson's Conservatives as the Red Wall continued to crumble.

It was a dreadful day for Labour everywhere except Wales where First Minister Mark Drakeford emerged the victor with a 5 per cent increase in vote share, despite the Welsh Labour administration's particularly poor pre-Covid health record.

One conclusion could therefore be that the success of the UK vaccine programme in the devolved nations has given an advantage to the incumbent through assumed gratitude. The flip-side of strong leadership is that when it comes with a powerful message on a highly divisive subject it can then galvanise the opposition, and that's what happened in the Scottish elections.

Having hammered the message about the right to hold a second independence referendum in the event of a majority, the SNP made it more urgent for those opposed to independence to support the party most likely to block it; and in most places that was the Scottish Conservatives and new leader Douglas Ross's unwavering determination to stick to the anti-referendum script.

Of all the results from an election, which was virtually impossible to predict with any accuracy because of the vagaries of the single transferrable vote system, it is arguably the Scottish Conservative performance which was the most remarkable.

The overall expectation was that half a dozen losses were to be expected and, with defeats in Ayr and Edinburgh Central on the first of the two-day count, that looked about right. In the end, the system did its job, with the loss of Ayr guaranteeing three seats on the South of Scotland list – helping to knock out two senior Nationalists, Paul Wheelhouse and Joan McAlpine in the process – and contributing to an unchanged total of 31 Tory MSPs.

It's all the more extraordinary when there was so much criticism of Scottish Conservative leader Douglas Ross and his campaign, internally as well as externally, with wistful contrasts with previous leader Ruth Davidson and a sense that the rigid 'say no to a second referendum' approach was wearing thin.

It was certainly wearing thin with political reviewers who gave him the thumbs down at every opportunity while praising new Labour leader Anas Sarwar. But the upshot was 100,000 more votes than in 2016 when Ruth Davidson's profile was at its highest, the EU referendum was still seven weeks off, and the Prime Minister was not booming Boris Johnson. So, 100,000 more Scots voted Conservative despite all that, plus the negative publicity about the Number 10 wallpaper bill, which BBC Scotland gleefully re-reported in its bulletins despite there being no specific Scottish angle to the story.

Why people vote for change

Looking back through recent electoral history there is a consistent thread, which too often banjaxes liberal-left observers who struggle to understand the appeal of a Donald Trump or Boris Johnson in anything other than dismissive terms about the intelligence or lack of it amongst their supporters.

The EU referendum defeat, the Trump victory in 2016, and the Johnson landslide in 2019 were not supposed to happen because commentators could not see that the simple message of a big change to cut through problems, which no-one had been able to solve for years, appealed to millions of people who had grown weary of nothing ever changing.

For a left-of centre party, it's understandable that Scottish Nationalists deny the same forces are responsible for the SNP's remarkable ability to maintain an iron grip on every Scottish election since 2007, insisting their nationalism is different from any other kind. But the SNP has been able to capitalise on the same sense of abandonment amongst the thousands of Labour voters their party took for granted.

If you are sitting in a crumbling terraced house in Durham, a trailer in Detroit, or in a damp flat in Drumchapel you are going to back the people who promise to blow up the system that has put you there. There is nothing new or remarkable in that, only to the extent that the power of a simple message strongly delivered by a charismatic and authentic figure is so regularly overlooked or derided by political snobs.

Devolution has created the perfect situation for an insurgent, which is also the establishment at the same time, in which the SNP can still sell a simple message that everything will be better if a dynamic new direction can be followed, but in Westminster has a convenient scapegoat for everything which goes wrong on their watch.

The Conservatives have the opposite problem in being the party of Westminster and the UK establishment which gets the blame, while trying to be the insurgents fighting against a Scottish establishment now controlled by Nationalists in the way it was once gripped by Labour.

Direct approaches

It's all very well for Conservative unionists to shake their collective heads at so many Scots believing the SNP has been responsible for the vaccine programme and the furlough scheme, the question is what can be done to counter it?

The UK Government has learnt the hard way how adept the SNP is at taking UK money and claiming the credit for its impact, or simply refusing to accept responsibility when it senses danger, as with the refusal to take over social security payments, so the approach now is to go direct to local authorities or public service providers and bypass the Scottish Government.

Whether this works in changing perceptions remains to be seen, and it is already being interpreted as 'dismantling devolution', but it will be hard for cash-strapped councils to turn down direct offers of investment, and will be difficult for the SNP to explain why they should, apart from a political principle about which most voters won't care.

An election-day survey from ex-Prime Minister Gordon Brown's thinktank, Our Scottish Future, found that 73 per cent of voters wanted better co-operation between Scotland and the rest of the UK – so where does that leave the SNP's decision to snub Sir Peter Hendy's Union Connectivity Review of infrastructure?

Perception is political reality and under both Alex Salmond and Nicola Sturgeon the SNP has expertly created the perception that Scotland is being done down and held back by the United Kingdom, to the extent that some SNP supporters believe the Scottish Government's own expenditure and revenue figures, which show a pre-pandemic deficit of some £15bn, is the work of a Westminster plot.

But if the SNP is seen to block the UK Government doing what it can to give the Scottish recovery the same boost as the vaccine programme just for the sake of political point-scoring, that perception will change.

About the contributor

John McLellan is a former editor of *The Scotsman* and *Edinburgh Evening News* and was director of communications for the Scottish Conservatives in 2012-13. He is an honorary professor of journalism at the University of Stirling, director of the Scottish Newspaper Society and is a serving Conservative City of Edinburgh councillor.

Upper-case Unionism vs lower-case unionism: Populism on the streets of Northern Ireland

The Good Friday Agreement seemed to have sorted the 'Northern Irish problem' – and then Brexit came along and produced a new border in the Irish Sea. The result has nightly rioting on the streets of Ulster. Gail Walker seeks the causes and the routes out

The death of Prince Philip on April 9, 2021 may have prompted a brief respite from the violence that had flared that spring in Northern Ireland in response to the growing unionist resentment at a Brexit deal that brought an Irish Sea border.

But only a fool would have thought that the few nights of relative quiet around his funeral were anything more than a temporary cessation of the trouble that erupted chiefly in Belfast, where the Police Service of Northern Ireland (PSNI) used water cannon for the first time in six years, but also in the much smaller eastern towns of Newtownabbey, Carrickfergus and Ballymena.

Unionism feels angry and betrayed, not only with the Northern Ireland Protocol but also the perception that the peace process is a one-way street that appeases nationalism, with a united Ireland as the inevitable destination.

Put bluntly, they see a Good Friday Agreement that was invoked during the Brexit negotiations to ensure nationalists were granted an invisible border on the island of Ireland while unionists were forced to accept an all-too-visible sea border between Northern Ireland and the rest of the UK.

Indeed, how this could be acceptable under the terms of the Agreement is a question that has left both the British and Irish governments floundering. If the assumption had been that loyalists would just suck it up, then that appears to have been a serious miscalculation.

Boris explains it?

With typical oratorical flourish prime minister Boris Johnson told BBC NI's *Spotlight* on 20 April that he wanted to end 'ludicrous barriers' to internal trade between Great Britain and Northern Ireland and that the Government was trying to 'sandpaper' the NI Protocol into shape.

Taoiseach (Irish Premier) Micheal Martin told the same programme the Brexit protocol was not a danger to NI's constitutional position within the UK.

Both leaders clearly intended to calm tensions, but their words represented no change in principle and only appeared to add to unionist frustrations.

Make no mistake, tensions in Northern Ireland are running higher than they've been for decades. The unionist summer marching season, largely suspended last year due to the pandemic, is just around the corner. This year the mood music is somewhat different. Some protest marches and gatherings have already taken place. Once again, for all the wrong reasons, Northern Ireland is making the news around the world.

Those images of a burning bus, its black plume of smoke staining the skies above Belfast, and of rival crowds lobbing petrol bombs were dramatic, even iconic – like the rioting youth silhouetted in front of the peace wall where someone had daubed 'there was never a good war or a bad peace'.

For some it's an all too easy visual shorthand for the impact of Brexit, though the reasons behind the violence are more complex than that.

But stories about Northern Ireland are often told elsewhere in clichés, or maybe it's just because the same story has been told so often now.

The story behind the trouble on the streets

That's always been the thing about Ulster. The focus is relentlessly on the violent minority, never the vast majority keeping their heads down and going about their everyday business, wishing they lived some place else or had the means to get out. The latter, however, don't make for gripping TV footage.

That's not to say the rioting isn't profoundly troubling. It is, because history shows us how a few people can set the narrative, ratcheting up tension at will. All of which points to a darker interpretation of recent events – that while no one wants the 'Troubles' back, some crave aspects of them. The conflict gave paramilitaries identity and importance. They were the centre of their small corner of the universe.

There's a dreadful truth that the violence lobs that status back at them. US President Joe Biden is worried about Lanark Way, the interface area in north Belfast where rioting has flared. That's quite a result for a group of teenagers over the Easter holidays albeit directed by sinister 'community representatives'.

There were always two parts to the Good Friday Agreement, just as it had two names – many unionists prefer to call it the Belfast Agreement. First, the legal bumph about governance and second the process of reconciliation. Over the past 23 years, reconciliation has never been on the agenda.

We are now at that part of the road where the tin can of sectarian hatred kicked by that agreement finally stopped rolling. The political forum that was meant to bring peace is in fact a nest of grievances, grandstanding, begrudgery and polite extremism. The Agreement's constructive ambiguity, its light touch with difficult concepts, has been replaced by a wrecking ball of stand-offs.

Even traditional non-sectarian issues such as schools' transfer tests, gay rights and abortion, now have absurd, inaccurate Orange and Green colourings.

It's easy to blame the politicians, but that's because many have played their part. It also has to be said, however, that peace granted a licence to the worst side of popular nature.

Reassured that nobody was actually that likely to shoot anybody any more, people felt emboldened to be as extreme as they wanted. The old 'Troubles' decency of trying to get by, offending as few people as possible, gave way to an in-your-face aggression that now dominates public discourse.

Is the new sea border the reason?

The idea that rioting youths are driven by complicated trade tariffs is laughable, but the anger over the Irish Sea border is real in wider unionism. Many feel Northern Ireland's constitutional status has been undermined and accuse the EU, Dublin and Westminster of breaching both the letter and spirit of the Good Friday Agreement.

The match that sparked the tinder was the decision by the Public Prosecution Service (PPS) not to prosecute Sinn Fein leaders – including the Deputy First Minister Sein Fein's Michelle O'Neill – who attended the funeral of senior IRA figure Bobby Storey in June 2020. Around 2,000 people lined the route in west Belfast and followed the cortege at a time when regulations only permitted up to 30 people to attend a funeral. For many the saga epitomised what's wrong with the peace process – that it 'always appeases republicans'. The fall-out has undermined confidence in the PSNI in particular and the legal system generally.

The victims are of course the serving police officers, scores of whom were injured during the recent rioting. They joined a service for peace-time and were promised everyone would support them. Instead, just like in the 'Troubles', they take the full impact of Ulster's political failures.

The start of April 2021 saw the 10th anniversary of the murder by dissident republicans of PSNI constable Ronan Kerr – a Catholic officer who came to symbolise the consensus around the new service. His face should have been prominent in the news agenda as yet another of those grim Northern Ireland milestones was marked.

Instead the reputation of the very force he served in was being traduced over the Storey judgment. Just as it had been trashed weeks earlier after a row between officers and relatives attending a commemoration of a Loyalist massacre at a bookies shop. Just as it had been trashed shortly before that for being consigned to observer-status as masked Loyalists paraded in east Belfast.

In mid-April 2021, a female Catholic police officer was forced out of her home by a suspect device in a nationalist town – the assurances given to young Catholics as they were urged by Sinn Fein to join the new police service, sound increasingly empty. No wonder people feel concerned about aspects of policing.

Time's up for the Union?
Being a unionist isn't easy in a place where people are constantly being told it's a numbers game and the egg-timer of history is running out. When people think they're being defeated, they get scared and they get angry. Real politics is about changing that perception. Unfortunately, unionist leadership was always about circling the wagons; reactive as opposed to strategic.

No one talks up the many benefits of the Union, such as an efficient Covid-19 vaccination programme that has proceeded at a much faster pace than that in the Republic. But yobs burning out a bus won't save the Union.

Political unionism has also cut adrift many thousands of small 'u' unionists alienated by the sectarianism that passes for debate at Stormont.

People in Northern Ireland are easily wound up. Sectarianism is rife. Bigotry surfaces quickly. Social media has brought us a whole new riot experience – the first Twitter Translink Bus Burning with drone footage!

The April turbulent weeks have reminded most people what really matters. They want peace and to get on with their lives. They want to live in a normal place where no one is above the law. The pull of that normality has got stronger over the year of the pandemic.

Unlike England, the Republic or even Scotland, Northern Ireland has had a decade of traumatic events, with a series of murders including that of journalist Lyra McKee, shot dead by the New IRA in Londonderry in 2019.

There is a sense that a period of stability and recovery would be most welcome. It's in this context that Sinn Fein pushing again for a referendum on Irish unity after a poll found 51 per cent of people in Northern Ireland wanted one in the next five years, was met with a less than enthusiastic response from many quarters.

Feeling the wind in her sails due to the strains pressed upon the Union of Great Britain and Northern Ireland by Brexit, Covid-19 and the rise of Scottish nationalism, Sinn Fein's Michelle O'Neill, Northern Ireland's deputy first minister, said there was an "unstoppable conversation under way" on the issue.

But anybody sensible would see that this is one conversation that needs to have the brakes applied, not for any anti-democratic reason but simply because the realities of life in Northern Ireland mean that such a poll would dangerously exacerbate tensions and undermine the hard-won peace.

Seriously, how do the very vocal supporters of such a poll really think that it's going to play out?

That it's going to be a Socratic dialogue with austere intellectuals nodding wisely, carefully balancing the arguments for and against, before reaching a decision as to what would be best – staying in the UK or joining the Republic?

Certainly, it would be the first time in the history of Ireland that such a historic move was settled in a calm, thoughtful manner.

Call me a cynic, but I'd suggest it's more likely we'd see people being wound up to breaking point, fearing their very identities are at stake. There's a real risk of low-level persistent disturbance, with all the old sores which no one has bothered attending to in two decades – victims and their families, truth and reconciliation, anniversaries, unresolved resentments everywhere one looks – breaking out once more.

The big talk and handshake moments of 'constitutional settlement' have already proved to be too unwieldy, clumsy, dependent on too many tins that can never be kicked far enough away, to address the micro details which is where the devils are in Ireland.

Besides, the idea that around one million Protestants, faced with the prospect of a united Ireland, would merely shrug and say "ah well, time up, nice while it lasted" sounds overly optimistic.

Michelle O'Neill talks about a 'conversation' but what's been happening is more of a monologue. And if it wasn't, would she even be prepared to listen? If people voted for the Union would she shelve the idea of Irish unity for another 25 years? I think not. We'd be back at this place as soon as opinion polls lurched again, or some new crisis was provoked somewhere, which would allow everyday politics to be abandoned again in favour of the politics of sash and the green flag.

In republican minds, the chat always goes like this -

Republican: "Let's have a united Ireland."

Unionist: "Yes, let's."

It's the politics of fantasy and comes from an explicit refusal to properly engage with the other side. As Scotland prepares for its second independence poll 'in a generation', to paraphrase an old IRA saying, in polls the Union has to be lucky all the time, a united Ireland only once.

The new reality

But that refusal to engage isn't just one way. Unionist reticence stems partly from feeling threatened and on the back foot. It's as if by not talking about a border poll, they can will the subject away. It's also about a perception that being a unionist isn't the right thing to be any more. Across wider unionism, people lack the confidence to put their heads publicly above the parapet, to say that's who they are and why it matters to them.

The main threat, however, comes from a failure of unionist leadership to embrace modern Northern Ireland, to see that if they only did so the future is there for the taking.

The old 'What we have we hold' is subject to the law of diminishing returns. This year Northern Ireland celebrated its centenary. It's a radically different place from how it was in 1921, 1971, 2001.

It's no longer the unionist-dominated state it was at its inception. The horror of the Troubles means there are those who shy away from the binary description of Green or Orange. Things are more complicated and nuanced for many.

Socially, the place has changed beyond all recognition – and crucially it's the failure of unionist parties to reflect that transformation that is their biggest obstacle in winning support for the Union.

Put bluntly, there remain too many caveats when it comes to voting for the main unionist parties. Yes, some voters from a unionist background hold strong views on issues including abortion and same-sex marriage, but others feel the direct opposite with equal intensity.

Voting unionist should be simply that – supporting the Union. It shouldn't mean having to sign up to a series of stances on social issues.

Upper and lower case unionists

For many, the unionist parties look 30 years out of date. What we might call 'lower case' unionists are embarrassed by their antics. So much so that a sizeable number of younger unionists have gone into a kind of internal exile – either not getting involved in politics or identifying themselves as on the centre ground.

The moderate, middle-ground Alliance Party took almost 17 per cent of the vote at the 2019 Westminster election. That's nearly one-in-five. Where are they strongest? In the unionist commuter belt. The idea that more than a handful of these voters is chomping at the bit to vote for a united Ireland is frankly ludicrous. These are unionists estranged not from the Union but from upper case Unionism.

When push comes to shove they're still, at heart, unionists. It's just a very different type of unionism from their parents – it's outgoing and liberal. They want to live in Northern Ireland the way they reckon they'd be living across the Irish Sea. Which is also why many young unionists in Ulster move over there the first chance they get.

Paradoxically, a border poll may give political unionism the shot in the arm it so desperately needs. Because then the question won't be are you voting for a particular unionist party (the DUP, UUP or TUV) but only this: do you want to stay in the Union with Great Britain?

That isn't just a question for unionists. The supposition that nationalists would vote as a monolithic bloc for a united Ireland is a nonsense.

Opinion polls have regularly shown that nearly a third of Catholics were prepared to see the Union continue. Brexit and other side issues may have whittled away at that but probably not to the extent some would hope.

Normal life continues

When it comes down to it, what really matters to people is their quality of life – decent jobs, good schools, a fit-for-purpose health service, how quickly they get their vaccine...

Which are exactly the issues many people are more focused on right now. Truth be told, they probably dread the thought of a border poll face-off and what it may unleash.

Many people, particularly those who lived through the 'Troubles', would reflect profoundly ahead of such a referendum. They might feel they're rubbing along OK with their neighbours, that it might be best to let things sit.

There's nothing inevitable about a united Ireland. Indeed, it's likely some of the 51 per cent in favour of a border poll in the *Sunday Times* survey in January 2021 included those convinced it won't be successful and who just want to get it over and done with for a generation.

Republicans deluding themselves with a simple sum – ostensibly that the DUP plus the UUP equals 100 per cent of all those in favour of the Union – may be on the verge of not an historic victory but an historic miscalculation.

Those making the case for staying in the UK need to talk to potential supporters of the Union from the nationalist tradition, but they also need to start engaging with the real lives of those in their traditional heartlands.

The internal coup in the DUP in May 2021, which saw the removal of Arlene Foster – the woman who had led it for six years and served as First Minister for that period – installed the comparatively little known hard-liner and agriculture minister Edwin Poots as leader. The cadre which managed the heave gained a tiny majority of the 36 electorate – Members of the Legislative Assembly (MLAs) and MPs – on May 15 in a situation still very much in flux. There is a clear tussle underway for control of the party between, crudely put, those (who number creationists and religious fundamentalists) seeking to 'consolidate' traditional hard core support and a more (in DUP terms anyway) 'liberal' wing, looking to build a much broader base for the union. That the trigger for the heave was Foster's less-than-enthusiastic performance in a vote to ban Gay Conversion Therapy seemed a significant indicator of how the lines subsequently came to be drawn.

Ironically, the DUP coup coincided with a moment of crisis within Sinn Fein, which took the extraordinary decision during that same week to 'sack' its entire party structure in Derry/Londonderry – including in effect firing two serving MLAs, supporters of one of whom, Martina Anderson, former MEP for the constituency, chose in an unprecedented challenge to SF leadership, not to go quietly.

Both parties face serious strains from within and it might be a kind of relief for both if the Assembly elections scheduled for May 2022 were brought forward to the autumn of 2021. A relief for everyone but the voters, that is, who have already shown themselves less than eager to engage yet again in a polling exercise which seems to achieve little or nothing by way of progress.

Nonetheless, one outcome could be a sufficient falling off in support for the DUP, thanks to a perceived entrenchment of hardline conservative views, that SF become the largest party in Northern Ireland. That would be an important moment in the centenary year of the state and one it would take a huge effort to reverse by any future poll.

There is an opportunity right now for leadership to occur, from within the main unionist blocs. It remains to be seen if there is any individual with sufficient ambition or vision to say those few important sentences which would transform the unionist future.

It's about owning that future, not harking back to old grievances or using old methods to highlight them. Northern Ireland's is a successful economy on a manageable scale which, for a start, is on the verge of beating the pandemic.

We have learned to hang together and not hang separately. The economy is small enough and well-upholstered enough by public subsidy for everybody to be able to have the best standard of living in these islands. Most people would rather have the jurisdiction work than not work.

It's time for unionism to start talking about that on every street corner. And that means also in every part of nationalist and republican west Belfast and all over the island and in London.

The union message isn't exclusive to Northern Ireland of course. But this is where the impact of that message on people is greatest and where the implications of getting it wrong – whatever 'it' may turn out to be – carry the highest tariff.

In this centenary year, Northern Ireland needs an advocate, a champion and a politics that is inclusive enough and expansive enough to sustain co-existence within porous boundaries and without.

It remains to be seen what the new normal is to look like in Belfast, because very few want the old one back.

About the contributor

Gail Walker is the *Belfast Telegraph's* editor-at-large.

How populism turned against devolution in Wales

Having persuaded the poorest UK nation, which had most to lose from leaving the EU to do just that, populists at both ends of the M4 have made scrapping the Welsh Parliament their next target. Martin Shipton reports

Constitutional change is meant to go one way, with the centre ceding power to the more local. But since the Brexit vote, and especially since Boris Johnson became Prime Minister, the movement has been in the opposite direction.

What's happening in Wales has been characterised as a Westminster power-grab aimed at rolling back devolution. This has been fuelled by the 2016 Brexit Referendum outcome, which had demonstrated how people could be lured to vote to leave despite the billions of pounds in EU aid the country had received.

The rise and fall of Abolish
With the UK out of the EU, the next aim of the populist iconoclasts is to close the Senedd down.

In 2016, at the final election before the Welsh Assembly became the Welsh Parliament, a small group that received minimal publicity and did little campaigning stood as the Abolish The Welsh Assembly Party and attracted 44,286 (4.4 per cent) of the nation's regional list votes – a significantly greater number than the Green Party, which totalled 30,211.

In 2021, at the first Welsh Parliament/Senedd election, Abolish was perceived as a true competitor – seen on the right as an antidote to increased levels of support for Welsh independence. In fact, Abolish frequently pointed out that opinion polls consistently showed greater support for shutting the Welsh Parliament down than for Wales becoming an independent state.

Abolish supporters were very active on social media, constantly sniping at their target and the pro-devolution parties. Many of the most prominent activists with Abolish had previously been Ukip and/or Brexit Party campaigners. More worrying, from the point of view of pro-devolutionists, was that they had Trojan horses in the Welsh Conservative Party.

In fact, there was polling evidence to show that a majority of Tory voters in Wales would vote to scrap the Senedd in a referendum. A YouGov poll in March 2021 showed that 59 per cent of them would vote to abolish it and only 25 per cent to keep it. It seems likely that many of them had not budged from their position of opposition to establishing the National Assembly at the 1997 devolution referendum, when the Yes campaign won with a whisker-thin majority of 6,721 votes.

Throughout the two decades and more of devolution the No camp has persistently conflated the institution and the executive, blaming the Assembly for every perceived shortcoming of the administration in a way that would be inconceivable with regard to Westminster or any other legislature.

Small wonder that a number of Tory candidates declared themselves as abolitionists, that pro-devolutionist MS Suzy Davies was deselected and that former Assembly Member Jonathan Morgan didn't even make a candidates' shortlist when he told a party panel he would vote to keep the Senedd.

What the abolitionists didn't have was the consistent support of a mainstream news outlet circulating in Wales in the way Leave campaigners had in the run-up to the 2016 referendum won by Brexiteers.

This is likely to have had an impact on what was ultimately to be a humiliating election result for them. Despite having been accorded major party status by BBC Wales, entitling them to participate in the main leaders' debate, they actually achieved a lower percentage of the regional vote – 3.73 per cent – than they had five years before. They won no seats, demonstrating that populism isn't always popular.

However, in what could be seen as a pincer movement, the UK government had applied its own pressure, using its 80-seat majority to stamp its authority on the devolved administrations, which were seen as likely hindrances to a project geared to bolstering 'global Britain' as a monolithic post-Brexit force on the world stage.

By the time the Senedd election campaign began in earnest, it was clear that serious constitutional clashes were in the offing.

Tensions in play

From the beginning of devolution in 1999 there had always been tensions between the administrations in Cardiff and Westminster.

For the first 11 years they were relatively manageable, with Labour – or Labour-led – administrations in power in both locations. What difficulties there were related largely to a lack of adjustment to devolution by individual Whitehall departments, notably the Home Office. Some Labour ministers were more sympathetic to the Welsh government than others, reflecting the jitteriness some felt about an institution that had taken over powers for which Westminster had been responsible before devolution.

When the Conservative/Liberal Democrat UK coalition came to power in 2010, there were inevitably concerns about how relations would be between the two administrations. Perhaps because of the presence of the Lib Dems, but maybe just because the new prime minister David Cameron didn't want to fight this kind of battle, things weren't as antagonistic as they could have been.

The term respect agenda was coined, referring to the desired nature of the relationship between the Tory-led government in Westminster and the Labour-led one in Cardiff.

Coalition in Cardiff

When a referendum was called in 2011 on the question of whether the then National Assembly should have primary law-making powers, the Conservative leader in Wales, Nick Bourne, campaigned with Labour First Minister Carwyn Jones for a Yes vote, which was duly delivered.

Nevertheless, the two governments didn't always agree, and on three occasions the UK Supreme Court was consulted to see whether the National Assembly had the legislative competence under the devolution settlement to make laws in certain areas.

In two of the cases – the right of the Assembly to remove the Secretary of State for Wales' right to confirm by-laws made by Welsh councils and the establishment of a body to regulate wages in the agricultural sector – the Supreme Court ruled in favour of the Assembly.

However, in the third case the Supreme Court decided that the Assembly did not have the power to introduce a law that obliged those who made compensation payments to workers who had contracted asbestos-related diseases to reimburse the NHS for the cost of caring for the victims.

Regardless of the outcomes, neither side could complain about the process, which saw disputes about whether the Assembly had legislative competence or not decided by judges in the most senior UK court.

Taxation and representation

A few years later, it was a Conservative government that delivered tax-levying and income tax-varying powers to Wales – the latter against the judgement of many Labour MPs, including the then shadow Welsh secretary Owen Smith, who saw the move as a 'Tory trap'.

But the deal – described as a fiscal framework – was negotiated in December 2016 by Mark Drakeford, then the Welsh government's finance minister, and David Gauke, then the chief secretary to the UK Treasury. By that time Theresa May had taken over as Prime Minister following Cameron's departure after his humiliating defeat in the EU referendum the previous June. That was the high point of the respectful co-existence between the two governments. Things could only get worse, and they did.

After an ill-judged decision to call a general election, Theresa May lost the Tories their majority, led her government into a cul-de-sac over Brexit and was eventually ousted by Boris Johnson in 2019 – an event that should immediately have signalled trouble for Welsh devolution.

At first, however, the new prime minister had internal party battles to fight. After taking a tough line with rebel MPs, Johnson secured the opposition's agreement to hold another general election, at which he won an 80-seat majority, giving him carte blanche to proceed as he pleased.

His main mission, of course, was to 'get Brexit done', and what became seen as a change of attitude for the worse by the governments of Wales and Scotland didn't take long to materialise.

Global not devolved Britain.

With his eye on a potential trade deal with the United States that could necessitate the lowering of standards in policy areas like the environment, food and animal welfare, Johnson sought to ensure that there could be no question of the devolved administrations being able to veto any such change.

Westminster's Internal Market Act gave the UK government the power to force the three devolved countries to allow overseas goods to be sold that would not meet EU standards. It also allowed the UK government to spend money on infrastructure projects in Wales, Scotland and Northern Ireland without reference to the devolved administrations, driving a coach and horses through the existing devolution settlements.

The UK Shared Prosperity Fund – meant as a replacement for EU regional aid money, from which Wales has benefitted enormously, especially in the devolved era – will be distributed by the UK government, not the Welsh government.

In March 2021 it was with a sense of anger and frustration that Wales' European transition minister Jeremy Miles reacted to the confirmation that the UK government would be bypassing the Welsh government again to distribute money in Wales from its levelling up fund, aimed at regenerating poorer communities. He said: "This is the UK government taking funding that would previously have been allocated to Wales to spend in line with the priorities this Senedd – elected by the people of Wales – has identified.

"This means decisions made by Whitehall departments with no history of delivering projects within Wales, no record of working with communities in Wales and no understanding of the priorities of those communities. In practice, this will mean that the UK government is taking decisions on devolved matters in Wales without being answerable to the Senedd on behalf of the people of Wales. We now face the prospect of a centralised, Whitehall-led approach instead of a regionalised, made-in-Wales approach."

He added it was important to remember that the current UK government had "an appalling record on providing Wales with even a fair share of UK spending, let alone the kind of funding needed to 'level up'."

First shots in a war of attrition?

First Minister Mark Drakeford, a former social policy professor whose reassuringly avuncular TV appearances during the pandemic had turned him into a popular figure with the majority, said Johnson's attempts to roll back devolution could end with the break-up of the UK – an assertion that got him a place on the front page of the SNP-supporting *National* paper in Scotland. We can expect a continuation of this war of attrition.

Johnson's priority seems to be to appease his supporters in England, few of whom have sympathy for Welsh or Scottish devolution, which they regard as a drain on the UK's resources.

More evidence has also emerged of an apparent attempt to do down Wales, with the UK government accused of discriminating against two Welsh local authority areas by excluding them from a list of priority places earmarked for regional aid spending intended to replace EU funds.

Caerphilly and Bridgend county boroughs contain some of the poorest communities in Europe, yet do not appear in the list of 100 priority areas likely to benefit from the Community Renewal Fund, a precursor to the UK Shared Prosperity Fund, which will be the main driver of regional aid grants in the future.

When the UK was in the EU, a region known as West Wales and the Valleys benefitted from billions of pounds of European aid because the earnings per head were less than 75 per cent of the EU average. This region included the county boroughs of both Bridgend and Caerphilly.

Caerphilly Labour MP Wayne David accused the UK government of giving resources to well-off areas like Richmond in North Yorkshire, where Rishi Sunak, the Chancellor, happens to be the MP, while deliberately excluding needy areas like Caerphilly and Bridgend..

Following or finding the data

The Welsh government said it had not been given access to the data used in deciding which areas should receive funding and which should not, adding: "What is most concerning however is the UK government taking decisions on devolved matters in Wales without being answerable to the Senedd on behalf of the people of Wales.

"We have also received no guarantee that Wales will receive its fair share of funding, with decisions being made in Whitehall departments with no history of delivering projects within Wales, no record of working with communities in Wales and no understanding of the priorities of those communities."

When Welsh government officials met Whitehall, civil servants asked them for details of how decisions had been made. It is understood relations had sunk so low that it was suggested at one point that the Welsh government should submit a Freedom of Information request to Westminster. Plaid Cymru leader Adam Price characterised the UK government's attitude to the Welsh government as 'indifference bordering on contempt'.

Constitutional crises are often spoken about but rarely come to much. This time, though, such a scenario may well have legs. Abolish's aim may seem outlandish now: Ukip had its beginnings at the fringe of politics, but changed the course of British history.

For now, Mark Drakeford's own version of the vaccine bounce may have seen him claim a renewed mandate for his 'nationalist-lite' agenda.

But with the future of the UK in doubt, the choice for the people of Wales could within a few years lie between a leap into the unknown with independence or assimilation into a greater England. Neither outcome can be taken for granted.

About the contributor

Martin Shipton is the political editor-at-large of the *Western Mail*, having previously been the paper's long-serving chief reporter. He has covered the Senedd (formerly known as the National Assembly for Wales) throughout its existence. He is the author of *Poor Man's Parliament: Ten Years of the Welsh Assembly* (Seren, 2011); *Political Chameleon: In Search of George Thomas* (Welsh Academic Press 2017); and *Mr Jones, The Man Who Knew Too Much: The Life and Death of Gareth Jones* (Welsh Academic Press, 2021.)

Life on the other side of the Red Wall

Is populism in play in rural areas as it is the cities? David Banks offers a view from England's most northern county

Beyond the political Red Wall that Boris built and northward still further, beyond the earthen rampart erected in the time of Hadrian, lies a land robbed by populism of any real democratic say in its own destiny. Beautiful rural Northumberland, containing in Berwick-upon-Tweed England's most northerly constituency, succumbed to its fate before Brexit gave rise to celebrity politics and before the great pandemic strangled whatever social life this sleepy backwater enjoyed.

The place where I now live was not Red Wall territory-turned-blue by the Brexit referendum of 2016, nor in the general elections of 2017 and 2019. It had already tumbled to the Tories in 2015 when Alan Beith, for four decades a popular Liberal Democrat MP and for a dozen years the party's deputy leader, 'defected' to the Lords. The county seat is now steadily captained by vociferous prime ministerial supporter and prominent Brexiteer Anne-Marie Trevelyan.

Local democracy has undoubtedly suffered, as much a result of the national *ennui* with politics as it has owed to anger generated by cuts in funding and services. If Westminster is viewed by the people of Northumberland as a foreign country then Morpeth, the sleepy hollow wherein meets the county council, is equally remote from me and my neighbours.

The ennui is catching, right down to the nursery level of local politics: when did my village last elect a parish council? It never happens: in place of what are deemed 'troublesome, expensive elections' the newest (preferably middle class) retired incomer to the village is immediately drafted to fill the vacancy left by the last incumbent to fall off the parish perch through boredom.

Anecdotally, life has become more difficult due as much to the social torpor brought about by Covid-19 as to the aftereffects of Brexit and its ensuing political upheaval. How else to explain the plight of an elderly couple, shielding with chronic underlying health conditions, who found nowhere to turn for help other than to *The Clarion*, the e-newspaper I produce, when their insurance company replaced their leaking bathroom with a temporary outside 'lavvy' in the garden for four weeks in dead of winter and then apparently forgot about them?

Little wonder: until the 2021 council election my local county councillor, the man charged with representing Northumberland County Council's Norham and Islandshires ward, lived for two years (quite legally, apparently) 150 miles away on the Isle of Man! Eight hours distant by rail and air or a nine-hour drive and ferry trip away. He claimed to attend to any issues raised by the electorates of the dozen parish councils in his 'diocese' by text and email but since he long ago stopped returning my 'impertinent' calls, goodness knows how the bathroom-less Jean Eisenhauer and her disabled husband Bernie – he is in his late 70s, has a pacemaker fitted and suffers epilepsy – could hope to make contact.

Across the other wall – Hadrian's
Being the northernmost English constituency makes Berwick the closest town to our cross-Tweed neighbours, the Scots, and exposes another issue brought on by the UK's political dissolution: that great national gift, the NHS, which has spanned my lifetime, has fallen prey to an unwelcome and disturbing fragmentation.

My wife and I, living on the English side of the Tweed but belonging to our closest medical practice on the Scottish side, waited in vain in each of the last two years to be summoned for our normal flu jabs only to discover on chasing up that we – along with other of our Scottish GP's patients living in England – had fallen through the cracks of the cross-border NHSes.

A few miles down the road, fellow Anglo-Scots NHS inbetweener Brian Watson read *The Clarion* report of my determined and ultimately successful campaign to have someone – *anyone* – give us our flu jabs and contacted me with a more serious concern.

"While I have received my vaccination invitation from NHS England (I am 64)," he wrote, "my wife Monica, 62, doesn't exist on either English or Scottish lists, even though she has an NHS number and has recently had breast and bowel cancer screening.

"She is in the Kafka-esque situation in which we often find ourselves in the Borders: English for some things, Scottish for others and precariously perched between the two health services. Any suggestions?"

Why ask me? For the same reason that the bathroom-less Eisenhauers had: like local democracy, the local media has gone to hell on a handcart. Few staff, few resources, centralised production and shared (i.e. cheaply-produced) copy between newspapers means councils and courts are no longer covered, expensive investigative journalism is a lost art and hard news has been replaced by dressed-up press releases.

Meanwhile, the action line – once a staple ingredient of the local rag, which would have been the automatic shoulder-to-cry-on for problems such as the Watsons' – has become an *in*-action line. Dead.

When politicians keep their distance from the voter and the press becomes too weak to wield even a downsized simple sword of truth in its readers' cause, then a broken-down retired editor's hobbyhorse provides some sort of last resort.

A smokescreen of 'anti-wokeness'

My friend and fellow writer, the educationist Dr Bernard Trafford[1], sees our political leaders laying a smokescreen of 'anti-wokeness', chauvinism and faux, flag-waving patriotism behind which lurks a cunning plan.

Implying that some sort of instruction had gone out to cabinet-ranking ministers to engineer photo-opportunities involving less-than-discreet displays of the union flag wherever possible, Trafford wrote[2]: "The Conservative government is consciously, if quietly, identifying itself with both nation and crown. The carefully judged branding suggests that the government actually embodies the UK and that it both speaks for and *is* the country: *"L'état, c'est nous"*.

"That invites the implication that, if you disagree with government, you're knocking your country. Criticism is characterised as unpatriotic, a line the Prime Minister and his cohort constantly push at the opposition in Parliament.

"This calculated populist strategy, of which government's current 'war on woke' forms part, provides a cloak for its shortcomings in, for example, tackling the pandemic. BBC presenters who question its flag-waving, the National Trust seeking to 'add context' to stately homes built on the profits of slavery, historians investigating statues of controversial (or downright wicked) historical figures. . . all are subjected to savage attacks, accused of hating their country or undermining its proud history.

"Populism, it appears, works as easily here in the formerly easy-going UK as in, say, Hungary or Poland, whose nasty right-wing regimes we are quick to deplore."

In my growing-up years of the 1950s and 1960s politicians, newspapers and broadcasters (and doctors with little more to establish their authority than stethoscopes and white coats) were regarded as unimpeachable sources. Today, in the pandemic era when trust in authority is vital, who do we believe?

The internet, largely unregulated and in the ownership of global powers far greater than mere governments, has replaced traditional media as the go-to information source; a report by the Office of Communications (Ofcom)[3] revealed that by 2019 50 per cent of 10-year-old children in the UK owned a smartphone. "Children who have never known a world without the internet [and whose] online and offline worlds are indistinguishable," commented the regulator's strategy and research group director Yih-Choung Teh.

Political leaders in their unprincipled trawl for power have recently offered more confusion than reassurance: "You're fake news!" became an empty political slogan that once bellowed by US President Donald Trump echoed around the world, further diminished a failing, financially-weakened news media in the eyes of the public. On mask-wearing to protect against coronavirus, he told America as the death toll mounted: "It's voluntary, you don't have to do it. I don't think I'm going to be doing it."

"Get Brexit done!" boomed British Prime Minister Boris Johnson, enthusiastically picking up the theme of replacing policy with a punchy slogan. 'Protect the NHS', won not only the Brexit Referendum but also formed the cornerstone of the UK's 'data-led' response to the pandemic. And still the death toll mounted.

Even Tories find populism distasteful

Populism has a lot to answer for, according to former Conservative MP and Cabinet Minister Rory Stewart. Speaking in a radio discussion[4] he said: "The line between populism and a normal democracy in Britain is a very thin one."

The former Secretary of State for International Development whose English west coast Cumbrian constituency owed more to Hadrian's Wall than any Red Wall regrouping, expounded on the cost of populism in the post-Brexit/Covid era: "The incredible success of the Brexit campaign and then of an election around 'Get Brexit Done' has made what used to be called popular styles of campaigning – three-word slogans and very, very simple messages – become absolutely mainstream.

"Basically we have created a politics which is about permanent campaign. And a lot of leadership problems are about people who are focused more on how to get elected than they are on the question of how to govern well. These politicians are not incentivised to focus on crises because they will gamble that [as such crises] are unlikely to happen on their watch they're not likely to put the time into really getting to know experts in these areas.

"I felt this with flooding [Stewart's constituency was deluged in the 2015 floods] and even with prisons [he was Prisons Minister 2018-19] . . . that my predecessors and colleagues had not really wanted [to get involved] because that wasn't who they were. They are professionals at charming and winning over voters. They're not people who are [expert] at running crisis management, so all the things that would be taken for granted if you were in this business – running exercises, training, setting up an ops room, acting quickly, gripping the situation . . . none of this is second nature to them and I think this is a real problem in democratic politics."

So how do we counter the celebrity politics that currently holds sway? What failure of the democratic system projects the likes of Trump and Johnson – publicity-loving 'bad lads' from all corners of the world of entertainment – into the number one posts in politics? While the United States' public replaced an extraordinary one-term President Trump with a more traditional figure in Joe Biden – bringing to a close a disturbing but temporary aberration – the UK continues to labour under the weight of prime ministerial scandal and talk of celebrity entryism (actor Lawrence Fox's run for London mayor, former newspaper editor and controversial TV host Piers Morgan tipped to 'do a Boris'?).

Will it provoke another Red Wall revolution to reshape British politics? Currently, an electorate pummelled by pandemic and dazzled by its wished-for celebrity democracy shows no sign of returning government to business as usual.

Notes

[1] Former headmaster of the Newcastle upon Tyne Royal Grammar School and chairman of the Headmasters' and Headmistresses' Conference; regular contributor to the Times Educational Supplement

[2] https://www.voiceofthenorth.net/patriotism-isnt-wrapping-flag-involves-looking-country-critically-admitting-shortcomings-working-make-better-place/

[3] https://www.ofcom.org.uk/__data/assets/pdf_file/0023/190616/children-media-use-attitudes-2019-report.pdf

[4] Lessons On A Crisis, BBC Radio 4, March 23, 2021

About the contributor

David Banks is the former editor of the *Daily Mirror* in the UK, the *Telegraph* in Sydney Australia, the managing editor of the *New York Post* and *New York Daily News*. He now lives in Northumberland where he writes the on-line *Clarion* and edits www.VoiceoftheNorth.net.

A tale of two challenges: how did the media report Brexit and Covid in south Asian communities?

Mainstream journalists are missing out on important stories in these dramatic times by not looking at stories through a racially diverse lens, says Professor Barnie Choudhury

If the events of last year have taught us one thing it is that black lives matter. And yet the mainstream media seems to have learned nothing. It talks a great game. The UK media is not bigoted, according to the Society of Editors.[1] And yet, it does not seem to understand that the stories it chooses to cover, the people it gets to write them, and its central characters are overwhelmingly and hideously white. Unless, of course, it chooses to write about asylum seekers, migrants sponging off our state and a certain mixed race royal. I do not need to do the maths. It is as clear as night follows day.

The media does not get racial diversity. And neither, it seems, does this government, which has the most racially diverse cabinet in our country's history. Vaccine hesitation is not, as I have been reporting, because of structural racism or a lack of trust specifically in this government.[2] Instead, it is the fault of immigrants to the UK, according to its equalities minister, Kemi Badenoch, British born to Nigerian parents who spent part of her childhood in Nigeria.[3] So, if our country's leaders, and lest we forget we voted them in, are racism-deniers, what hope is there for the fourth estate whose job it is to hold them to account?

Why diversity?

The media's inability to understand that today's Britain is a melting pot of races, religions, languages and cultures probably explains many things. Among them the apparent strategic approach to newsgathering which should put diversity at its heart. Diversity of thoughts. Diversity of opinions. Diversity of writers. Diversity of subjects. Diversity of case studies. It is probably why mainstream media is bereft of diversity discourse about the two biggest news stories in the UK; Brexit and the pandemic.

When it comes to mainstream media, I have still to see, hear or read why some south Asian businesses voted for Brexit, how they have been getting ready for life outside the European Union and what impact the rush to sign a deal has cost them. When it comes to Covid, I am left wondering why mainstream media has singularly failed to profile hoteliers, construction companies and restaurants whose leaders have a black or brown skin tone. It is as if we, black and south Asians, are not important enough to warrant a mention, even though almost one in five of us is of colour, who contribute to our economy, our culture, and our shared history.

What are we missing?

Had mainstream media and journalists deigned to walk into our south Asian communities, going further than ordering a curry takeout on a Friday night, they would have found some great stories. How about a top line where south Asian entrepreneurs reveal how European Union 'red tape' is causing a 'nightmare' for their businesses? Or perhaps how projects are being delayed because of paperwork and uncertainty over what is needed? Or how they felt the government's entire approach to negotiations was nothing more than 'a wing and a prayer' and left them in 'confusion'? Or, and this is the kicker, Boris's teams did not make a single effort to engage these kinds of small-medium sized enterprises (SME) leading to a lack of diverse thought?

"We didn't have clarity on forms until the very end, although we were told which forms existed, but we were not sure whether we need to do it, or don't to do it," said Bharat Shah[4] from Sigma, an independent pharmaceutical company. "But it's going to be a much slower process. At the moment, it is a little bit of a nightmare."

It is a similar story in retail. Bestway Wholesale, a company established in 1976, agreed the bureaucracy was confusing. It has a UK turnover of £2.5bn. Across Britain, it has 65 Bestway and Batleys depots and supplies more than 70,000 independent retailers and 40,000 catering and food service outlets. So, you would have thought broadcasters and newspapers would have been clamouring to get its views? They would have got some great lines.

"We have found some difficulty in exporting to the EU," its managing director, Dawood Pervez[5] told *Eastern Eye*. "We've been told by some people that they're required to have HS [health and safety] codes and origin on the invoice. Others say HS codes origin, cube size, weight on the invoice. So, you're getting a lot of different answers from a lot of different places."

And remember how much was made of the hotel trade. Have any of you heard of Surinder Arora?[6] No, well he is the billionaire who runs the Arora Group, which specialises in hotels near airports. "We've got a couple of hotels in Gatwick, that are under refurbishment, and I think this is where we are finding getting the materials is taking longer," he said. "So, for example, some of your bathroom tiles or other fittings may be coming in from Italy or Spain or Portugal and they're taking a lot longer and we just have to work through it."

Stark headline views

In the rush to get something on air or in print or online, journalists go to their trusted sources. And if you have not got diverse names – let me rephrase that – if you have no idea how to cultivate racially diverse names, then you really will miss out on diverse views. Views where business leaders candidly painted a picture of government confusion in the lead up to Brexit. Why? Because the government refused to include them in the talks or allowed them to advise it, leading to just the opinions of big business and 'the usual suspects'. They are urging ministers to include them in future discussions concerning the country's economic recovery.

"It [the government] was bombarding people with so much information, not timely, but all speculative," said Shah. "We were prepared for a no-deal Brexit, in that sense a £40m, £50m turnover gone. There would be redundancies, there would be closure of some of our businesses. We lobbied a lot of people in Parliament and a lot of other pharmaceutical bodies on intellectual property. Honestly, it was a brick wall, we hardly got any feedback."

And his industry also has huge concerns about something called 'parallel imports'. A quick search on Google suggests not one single mainstream news outlet or national newspaper has picked up on this important story. This is where companies can import, often cheaper, generic medicines to the UK, relabel them and resell them at a profit.

"Parallel importation is very, very critical for the UK, pharmacy industry," said Sam Patel,[7] executive director of Day Lewis, one of the largest independent pharmacy chains in the UK and Europe. UK pharmacies up and down the country rely on the ability for the supply chain to procure medicines directly from Europe under licence for repackaging into UK packs."

He told me the supply chain had been very resilient because 'manufacturers have had to take leaps of faith, building up stockpiles to ensure that there's continuity of supply from Europe'.

By why should the government or media care? "What's really critical is that the UK government doesn't backtrack or change the guidance particularly around how intellectual property and trademarks are legislated to ensure parallel importation could continue since our departure from the EU," he added.

And here comes the important bit, fellow journalists. "Because in the absence of the ability for the pharmacy industry to bring in products from Europe," said Patel, "You may see shortages in the market and that could have serious health consequences for our patients."

Bharat Shah, co-founder of Sigma, laid out the facts. "Our business of parallel export was roughly about £2m a month," he said. "That is very little compared to a lot of other operators. There are no figures but we in our industry accept it is at around £600-£700m a year. Quite a lot of people are involved in that business. If those businesses are not going to operate, businesses close with people being made redundant."

Good job some of us speak to south Asian and black people, eh?

Covid coverage

It is the same with the coverage of the pandemic. Until recently the media has not given one hint black and Asian people featured in its thinking. That is despite months of pointing out 90 per cent of doctors who died on the front line were people of colour,[8] that some ethnic minorities were twice as likely to die from the virus. No, nothing happened until the story of 'vaccine hesitancy' cropped up.[9] After that the media was all over it, like the proverbial rash. Even then it was how certain communities were putting the country at risk and the negative spin continued, unrelenting.

But journalists only needed to walk up and down the Belgrave Road in Leicester and pop into the local shops which were open to get a sense of relief. Bobby's is the oldest vegetarian restaurant in the city. It is run by one of the sons of its founder. Dharmesh Lakhani[10] had to close his restaurant during lockdown one at the end of March 2020. Business is down and some of the things he does today are loss leaders. Yet, refreshingly, he blames no-one.

"I am really grateful for the help we've received in terms of grants from the government as small businesses and also the availability of a bounce back loan which many small businesses have taken up and I have as well," he said. "But these were necessary to get us through this period, however uncertain it is. We're just trudging along, trying to keep as little in the red as we can, let's put it that way."

Like many businesses, Lakhani has also had to furlough some of his employees. But see what it means to him. "Furlough has been really, really good in terms of colleagues can come back. They have job security, so long as we get open again."

Negativity sells in news. We know that. But sometimes hearing diverse opinion, where businesses are not trashing the government, are doing their best and are grateful to have work make a refreshing change from your usual gloom and doom, in-your-face, reporting.

Not business as usual

Covid coverage by mainstream media has also lacked those stories which show some south Asian businesses have also had to think outside the box. Friends Tandoori, a restaurant in the Clarendon Park suburb of Leicester, opened at the worst possible time. Friends operated in Belgrave for 26 years but closed in 2008. Its new venture launched in September 2019.

It takes time to establish any new venture, especially after an absence of more than a decade. But six months in, Friends had to close because of lockdown. It then reopened and just when Navratri and Diwali happened – the two massive south Asian religious festivals – it closed again, serving takeaways. Worse, Valentine's Day was a wash out, despite the attempts of brothers and owners Manmohan, Manjit and Surjit Pabla.

"For Valentine's, we sort of decked it out with all the hearts and stuff and whatever and this Sunday we're going to be doing something new again, something different," said Manjit Pabla.[11] It just keeps passing trade, keeps their eyes on the window and keeps us in the public mind."

And if you do not speak to south Asian restaurateurs, you will never get a sense of how much Covid has affected businesses now only selling takeaways. "We're selling food," Pabla conceded. "But you're not then selling, for example, the aperitif. You're not selling the wines and the drinks and cocktails, or coffees and desserts to push up the spend per head."

Media's role in history

If journalists write the first draft of history, then academics try to analyse what is going on. But many academics rely on news and contemporary events to give them ideas and set out the historical importance. I bet 30 years from now, few academics will have written about the experiences of south Asian businesses pre and post-Brexit.

Reporting superficially the story of the day is not good enough. What we must do is embrace the idea that the more different voices, from different walks of life, different experiences, can only enhance what we do. Unless we grasp that fundamental axiom, we will continue to fall into the trap of seeing our world through a white lens. What we need is to show how that light refracts into beautiful colours, a metaphor for diverse reporting, missing so much in our current mainstream media.

Notes

[1] Murray, I. (2021) UK media not bigoted: SoE responds to Sussexes' claims of racism. *Society of Editors*. Available at
https://www.societyofeditors.org/soe_news/uk-media-not-bigoted-soe-responds-to-sussexes-claims-of-racism/. [Accessed 14 March 2021]

[2] Choudhury, B. (2021). Acknowledge NHS structural racism. *Eastern Eye*. Available at https://www.easterneye.biz/acknowldge-nhs-structural-racism/. [Accessed 14 March 2021]

[3] Singh, A. (2021) Historic medical racism 'not a reason' for vaccine hesitancy, equalities minister claims. *Huffington Post*. Available at https://www.huffingtonpost.co.uk/entry/kemi-badenoch-vaccine-hesitancy-medical-racism_uk_6048fd48c5b60e0725f48856. [Accessed 14 March 2021]

[4] Shah, B. (2021) Questions on Brexit. [interview] Interviewed by Barnie Choudhury 19 January 2021

[5] Pervez, D. (2021) Questions on Brexit. [interview] Interviewed by Barnie Choudhury 19 January 2021

[6] Arora, S. (2021) Questions on Brexit. [interview] Interviewed by Barnie Choudhury 20 January 2021

[7] Patel, S. (2021) Questions on Brexit. [interview] Interviewed by Barnie Choudhury 20 January 2021

[8] Choudhury, B. (2020) Dereliction of duty. *Eastern Eye*. Available at https://www.easterneye.biz/exclusive-dereliction-of-duty-government-failing-asian-doctors/. [Accessed 20 March 2021]

[9] Choudhury, B. (2021) Acknowledge NHS structural racism. *Eastern Eye*. Available at https://www.easterneye.biz/acknowldge-nhs-structural-racism/. [Accessed 20 March 2021]

[10] Lakhani, D. (2021) Questions on Brexit. [interview] Interviewed by Barnie Choudhury 26 February 2021

[11] Pabla, M. (2021) Questions on Brexit. [interview] Interviewed by Barnie Choudhury 19 February 2021

Note on the contributor

Barnie Choudhury is a communications consultant and writes for *Eastern Eye*, Britain's leading south Asian national newspaper. He was a BBC journalist for 24 years and won several industry awards for his reporting of diverse communities. He is a professor of professional practice at the University of Buckingham.

Section five
Boris and Brexit

***

The role played by the beastly Europeans and their Euromyths

John Mair

On January 31, 2021 the United Kingdom left the European Union nearly five years after the Leave side had won the EU Referendum. In the words which drove him to the 2019 historic general election victory Boris Johnson was 'Getting Brexit Done'. Britain was out of the world's biggest economic trading bloc after over four decades. The United Kingdom was now truly an offshore economic island 'free' of EU restrictions.

The Brexiteers – especially those in the Conservative Party – had won their long march to what they considered to be freedom from Euro-bureaucracy. In essence, the Brexit debate had become an internal Tory party debate; Labour had, by and large, accepted the Remain status quo as a party. What had begun as a Eurosceptic, indeed revanchist, sect within the governing party had grown to a hard majority, led by the soi-disant European Research Group of MPs.

Prime Minister Boris Johnson was the willing leader of the pack, even if late at this party. His main messages in the 2016 Referendum, when he led the Leave campaign, and in the 2019 General Election, when he was then Prime Minister, was that Britain had to be out of Europe. Now it was.

The Brexit story is in (too) many ways a Boris Johnson story. This section attempts to link the two.

James Mates is one of the more distinguished British broadcasters, always at Independent Television News, for whom he has worked for nearly 40 years. He has been its Europe Editor since 2012.

The role played by the beastly Europeans and their Euromyths

In the lead chapter of this section – *Are the 'beastly Europeans' really 'trying to do us in?'* – he tackles the vexed question of why Europe has lost salience. The pandemic has wiped EU issues from the front pages. Some of us don't care, others still don't know much about the issues.

Mates argues the media need to focus on Brexit and its consequences, even if a populist UK government would rather they didn't. He is firm and to the point. "How the press and television should deal with this is a problem on two levels. First the specific: how to tell our audiences that Brexit is far from over (in fact it had barely begun) and if you haven't been playing attention already the time to start paying attention is now.

"And then second: how to report in a world where Governments and their supporters actively want you *not* to report. How to ensure that, as the *Washington Post* might put it, democracy doesn't die in darkness."

Will Hutton is one of the more prominent 'public intellectuals' in the UK. He is of the Labour persuasion. His seminal book, *The State We're In,* provided intellectual ballast for (Tony) Blairism. Hutton has advised other Labour Party leaders since. His position on Europe is crystal clear; he is an unreconstructed Remainer. He views Prime Minster Johnson as being 'economical with the actualité', but still a hero to the right-wing press.

Hutton sees them as Brexit biased by nature, leading up to the 2016 Referendum and since then well into 2021. He does not mince his words in *How Britain was let down by its press over Brexit – and how that can change.* "Truths that qualify and obstruct the chosen narrative become embarrassing, maybe even showing it up as so far from the truth that the authority and credibility of the disseminator is undermined."

Some of the best eyes on Brexit and its effects in the UK often come from the foreign correspondents based in the country. Deborah Bonetti is Director of the Foreign Press Association in London. Yet she has a foot in both camps. Born in Italy, she has spent half her life in the UK.

Bonetti has observed the difficult UK/EU marriage finally become a divorce after acrimonious discussion. It was almost inevitable.

In her chapter *Did the British ever understand the European project?* she explores the turbulence. She says: "...while Britain can still proudly feel European, it is a Europe of the mind it really feels part of, rather than a Europe of realities. The values of democracy, personal freedom, human dignity, active civil society, market economy and the rule of law are all part of its DNA. Just not a willing abdication of its sovereignty."

Dr Steven McCabe of Birmingham City University's Centre for Brexit Studies is another firm Boris sceptic. He dates the PM's 'truth problems' back as far as schooldays at Eton where he adopted the moniker 'Boris' rather than his real first name 'Al'. In his chapter, *Al promised you a miracle – life under 'greased piglet'*

Johnson, McCabe sees Johnson as a classic clown and "Like the greatest entertainers, especially magicians, it is intended to distract from the trick whilst keeping the crowd happy."

The same theme of prime minister as comedian is explored in the chapter *Deceptively silly – the role of the cucumber in Boris Johnson's ideology* by journalist turned academic Imke Henkel, of the University of Lincoln.

For Henkel, the PM's problem with the truth and 'Euromyths' started when he was the *Daily Telegraph* correspondent in Brussels in the 1990s and embellished the 'bent bananas' and the 'downsizing of condoms' stories inter much alia. They became fact or Euromyths.

As she puts it: "The stories about the alleged ban of bent bananas or downsizing of condoms are ideological speech. In that sense they resemble propaganda. Boris Johnson uses the same narrative techniques – the same storytelling – in his newspaper columns and political speeches: the £350m-bus and the 'Taking Back Control' slogan are expressions of a Eurosceptic British supremacy myth. As myth they hide the ideology they articulate."

Finally, in this section, Associate Professor Alistair Jones in *Getting Brexit done and the future of the UK-EU relationship* looks forward. Boris Johnson's populist slogan 'Get Brexit Done' may have won him the 2019 general election but the unrealistically easy call to arms which played well through the media disguised a reality of future problems for the UK, EU and Ireland which the PM seems unable to acknowledge.

Those we left in the EU are wary to say the least. "There is little trust of Johnson and his government. Having seen Johnson distort and mislead over the results of the Withdrawal Agreement, linked to his absolute lack of grasp over detail, leaves the EU in something of an uncomfortable position… from the EU perspective Brexit was not wanted or desired, but the EU appears a little more up to the mark in preparing for it. The problem is the British approach to everything, that British exceptionalism."

Brexit is or could become a mess for the UK. It is a mess of our (and Boris Johnson's) making.

Are the 'beastly Europeans' really 'trying to do us in'?

The pandemic has wiped EU issues from the front pages. Some of us don't care, others still don't know much about the issues. ITV News Europe Editor James Mates argues the media need to focus on Brexit and its consequences, even if a 'populist' UK government would rather they didn't

Well, we 'Got Brexit Done!'. Didn't we? Can we all forget about Europe now? Not completely, obviously, but surely the papers and TV can stop banging on about it ALL the time. Four years of Brexit? I never want to hear that word again.

I may be being a tiny bit unfair, but that, I suspect, is the attitude of 95+ per cent of the British public right now and, more worryingly, roughly the same proportion of our news editors and foreign desks. For sure, the small matter of a global pandemic and a more than a hundred thousand of our fellow citizens dead has wiped Brexit from the front pages. But we have been living through the greatest dislocation in our economic life since World War II, and it has generated barely a mention on the front pages for months. Occasionally the FT or the business pages will point out that our exports to the EU have fallen somewhat, by more than 60 per cent in fact, and a Government Minister will mumble something about 'teething troubles, only to be expected you know', and we doze off again and get back to debating Harry and Meghan.

'Boiling the frog'

And the worst of it is that this is exactly how the Government wants things to be. Call it 'boiling the frog', or skilful news management, or just dumb luck that the consequences of Brexit should be overshadowed by an even greater crisis. But whatever you call it, it is a gift to those who are happier talking about something else – anything else – rather than the impacts of the decision they took to effect the most radical split possible from our neighbours and former partners.

How the press and television should deal with this is a problem on two levels. First the specific: how to tell our audiences Brexit is far from over (in fact it had barely begun) and if you haven't been playing attention already the time to start paying attention is NOW. And then second: how to report in a world where governments and their supporters actively want you *not* to report. How to ensure, as the *Washington Post* might put it, democracy doesn't die in darkness.

The biggest problem with reporting post-Brexit Europe is the exact same problem as reporting pre-Brexit Europe: the quite astonishing lack of knowledge in UK politics and media about how the EU works, what motivates its leaders and why its institutions react the way they do. I have written before about the obsession of our political class with US politics, society and jurisprudence, matched in equal and opposite degrees by indifference to the European equivalents (Mates, 2017). It was a degree of indifference that made Brexit possible, and if it continues unchanged it will make more likely a raw and bloody sore running down the channel for many years to come. Possibly down the Irish Sea as well.

A 'culture war without end'?

Playing 'the beastly Europeans are trying to do us in' card has been a staple of governments of both colours since the moment we joined the Common Market. But as members this was largely a way to blame Brussels for anything unpopular while claiming credit for the opposite. Now it is in danger of becoming a governing philosophy, a deliberate stoking of a 'culture war without end' that will make criticism of the Government somehow 'unpatriotic' in the face of a 'hostile' EU allegedly determined to ensue Brexit is a 'failure'. I would point in evidence to the decision to replace the more emollient Michael Gove with the hard-line David Frost in charge of future dealings with the EU; the initial refusal (uniquely in any Western country) to deny full diplomatic status to the EU ambassador in London; the unilateral extension of the 'grace period' for the Northern Ireland protocol on the grounds of the EU's alleged intransigence and unreasonableness. This is not to say Brussels hasn't been contributing to the atmosphere with its own unilateral moves over Northern Ireland and some ill-judged lashing out in the 'vaccine wars', but there is little doubt it suits the UK Government to actively frame all reporting of Brexit and its aftermath in these terms.

Which creates quite a problem for those who have been on the frontline of reporting Brexit. First, the difficulty of cutting through the pandemic and trying to differentiate the effects of Brexit from those of Covid. But secondly trying to avoid the Government's framing of Brexit impacts as the products of an unreasonable, pettifogging Europe that is out to get us. Hopefully the former will fade as the vaccines kick in, although there will be months if not years in which negative Brexit impacts will be put down to Covid. The latter is going to be much longer battle in which understanding how Europe works and why it works that way are going to be crucial.

The most urgent issue is likely to be Northern Ireland, not least because of the impact the Protocol and its associated checks are already having in reigniting Loyalist anger, even violence. The reporting of this is going to be a challenge. Maybe the most important thing to understand is that the Northern Ireland Protocol is not a fiendish plot by the EU to punish and then split the UK, but something that is working exactly as it was written and designed to work. There are no unintended or unforeseen consequences at play here. Everything was predicted and warned about but signed up to none the less because it did two things: 'Got Brexit Done' and permitted the scrapping of Theresa May's hated Northern Ireland 'Backstop'. A Venn diagram of those demanding it be scrapped or renegotiated would be an almost perfect subset of those who supported and even voted for it in the first place.

A place in the sun
The same is true of countless other Brexit impacts. Let's take the example of Britons being forced home from lives in the EU, or others having to abandon their dreams of a retirement in the sun. These are not accidents; this is happening by design. It is precisely what British negotiators and politicians knew would happen but insisted upon because of the desire to restrict the access of EU citizens to the UK. The inability of British musicians or other creatives to work temporarily in the EU, the loss of opportunities to work as chalet staff through a French ski-season, the impossibility now of UK families employing *au pairs* from Europe to help with child care. None of these are unforeseen consequences, every one of them was pointed out and considered and pushed ahead with anyway.

Which is fine. The UK voted for Brexit and it has been the job of the Government and its negotiators to make (often tough) decision on how Brexit should look. What is not fine is the attempt being made to paint these consequences as 'post-Brexit European curmudgeon'.

When I reported, earlier this year, on the forced departure of British immigrants (let's not sugar-coat with ex-pats) from Spain, an official from the Foreign Office spent most of the next day trying to persuade first me, then my bosses – going steadily up the ladder – that these were not real problems at all, that UK citizens had all been protected by the Withdrawal Agreement and everything would be sorted out. A flood of subsequent reporting elsewhere in the British media established beyond question that these problems were real and British citizens living in the EU were facing real issues in being allowed to remain there. Making the attempted 'spin' worse was that the attempts to downplay this issue were made not by an appointed Special Advisor (the ones who are meant to fight political battles) but a civil servant (the ones who are not).

The denial of temporary work-permits to musicians was initially blamed by the UK Government on the EU playing hard-ball. It turned out UK negotiators had been offered exemptions for temporary creative workers but had turned them down. And so on. The reporting of these issues requires proper knowledge in order to challenge a narrative being pushed in London. Equally, knowledge of the EU's treaties and structures (often pretty inflexible, as they have to be when trying to bind in 27 heterogeneous countries) is needed to counter the idea that 'well, they could just do 'X' if they wanted to and if they weren't being so awkward'. Too often we hear the enforcement of provisions of the Withdrawal Agreement or the Trade and Co-operation Agreement described as 'Brussels red-tape', or 'revenge for Brexit' or 'teething problems' without proper challenge. Sometimes without challenge at all.

Dealing with a President who lied

The difficulties faced when applying traditional reporting methods to the coverage of 'populist' governments are not new, and go way beyond Brexit. For four years the press in the US struggled, and frankly failed, to establish new terms of engagement with the Trump administration. How do you deal with a President who brazenly lies? Can you say 'the President lied'? How do you deal with officials who abandon regular press briefings? Who will speak only to chosen and sympathetic outlets? Who regard the relations with the media as performative displays in a culture war without end? No one was prepared for it. Despite the evidence of the campaign, no one believed this would be how Trump governed.

Only by the end of 2020 did the reporting catch up with what had become a political reality, and then only when the lies about election fraud became so egregious, so dangerous and so clearly aimed at clinging to power in the face of a decisive defeat at the polls. It was only at this point the lies were called what they were, that the portrayal of politics as a battle between competing narratives of equal validity was finally abandoned, that there is no balance to be weighed when it comes to urging your supporters to storm the legislature. No 'he said, she said'. But it took an attempt to overturn a democratic election to get there.

Trump is, however, only the most extreme example. The definition isn't easy, but in describing a government as 'populist' one is talking about an administration that abandons norms and conventions, harnesses the power of the state to the propagation of their own political narrative and seeks to remove constitutional constraints on their own actions. That list is not exhaustive. These are traits that have been easy enough to find in the current UK Government, whether it be the unconstitutional attempt to prorogue Parliament, the apparent removal of all sanction for breaches of the ministerial code, the determination to restrict judicial review of their decisions, the politicisation of the Government information machine. This list, too, is not exhaustive. It all indicates British journalism is facing challenges of the same type (even if not to the same degree) as our colleagues in the US.

The spin that backfired

There are some encouraging signs. Let's examine an example from early 2021, in the publication by the Government of an 'independent' report into the state of race relations in the United Kingdom. Leave aside the fact No 10 hand-picked those writing the report (to an extent all governments do that), it was the manner of release that went way beyond traditional news management. The report summary was released at 5pm one evening with the full report to follow the next morning. The pre-release summary contained a most unusual 'do not approach' embargo clause, forbidding journalists from gathering other reaction ahead of embargo time. This type of embargo is rarely used, and only for matters like New Year's Honours nominees etc. In the event the embargo was widely ignored.

So journalists were presented – close to deadline time – with the Government's *own* summary of a long report, with no ability to read, let alone challenge the full report, and an injunction to seek no further views on it before writing the stories that were to lead many papers and bulletins the next day. This is not normal.

The attempt garnered one day of good headlines, before degenerating into a mass of recrimination and complaint that the conclusions were perverse, the methodology flawed and even collaborators named who had never actually participated. So in that sense the spin backfired, and – as soon as they were able – the press did their job. But this single example is not the first and will certainly not be the last.

The politicisation of the No 10 information operation is real and presents journalists with plenty of challenges. Boris Johnson brought in his own press team, largely drawn from the Vote Leave ranks that had fought the EU Referendum. Remember it wasn't so long ago a British Prime Minister (John Major) chose a civil servant to run his communications (Christopher Meyer), a man who then filled the role with such rectitude that Tony Blair subsequently saw fit to appoint him ambassador to Washington. Different times.

And while this has happened, a number of scandals that in recent memory would have rocked a government to its core have been ridden out with barely a tremor. The handing of hundreds of millions in PPE contracts to Tory donors, the targeting of 'levelling-up' money at Tory held marginals, the undeclared friendship with Jennifer Arcuri and the tax-payers' money that came her way, the gift of foreign holidays and domestic refurbishments to Boris Johnson personally, without there being any record of who paid or how much. Correlation is not causation, and maybe it is just the weight of Covid news that allowed so much else to slip from public view, but there should be a real concern that the politicisation of information and standards is creating a new normal of 'we won, we're in charge, get used to it'.

Reporting can take time to find its feet when confronted with people who don't play to long accepted rules. Trump never did become 'presidential', it was journalism that had to adapt to him. Maybe populist governments never will fall into line with long-established conventions or traditional standards of behaviour. Confronting this can feel like a loss of neutrality, a taking of sides, but there are things journalism should never be neutral about. One of those things is accepted facts. Journalists should not be neutral about reality.

Reference
Mates, James, (2017) 'In love with America, indifferent to Europe: UK journalism's westward squint', in Mair, J., Clark, T., Fowler, N., Snoddy, R. and Tait, R. (eds), *Brexit, Trump and the Media*: Bury St Edmunds: Abramis pp 225-229.

About the contributor
James Mates is Europe Editor of ITV News who has been covering events and crises (mostly crises) in the EU and the Eurozone since the Greek crisis broke out in 2011. For more than three decades he has been covering global hotspots, including postings to Tokyo and Moscow. For five years at the end of the last century he was Washington Correspondent, watching the Clinton administration implode under the Lewinsky scandal, the US Supreme Court make GW Bush president, and then the world change on 9/11.

How Britain was let down by its press over Brexit – and how that can change

Britain's experience with the Brexit debate has shone a light on the inadequacy and commitment to truth of both its press and politicians. A new approach is needed – and is imminent – argues Will Hutton

A great country has ruptured a deep association of 44 years extending from trade to security with almost all the countries of the continent of which it is part. The economic and political damage of this will grow in intensity, while any gains will be paltry. A majority of its working population, keenly aware of the depth, breadth and value of the ties that bind Britain to Europe and wary of the cost of breaking them, voted for the UK to stay in the EU on June 23, 2016. But the vast majority of the over 65s, largely insulated from such risks and with the time to read our newspapers, voted to Leave, their votes pipping those who were younger.

It was not only a generational divide, but a chasm of understanding between those who read the right-wing press and those building businesses and careers in the real world. Now a slow burn calamity is unfolding before our eyes, one which has many causes but for which the necessary precondition is the extraordinary one-sidedness and distortions of the British media.

The British press – telling the truth?
It is a cardinal democratic principle that news reporting should abstain from overt partisanship and aim for impartiality. A media that becomes an open advocate for a political party or major issue is no longer 'media' in the sense of being a reliable conduit for information of whatever kind; necessarily facts and events that don't fit the position it has adopted have to be downgraded or at worst just plain ignored. Truths that qualify and obstruct the chosen narrative become embarrassing, maybe even showing it up as so far from the truth that the authority and credibility of the disseminator is undermined. In which case it has to double down and ignore reality altogether, while vastly exaggerating what scraps of information there are that might confirm its position.

The reading, listening and watching public is disarmed: it has literally no idea what is going on. Worse, the political process is polluted. The favoured political party or cause starts to rely on uncritical support for whatever it says, corrupting its own fealty to making a case honestly. It can get away with any old lies or misconduct knowing it will only be challenged by those on the margins – 'voices off' that can be ignored and derided. A shared understanding of what is happening is the fundamental precondition for a functioning democracy and the good governance that ensues; a press that drops impartiality attacks that foundation. Brexit is a prime exemplar.

British 'impartiality' vs US 'freedom'

Partisanship now defines the contemporary media in Britain and the USA. Ever since the Fairness Doctrine, requiring broadcast output to be balanced, was abolished by President Reagan in the US in the 1980s on the specious grounds that there was no truth only many truths, and audiences should be free to choose the truth that most conforms to their prejudices, much American media has increasingly dropped any pretence at trying to convey reality accurately.

Donald Trump built his particular politics and presidency on insisting anything that did not conform with his worldview was 'fake news', while everything he did was to 'Make America Great Again' whose sincerity could not be doubted. In the end he came to believe his own narrative – spectacularly that he was the victim of gigantic voter fraud in the 2020 Presidential election – leading, inevitably, to his disaffected supporters storming Congress on January 6, 2021. Even now many Republican voters, and sadly elected Republican politicians, believe the 'fraud' trope, and use it as an excuse to indulge naked voter suppression. The integrity of American democracy is at stake.

Britain's Brexit insurrection?

Britain has aped the same decline, with its partisan press a principal driver. The drama of Brexit is less vivid than the scenes on the Capitol but in many ways just as insidious. Economy with the truth, uncritically repeating misinformation and sometimes lies or simply failing to report at all characterises much of our media coverage of Brexit, the approach extending to a failure to probe the dissimulations straying into plain falsehoods of the Boris Johnson Government. Occasionally some stories, like the opulent refurbishing of the Number 10 Downing Street flat financed in undisclosed ways, are so juicy it is obvious that failure to report them will threaten a paper's credibility, but even while the *Sun* and *Mail* on April 29, 2021, were prepared to splash on the story that the Prime Minister was to be investigated by the Electoral Commission for potential wrong-doing over the financing of his flat renovations, neither the *Telegraph* nor *Express* could bring themselves to break the rule that a Tory leader is never given a hard time. The story was downplayed. For the unwritten rule is that reporting is done within a framework that indulges the Conservative Party, in particular its right-wing, and abuses the Labour Party.

David Cameron and George Osborne were shocked, campaigning to Remain in Europe in 2016, how it felt to be at the receiving end of Britain's right-wing press. The *Daily Mail* alone ran anti-EU immigrant stories on almost every front page in the three-week run-up to the Referendum. Its aim, along with the *Sun, Express* and *Telegraph,* was not to frame the argument in the public square over the EU with the best information for and against that could be mustered. It was wholly to reshape the public square so only one argument would seem valid, and then to enter it as one the most vociferous exponents of the Leave case. This is not a free press; this is press as propaganda.

Getting Brexit Done - but at what cost?
The approach has continued in the first months of 2021 after the signing of the Trade and Co-operation Agreement – the much vaunted zero tariff, zero quota trade 'deal'. Beyond the *FT, Observer, Guardian, The i* and Channel 4 News there has been an absence of forensic examination about the widening ruptures caused by interpreting sovereignty – the dream of the Brexiteers – so it means complete refusal to compromise over regulatory standards or accept the adjudication of third parties in trade disputes.

The fantasy is that all matters in trade in goods and services is the price, thus justifying the zero tariff/zero quota nature of the deal, and ignoring the vital importance of the intrinsic attributes and capacities of the goods and services themselves – their impact on the environment, their safety, their durability, their inter-operability, their reliability, what recourse is offered if they fail to meet buyers' expectations and so on.

These 'non-tariff' barriers to trade are commonly understood to be four times more important than any tariff in determining trade flows, and crucial in industries like life sciences, the creative industries, financial services, complex manufacturing, business services, logistics. These are industries in which Britain has a comparative advantage – indeed the financial services and creative industries employ more than a million people each ranking as among the country's biggest employers – and which membership of the Single Market, which seeks to align such regulations around the best standards to such an extent they have become world standards in many industries, hugely benefited.

Britain's media disregarded discussion of leaving the single market and the vital importance of eliminating or reducing non-tariff barriers to trade as 'Project Fear' in the Referendum campaign and wilfully ignores it now. Thus in the first four months of Brexit, three in five firms, according to LSE's Centre for Economic Performance, report that Brexit is causing them problems in trading with Europe through having to demonstrate they still conform with the EU's regulatory standards, at best experiencing severe delays through customs and regulatory checks and at worst being unable to export at all. A fifth of small firms have halted exports to the EU completely, among them exporters of perishable food products like shellfish or cheese, so that overall export levels are significantly down on the comparable period in 2020. Many are being compelled to establish operations within the EU. The New Financial think tank reports 440 financial firms have set up hubs in the EU so they can trade within the single market, transferring £900bn UK bank assets and £100bn of funds under asset management to cities like Dublin and Amsterdam. Amsterdam has now supplanted London as Europe's top share trading centre. Their surveys indicate much more is to come. Foreign Direct Investment into the UK reached a peak in 2016 but has been trending lower ever since with the Government in increasingly desperate moves to shore up interest.

All of this would be complete news to any consumer of Britain's mainstream media. It does not conform with the narrative that any problems are teething problems and Brexit has created all kinds of new trading and investment opportunities. Yet even the much-vaunted deals struck with Japan and others, which in any case are largely roll-overs mirroring the trade deals the EU has already struck, offer none or only trivial advantages. Instead of proper criticism, even mockery of the official line, Britain's fawning media repeats it faithfully.

The Irish question – bordering on confusion?

The creation of the regulatory border down the Irish Sea between Northern Ireland and the British mainland is a mystery to most of the public. Most accept the consensus right-wing media line that if the EU was less intransigent and accepted British standards and regulations, goods and services could flow from Britain to Northern Ireland to Ireland and back again without any problem. It is those dastardly foreigners again up to no good. But in which case, rather than Britain leaving the EU, the EU would have joined Britain so British standards and regulations would become the norm in the Irish Republic and by inference the rest of the EU. Boris Johnson, after all, swore there would be no border in the Irish Sea to check that British goods and services complied with EU standards – so it must be the EU's fault. Even he wouldn't brazenly lie, would he?

Only Johnson knows whether he knowingly lied, did not understand the single market or simply hoped something would come up to save him when he brazenly declared there would be no border in the Irish Sea – but what is dismaying is how so few senior politicians, let alone the wider public, begin to understand the issue. EU lead negotiator Michel Barnier writes in his memoir *The Grand Illusion* that leading Brexiters, notably Johnson and Dominic Raab, simply did not understand the complexities of managing the Irish border – in particular why the May Government had negotiated the infamous backstop to prevent a border in the Irish Sea. Why would they? They knew the wider public knew nothing and the press was slavishly behind them, explaining nothing. Even the BBC is reluctant to depart from the wider media discourse. Brexiters could posture as they liked, insisting Britain was taking back control and lie about the existence of a new border in the Irish Sea.

Yet already the 'protocol' in the treaty that provides for regulatory checks before goods and services reach Northern Ireland has become toxic in Northern Ireland's unionist politics and communities, a proximate cause of the downfall of Arlene Foster, leader of the DUP.

The frail Good Friday Agreement, built on Ireland and Britain's shared membership of the EU, looks in peril. Theresa May, struggling to keep no border but have only a backstop if there were proven problems, was more honest about the issue – but Johnson accused the backstop of being a surrender of sovereignty and resigned from the cabinet to right-wing media applause. Now we watch the potential re-ignition of violence in Northern Ireland, and a potentially successful vote in Northern Ireland in favour of Irish reunification. A degenerate biased press is triggering not just the banalities of lost trade and slow economic growth, but the disintegration of the British state.

Does it matter?

The conventional wisdom is that this mismatch between reality and rhetoric does not matter. Johnson's charm and ebullience seems to make him impervious to charges that he lies and dissimulates, and Brexit is a slow-motion disaster. Red Wall voters judge him by his actions – he got Brexit done, delivered a successful vaccine roll-out and in parts of the north – notably Teesside under its Heseltinian mayor Ben Houchen – is delivering an industrial renaissance. Johnson retains an opinion poll lead and the Tory performance in the English council elections was remarkable for a government in mid-term. The Tories not only won the Hartlepool byelection, they did so with 51.9 per cent of the vote. Houchen won the Tees Valley mayorality with 73 per cent of the votes cast. Must Remainers give up making the case for Europe, concede that swathes of voters believe Brexit will change their lives for the better whatever the evidence and that the rupture with the EU is unchallengeable?

Yet reality will out. A sixth of Britain's annual output represented by exports to the EU, a third of its investment and the growth prospects of its most dynamic industries depend on the closest possible economic links with the EU. Brexit will be long term depressive and reversing it will become a live issue in British politics. Nor is Tory hegemony quite as solid as it seems at first glance. In the May 2021 local elections, despite a lacklustre campaign and an absence of a compelling vision, Labour has closed the poll gap with the Tories. It holds 11 out of 13 English mayoralties and won decisively in Wales. As importantly the Greens advanced across England, Wales and Scotland and the Lib Dems outperformed their poll rating. Despite the success of the vaccine roll-out and optimism about an economic recovery, progressive pro-EU parties in aggregate outpolled the Tories.

What is required is the creation of a great coalition around a common programme that will include voting and media reform, and the rejoining of the single market and customs union as a prelude to EU full membership. In a first-past-the-post voting system, progressive votes have to cohere around one candidate. Everybody knows the only economic future is to build a series of economic superclusters in our cities and towns which can grow by seamlessly trading with Europe. The rest is chatter. A biased and toxic media can only damn the waters of truth for so long. They will burst over us, and soon.

Note on the contributor
Will Hutton is a columnist on *The Observer*, which he edited between 1996 and 2000. He is author of a number of best-selling economics and politics books including the seminal *The State We're In* and most recently, with Andrew Adonis, *Saving Britain*. He has just demitted the office of Principal of Hertford College Oxford University. He becomes president of the Academy of Social Sciences in June 2021.

Did the British ever understand the European project?

Deborah Bonetti was born in Italy but has spent half her life in the UK. She runs the Foreign Press Association in London and has observed the difficult UK-European marriage finally become a divorce

There is an argument, excellently discussed in Robert Tombs' *This Sovereign Isle*, which goes: "the British have always been and felt part of Europe. To say otherwise is simply wrong."

I understand that, historically, that may prove correct. But – define the British and define Europe now. Both concepts have become arguably more fluid, elusive, subject to change and interpretation than ever before. And as Professor Tombs says in the first line of his book: "Geography comes before history" – and that alone places Britain on the very edge of continental Europe.

Being an island, made up of different nations and poised on the edge of the great European continental plate means that Britain is near but crucially not part of the rest of continental Europe.

This is not a contentious point of view, it's simply a fact. And to Europeans in general, Britain feels very different in a multitude of ways: culturally, historically, socially, politically and of course religiously too.

Did this bring about Brexit? We shall see.

On the continent, it may be true that we squabble with our neighbours (see the two world wars) but, especially since the foundation of the European Union and its predecessor bodies, born to keep that very peace which eluded us for too long, we've somehow learnt to live with each other.

Most of the time, we even get along. We also know how our neighbours think and act, we recognise each others' behaviours and are comforted by the fact that we consider each other predictable. We 'trust' our neighbours with keeping our democracy and are unworried, by and large, by questions of sovereignty. The Brits on the other hand are different and, to most of us, an unknown quantity.

Continental love unrequited

While there is continuous and repeated cultural exchange with most of the other countries in Europe, the curiosity and fascination that there is towards Britain is rarely reciprocated. For example, continentals tend to know a lot about who's who in most other European countries. We read each others' authors, we know each others' songs and sayings, we even eat and celebrate in similar ways. Our languages may be different but our meanings are often the same. Does this hold true of how we relate to Britain? Hardly.

British soft power is legendary. Everyone in the world has to be able to speak English to get anywhere. Everyone knows who the Queen is, or who Shakespeare, Charles Darwin, Isaac Newton or even JK Rowling are. How many people in Britain are aware of, say, Pirandello, Stendhal, Saramago or Schiller? The insularity of the culture here is striking to someone crossing the Channel.

That does not mean that we continentals don't like you; opposites attract. Rather that while we can't get enough of the stories that come out of your weird and wonderful country, full of castles and legends, flying nannies and pipe-smoking detectives, you simply don't requite our love.

There is an endless curiosity on the continent, and indeed the world, about Britain. That is why the highest concentration of foreign journalists on the planet is to be found in London, at the FPA (the world's oldest and largest association of foreign correspondents); but that passion and curiosity is rarely returned.

You seem to be looking for friends away from Europe, both west (there is an obsession with America) and east, with the new tilt towards Asia and the Indo-pacific region announced by the UK Government recently. Your nearest should be your dearest, but that's not how things are between us, unless we take 'dear' as meaning expensive in the brave new world post-Brexit.

My split life

I was born in Milan, Italy, an industrial and industrious city, famed for its fashion in the rest of the world and, in the rest of Italy, for its workaholism and boasts of being the 'most European' city in the country. That is meant as a compliment.

For most Italians, the EU was and still is a great project, despite the recent vaccine debacle, which has exposed worrying fissures. The EU would (in our collective minds) drag Italy out of its small-minded, inward-looking preoccupations and finally set it free to stand on the world stage with like-minded allies. It would get rid of the Bourbonic bureaucracy that can feel at times insurmountable and help obliterate the last traces of mafia and corruption secretly surviving in the depths of the country.

That's what we signed up to: a union of like-minded nations that would look out for each other, make us feel safe and secure and make us 'live our best life'.

But that's not what Britain signed up to at all: after much deliberation on whether to join or not, what it only and ever really wanted with the EU was a transactional relationship, a free market. No love or fuzzy feelings towards us, no 'making each other better' rhetoric, nor any real belief that Europeans could be trusted to make rules, let alone obey them. In a nutshell: the British only wanted one thing (free trade), not a lasting relationship with the continent.

And to be fair, we are sometimes just too much for you. Having lived in Britain over half of my life, I still get to hear how 'fiery' we Italians are; how we have a 'lust for life' and how much we savour living our decadent and uninhibited (though maybe not as much as the French) *dolce vita*.

I have been told countless times how beautiful a country Italy is, what great food and wine and beaches and people it has… I bet you say that to all Europeans. We're a great place to go on holiday or buy a second home, but not too much more than that. And that is because you think we are like a different species.

Rob Temple, in his funny book *Very British Problems,* sums up how the 'awkward Brits' feel compared to us continentals: "Spare a thought for those (of us) living abroad, surrounded by relaxed, uninhibited extroverts, going about their daily lives with barely a single unnecessary apology passing their lips."

What we really think about you

What we continentals feel about Britain, however, is more complex and deep. Because you are so different, we want to know more. In the complex list of ingredients that make up our relationship with Britain, there is a lot of admiration, curiosity, envy, gratitude (for the two world wars in particular) appreciation and even trust. But there is also a belief in various countries that you are still the 'perfidious Albion' of yore, superior and ever so slightly xenophobic.

You also never accepted being part of the Euro. Another slight towards the great European project but, as it turns out, your saving grace when deciding to exit the EU completely; something that many of the countries who are now part of the single currency can only ever dream of. Exiting the EU while being inside the Euro-zone would translate into certain economic catastrophe, something one might call a disincentive.

So, were the seeds for Brexit sown eons ago, with Britain detaching itself from the continental shelf, then creating an empire, then using its language to colonise the rest of the world in peace time? Was it all there from Boudicca down to Boris? I believe so.

President Charles de Gaulle was correct when he said (in a 1970 speech): "Our neighbours across the Channel, being made for free trade by the maritime character of their economic life, cannot possibly agree sincerely to shut themselves up behind a continental tariff wall." Britain should never have joined. It was never going to do well inside the EU and arguably never truly accepted the tenets of its foundation.

Over the years, Britain has felt more and more like its membership of the EU was the equivalent of an abdication of democracy, with mounting levels of frustration all across the population.

Everything in this country's identity naturally rebels to what many now identify as the 'faltering utopia' of the EU and, while Britain can still proudly feel European, it is a Europe of the mind it really feels part of, rather than a Europe of realities. The values of democracy, personal freedom, human dignity, active civil society, market economy and the rule of law are all part of its DNA. Just not a willing abdication of its sovereignty.

Note on the contributor

Deborah Bonetti is an Italian journalist and UK correspondent for the daily newspaper *Il Giorno* (based in Milan) as well as the director of the Foreign Press Association in London. She is chair of the Foreign Lobby of International Journalists and observer on the National Committee for the Safety of Journalists (in the UK). She has dual nationality.

Al promised you a miracle – Life under 'Greased Piglet' Johnson

The rise and achievement of power by Prime Minister Boris Johnson has been remarkable, given his well-publicised flaws, argues Steven McCabe, but the self-caricatured buffoon's relative political success so far does not mean the enthusiastic former Classics student doesn't have to worry about being stabbed in the back

That Boris Johnson is proving to be a controversial Prime Minister should come as little surprise. A willingness to break rules and unshakeable self-belief that norms expected of others did not apply to him have been among Johnson's consistent personality traits (Oborne, 2021). A key aspect of creating 'brand Boris' has been the lovable buffoon schtick which serves to make him seem much less elite than his background might suggest. A desire to be outside of convention and, when considered expedient, willing to rail against 'the establishment' has served Johnson well. Becoming Prime Minister, his long-cherished dream, has been achieved by assiduously proffering views through his ability to access the media that are explicitly intended to be populist (Purnell, 2011). But will the man who has promised so much be able to deliver?

The 'magnificent scoundrel and his lying machine'
Boris Johnson is a gift to the media who have happily reported on a litany of his misdemeanours. Johnson has no compunction in 'departing from the truth'. Curiously, where other politicians might squirm under the intense scrutiny of press examination of their past, Johnson appears to thrive. As James Smith, author of *Other People's Politics: Populism to Corbynism,* published in 2019, writing in *Tribune Magazine* asserts, Johnson has employed falsehood to achieve political and, it might be argued, more crucially, personal ends but without 'higher moral purpose' through giving the impression of being a man of the people (2021). Even in his vaguely sympathetic biography, *The Gambler*, Tom Bower acknowledges Johnson's failings and, significantly, that on at least two occasions, he's been dismissed for

untruthfulness (2020). *The Times* sacked him for inventing a quote when he was a trainee journalist. Later he was sacked as a shadow minister by Conservative Party leader Michael Howard for lying about an affair.

Johnson's aspirations to become PM had long been questioned by a range of those who had come into close contact with him. Former editor of *The Daily Telegraph* and eminent historian Sir Max Hastings, in an excoriating comment piece shortly before Johnson became leader of the Conservative Party, and therefore, PM, makes clear his disdain for someone he clearly feels unfit to assume such a position (2019). Hastings claimed Johnson 'cares for nothing but his own fame and gratification' followed others in which he, as well as former minister Michael Heseltine, argued he used celebrity as a platform to cultivate popularity. Tales of Johnson's willingness to depart from agreed speeches caused consternation among policymakers who dreaded his ability to say whatever he felt pleased the audience he was trying to convince (Knight, 2019).

That Johnson was a consummate crowd-pleaser and entertainer, though appalling those who considered him unable to master the detail required of a serious politician, recognised his 'Heineken' factor made him an asset (Montgomerie, 2012). Despite setbacks which would have ended the ambitions of most others, such was Johnson's standing among many Conservative MPs, immediately after the EU Referendum result in 2016, resulting in PM David Cameron's resignation, he felt compelled to stand to replace him. It is significant his attempt to become PM was derailed by Leave ally and former Cabinet colleague Michael Gove, who infamously stated Johnson could not 'provide the leadership or build the team for the task ahead' (Cooper, 2016).

One hurdle not enough to stop Boris

Unperturbed, Johnson used his rehabilitation under eventual leadership winner, Theresa May, in whose cabinet he became Foreign Secretary, to revive his leadership ambitions. Many contended that, finally, given high office, Johnson's failings would be exposed. Victoria Honeyman in *The Conversation*, just after his resignation as Foreign Secretary over opposition to what May proposed in terms of a future relationship with the EU, examined what she saw as his 'litany of blunders and poor diplomacy' (2018). May's inability to achieve Parliament's approval for her Brexit deal with the EU was undoubtedly made impossible by so called 'Spartans' in the peculiarly-named European Research Group, creating an impasse (Ashford, 2019). The Spartans looked to an alternative leader who would be willing to confront the EU and deliver what the people wanted, departure from the EU on as onerous, 'hard Brexit', conditions – ideally with no deal – as possible. This was Johnson's moment.

Ambition achieved – Johnson as PM

In becoming leader of the Conservative Party and thus Prime Minister in July 2019, Johnson, had achieved despite what his many detractors in the media and, notably, within his own party, considered impossible for a man so wedded to the cult of his own personality. Some commentators believe Johnson displays classic symptoms of narcissism. Psychologist, Chantal Gautier, agrees with those who believe Johnson is driven by his own ego which, when combined with 'power, arrogance, cockiness' and a desire to be 'seen to be right' can lead to delusion (2019). Nonetheless, in becoming leader, Johnson recognised he had inherited precisely the same situation that had confounded his Predecessor. In breaking an impasse of fulfilling the 'will of the people' who had voted to leave the EU in June 2016, he had licence to do it his way. Writing in *The Atlantic*, Tom McTague explains Johnson's very ascendancy had been possible exactly because of his refusal to comply with 'constraints that usually apply' (2019).

'Enemies of the people'?

Parliament's agreement required the consent of those who had long argued the UK must be free of EU interference. It was to these Johnson looked. Those deemed insufficiently supportive of his approach, including many judges, as well as senior MPs, were treated as enemies opposing the will of the people. In 2016 this had been an accusation made against the High Court judges who ruled Theresa May could not trigger Article 50, allowing the UK to leave the EU, without the consent of Parliament (Blitz, 2016). Spurred on by those who considered doubters in the wisdom of leaving the EU to be equally subversive, as Taylor contends, many tabloids followed this line of attack on so called 're-moaners' (2019). This allowed Johnson, ever the populist, to draw succour for his actions in expulsions, illegally proroguing Parliament, and in making a range of promises to those whose support he needed.

One such promise, that there would not be a border between Great Britain and Northern Ireland, is proving especially troublesome. Those with any experience of the issues surrounding this part of the UK usually tread extremely carefully when dealing with issues surrounding its status (see Mair *et al*, 2019).

In winning the December 2019 General Election, Johnson repaid the faith Conservative Party members had put in him as leader. Promises made during the election to 'Get Brexit done' and to 'level up' produced the largest majority since Margaret Thatcher. In any Cabinet the leader is 'first among equals', this appears not to apply in Johnson's case. With resonance to his hero, wartime leader Winston Churchill, Johnson believes his influence to be omnipotent. Those unable to share his view are deemed as having no place. As such, it may be said, Johnson shares character traits with former American President Donald Trump, someone who, when Johnson was serving as populist Mayor of London, he'd once dismissed as being 'clearly out of his mind' and 'unfit to hold the office of President of the United States" (Mackey, 2019).

Is Boris the new Trump?

Comparison with Trump may seem trite. Nonetheless, beyond aspects of their upbringing in which their sense of entitlement and self-belief was encouraged by their fathers and which have led to narcissistic tendencies, both share a penchant for engaging in populism which ensured the election of both. In Trump's case, the rhetoric of Making America Great Again, used in his successful 2016 campaign, and coming months after the vote to leave the EU in the UK, were emulated by Johnson in winning win the 2019 election with 'Get Brexit done'. What both also share is apparent disdain for engaging in the minutiae of the processes and protocols of running a country. Such deficiencies may not appear important in securing the support of disgruntled voters, but likely to be exposed during an unanticipated crisis as with the Covid-19 pandemic.

Crisis, what crisis? Confused messages and the whiff of incompetence

In assembling his Cabinet in early 2020, many political commentators expressed the belief it was not one blessed with an 'embarrassment of riches'. Questions were asked how a Cabinet clearly in thrall to Johnson and shorn of the talent of those who had left because of opposition to Johnson would cope? But in the wake of his election win, he was apparently untouchable. As Johnson had shown, appealing to those dissatisfied with the way elitist government operates can pay dividends. Indeed, Johnson knew the importance of the instincts of his then closest political adviser Dominic Cummings who, as the media reported, exalted in his reputation as a Svengali and Rasputin figure who had contempt for systems of government, especially the civil service (BBC, 2020). Cummings, who Johnson relied on, possessed what seemed like an uncanny ability to read the runes and understand what the public wanted (McCabe, 2020).

Johnson, who had promised to 'get Brexit done' though his 'oven ready' deal might have expected more scrutiny by the media during 2020. After all, public opinion, emphasised by the election in December 2019, strongly indicated their desire for the Brexit process to end so they could, it might be assumed, enjoy the benefits proclaimed by the PM. But Brexit, challenging as it surely was likely to be, was subsumed by the worst health crisis to confront the UK Government for a century. Dealing with coronavirus, which could only be arrested by curtailment of normal activity (lockdown), did not fit well with a dilettante PM who had previously exalted in his libertarian – some would argue libertine – credentials.

Coping with the Covid crisis

Though Johnson had been given warning by countries already being ravaged by the virus of the need to implement 'lockdown', as Elgot (2021) describes, Johnson's government was paralysed by panic. One adviser called No 10 a 'plague pit' and Johnson's approach, at best, lackadaisical and incompetent. Hardly a surprise, it might be said, but going on holiday and missing vital Cobra meetings dealing with the impending crisis hardly suggested someone taking the crisis with the seriousness it deserved. Much of media has branded Johnson's government's handling of the pandemic as woeful (Calvert and Arbuthnott 2021).

Hesitation in announcing lockdowns combined with confused messages including, as many argued, a ludicrously optimistic suggestions by the PM that the pandemic was over by July 2020, undoubtedly cost many tens of thousands of lives. As McCabe (2020a) describes, compelling evidence showed 'Eat Out to Help Out', which cost the taxpayers £849 million in the summer of 2020, ensured a resurgence in infection. To have experienced one of the worst rates of death of any country combined with a phenomenal decline in the economy might be argued to be endemic of the inexperience of a Cabinet dealing with unprecedented events (Mellor, 2021).

As reports of corruption and cronyism emerge, it seems Johnson's popularity might, as his critics had long predicted, start to decline, particularly among those who had voted for his 'miracle' in 2019. Speculation about Johnson's future mounted leading many to believe he would be deposed. Unless he experienced his own miracle he would be replaced. But this miracle arrived in the success of the vaccination programme, allowing the promise of a return to normality that, it was stressed, would not have been possible had the UK still been a member of the EU (McCabe, 2021).

Ever get the feeling you've been cheated?[1]

The Observer's Andrew Rawnsley describes Labour's leader of the Opposition Sir Keir Starmer's inability to get answers from Johnson during Prime Minister's Questions in the House of Commons as being like trying to catch a 'greased piglet' (2021). Rawnsley argues, despite what he regards as Johnson's 'catastrophic mishandling of the pandemic', his popularity, primarily because of the success vaccination is having, has seen his ratings dramatically improve. Many ask the same question Rawnsley poses: "Might this serial bungler even emerge as the political winner of the crisis?"

In an excellent distillation of Johnson, Docx presents a compelling thesis that Johnson's act of being a seen as a clown is one he's perfected since his days at Eton and which included a change of name from 'Alexander' to 'Boris' (2021). Like the greatest entertainers, especially magicians, it is intended to distract from the trick whilst keeping the crowd happy. There is, of course, the question of how long what increasingly seems like a deception by Johnson, who is accused of allowing the imposition of draconian legislation and enabling his friends to become even wealthier, can last. Will his explicit use of populism begin to wear thin among those who discover there will be no miracles for them? Herein lies the greatest threat.

Historian Simon Sebag Montefiore stresses: "All tyrannies are virtuoso displays, over many years, of cunning, risk-taking, terror, delusion, narcissism, showmanship, and charm, distilled into a spectacle of total personal control." Docx concludes: "Masks change, not archetypes. The fool still holds the stage. And pitiful ambition is precisely what we are watching." Perhaps Johnson, a student of classics will be aware of the fate of Publius Clodius Pulcher, a populist demagogue of ancient Rome who refused to play by the rules. The more audacious Clodius became, the more the Roman public loved him. Eventually, Rome's elite tired of him and grew to despise his behaviour. He was killed by an enemy, Annius Milo, on the Appian Way. History is replete with many such populist leaders who promise much, fail to deliver, and are brutally deposed. Johnson should beware.

Note
[1] Uttered by Sex Pistols' disillusioned lead singer Johnny Rotten at the final concert of their US tour on January 14th 1978

References
Ashford, J. (2019), 'Who are the Tory 'Spartans'?', *The Week*, 5th November, https://www.theweek.co.uk/104166/who-are-the-tory-spartans accessed, 8th March

BBC (2020), 'Dominic Cummings: Who is Boris Johnson's senior adviser?', *BBC Politics Website*, 13th November, https://www.bbc.co.uk/news/uk-politics-49101464 accessed 2nd March

Blitz, J. (2016), 'Brexit Briefing: Enemies of the people?' *The Financial Times*, 4th November, https://www.ft.com/content/010325da-a28a-11e6-82c3-4351ce86813f, accessed 19th March

Bower, T. (2020), *Boris Johnson: The Gambler*, WH Allen, London

Calvert, J. and Arbuthnott, G. (2021), *Failures of State: The Inside Story of Britain's Battle with Coronavirus*, Mudlark, London

Cooper, C. (2016), 'Michael Gove to stand in Tory leadership contest and says 'Boris is not a leader", *The Independent Website*, 30th June, https://www.independent.co.uk/news/uk/politics/michael-gove-stand-tory-leader-a7110591.html, accessed, 20th March

Docx, E. (2021), 'The clown king: how Boris Johnson made it by playing the fool', *The Guardian*, 18th March 2021, https://www.theguardian.com/news/2021/mar/18/all-hail-the-clown-king-how-boris-johnson-made-it-by-playing-the-fool?CMP=Share_AndroidApp_Other accessed 19th March

Elgot, J. (2021), "No 10 was a plague pit': how Covid brought Westminster to its knees', *The Guardian*, 12th March, https://www.theguardian.com/politics/2021/mar/12/no-10-plague-pit-how-covid-brought-westminster-to-its-knees accessed 14th March

Gautier, C. (2019), 'As a psychologist, I look at Boris Johnson and I worry for Britain', *The Independent*, 3rd September, https://www.independent.co.uk/voices/boris-johnson-brexit-no-deal-leadership-charisma-ego-a9090086.html accessed 28th February

Hastings, M. (2019), 'I was Boris Johnson's boss: he is utterly unfit to be prime minister', *The Guardian*, 24th June, https://www.theguardian.com/commentisfree/2019/jun/24/boris-johnson-prime-minister-tory-party-britain accessed 10th March

Honeyman, V. (2018), 'Boris Johnson's record as foreign secretary is stained by litany of blunders and poor diplomacy', *The Conversation*, 10th July, https://theconversation.com/boris-johnsons-record-as-foreign-secretary-is-stained-by-litany-of-blunders-and-poor-diplomacy-99649 accessed 17th March

Knight, S. (2019), 'The Empty Promise of Boris Johnson', *The New Yorker*, 13th June, https://www.newyorker.com/magazine/2019/06/24/the-empty-promise-of-boris-johnson accessed 11th March

Mackey, R. (2019), 'Donald Trump Praises Boris Johnson, Who Once Called Him "Unfit to Hold the Office of President of the United States"', *The Intercept*, 23rd July, https://theintercept.com/2019/07/23/boris-johnson-donald-trump-unfit/ accessed 14th March

Mair, J., McCabe, S., Fowler, N. and Budd, L. (2019), *Brexit and Northern Ireland, Bordering on Confusion*, Bite-Sized Books, Goring on Thames

McCabe, S. (2020), 'The Curious Role of 'Despicable Genius' Dominic Cummings', in *Pandemic, Where Did We Go Wrong?* edited by J. Mair, Bite-Sized Books, Goring on Thames

McCabe, S. (2020a), 'Did 'Eat Out to Help Out' Result in the Country 'Getting Stuffed'?', in *Pandemic, Where are We Still Going Wrong?* edited by J. Mair, Bite-Sized Books, Goring on Thames

McCabe, S. (2021), 'Does Vaccination offer Johnson a Way out of the Pandemic?' in *Pandemic, A Year of Mistakes?* edited by J. Mair, Bite-Sized Books, Goring on Thames

Mellor, J. (2021), 'Covid: Government's furlough scheme handing millions to tax exiles and foreign states', *The London Economic*, 20th March, https://www.thelondoneconomic.com/news/covid-governments-furlough-scheme-handing-millions-to-tax-exiles-and-foreign-states-259523/ accessed 21st March

Montgomerie, T. (2012), 'Boris, "the Heineken Tory" who reaches parts of the electorate that other Conservatives don't', Conservative Home Website, https://www.conservativehome.com/thetorydiary/2012/04/boris-the-heineken-tory-who-reaches-parts-of-the-electorate-that-other-conservatives-dont.html accessed 21st March

McTague, T. (2019), 'Boris Johnson Meets His Destiny', *The Atlantic*, 22nd July, https://www.theatlantic.com/international/archive/2019/07/boris-johnson-profile/594379/ accessed 16th March

Oborne, P. (2021), *The Assault on Truth: Boris Johnson, Donald Trump and the Emergence of a New Moral Barbarism*, Simon & Schuster, London

Purnell, S. (2011), *Just Boris: The Irresistible Rise of a Political Celebrity*, Aurum Press Ltd, London

Rawnsley, A. (2021), 'Why Boris Johnson, the greased piglet, is eluding the grasp of Keir Starmer', *The Observer*, 7th March, https://www.theguardian.com/commentisfree/2021/mar/07/labour-must-not-let-boris-johnson-emerge-as-covid-hero accessed 9th March

Smith, J.A. (2019), *Other People's Politics: Populism to Corbynism*, Zero Books, Winchester

Smith, J.A. (2021), 'How the Media Made Boris Johnson', *Tribune Magazine*, 14th February, https://tribunemag.co.uk/2021/02/how-the-media-made-boris-johnson, accessed 10th March

Taylor, R. (2019), 'From Euroscepticism to outright populism: the evolution of British tabloids', *London School of Economics Blog*, 4th January, https://blogs.lse.ac.uk/brexit/2019/01/04/from-euroscepticism-to-outright-populism-the-evolution-of-british-tabloids/ accessed 5th March

About the contributor

Dr Steven McCabe is Associate Professor and Senior Fellow, Centre for Brexit Studies and Institute of Design and Economic Acceleration (IDEA), Birmingham City University, and writes/comments regularly in the national and international press on politics and the economy. As well as being joint editor of *Brexit and Northern Ireland, Bordering on Confusion* and *English Regions After Brexit: Examining Potential Change through Devolved Power,* (published by Bite-Sized Books respectively in 2019 and 2020), in the past year he has written a number of chapters for texts examining the impact of the pandemic.

Deceptively silly – the role of the cucumber in Boris Johnson's ideology

Imke Henkel examines the rise of the Euromyths and how they have shaped UK politics for 30 years

In May 2016, Brexit campaigner Boris Johnson addressed a small crowd which had assembled to watch him launch his soon-to-become infamous battle bus (the '£350m a week for the NHS' one).

"It is absolutely crazy," cried Johnson, "absolutely crazy that the European Union is telling us how powerful our vacuum cleaners have got to be, what shape our bananas have got to be, and all that kind of thing." (*Daily Telegraph*, May 12, 2016 video 00:01:07–00:01:22 [accessed on May 15, 2019, no longer available.]) The European Union, of course, never said or demanded anything of the sort.

Johnson's claims were false. The assertion that the EU allegedly forbade the British people to use powerful vacuum cleaners or to sell (or buy) bent bananas are examples of the so-called Euromyths. Since around 1990, these Euromyths appeared in the UK press as deceptively silly news stories that made false claims like the one that European regulators banned bent bananas or that they imposed too small condoms on British men.

It was always well known that these stories were false. Over 25 years, the EU published a blog that debunked the lies. Many UK mainstream media published refutations (e.g. Sebestyen, 1996, Smith, 2017). Repeatedly. Constantly. It did not matter. The liars shrugged and repeated their lies.

Back on the day in May 2016, just about a month before Britain voted to leave the EU, Johnson's audience met his false contentions with chuckles. They knew and recognised the Euromyths genre. By the time of the Brexit Referendum, it had been around for a quarter of a century. It was effective and it helped to turn voters against the EU. Remarkably, it did so despite the constant debunking of the false claims. Most people did not believe the lies. They still were persuaded by the Euromyths.

Why did the Euromyths persist?

The answer to this question goes some way to understand the British Eurosceptic discourse since the late 1980s. It also sheds light on the former journalist, now Prime Minister's Euroscepticism. More seriously, it reveals how Johnson's style of political communication is constructed to convey an ideology.

I start my answer with a closer look at the Euromyths news stories. They were persuasive, I argue, because they were told in a specific way. They only pretended to be news stories. They used all the paraphernalia of news reporting – inverted pyramid, reporting 'facts', quoting conflicting views etc. – as an empty gesture.

I explain this in more depths in my recently published book *Destructive Storytelling* (Henkel, 2021), where I use Critical Discourse Analysis (Fairclough, 1992) to show that Euromyths news stories counteract the factual news discourse with a conversational discourse (directly speaking to the audience) that creates a metadiscourse and thus undermines the importance of truth.

Like a Shakespearean comedy, Euromyths news stories incorporate the voice of a jester. There is a constant jester's aside that creates an understanding between the author of the article and their audience (cf. Mullini, 1985). This jester's voice builds the metadiscourse that runs counter to the news story discourse. Thus, it undermines the news story's claim to truth.

It is this jester's voice that Johnson's audience heard back in May 2016 (and on many other occasions) and that made them chuckle. The jester's voice renders factual accuracy irrelevant. With a wink of the eye, its metadiscourse invites its audience to dismiss any concerns about the factuality of the reported news story and to listen instead to the 'real meaning'. This 'real meaning' is what the French philosopher and linguist Roland Barthes has described as 'myth'. The myth conveys an ideology. I will come back to this.

The cucumber takes centre stage

First, though, I want to show how this works, discussing a sample Euromyths news story. On May 7, 1993, the *Daily Mail* published an article headlined '*Brussels sprouts the curve-free cucumber: Go straight or else, EC warns growers*' (Pendlebury, 1993). The news story wrongly contends that the EC (European Commission) wanted to ban curved cucumbers. The article does most of the things reporters still learn in journalism school about news writing that intends to assert its 'objectivity' and truthfulness (Harcup, 2009): it quotes people from both sides, representing conflicting views; it reports facts using details as supporting evidence; it withholds the reporter's view and instead uses quotes to report these views 'objectively'.

The American sociologist Gaye Tuchman has described such practices as 'strategic rituals of objectivity' (Tuchman, 1972). Journalists use them, Tuchman observed, to fend off complaints against their reporting. To protect themselves not least against libel suits, journalists use such "strategic rituals of objectivity," writes

Tuchman, "almost the way a Mediterranean peasant might wear a clove of garlic around his neck to ward off evil spirits" (1972, p. 660).

As Pendlebury's cucumber-article in the *Daily Mail* employs these objectivity-rituals, it anchors the story in the factuality-signalling news discourse. By employing the rituals of objectivity, the *Daily Mail* news story makes a claim to 'truthfulness'.

However, it also does something else. The cucumber article opens with a lead that includes the audience in assumed shared laughter: "We laughed when they tried to ban prawn-flavoured crisps and the green colouring in mushy peas" (Pendlebury, May 7, 1993).

This opening runs against the inverted-pyramid structure common in objectivity-signalling news reporting: the cucumber story prioritises the simulated agreement with its audience, not the most important fact. The simulated conversation also runs against the strategy of objective reporting to withhold the reporter's voice. Although the reporter of the cucumber story uses on other occasions quotes to express his own views, he also, like in this instance, directly offers his views, and, echoing the laughter in the lead sentence, he speculates that the alleged regulation is "a directive the late [comedian] Frankie Howerd would have loved." (Pendlebury, 1993)

Furthermore, the reporter imagines comical scenes ("Ministry of Agriculture inspectors, stalking New Covent Garden, tape measures at the ready"), inserting a fictional, absurd image in the news story. The reporting is also riddled with comical words, with occasionally added sexual innuendo (the allegedly outlawed deformation of cucumbers is dubbed 'kinks', the surmised ban will not allow them 'to droop'. [cf. Sexis-Lexis.com, 2016])

The comical language is used to construct an agreement between the reporter's voice – acting like a Shakespearean jester – and its readers. This audience is identified as the 'British people': the supposed regulation is not just mocked by the reporter/jester in agreement with the readers, it equally meets the 'ridicule from Britain's £44m cucumber industry', and the 'amused contempt' from cucumber growers 'in deepest Essex', where one of the British cucumber growers is quoted with the request "Am I allowed to laugh?"

The funny, taunting Britons are, at the same time, hard-working ("families, not co-operatives, with a small acreage, getting up early in the morning and picking the cucumbers themselves") that beat the "tough Dutch and Spanish competition." The incorrect news story about the European Commission's alleged ban of curved cucumbers is used to tell the 'real' story of a funny superior British people beating weak (only held up by subsidies) and humourless Europeans.

How ambiguity develops myths

I argue that the ambiguity between a news discourse enacting objectivity rituals and a metadiscourse that, in an aside, tells the 'real' story, turns the news story into a myth in Roland Barthes' sense.

Barthes describes myth as a type of speech that thrives on the ambiguity of language use. He developed his theory of myth in his essay '*Myth Today*' ('*Le mythe, aujourd'hui*'). First published in 1957, it accompanied a collection of 53 already previously printed articles that, as Barthes explains in the preface, "were written [...] to reflect regularly on some myths of French daily life (Barthes, 2013 [1957], p. XI). He developed his concept of myth to reveal the ideology of the French bourgeoisie. His central argument is that myth naturalises what is a historical-political phenomenon. Myth depoliticises political phenomena. Myth annihilates the socially constructed, historic-political origin of things. Thus, myth becomes ideology.

Building his semiotic understanding of myth on Ferdinand de Saussure's analysis of language as a semiological system, Barthes defines myth as a 'second-order semiological system' (2013 [1957], p. 217). He famously uses the example of a *Paris Match* cover-photo to explain his theory. The photo shows a black man in French uniform saluting the French flag. Whereas the photo signifies on the first semiological level just what you see: a black French soldier saluting, on the second semiological level it turns into a sign for the myth of the great, all nations and people embracing French Empire. It becomes ideology.

The analysis of Euromyths news stories reveals the same structure. The cucumber story uses the supposed ban of curved cucumbers as an 'alibi' (Barthes, 2013 [1957], p. 239) for British superiority over the EU. This is how the Euromyths news stories use, in their false reporting, the allegedly absurd EU regulations: they become an alibi for British superiority. As myth they create an articulation for a Eurosceptic ideology. This is why Euromyths news stories kept being published despite being consistently debunked. They offered an articulation for a Eurosceptic supremacy myth in disguise.

The ideology, hidden in silly news stories, speaks to the British public. The alleged ban of bent bananas, which has become iconic for the Euromyths falsehoods, provides a succinct example.

During a debate on BBC Question Time in February 2017, a woman in the audience explained that the sight of straight bananas made her vote for Brexit: "I'm just sick of the silly rules that come out of Europe." (Annie Ludlow, 2017, February 2, *00:00:10–00:00:16*). When challenged by presenter David Dimbleby ("It was bananas what did it, was it, for you?"), the woman confessed: "It was more than bananas. [...] it's opportunities out there that I feel we need to see as a country" (Annie Ludlow, February 2, 2017, *00:00:26–00:00:31*). The Euromyths (bananas) articulate the longing for national grandeur. I discuss another example in more detail in my book.

Alibis for ideology

The hidden ideology is what renders factual accuracy irrelevant. Why fact checks do not work. They are impotent if the falsehood is but an alibi for an ideology. The stories about the alleged ban of bent bananas or downsizing of condoms are ideological speech. In that sense they resemble propaganda.

Boris Johnson uses the same narrative techniques – the same storytelling – in his newspaper columns and political speeches: the £350m-bus and the 'taking back control' slogan are expressions of a Eurosceptic British supremacy myth. As myth they hide the ideology they articulate.

However, contrary to what he himself has claimed and to what has been often repeated, Johnson did not invent the Euromyths. Instead, he jumped on the rolling bandwagon, back in Brussels in the late 1980s when *Daily Telegraph* editor Max Hastings offered him the job as Brussels correspondent, after the *Times* had sacked him for making up a quote. Johnson kept writing false stories for the *Telegraph*. But he did not invent the specific genre of the Euromyths news stories as an archive search of his *Telegraph* stories shows. He was not that creative. Just opportunistic.

Johnson did, though, make most effective use of silly stories to express the Eurosceptic British supremacy myth that, if articulated directly, would have placed him in the far-right political wilderness. Moreover, Johnson's Eurosceptic supremacy myth employed the populist dichotomy, as defined by Cas Mudde, of "two homogenous and antagonistic groups, 'the pure people' and 'the corrupt elite'." (2004, 543)

The silly stories of bent bananas and too small condoms, which Johnson kept repeating in his Brexit campaign, pitched a funny, hard-working strong British people against a weak and corrupt EU. The populist dichotomy helped his Eurosceptic message to become powerful. The falsehood proved to be irrelevant.

References

Annie Ludlow. (February 2, 2017). Brexit bananas about Question Time on BBC 1. [YouTube video]. Annie Ludlow. Retrieved from https://www.youtube.com/watch?v=MrGMTdsj_tk

Barthes, R. (2013 [1957]). *Mythologies* (R. Howard & A. Lavers, Trans.). New York: Hill and Wang.

Fairclough, N. (1992). Discourse and social change. Cambridge: Polity.

Harcup, T. (2009), *Journalism. Principles and practices* (2nd edition). London, Sage

Henkel, I. (2021) *Destructive Storytelling. Disinformation and the Eurosceptic Myth that Shaped Brexit*. London: Palgrave Macmillan.

Mudde, C. (2004), The populist zeitgeist", *Government and Opposition, 39*(4), p. 541-563.

Mullini, R. (1985). Playing the fool: The pragmatic status of Shakespeare's Clowns. *New Theatre Quarterly, 1*(1), 98–104.

Pendlebury, R. (May 7, 1993). Brussels sprouts the curve-free cucumber: Go straight or else, EC warns growers. *Daily Mail*, p. 9

Sebestyen, V. (August 5, 1996). If the baddies of Brussels are back it must be August. How the Euro scares of summer turn into the myths of autumn. Evening Standard, p. 13.

Sexis-Lexis.com. (2016). Sexis-Lexis.com. Dictionary of sexual terms. Retrieved October 18, 2020, from http://www.sex-lexis.com/.

Smith, A. (October 9, 2017). Here's a handy list of every myth about the European Union since 1992. Mirror Online. Retrieved from https://www. mirror.co.uk/news/politics/heres-handy-list-every-myth-11315766

Daily Telegraph. (May 12, 2016). Boris Johnson began his Vote Leave campaign on bus made in Germany. *Daily Telegraph*. Retrieved from https://www.telegraph.co.uk/news/2016/05/11/boris-johnson-began-his-vote-leave-campaign-on-bus-made-in-germa/

Tuchman, G. (1972). Objectivity as strategic ritual: An examination of newsmen's notion of objectivity. American Journal of Sociology, 77(4), 660–679

About the contributor

Dr Imke Henkel is senior lecturer in journalism at the University of Lincoln and a former political journalist who wrote for leading German national newspapers including *Sueddeutsche Zeitung* and *Die Zeit*. She was also the UK and Ireland correspondent for the German news magazine *Focus* for ten years. She has just published the book *Destructive storytelling: Disinformation and the Eurosceptic myth that shaped Brexit* with Palgrave Macmillan.

Getting Brexit done and the future of the UK-EU relationship

Boris Johnson's populist slogan Get Brexit Done may have won him the 2019 General Election, says veteran UK-EU watcher Alistair Jones, but the unrealistically easy call to arms which played well through the media disguises a reality of future problems for the UK, EU and Ireland which the PM seems unable to acknowledge

The 2019 General Election cry from Boris Johnson of Get Brexit Done seemed to resonate with many voters. Parliament had been blamed for failing to ratify the Withdrawal Agreement and failing to agree on any form of relationship with the EU. Thus a new Conservative Government was needed to enforce the will of the people from the 2016 EU Referendum.

But this is an awfully narrow, if not inaccurate, narrative. It excludes the fact the Second Reading of the Withdrawal Agreement Bill was passed. The Second Reading of a Bill discusses the thinking behind the legislation. The Third Reading, which looks at the detail of the Bill, was pulled by Johnson. With hindsight, although many commentators made this point at the time, it was withdrawn because so much of the detail of the Agreement was unpalatable to Brexiteers and to 'Remoaners' alike. Parliament – and remember, we live in a parliamentary democracy not a prime ministerial democracy – is the source of all political power in the UK. Parliament is the legislature, as well as being the body which scrutinises the Government. Parliament holds the Government to account. Johnson knew full well Parliament would not vote for his Withdrawal Agreement when they saw the actual detail. Both Brexiteers and Remoaners would propose amendments to the deal, and it would again stall in Parliament.

After the election, the Bill was rammed through Parliament at high speed. The Lords proposed a couple of amendments but these were thrown out. There was negligible scrutiny, in fact, less than had been promised prior to the election. Johnson had 'got Brexit done'. Except, of course, he hadn't. The UK had left the EU, entering a transition period that would last 11 months, after which...

nobody knew what would happen. Leaving the EU is an event; Brexit is a process. That process started with the acceptance of the Withdrawal Agreement and will continue through every new trade deal or renewal of deals.

Even after the passing of the Withdrawal Agreement there were concerns being expressed by Brexiteers about the detail. Iain Duncan Smith 'bemoaned the fine print in the Withdrawal Agreement which could keep the UK hooked into the EU's loan book indefinitely' (Peat, 2020). This from an ardent Brexiteer who voted for the Withdrawal Agreement legislation. It highlights the lack of scrutiny undertaken by many, something which Johnson anticipated with his huge Parliamentary majority. There were concerns over how much money the UK would continue to contribute into the EU budget, the access of EU fishing boats into UK waters, and so many other matters of detail. Too late, but Johnson had 'got Brexit done'.

The future relationship does not really look good for the UK. One of the mantras from the EU Referendum was 'take back control'. It was, in effect, all about sovereignty. In leaving the EU, the UK stops sharing aspects of sovereignty, even though it had never been given away. The 'taking back' of sovereignty comes at a price. This price depends on the future relationship with the EU. What was clear in everything the Johnson Governments have negotiated, is the emphasis not just on 'regaining' sovereignty but also diverging from the EU. The future relationship must be markedly different to that as an EU member.

This issue of divergence is a problem. In many of the arguments around the future relationship between the UK and the EU, there were suggestions of using the Canadian model. Canada has been negotiating a trade deal with the EU for a number of years (see EU Commission, 2020). This trade deal is all about convergence, bringing the EU and Canada closer together economically and in trade. With the UK leaving the EU, it is about divergence, the UK removing itself from alignment with the EU's practices. Consequently, a Canada-style trade deal was never really a starting option.

The clearest example of the problems that will continue for the UK-EU future relationship is encapsulated in the Northern Ireland-Republic of Ireland border. During the EU Referendum campaign, this concern was dismissed by the Leave team. Johnson said Brexit would leave the border situation unchanged (BBC, 2016). This was either a brazen lie or an example of the extent to which Johnson did not understand how the Single Market of the EU operated. If the UK was to leave the Single Market, a border would have to be established. Any goods entering the Single Market would require completed paperwork, such as customs declarations, which would have to be produced prior to entering the Single Market. The problem was the Good Friday/Belfast Peace Agreement, which stipulated there would be no border on the island of Ireland. For the latter to remain true, a border would have to be established between mainland Great Britain and Northern Ireland, something which was wholly unpalatable to most Brexiteers and to the Democratic Unionist Party (the dominant Unionist party in Northern Ireland which would be propping up the future minority Theresa May Government).

Today, despite Johnson repeatedly saying it does not and will not exist (Stewart et al, 2019; Blevins, 2020; Heffer, 2021), there is now a border within the UK, down the Irish Sea. Goods leaving Great Britain for Northern Ireland will have to meet the criteria for entering the Single Market, as Northern Ireland has remained in the Single Market while also remaining within the UK. There is now more speculation of this being the first step in the reunification of the island of Ireland, subject to the obligatory referenda in both Northern Ireland and the Republic of Ireland (O'Leary, 2021).

Yet within the Northern Ireland Protocol of the Withdrawal Agreement, there is even more room for destabilising the future relationship between the UK and the EU. Article 16 of the protocol has already been activated and deactivated, as well as other threats to use it. This Article allows either signatory 'to take unilateral action if the implementation of the agreement gives rise to negative consequences' (Rice, 2021). These consequences could be economic, environmental or even societal, although any action must be linked directly to where the problem has arisen.

Johnson has already threatened to activate Article 16 on two occasions, on 13 January 2021 and 3 February 2021. The European Commission activated Article 16, and deactivated it within three hours, on 29 January 2021 over vaccines for the Covid-19 virus. This act by the Commission was carried out unilaterally. The UK and Irish Governments were not informed in advance of the activation. It was a monumental blunder by the Commission President, Ursula von der Leyen. The reality is a distinct lack of trust between the two sides. This lack of trust is what will influence the future relationship.

Oliver (2018) has noted how much of the debate around the future relationship between the UK and the EU has focused on the economic relationship and on trade. This is the tangible aspect of the relationship: goods moving between the UK and the EU, or not, as the case may be. Such a perspective neglects the financial sector, which was not included in the post-Brexit trade agreement signed on Christmas Eve 2020. Wyman (2016, 6) estimated a quarter of all of the financial sector's revenue came directly from business related to the EU. Leaving the Single Market, and losing all forms of equivalence, could see business with the EU halve, tens of thousands of jobs lost, and cost billions in tax revenues for the UK Government. These redundancies will be visible, but the trade in the finance sector is not as obvious as lorries crossing the English Channel.

What has been noticeable in the debates around the future relationship between the UK and the EU, is the extent to which it has been inward looking in the UK. Throughout the EU Referendum, and thereafter, the case was very much around how the EU would be falling over backwards to do a deal with the UK. Alongside this, there was this perception of the UK bestriding the world. All of this highlighted what has been termed 'British exceptionalism'. Such a perspective highlights how Britain won the war singlehandedly against Nazi Germany, how Britannia ruled the waves and how the Empire was so beneficent to the subjugated. Membership of the EU constrained the UK from performing this global role, hence the need to leave the EU (see Tilford, 2017; Dadow, 2018; Crozier, 2020). All of this is an absolute misrepresentation of history. Yet the way the future relationship with the EU is portrayed, is through such a lens.

So what does the future hold for UK-EU relations? There is a distinct lack of trust on both sides. There is widespread speculation among Brexit-supporting media outlets that the EU will do what it can to ensure Brexit fails (Neilan, 2020; Adye, 2021; Farrell, 2021). This is a rather far-fetched supposition because trade between the two is significant. A failing Brexit would hurt many EU member states. Yet that must be balanced by the fear in the EU of other members leaving. There is speculation of the Czechs, Dutch and Poles all waiting to see the extent to which Brexit is successful, and whether or not they could leave as well.

Conversely, there is little trust of Johnson and his government. Having seen Johnson distort and mislead over the results of the Withdrawal Agreement, linked to his absolute lack of grasp over detail, leaves the EU in something of an uncomfortable position. Laurent (2020) provides a list of reasons as to why the EU does not trust Johnson. During the negotiations, there were endless attempts to divide the EU, or to refuse to accept the rules around state aid, or even to accept the need for a border between the EU Single Market and the UK, and to then blame the EU for not acceding to British demands. This was before the UK threatened to breach international law through the Internal Market (UK) legislation, or deciding it wanted to unilaterally extend the grace period in the Withdrawal Agreement and the post-Brexit Trade Deal because of problems in getting supplies into Northern Ireland.

The future looks somewhat bleak, and this is without comparing the Erasmus+ scheme to that of the planned Turing scheme which enable academics and students to study in Europe, or the need for European Travel Information and Authorisation System (ETIAS) visas to enter the EU from 2022. Throw in all the non-tariff barriers to trade (which Johnson wrongly said would not exist in his announcement of a post-Brexit trade agreement) and the situation gets markedly worse.

From the EU perspective, it looks little better. Brexit was not wanted or desired, but the EU appears a little more up to the mark in preparing for it. The problem is the British approach to everything, that British exceptionalism again. Demands are made of the EU but with negligible concessions offered in return. Government adviser Lord Frost, like Johnson, appears to believe a good negotiator is one who stands their ground and forces the other side to budge. In such a game of hard ball, the EU could walk away as it has far less to lose. And this is the basis for the future relationship as things currently stand.

At best, the future relationship is likely to be terse. At worst, there will be court cases and disputes as both sides try to manipulate the various agreements to suit their own needs and wishes. If it is an absolute disaster, there is speculation the UK could re-apply to join the EU. The EU member states would have to be unanimous in accepting such an application, and that will be highly unlikely for at least a generation.

References

Adye, J. (2021); "EU is not a friend but an adversary - Brussels wants Britain humbled" *Daily Express* 15 March 2021

BBC (2016) "Boris Johnson: Brexit would not affect Irish border" 29 February 2016.

Blevins, D. (2020); "The PM said there would be 'no checks' but there will be" Sky News, 20 May 2020.

Crozier, A. (2020); "British exceptionalism: pride and prejudice and Brexit" *International Economics and Economic Policy* vol. 17, pp. 635-658

Daddow, O. (2018) "Brexit and British exceptionalism: the impossible challenge for Remainers" https://blogs.lse.ac.uk/brexit/ (last accessed 19 March 2021)

EU Commission (2020); "EU-Canada Comprehensive Economic and Trade Agreement (CETA)". Available at: https://ec.europa.eu/trade/policy/in-focus/ceta/index_en.htm (last accessed 17 March 2021)

Farrell, K. (2021); "'They can't bear it!' Habib in scathing rant at EU plot to 'damage' Brexit Britain success" *Daily Express* 5 February 2021

Heffer, G. (2021); "Brexit: Boris Johnson says he'll consider triggering Article 16 of Northern Ireland Protocol" Sky News, 3 February 2021

Laurent, L. (2020); "You Can't Blame the EU for Not Trusting Boris Johnson" *Bloomberg Opinion* 16 October 2020

Neilan, C. (2020); "EU wants to 'punish' Britain with unacceptable trade deal, Boris Johnson tells Cabinet" *Daily Telegraph* 10 December 2020

O'Leary, B. (2021); "A referendum on Irish unity is coming, whether we like it or not" *The Irish Times*, 19 March 2021

Oliver, T. (2018); *Understanding Brexit: A Concise Introduction* (Policy Press, Bristol)

Peat, J. (2020); "Iain Duncan Smith up in arms over Withdrawal Agreement "fine print"" *The London Economic* 4 August 2020.

Rice, C. (2021); "Explainer: Article 16 of the Northern Ireland Protocol" UK in a Changing Europe. Available at: https://ukandeu.ac.uk/explainers/article-16-of-the-northern-ireland-protocol/ (last accessed 19 March 2021)

Stewart, H., Rankin, J. and O'Carroll, L. (2019); "Johnson accused of misleading public over Brexit deal after NI remarks" *The Guardian* 8 November 2019

Tilford, S. (2017); "The British and their exceptionalism" Centre for European Reform. Available at: https://is.muni.cz/el/phil/podzim2020/AJL27087/um/Tilford__Simon_The_British_and_their_exceptionalism.pdf (last accessed 19 March 2021)

Wyman, O. (2016); "The Impact of the UK's Exit From the EU on the UK-Based Financial Services Sector" Marsh and McLennan Companies

About the contributor

Alistair Jones is Associate Professor in Politics and a University Teacher Fellow at De Montfort University in Leicester. He is a leading expert on Britain's relations with the EU and author of *Britain and the European Union* (2016), *The Resurgence of Parish Council Powers in England* (2020) and *Contemporary British Politics and Government* (2015 with Phil Cocker).

Section six
The new populism and the media
***

The undermining of truth in a changing and unreliable media environment

Raymond Snoddy

This book, and previous contributions in what is now a trilogy, have been a little unusual in that quite deliberately they come to no fixed conclusion. About 45 media academics, journalists who have become media academics and practicing journalists, reveal their separate thoughts, analysis, reporting around the main theme, and come to, yes, individual conclusions, some as up-to-the minute as a book can ever be.

This final section is reserved for the broader approach, such as the likely impact of artificial intelligence, not just on the future of information but of democratic society itself in this decade, from Dr Alex Connock.

And then finally can we discern a possible solution to the near existential threat posed by false information, alternative facts and, sometimes, lethal conspiracy theories?

The crisis has been long in the making and comes, Ken Goldstein argues, not just from the rise of the internet and the social media giants but from the simultaneous destruction of much of the traditional media. The vacuum created has seriously weakened the main countervailing force against online falsehood.

There is also room for the quirky. Could it be that there are some similarities between the pitch demonstrations at Manchester United's Old Trafford ground against the actions of the club's foreign owners, and the storming of the US Capitol, even though no-one was seriously injured in Manchester and one was about football not politics?

Veteran football correspondent Jim White of the Daily Telegraph thinks there are.

Oxford academic Connock tells the extraordinary story about how an artificial intelligence (AI) system revealed in 2017 that neo-Nazis were planning to gather in Charlottesville, Virginia for a Unite The Right Rally. The same system was able to warn about potential revolutionaries arriving in Washington in January 2021. It was not the FBI, although the agency may well have also known, but the User Knowledge Operations Team of AirBnB, the room letting service who tracked the movements.

AI, which has already been successfully used in social marketing, and politics has now moved on to conspiracy marketing. An increasing number of research findings suggest a small number of social media account holders, reaching only a small number of users, are still dangerous because their audiences contain the minority prepared to act on the false information. When Donald Trump's Twitter account was closed there was a 73 per cent decline in hate speech on Twitter, while another study found two thirds of anti-vaccine content shared on Twitter and Facebook was derived from just 12 people. For Connock, however, the danger and the implication of AI for society is just beginning.

The US National Security Commission on Artificial Intelligence found the threat from AI went far beyond driving social information around the Capitol riot but 'as an existential threat to the liberty of individuals as a whole'. Adversaries tooled up with AI, foreign as well as domestic, will use misinformation campaigns not just to send one powerful generalised message to a million people. "The new AI tools will send a million individualised messages – each configured on the basis of a detailed understanding of targeted individual's digital life, emotional state and social network," Connock warns.

The degree to which actors at state, corporate, insurgent group and individual level, exploit such potential and the enabling flaws in current high tech and social media companies, will be an enduring theme of the 2020s. Former television executive and BBC Trust member now a journalism professor, Richard Tait, fears independent reporting is not just under threat in EU countries such as Hungary and Poland but also in the UK as a result of the populist government of Boris Johnson. Public service broadcasting, with its commitment to accurate and impartial journalism, Tait believes, falls into the hit list of populist governments alongside an independent judiciary, an unpoliticised civil service, even an effective Parliament. He notes the BBC had a public trust level of 64 per cent, before the May 2021 crisis over Martin Bashir's Panorama interview with Princess Diana 26 years ago. Such a rating was twice that of the *Daily Telegraph* and the *Daily Mail* and four times that of *The Sun*.

Yet there are repeated attacks on the BBC's impartiality by both public, populist press and politicians even though Ofcom, the communications regulator, has found no evidence to support attacks. In 2017 Ofcom analysed 300 complaints about BBC impartiality and found none of them justified. In 2020 it considered, in its role as the final court of appeal, 230 complaints, and again found none justified. Tait believes, apart from the impact of the Bashir affair, and likely political attacks both traditional and contemporary on public service broadcasters, the BBC will have to come to terms in future with a new journalistic minefield, reporting 'culture wars' with impartiality.

This too could be a very divisive area as populism takes on controversies over gender, race, identity and history.

Professor Julian Petley of Brunel University, a former journalist, has come to the conclusion it is no longer enough to refer to the majority of the British national newspaper industry as the 'Tory press' but, at the very least, a populist press, or even more precisely 'an authoritarian populist press'. Such newspapers present 'common sense' explanations of the working of the world as if they were the natural wisdom of the ages. "Of course they are no such thing. Rather they are the deep-rooted products, of culture and history," he emphasises.

Petley has concerns about the launch of GB News, a new 24-hour television news channel in the UK chaired by Andrew Neil, the political broadcaster and former editor of the *Sunday Times*. "The fear is that GB News may do to broadcast news in the UK what Murdoch did to the UK press after he purchased the *News of the World*, *The Sun*, *The Times* and the *Sunday Times*, that is lead other channels to compete with it on its own terms," Petley argues. There are already concerns popular national newspapers are increasingly setting the news agenda of the BBC. Anything that further encourages this process – and Petley fears GB News might do that – "would be a disaster for trustworthy journalism, informed debate and, ultimately, for democracy itself in this country."

Dr Sara McConnell, a former *Times* journalist who now teaches journalism at the University of Sheffield, also emphasises research that warns journalists not to see populism as a short-term phenomenon. Rather it is located in deep-seated and long-term trends of distrust in politicians, a perceived destruction of national identity and established ways of life, relative deprivation and 'left-behindness'. Such factors have led to Trump and Johnson, McConnell believes. What is arguably new is the extent to which leaders like Trump and Johnson gaslight journalists and the public telling lies 'they know must be called out and engage in a form of censorship by refusing to submit to scrutiny from all sections of the press, rather than just friendly media like Fox News in the US or the tabloid press in the UK'.

Elena Cosentino, director of the International News Safety Institute, brings to the fore one aspect of political reporting in the time of Trump, which could get overlooked – the increasing threat to the lives of journalists denounced as 'traitors' for doing their jobs. Cosentino tells how a week before the 2020 presidential election representatives from 40 leading news organisations from around the world took part in what turned out to be a very alarming online meeting. One representative was full of foreboding if there were no clear winner and one side prematurely claimed victory. Armed right-wing militia groups might come out to 'defend the White House' or storm state capitols. This was what turned out to an accurate prediction about the US, for goodness sake, a country with a much-admired constitution guaranteeing media freedom. The fact journalists were having to prepare for an election in America as if it were Iraq 'almost beggars belief', Cosentino observes.

By 2020 the curve recording attacks on journalists had already started to shoot up vertically. "A perfect storm of pandemic denialism, emboldened white supremacy and police brutality at Black Lives Matters protests" had led to a record 400 journalists being physically assaulted in the first ten months of the year. This was more than three times the combined total for the three years since 2017. The Trump presidency had purposefully, obliterated, tweet by tweet a large portion of American trust in the news industry and raising to record highs society's threshold of tolerance for violence against journalists. There is no room for complacency. Although President Biden appears more tolerant of the media, one of his first decisions was to refuse to sanction the Saudi crown prince Mohammed bin Salman in relation to the murder in Istanbul of Jamal Khashoggi, a journalist who sought protection in America.

It has famously been said that some people believe football is a matter of life and death. It is far more important than that. Football writer Jim White believes there are parallels between the pitch invasion at Old Trafford, which caused the Manchester United v Liverpool match to be postponed, and the invasion of the US Capitol.

Like the Capitol demonstrators the Manchester United supporters organised their demonstration on social media and found little by way of security standing in their way. Once the fans got onto the pitch it became less of a demonstration 'and more a trespass on territory infused with emotional heft'. But, according to White, it was difficult to justify the expansive scale of the subsequent coverage as 'mayhem', given there were five deaths in the storming of the Capitol while in Manchester one policeman received a gash under his eye from a thrown traffic cone. At least the fans' voice was heard in their protest against the Glazers, the American owners of the club, and they have found a route to prominence in future. From now on groups of supporters know how to communicate their intent: get on the pitch and get the game postponed. "That might be the most challenging lesson of the Old Trafford insurrection," concludes White, who does not say whether he thinks the US Capitol insurrectionists might have learned a similar lesson.

Clive Myrie, the BBC television journalist who has covered six US presidential elections, worries that in America opinion can be dressed up as news and many Americans want their views affirmed not challenged. No less than 56 per cent of

Americans believe journalists and reporters lie, with 58 per cent convinced most news organisations are more concerned with supporting an ideology or political position, rather than informing the public. As a result the news channel most trusted in the US is not Fox News, Bloomberg, MSNBC, or even PBS but the 'heavily regulated' BBC.

Myrie quotes the American Fairness Doctrine that insists broadcasters must use their licences to serve the community as a whole. "Broadcasters must provide adequate coverage of public issues and ensure coverage fairly represents opposing views," the doctrine states. The Fairness Doctrine was abolished by President Reagan 40 years ago.

Finally, a long look at what is to be done about false information and conspiracy theories that appear to be tearing societies apart and undermining democratic political systems, from Canadian media consultant and expert on media economics Ken Goldstein. You cannot understand the impact of misinformation, Goldstein argues, without realising that the current situation is not only the result of the addition of new media of all types but the result of the subtraction of old media that once served as a common core for information about public affairs. The collapse of the traditional media model, for newspapers in particular, with the exception of major players such as the *New York Times*, the *Washington Post* and *The Guardian*, 'has created a vacuum that now is being filled by purveyors of alternative facts'.

Goldstein, after a decade when debate has swirled around getting Google or Facebook to compensate traditional media or looking again at copyright issues, or tax credits for traditional media, believes there is no single solution. Deal with the specifics, some of which have merit, but a broader approach is necessary. Society needs to spend more time on where the industry might be in five to ten years, which possible future would be best for public policy goals and what would be the best combination of corporate structures and public intervention to achieve such a benign outcome. "There is an urgent question that needs an answer: How will a modern democracy function if we all have less in common?" Ken Goldstein asks.

Artificial intelligence and extremist content: a recipe for insurgency

An army marches on its stomach, said Napoleon. What fuelled insurrectionists in Washington DC on January 6, 2021, was an off-menu medley of misinformation, online tactical coordination and holiday rental bookings. The would-be revolutionaries were unfettered by reason, regulators or tech platforms. Though few in absolute numbers, they grew their traction by algorithmic amplification in social media. To combat their misinformation, taking down accounts has worked, but next generation AI technologies raise new threats. To borrow a Trumpism, if you don't fight like hell, civil society could soon again be at risk, says Said Business School's Alex Connock

Let's start with a quiz question: what kind of organisation would you expect to have a security unit like this under their control? "We have an investigation team called the User Knowledge Operations Team… comprised of former law enforcement officials, people in cybersecurity, people from the US Government and around the world. Basically what happens when people post information publicly, that they're intending to join a hate group rally or something they have an intention that we think is nefarious, we will investigate. There are a few that are places where neo-Nazis congregate online and we do monitor those forums."[1]

We accept that professional security watchers – say the NSA or FBI – would have units like that. They design AI systems to proactively trawl social media and other platforms and identify risky outliers – people far outside the statistical norm of who would normally buy peroxide in bulk, for instance, or transatlantic flyers without any luggage. Agencies look ahead to potential flashpoints and seek to thwart bad actors. But this isn't their team.

We are equally aware major hardware companies like Apple or Facebook would also employ ex-national security people to handle their own rapidly-growing cyber risks and protect their IP. To understand the dangers we have only to read Nicole Perlroth's extraordinary 2021 book *This is How They Tell me the World Ends*, exposing the global, criminal and geopolitical cyber war at escalating scale for countries, corporations and now individuals[2]. Need an iPhone hack to crack activist correspondence with local journalists?[3] A teenager could sell you one for $100,000 in a Buenos Aires coffee shop. But this isn't a hardware company's team either.

The answer? A zeitgeisty, new-economy rental site, provider of party homes from Miami to Amsterdam does this kind of proactive security analysis too. The 'User Knowledge Ops Team' was described by Brian Chesky, CEO of the funky Airbnb. The work of that unit has been serious and ongoing; as it turned out, proving pivotal to the security of the free world. Airbnb was as alert for the arrival of potential revolutionaries in Washington DC this January as the FBI. "So in 2017, that summer, we started hearing that on forums, neo-Nazi forums, neo-Nazis were talking about booking Airbnbs in Charlottesville, Virginia, for the... Unite the Right rally. So we went to law enforcement. And we ban anyone that we could find that was… a neo-Nazi…we didn't just make a new policy or new decision on January 6 in the wake of the Capitol insurrection we've been doing this actually for five years."

Airbnb and insurrection

When national security depends on a millennial holiday rentals site and the real stupidity of the crowd combines with the scaled-up sophistication of Artificial Intelligence, democracy is at risk.

Airbnb's best efforts notwithstanding, Washington's Capitol complex was invaded on January 6, 2021, after then President Donald Trump made repeated, extensive and unproven claims of election rigging. He said to a rally of supporters: "If you don't fight like hell, you're not going to have a country anymore."[4] The crowd *did* fight like hell. Like many of history's pivotal mobs, it was both opportunistic and well-planned. The mob aimed to reverse Trump's defeat in the 2020 US presidential election by thwarting the joint congressional session to ratify the Biden victory. Such was the violent insurrection that five people died[5] (including police officer 42-year-old Brian Sicknick) and almost 150 were injured.

Social media played a role in the inspiration of the attack – with militia groups coordinating online and deploying quasi-military tactics. At least 12 of the people charged[6] around the insurrection were overt followers of the QAnon conspiracy movement, using the full suite of social tools from Instagram to Telegram. Conspiracy charges were eventually brought against members of two far-Right groups: the nationalist Proud Boys (four charged by February, and 11 in total arrested) and the Oath Keepers militia (five arrested.) Other groups represented included the Three Percenters and white supremacists Patriot Front. But Cynthia Miller-Idriss from American University's Extremism Research Lab said (to the *New York Times*): "The majority appear to be individuals who are not card-carrying members."

Who influenced the mob?

Amongst influencers, there is leverage of scale. In e-commerce, a single influencer such as Kylie Jenner with 223 million followers can command $986,000 per post.[7] From Obama's 2012 election onwards what has worked in social marketing has also worked in politics – and now in conspiracy marketing. A study on Twitter published in the AAAS journal Science by Nir Grinberg and others[8] (January 2019) found that in the 2016 election whilst 'fake news accounted for nearly six per cent of all news consumption', it was heavily concentrated in a surprisingly small number of accounts. "Only one per cent of users," the report said, "were exposed to 80 per cent of fake news, and 0.1 per cent of users were responsible for sharing 80 per cent of fake news." Fast forward to January 2021 and the few thousand people who wanted to take over American democracy may not have been indicative of a concomitant level of actual support.

The algorithmic focus of the social networks employed pushed supportive content disproportionately to the fore and that tendency of the recommendation engines to amplify is what continues to drive the threat. Misinformation does not need to be universally accessed, or even that widely propagated, to gain traction. It is created by a limited number of players and viewed by a limited number of players, but among them are the few prepared to act on it.

The same logic can be played in reverse – and has been. Twitter suspended over 70,000 QAnon related accounts[9] on January 11, 2021, after the storming of the US Capitol. Taking out just one player from the movement can have a dramatic influence on the network effect. Of the 350 insurrectionists charged by March 2021, according to NPR's investigations team,[10] 12 per cent said they were specifically inspired by Donald Trump. "If Trump tells us to storm the f***in capital Ima do that then!" one defendant wrote.[11] When Trump's account was closed, Zignal Labs charted a 73 per cent decline of hate speech on Twitter after the removal of one (his) single account.[12] The research firm reported in January 2021 that discussion of 'election fraud' dropped 72 per cent from 2.5 million mentions on social media platforms to 688,000. Hashtag #FightForTrump fell by 95.5 percent, and #HoldTheLine 94.3 percent (according to *The Hill*, January 2021.)

From the Capitol to the anti-vaxxers

Similarly, albeit with different content from the conspiracy suite, the Centre for Countering Digital Hate (CCDH) found two thirds of anti-vaccine content shared on Twitter and Facebook was derived from just 12 people.[13] These included Robert F Kennedy Jr, son of the former US Attorney-General Robert Kennedy. In a line much quoted on radical memes, he said, in similar language to Trump: "We are the happy few, the band of brothers and sisters. We know what our job is in this life. We know that we're part of this battle. We have to fight and we have to die with our boots on if necessary."[14]

Nonetheless, the disinformation survives, aided by the impressive versatility of conspiracy thinking. Undaunted by the inconvenient truths of its previous predictions not panning out – for instance, the failure of Trump to pull the election out of the bag at the eleventh hour, or the lack of proof for a global, elite-led child abuse network from the entirely innocent Comet Ping Pong pizza restaurant in Washington's Chevy Chase neighbourhood – QAnon followers settled upon March 4 as a new date[15] for 'the storm', on which Trump would seize power from President Biden. Department for Homeland Security Officials sent warnings to police nationwide that fanatics had 'discussed plans to take control of the US Capitol and remove Democratic lawmakers'.[16] When that didn't pan out, some QAnon followers on Telegram posited that the coup had indeed happened – and that Bill Gates and others in fact had been arrested, executed and cloned.[17] Others still moved the date back: "It will be much much sooner than in four years. We are talking about days (weeks max)."

How rumours spread

Like a virus jumping hosts, the conspiracy also hops platforms to survive. The *New York Times* reported (March 25, 2021) after *Twitter* suspended Steve Bannon's account in November 2020, on the flimsy grounds that the former Trump adviser had proposed on his War Room podcast that several officials be beheaded[18] and their heads placed 'on pikes' on two corners of the White House like in 'the old times of Tudor England', Bannon maintained large audiences via Apple and Google podcast services. On March 28, 2021, Bannon was still available in the Google Podcasts library.[19] The report cited 25 white supremacists and pro-Nazi podcasts serving up conspiracies that were still available on Google podcasts: "This is a hit on America," he said. "They steal the election, they give us the pandemic and here comes open borders. This is all part of the globalist thing." Even extreme-right-wing icon Alex Jones, his channel long-deleted from Google-owned YouTube, still kept his listing on Google Podcasts on March 26, 2021, for his relentless diatribe.[20] "We've highlighted the fact that liberals are liars and they know it. Most of them are ugly people also, just as a side note."

Professor Rasmus Kleis Nielsen of the Reuters institute for the Study of Journalism at Oxford University, outlined the overall risk in a March 22, 2021, presentation at the BBC Trust in News Conference.

"We are in the middle of a complex information disorder where credible, trustworthy news and other kinds of information competes with various kinds of false and misleading material. This contributes to confusion and many other problems and at worst poses the risk of physical harm or undermining the integrity of elections."[21]

Are algorithms neutral?

The abilities of artificial intelligence to both sense the environment at scale and drive engagement through the provision of targeted services to individuals will most likely be a defining dynamic of the 2020s across all industries, politics, medicine, education and the battlefield. Recommendation and machine learning are the reason why a listing for your song on *Spotify Discovery Weekly c*an be worth a six-figure sum; or even the reason why the British Army is pivoting from tanks to AI-driven drones in its 2021 Defence Command Paper.[22] A taxi app can see whether your phone battery is low when you log in and price a quick pick-up at a premium. A bank can correlate the number of times you hit the backspace when filling in a loan form with the likelihood you would eventually pay it back. And a Harvard Business School study (JM Logg et al, 2018) on algorithm appreciation showed: "Lay people adhere *more* to advice when they think it comes from an algorithm than from a person."[23]

There is certainly a movement amongst US legislators – some of whom, like Alexandria Ocasio-Cortez, have said (January 13, 2021[24]) they perceive themselves to have had a near-death experience at the hands of the rioters – to address, at source, both the power of the algorithm over hate speech and the platforms that disseminate it. "You failed to meaningfully change after your platform has played a role in fomenting insurrection and abetting the spread of the virus and trampling American civil liberties,"[25] said the Democratic representative Frank Pallone, chair of the Energy and Commerce Committee. He was speaking to three of tech's most powerful players – Facebook's Mark Zuckerberg, Google's Sundar Pichai and Twitter's part-time boss Jack Dorsey, who were testifying in a six-hour hearing to two committees of the House of Representatives on social media's role in promoting extremism and misinformation, on March 25, 2021.

"The Capitol Hill attack started and was nourished on your platforms. Your business model itself has become the problem and the time for self-regulation is over. It's time we legislate to hold you accountable," said Pallone.[26] Emphasising the idea of dangerous algorithms that organically feed their own demand, California Democrat Doris Matsui said: "Big tech is handing our children a lit cigarette, and they become hooked for life."[27]

Legislation proposed in March 2021 to protect Americans from dangerous algorithms included an online Consumer Protection Act, and amendments to section 230 of the Communications Decency Act, which (pivotally to their business model) shields liability for social media companies. Such new legislation, if passed, could introduce liability for platforms if their algorithms amplified misinformation that drives violence. Michael Doyle, a Pennsylvania Democrat, said: "Time after time you are picking engagement and profit over the health and safety of your users, our nation and our democracy… We will legislate to stop this. The stakes are simply too high."[28] Zuckerberg pointed out Facebook has global fact- checking, with multi-language teams in over 80 countries.[29] He batted back suggestions that Facebook was responsible for the riots through a permissive environment for misinformation, hate speech and online extremism. "The responsibility here lies with the people who took the actions to break the law and… also the people who spread that content, including the [former] President [Donald Trump], but others as well."[30] During the session, only one of the three executives accepted any partial responsibility for the social media that fuelled the insurrection on January 6: Twitter's Jack Dorsey. He said he will not ban racist hashtags, because of their contextual nuance.[31] That is indeed a common problem in the use of natural language processing, which is imperfect at spotting sarcasm,[32] for instance. "A lot of these hashtags contain counter speech," Dorsey said. Or there could be posts which were actually refuting the racism the hashtags initiated, that might get taken out. Meanwhile Zuckerberg similarly said hate speech policies at Facebook are 'nuanced' and they have an obligation to protect free speech. He also said claims Facebook's advertising-driven business model amplified provocative and polarising speech were 'not accurate,' adding: "I believe that the division we see today is primarily the result of a political and media environment that drives Americans apart."[33] That balance of correlation vs. causality will again define the era of AI engines designed to filter and differentiate the two dynamics at epic scale – in everything from hair care product purchases to military confrontation and the relationship between pollution and global warming.

Zuckerberg spoke positively about some reform to Section 230, a law that exempts platforms from legal responsibility for what is posted by users. Meanwhile, Dorsey put forward his plan of allowing for an open protocol shared by tech platforms to create more transparency surrounding how content is moderated. He also said Twitter would like to open its moderation operations up to outside researchers for review. Predictably, activists slated what they saw as the CEOs' failure to take overall responsibility. "Mr Zuckerberg and the other tech CEOs couldn't even muster a 'yes' or 'no' to the simple question of whether they're responsible for how their platforms amplified disinformation that fuelled the insurrection,"[34] said Fadi Quran, the campaign director at Avaaz and member of activism group, the self-styled Real Facebook Oversight Board (quoted in *The Guardian*, 25 March.)

AI transparency (or the lack of it)

At the core of the matter, Congressional leaders were looking for more transparency and auditing of what they called the platforms' 'secretive algorithms'. That comes down to the who, and the why.

Clarity could derive from exploring 'who' is writing the code – who's doing the AI and who's good at it. The Stanford University Artificial Intelligence Index Report, 2021[35] shows AI has a diversity challenge: "In 2019, 45 per cent of new US resident AI PhD graduates were white – by comparison, 2.4 per cent were African American and 3.2 per cent were Hispanic." It also describes how China has for the first time overtaken the US in AI journal citations, as well as the total number of journal publications.

Alternatively, transparency could lie in the 'why' – the objectives algorithms are designed to achieve. When the congressional committee members suggested to Zuckerberg he might expose Facebook's algorithms to scrutiny he demurred, on privacy grounds, adding that it was an 'important area of study'.[36] Jack Dorsey agreed 'giving people more choice' about algorithms that served them up content was vital in the fight against misinformation. The lack of transparency in AI goes far beyond social platforms and will be a defining issue in the 2020s. Much of AI is already so 'black box' that even its creators don't know what is driving the outcomes. So-called 'unsupervised learning' techniques will produce answers without anyone having the means of discovering how those answers have been arrived at.

What's coming next?

The US National Security Commission on Artificial Intelligence report[37], released in February 2021 is an extraordinary must-read, for its clear-minded statement of the existential threat of AI – not as a driver of social misinformation around the Capitol riot, but as an existential threat to the liberty of individuals as a whole. This is partly because of the adoption of AI technologies that have been developed in the marketing industry (profiling, tracking, retargeting) but now exploited for different purposes in wider society, potentially dystopian ones. As the report states: "Ad-tech will become Natsec-tech."

The US Government 'still operates at human speed, not machine speed', in a kind of technical version of the long delay in calling the National Guard into the Capitol despite streamed real-time evidence of a pitch invasion, or the scepticism many in Congress still express towards enhanced security. Representative Matt Gaetz from Florida dismissed General Russel Honoré's proposed security upgrades in the wake of the Capitol attack in the following politicised terms: "Pelosi hired a bigot to hunt MAGA."[38] (February 2021)

The report predicts that adversaries, tooled up with AI, will use misinformation campaigns not just to send one powerful if generalised message to one million people (like, say Trump did or indeed many 20th century propagandists). The new

AI tools will send a million individualised messages – each configured on the basis of a detailed understanding of targeted individual's digital life, emotional state, and social network. In other words; the Cambridge Analytica-powered psychographic approach of the US 2016 election would be scaled out, but across more tools, with far better information, in real time, and potentially directly powered by foreign countries, rather than via proxy. The report adds:

"Most concerning is the prospect that adversaries will use AI to create weapons of mass influence to use as leverage during future wars, in which every citizen and organization becomes a potential target."

New York University's Professor Scott Galloway summarised the March 2021 Congressional appearance by the leaders of Facebook, Google and Twitter like this: "Wouldn't you love it if one of them got up and said: 'So okay, so this is what we do… we have determined that the most damaging… content actually creates engagement because our species is really flawed'."[39]

The degree of that flaw, and the degree to which actors at state, corporate, insurgent group and individual level exploit it, will be a theme of the 2020s, and a continuing issue for tech companies. As Brian Chesky of AirBnB puts it: "I think there is a reckoning that has occurred. And I think people are coming around to the idea that the path we've been on is unsustainable. And so having talked to most tech leaders. I think most of them are coming around, but… some are kind of in my mind may be dragging their feet."

Notes

[1] Air BnB Has a Hate Problem Too. Sway Podcast, New York Times, March 18 2021. https://www.nytimes.com/2021/03/18/opinion/sway-kara-swisher-brian-chesky.html

[2] This Is How They Tell Me the World Ends. Nicole Perlroth, published 18 February 2021.

[3] https://www.newyorker.com/magazine/2021/02/08/the-next-cyberattack-is-already-under-way

[4] https://www.npr.org/2021/02/10/966396848/read-trumps-jan-6-speech-a-key-part-of-impeachment-trial?t=1616953584097

[5] https://www.theguardian.com/us-news/2021/jan/08/capitol-attack-police-officer-five-deaths

[6] https://www.nytimes.com/interactive/2021/02/04/us/capitol-arrests.html

[7] https://www.hopperhq.com/blog/instagram-rich-list/

[8] https://science.sciencemag.org/content/363/6425/374.abstract

[9] https://www.theguardian.com/technology/2021/jan/12/twitter-suspends-70000-accounts-sharing-qanon-content

[10] https://www.wbur.org/npr/965472049/the-capitol-siege-the-arrested-and-their-stories

[11] https://www.npr.org/2021/02/09/965472049/the-capitol-siege-the-arrested-and-their-stories

[12] https://thehill.com/policy/technology/534587-internet-misinformation-dropped-73-percent-following-trumps-suspension-from

[13] https://inews.co.uk/news/technology/two-thirds-anti-vaxx-social-media-content-linked-just-12-people-926364

[14] https://childrenshealthdefense.org/news/the-truth-about-vaccines-2020-vaccine-roundtable-part-2-video-and-transcript/

[15] https://www.bbc.co.uk/news/blogs-trending-56260345

[16] https://www.nbcnews.com/news/us-news/extremists-discussed-plans-remove-democratic-lawmakers-fbi-homeland-security-bulletin-n1259467

[17] https://www.deccanherald.com/international/another-qanon-deadline-passes-with-little-fanfare-958271.html

[18] https://www.theguardian.com/us-news/2020/nov/06/steve-bannon-banned-by-twitter-for-calling-for-fauci-beheading

[19] https://podcasts.google.com/feed/aHR0cHM6Ly9saXN0ZW4ud2Fycm9vbS5vcmcvZmVlZC54bWw=

[20] Alex Jones Show Podcast, Google Podcasts. Accessed 27 March 2021. https://podcasts.google.com/feed/aHR0cHM6Ly9yc3MuZ2NubGl2ZS5jb20vYWxleEpvbmVzL2ZlZWQueG1s

[21] https://reutersinstitute.politics.ox.ac.uk/risj-review/how-evidence-can-help-us-fight-against-covid-19-misinformation

[22] https://rusi.org/commentary/requiring-perfect-alignment-uk-2021-defence-command-paper

[23] https://www.hbs.edu/ris/Publication%20Files/17-086_610956b6-7d91-4337-90cc-5bb5245316a8.pdf

[24] https://www.theguardian.com/us-news/2021/jan/13/alexandria-ocasio-cortez-aoc-capitol-attack-instagram-live-video

[25] https://www.irishtimes.com/business/technology/tech-bosses-grilled-over-capitol-riots-and-hate-speech-by-us-congress-1.4520759

[26] https://www.reuters.com/article/us-usa-congress-tech/big-tech-ceos-told-time-for-self-regulation-is-over-by-u-s-lawmakers-idUSKBN2BH1B0

[27] https://www.morningstar.com/news/dow-jones/2021032511651/big-tech-draws-comparison-to-big-tobacco

[28] https://www.post-gazette.com/news/politics-nation/2021/03/25/Mike-Doyle-Big-Tech-CEOs-Facebook-Twitter-Google-YouTube-Instagram-disinformation-social-media-house/stories/202103250172

[29] https://www.bbc.co.uk/news/technology-56523378

[30] https://www.ft.com/content/39a699fc-1730-4a5d-b43e-634ebe189d79

[31] https://finance.yahoo.com/video/twitter-ceo-dorsey-takes-blame-180847426.html

[32] https://www.theatlantic.com/technology/archive/2015/01/why-cant-robots-understand-sarcasm/384714/

[33] https://www.rev.com/blog/transcripts/mark-zuckerberg-opening-statement-transcript-house-hearing-on-misinformation

[34] https://www.irishtimes.com/business/technology/tech-bosses-grilled-over-capitol-riots-and-hate-speech-by-us-congress-1.4520759

[35] https://aiindex.stanford.edu/report/

[36] https://www.washingtonpost.com/technology/2021/03/25/facebook-google-twitter-house-hearing-live-updates/

[37] https://www.nscai.gov

[38] https://www.newsweek.com/matt-gaetz-leads-gop-charge-against-bigot-russel-honore-head-capitol-security-review-1573362

[39] https://podcasts.apple.com/us/podcast/microsoft-discord-goldman-sachs-junior-bankers-listener/id1073226719?i=1000514490768

About the contributor

Dr Alex Connock is Fellow in Management Practice (Marketing) at Said Business School, Oxford University, and co-director of the Oxford Diploma in Artificial Intelligence for Business. He is currently writing a book on '*Media Management and Artificial Intelligence*' due for publication by Routledge in 2022.

'Enemies of the People?' Will populism be the death of impartial journalism?

Across the world, populist governments have been bad news for good journalism – demanding and rewarding slavish obedience, suppressing independent reporting where they can, denouncing it as 'fake news' where they cannot. Richard Tait asks where the UK's current experiment in populist government will leave the British tradition of impartial broadcast journalism

It is not hard to find evidence around the world of the toxic effect of the rise of populism on good journalism – journalism which sees an important part of its role as holding power to account in the belief that, in the words of *Washington Post*'s slogan, 'Democracy Dies in Darkness'. In at least two EU countries, good journalism is fighting for its life – in Hungary the government has forced most media ownership into the hands of its friends, 'achieving a degree of media control unprecedented in an EU member state' (IPI, 2019); in Poland the government is nationalising independent media companies; in both countries public service broadcasting has reverted to the state control of the communist era (MFFR, 2021).

The current UK Government does not need to adopt the tactics of Fidesz or the Law and Justice party to make sure its friends are in charge of most of the national press – they already are. The Eurosceptic titles which control 80 per cent of the national newspaper market played a decisive role in the 2016 EU Referendum result, the failure of the May Government and the election of Boris Johnson's populist administration which achieved the form of Brexit they favoured. In Britain, the real media battleground for a populist government wanting to consolidate its grip on the media is broadcasting. In the UK, as in most countries, television news is the populist voter's news media of choice (Fletcher, 2019) and broadcasting is still by far the most trusted source of accurate and impartial news, with the BBC just ahead of ITV News and Channel 4. The BBC's Trust score of 64 per cent is twice that of the *Daily Telegraph* and *Daily Mail* and four times that of *The Sun* (Reuters, 2020).

Public service broadcasting, with its commitments to accurate and impartial journalism, falls only too clearly into the populist hitlist of obstacles to be rubbished and removed. Like an independent judiciary, an unpoliticised civil service, even an effective parliament, public service broadcasters are widely portrayed as part of a corrupt 'elite' conspiring to thwart 'the will of the people' (Holtz-Bacha, 2021).

'Undermining of the BBC'

The Government's attacks on the BBC's funding and Channel 4's licence off the back of a decisive election victory were notable not only for the level of threat (Groves, Revoir, 2020) but also for their total disregard for any of the review processes which are meant to protect the broadcasters from continuous interference and bullying. The BBC had recently been through an exhaustive charter review which had confirmed the licence fee and rejected decriminalisation; Channel 4's status, too, had recently been reviewed and settled. This did not stop the Government re-opening the same issues and announcing boycotts of programmes which had displeased it. The similarities with Donald Trump's tactics in the US, and the discovery of a 2004 blog from the New Frontiers Foundation, where Dominic Cummings was director, arguing for the 'undermining of the BBC' and the creation of a Fox News equivalent in the UK suggested a project straight out of the classic populist play book (Mason, 2020).

The pandemic brought a (temporary) pause to much of this. The period of the pandemic demonstrated the huge value and impact of trusted public service broadcast journalism, providing a unique national platform for key announcements and briefings as well as big audiences for news bulletins and current affairs which helped audiences distinguish between accurate and impartial reporting of the key issues and the horrible mélange of dangerous, misleading nonsense all over the social media platforms (Lawson, 2020). The bulletins tracked the success of the NHS vaccination programme nightly, with the good news of the UK's exceptional progress in terms of numbers vaccinated. An Opinium poll in April found 'incredibly strong' approval of Government handling of the vaccination programme at 72 per cent (Opinium, 2021). Together with the reductions in Covid cases and deaths, also reported nightly, the figures created the sense of the worst being over – a 'vaccine bounce' which neutralised opposition criticisms of Boris Johnson's earlier handling of the crisis and helped all three governing parties in London, Cardiff and Edinburgh in the May 6 elections.

'Detached from a lot of viewers'?

However, as the pandemic fades, Boris Johnson seems to be returning to his previous hostility to the BBC – he told the 1922 committee of Tory MPs at its March 23 meeting where he attributed the success of the vaccine programme to 'greed' that the BBC was 'detached from a lot of viewers' and adding that its management should 'move more in line' with the Government's point of view

(Pickard, 2021). The BBC faces a number of threats – the most immediate is that its reputation is 'undermined' in the same way as Donald Trump has destroyed many Americans' trust in much broadcast news (Mangan, 2018). At the heart of this are arguments over impartiality. The complaints were not just coming from the politicians – the BBC's 2019 Annual Plan had admitted 'perceptions of BBC impartiality have weakened' (BBC, 2019).

In March 2020 the BBC's new director-general, Tim Davie, the corporation's most experienced crisis manager, having survived the Ross/Brand scandal as director of audio and music and run the BBC very effectively as acting DG in 2012 after George Entwistle's resignation, rightly made impartiality his first priority (Davie, 2020). The BBC was making too many mistakes in this area – there were rows over Andrew Neil's criticism of Boris Johnson's refusal to be interviewed ahead of the general election (Badshah, 2019), and Emily Maitlis telling *Newsnight* viewers there was no argument over Dominic Cummings' drive north – 'he broke the rules' (BBC, 2020a). The Government was outraged at the time but ministers, in one of those populist U-turns George Orwell described so prophetically in *1984*, now attack Cummings' trip north as evidence of his unreliability in their arguments with him over how well Johnson dealt with Covid last year (Cecil, Murphy, 2021). Two *BBC Breakfast* presenters, Dan Walker and Naga Munchetty, got in a damaging tangle while musing live whether the President of the United States was a racist (BBC News, 2019). And then there was coming to terms with ensuring impartiality and accuracy on social media.

It's only a tweet

As Gary Gibbon, the political editor of Channel 4 News, has pointed out, the political parties (and their media allies) trawl the social media accounts of journalists for 'paint trails' – checking posts, tweets and likes for evidence of bias (Gibbon, 2020: 63). BBC journalists' output on social media is often not subject to the same careful editing as a news bulletin item or a current affairs investigation – but once out there, it represents the BBC's view and has to be judged by the same rigorous editorial standards of accuracy and impartiality as the rest of the BBC's output. 'It's only a tweet' does not quite cut it as an excuse for mistakes and giving the impression of partiality. The BBC acted on a report by Richard Sambrook, my former Cardiff University colleague, and tightened up the guidelines. And, as in the aftermath of the Hutton debacle of 2004, the BBC has turned to a comprehensive training exercise – to ensure all its staff, long established or recent recruits, really understand what accuracy and impartiality mean for the BBC's output (BBC, 2020b).

But on the central issue of political impartiality, Davie has defended the BBC's performance: "Overall, I am very proud of the BBC. Its record on impartiality is exceptional" (DCMS Committee, 2020b). The BBC's problem is far deeper than a few presenters going off-piste, serious though that is: Boris Johnson's Government thinks its journalism has an institutional left-wing bias. For many years this view has been enthusiastically supported and promoted by the majority of the national newspapers and right-wing think tanks (Barwise, York, 2020: 123-160). Now the UK has a populist government with an unassailable majority which believes the BBC should 'move more in line' with the Government's point of view. But before accepting these assertions it is worth analysing the evidence for and against the proposition that the BBC is institutionally biased.

The world according to Ofcom

The first place to look for evidence is the regulator. Since 2017 Ofcom has been the final arbiter of the impartiality and accuracy of BBC journalism. It has published two reviews of BBC journalism in the last couple of years. In October 2019 it found BBC journalism was seen as trusted and accurate by 71 per cent of regular viewers. Although the impartiality rating was lower at 59 per cent, Ofcom thought that reflected the greater polarisation of the audience and viewers' dislike of 'false equivalence' between opposing views of unequal factual weight. It also found some viewers were being influenced by media attacks on the BBC's journalism. Ofcom pointed out that since 2017 it had not found any BBC journalism in breach of impartiality. It had analysed 300 complaints about BBC impartiality and found none of them justified. It had assessed 'an extensive amount of content' on Radio 4's coverage of Brexit as part of a complaint the BBC was biased against the UK leaving the EU – it rejected the complaints, saying 'the content did not warrant further investigation (Ofcom, 2019: 11-18)

In November 2020, Ofcom's most recent annual report on the BBC found virtually the same levels of audience ratings for accuracy, trust and impartiality. It repeated its advice to the BBC to be bolder in its journalism and suggested ways it could improve its performance but again reported no evidence the BBC was in breach of its broadcast standards – it had considered 230 complaints as the final court of appeal and found none of them justified (Ofcom, 2020a:6). In many ways, Ofcom's findings were quite similar to those of the rounds of independent impartiality reviews which the BBC governors and then the BBC Trust commissioned between 2004 and 2016 which had used academic content analysis (from universities such as Loughborough and Cardiff) and external assessors, or panels of assessors, with expertise in areas such as business, science, diplomacy, statistics to assess the BBC's coverage of controversial areas. They also found the BBC's journalism was far from perfect and needed to be sharper and better informed, but it largely succeeded in being impartial. And Ofcom's findings that audiences really appreciated accuracy, trust and impartiality in broadcast journalism and thought the BBC needed to try harder rather than give up, echoed earlier research into attitudes to impartiality (Tait, 2020: 242-3).

A brief history of News-watch

So what is the evidence to support the widely held assertion among conservative politicians that the BBC is biased? The simple answer appears to be... David Keighley. I knew David Keighley as an affable BBC PR in the 1980s. He went on to be TV-am's director of public affairs and then a media consultant. In 1999, Lord Pearson of Rannoch, the Eurosceptic Conservative peer who was later the leader of UKIP, asked him 'can you help us and perhaps put the spotlight on in a way that has never been done before what is going on at the BBC, why they are so biased' (Keighley, 2017).

For the last 20 years, first with Minotaur Media Monitoring and now with News-watch, Keighley and his business partner Kathy Gyngell, a former television producer, have produced around 40 reports on BBC journalism which certainly meet the original brief, denouncing the BBC's journalism as hopelessly biased (News-watch, 2021). Whether they merit the often enthusiastic publicity and credibility which they have been given by politicians and conservative newspapers is perhaps more open for debate.

There are a reasons to be cautious. First, their own political views are scarcely mainstream. Keighley is on the editorial board of *The Conservative Woman*, a political website where Kathy Gyngell is editor. *The Conservative Woman* is currently some way to the right of the Government – attacking it for 'vaccine fascism' (Gyngell, 2021a) appealing to 'every Conservative' to vote for Laurence Fox, the Reclaim Party candidate in the May 6 London mayoral election, rather than the official Conservative candidate Shaun Bailey (Gyngell, 2021b); denouncing the Business Secretary, Kwasi Kwarteng, for his 'Green ideology' and support for veganism (Keighley, 2021).

And the research appears to be funded as well as commissioned by those who have already made up their minds about the BBC's journalism – with £210,000 coming from 2013 to 2018 from the Institute for Policy Research, a major funder of right-wing and centre-right think tanks often hostile to the BBC (Desmog, 2020). Patrick Barwise and Peter York, in their recent analysis of the BBC's critics, place News-watch firmly in the company of the free-market think tanks in and around 55 Tufton Street, London SW1, who have as their common characteristics Euroscepticism and hostility to the BBC (Barwise, York, 2020:105-125). They are critical of News-watch's credentials and lack of transparency over its methodology: 'we think the real mission of News-watch is to generate a limitless stream of material to be used in Eurosceptic 'hit jobs' on the BBC's coverage of the EU and Brexit' (Barwise, York, 2020: 147).

'Meet the new boss'

But when the BBC's new chairman, Richard Sharp, appeared before the House of Commons DCMS committee for his pre-appointment hearing in January 2021, he gave little support to the News-watch view of the BBC. He told the committee: 'I am considered to be a Brexiteer' – but said the BBC's Brexit coverage had been impartial. He did feel *Question Time* had had more Remainers than Brexiteers – but 'in terms of the breadth of the coverage, I thought it was incredibly balanced in a highly toxic environment that was extremely polarised' (DCMS, 2021: 4). He opposed decriminalisation of the licence free and thought public service broadcasting 'was a precious thing for the world', leading the chair of the committee, Julian Knight, to comment: 'It is quite interesting: no to decriminalisation, and you think the BBC's Brexit coverage was not biased in any way. So it feels to me like it is meet the new boss, the same as the old boss, in that respect' (DCMS, 2021: 21).

Richard Sharp's appointment had come after some fevered speculation last autumn that Boris Johnson was going to appoint Lord Moore, the former *Daily Telegraph* editor, with controversial views on race, gay marriage and Muslim immigration, as 'a strong chairman who will hold he BBC to account' (Heffer, 2020). Populist governments around the world have been putting their supporters on to the boards of public broadcasters to curb their journalism (Economist, 2021). This looked, fairly or unfairly, like a pretty crude power grab. Moore's mooted candidature did not survive Julian Knight saying Moore's conviction in 2010 for failing to pay for his TV licence (as a protest against the BBC not sacking Jonathan Ross) put him 'completely beyond the pale' (Siddique, 2020).

Richard Sharp was a less controversial appointment in that respect. He had enjoyed a very successful career at Goldman Sachs and is a friend of the Chancellor, Rishi Sunak – but then the same was true of Gavyn Davies who became BBC chair in 2001 after a very successful career at Goldman Sachs and was a friend of the then Chancellor, Gordon Brown. And Gavyn Davies had defended the BBC against the Government, resigning in 2004 after a huge row with No. 10 over Andrew Gilligan's report on weapons of mass destruction (Davies, 2004).

Standing up for the BBC

The truth about the chair of the BBC is it is a great honour and a huge responsibility – and in my experience, working for or with quite a few of them, by the time they get appointed they have achieved a lot in their lives and the epithet 'government poodle' is not one they need or want to add to their CV. To be a good chair of the BBC you have to challenge the organisation to improve its performance but also stand up for its independence, and that inevitably means some friction with the government of the day. I do not think it is a coincidence only one BBC chair over the last three decades has served a second term. It is hard to avoid the conclusion one reason is that the government of the day is *always* looking, to some extent, for a chair 'more in line' with the Government's thinking – and is usually disappointed.

That one exception to that rule was Marmaduke Hussey, who served for ten years and still divides opinions. The official historian of the BBC calls him 'resolute and charismatic' – but also says he was appointed in 1986 with a brief from the government to fire the director general and 'sort it [the BBC] out' (Seaton, 2015: 330). Hussey was reappointed in 1991 at a time when the Conservative government, shaken by the fall of Mrs Thatcher, was apparently 'locking politically correct appointees into quangos in case Labour won the election' (Horrie, Clarke (1994:199). To his three DGs Hussey seems to have been, or become, a nightmare – he fired Alasdair Milne, who found him duplicitous and 'terrible' (Milne, 1988: 198-202); pushed out Michael Checkland, who responded that Hussey was too old and out of touch, thinking FM meant 'fuzzy monsters' (Horrie, Clarke, 1994: 229-30); and tried (and failed) to fire John Birt, who said the arrival of Christopher Bland as Hussey's successor was the beginning of his happiest period at the BBC (Birt, 2002: 424).

Here come the culture wars

In the short term, the new chair and DG will have to steer the BBC through the serious crisis for the BBC's journalistic reputation provoked by Lord Dyson's report and prepare for the mid-term charter review. But there are other difficult editorial challenges ahead. As the political (though perhaps not the economic) arguments over Brexit begin to fade, the BBC will need to pay more attention to where it stands in reporting the 'culture wars' with due impartiality. This is already proving a very divisive area (Eatwell, Goodwin 2018: 44-86). Populism in many parts of the world has taken issues of gender, race, identity and history and weaponised them. Boris Johnson's Government has taken very clear positions on all of these and more – statues, flags, 'no platforming' at university. The Labour Party seems to be having an anguished internal debate about where it stands in these areas, and whether, given its supporters seem so divided over what they think (Mattinson, 2021:128-133) it really wants to fight on this battleground at all (Blair, 2021). And the BBC has come under attack from its critics for bias here as well – in being hopelessly 'woke' – with predictable and partisan positions.

A couple of fascinating panel events, run by *Tortoise* (Harding, 2021) and *ReNews* (ReNews, 2021), analysed the increasingly divisive and often toxic impact of these issues in newsrooms, particularly among younger staff, in the US and UK. Some newspapers also seemed under pressure to take sides because of their growing dependence on subscribers who themselves had very strong views in one direction or other. In the *ReNews* session, the BBC's director of news, Fran Unsworth, stressed the BBC was not going down that road – the universal licence fee brought with it a commitment to rigorous impartiality in this area: "If everybody pays then everybody has a right to see their views, their opinions, their beliefs reflected in our output… one person's social action is not the same as another person's social action, so it is our job as editors to really explain to our journalists what their role is. It isn't to make everyone think the same, because nobody can think the same. It is to help the public and audiences live with their inevitable differences' (ReNews, 2021).

The end of impartiality?

It is hard to think of a better definition of impartiality and the case for continuing to require all broadcast journalism to be impartial. But over the next few years that principle is likely to be challenged as never before. The Ofcom review of public service broadcasting will stress the importance of trusted, accurate news on public service channels (Ofcom, 2020). However, the Government has set up a panel to advise ministers (Terms of Reference, 2020), and one of its most senior members, Lord Grade, has already argued impartiality rules should be relaxed, allowing newspapers, for example, to have their own channels reflecting their editorial views (Waterson, 2020).

To see where that would lead you only need to look at GB News, which at time of writing is about to launch, a news channel owned and generously (it's a tough market) backed by mainly international investors, who apparently want a different approach to news (Ellson, 2021) and run by Andrew Neil who promises a 'Wokewatch' segment in his flagship evening show and believes the competition 'all come from various shades of left' (Duffield, 2021). GB News looks to be a highly professional outfit, hiring experienced people. Its output is currently under Ofcom rules on impartiality and accuracy – but for how long if the Government decides on deregulation? Would it then move more towards the Fox News model Dominic Cummings envisaged more than 15 years ago? And would other players with equally deep pockets and strong views on the agenda also fancy the prestige and influence of owning a news channel?

I have always argued for the value of rules on impartiality since the idea of relaxation was first floated 20 years ago and although the media environment has changed dramatically. I have not changed my mind about impartiality's role in our democracy and our society. It is probably the most important (perhaps the last) public good we have inherited from the analogue age of public service broadcasting (Tait, 2008: 110-115). But it is for you, our readers, to decide whether, on the evidence of this book, the advance of populism means impartiality is now a lost cause or a value which is now all the more vital to defend.

References

Badshah, Nadeem (2019) BBC's Andrew Neil lays down gauntlet to Boris Johnson over interview, The Guardian 4 December 2019. Available online at https://www.theguardian.com/politics/2019/dec/05/bbcs-andrew-neil-lays-down-gauntlet-to-boris-johnson-over-interview, accessed 10 May 2021

Barwise, Patrick, York, Peter (2020) The War Against the BBC, London: Penguin.

BBC (2019), BBC Annual Plan, 2019-20, March 2019, BBC: London. Available online at https://downloads.bbc.co.uk/aboutthebbc/reports/annualplan/annualplan_2019-20.pdf, accessed 4 May 2021.

BBC (2020a), Newsnight 'breached BBC impartiality guidelines' with Cummings remarks, 27 March 2020. Available online at https://www.bbc.co.uk/news/entertainment-arts-52824508, accessed 24 May 2021.

BBC (2020b) New measures reaffirm BBC's commitment to impartiality, 29 October 2020.Available online at https://www.bbc.co.uk/mediacentre/latestnews/2020/impartiality-measures, accessed 10 May 2021.

BBC News (2019) Naga Munchetty on Trump 'go home' comment, 27 September 2019. Available online at https://www.bbc.co.uk/news/av/uk-49852788, accessed 22 May 2021.

Birt, John, (2002) The Harder Path, London: Time Warner, 2020.

Blair, Tony (2021) Without total change Labour will die, *New Statesman,* 11 May 2021. https://www.newstatesman.com/politics/2021/05/tony-blair-without-total-change-labour-will-die, accessed 24 May 2021.

Cecil, Nicholas, Murphy, Joe (2021) PM Steps up War of Words with Cummings: Minister Highlights Aide's Barnard Castle Trip Three Times as Crisis Deepens, *Evening Standard,*

27 April 2021.

Davie, Tim (2020) Tim Davie's Introductory Speech as BBC Director General, 3 September 2020. Available online at https://www.bbc.co.uk/mediacentre/speeches/2020/tim-davie-intro-speech, accessed 6 May 2021.

Davies, Gavyn (2004) Gavyn Davies resignation statement, 28 January 2004. BBC Press Release. Available online at Mangan, Dan (2018) https://www.cnbc.com/2018/05/22/trump-told-lesley-stahl-he-bashes-press-to-discredit-negative-stories.html, accessed 25 May 2021.

DCMS Committee (2020a) The Work of the BBC: 12 March 2020. Available online at https://committees.parliament.uk/event/328/formal-meeting-oral-evidence-session/, accessed 27 April 2021.

DCMS Committee (2020b) The Work of the BBC, 29 September2020.Available online at https://committees.parliament.uk/oralevidence/955/html/, accessed 10 May 2021.

DCMS (2021) Pre-appointment hearing for Chair of the BBC, 14 January 2021. Available online at https://committees.parliament.uk/publications/4318/documents/43836/default/, accessed 23 May 2021.

Desmog (2020), News-watch. Available online at https://www.desmog.com/news-watch/, accessed 15 May 2021.

Duffield, Charlie (2021) GB News launch date: When does Andrew Neil's new TV channel start? Everything we know so far, *i News,* 24 May 2021Available online at https://inews.co.uk/news/uk/gb-news-launch-date-tv-channel-andrew-neil-new-when-start-latest-news-947550, accessed 25 May 2021.

Eatwell, Roger, Goodwin, Matthew (2018) National Populism, the Revolt against Liberal Democracy, London: Penguin.

Economist (2021) Populists are threatening Europe's independent public broadcasters, *The Economist,* 10 April 2021.

Ellson, Andrew, *GB News* is Britain's newest current affairs channel but most backers are based abroad, *The Times*, 22 May 2021, available online at https://login.thetimes.co.uk/?gotoUrl=https://www.thetimes.co.uk/article/gb-news-is-britains-newest-current-affairs-channel-but-most-backers-are-based-abroad-vjrtwbvtq, accessed 24 May 2021.

Fletcher, Richard (2019) The Rise of Populism and the Consequences for News and Media Use, Reuters Digital News Report, 2019. Available online at https://www.digitalnewsreport.org/survey/2019/the-rise-of-populism-and-the-consequences-for-news-and-media-use/ accessed 28 April 2021.

Gibbon, Gary (2020), Permission not to Engage, in Mair, John et al (eds), Brexit Boris and the Media, Bury St Edmunds: Abramis pp 61-65.

Groves, Jason and Revoir, Paul, (2020) Downing Street threat to BBC: pick the right boss to replace Lord Hall as director general... or we'll fire them, Daily Mail, 21 January 2020. Available online at https://www.dailymail.co.uk/news/article-7913609/Downing-Street-threat-BBC-Pick-right-boss-replace-Lord-Hall-fire-them.html, accessed 27 January 2020.

Gyngell, Kathy (2021a) Today's talking point, *The Conservative Woman,* 24 April 2021. Available online at https://www.conservativewoman.co.uk/todays-talking-point-81/, accessed 15 May 2021

Gyngell, Kathy (2021b) For the sake of truth and honesty, vote Laurence Fox for London mayor, *The Conservative Woman,* 5 May 2021. Available online at https://www.conservativewoman.co.uk/for-the-sake-of-truth-and-honesty-vote-laurence-fox-for-london-mayor/, accessed 15 May 2021.

Harding, James, (2021), Cancel culture and the battle for truth, *Tortoise,* 13 April 2021. Available online at online https://www.tortoisemedia.com/audio/cancel-culture-and-the-battle-for-truth/, accessed 24 May 2021.

Heffer, Greg, (2020) Government wants 'strong' BBC chair - amid reports Boris Johnson's old boss Charles Moore will get role. Available online at https://news.sky.com/story/government-wants-strong-bbc-chair-amid-reports-boris-johnsons-old-boss-charles-moore-will-get-role-12083360, accessed 16 May 2021

Holtz-Bacha, Christina (2021) The kiss of death: Public service media under right-wing populist attack, European Journal of Communication, 1:17, 2021. Available online at https://journals.sagepub.com/doi/pdf/10.1177/0267323121991334, accessed 22 May 2021.

Keighley, David (2017) David Keighley - BBC Bias and Trying to Make the Corporation More Accountable, speech to Traditional Britain Group, 22 November 2017. Available online at https://www.ofcom.org.uk/__data/assets/pdf_file/0025/173734/bbc-news-review.pdf, accessed 15 May 2021

Keighley, David (2021) The poor can't afford to eat Kwasi's Greens, *The Conservative Woman,* 26 April 2021. Available online at https://www.conservativewoman.co.uk/the-poor-cant-afford-to-eat-kwasis-greens/, accessed 15 May 2021.

Holtz-Bacha, Christina (2021) The kiss of death: Public service media under right-wing populist attack, European Journal of Communication, 1:17, 2021. Available online at https://journals.sagepub.com/doi/pdf/10.1177/02673231211991334

Horrie, Chris, Clarke, Steve, Fuzzy Monsters, Fear and Loathing at the BBC, London: Heinemann.

IPI (International Press Institute) (2019), Conclusions of the Joint International Press Freedom Mission to Hungary, 19 December 2019. Available online at https://ipi.media/wp-content/uploads/2020/02/Hungary-Conclusions-International-Mission-Final.pdf, accessed 25 April 2021.

Lawson, Mark, (2020) 2020 vision: how Covid news topped the TV ratings, *Guardian*, 23 December 2020. Available online at https://www.theguardian.com/tv-and-radio/2020/dec/23/tv-news-2020-covid-ratings-dominic-cummings, accessed 29 April 2020.

Mangan, Dan (2018) President Trump told Lesley Stahl he bashes press 'to demean you and discredit you so ... no one will believe' negative stories about him, CNBC, 22 May 2018. Available online at https://www.cnbc.com/2018/05/22/trump-told-lesley-stahl-he-bashes-press-to-discredit-negative-stories.html, accessed 15 May 2021.

Mason, Rowena (2020) Dominic Cummings think tank calls for 'end of the BBC in current form', *The Guardian*, 21 January 2020. Available online at https://www.theguardian.com/politics/2020/jan/21/dominic-cummings-thinktank-called-for-end-of-bbc-in-current-form, accessed 28 April 2021.

Mattinson, Deborah (2020) Beyond the Red Wall, London: Biteback.

Milne, Alasdair (1988) DG, The Memoirs of a British Broadcaster, London: Hodder & Stoughton.

MFFR (Media Freedom Rapid Response) (2021) Democracy Declining: Erosion of Media Freedom in Poland, Vienna: IPI. Available online at https://www.article19.org/wp-content/uploads/2021/02/20210211_Poland_PF_Mission_Report_ENG_final.pdf, accessed 25 April 2021.

News-watch (2021) Monitoring Projects and Reports. Available online at https://news-watch.co.uk/monitoring-projects-and-reports/, accessed 15 May 2021

Ofcom (2019) Review of BBC News and Current Affairs, 24 October 2019. Available online at https://www.ofcom.org.uk/__data/assets/pdf_file/0025/173734/bbc-news-review.pdf accessed 14 May 2021.

Ofcom (2020a) Ofcom's Annual Report on the BBC, 2019/20 Available online at https://www.ofcom.org.uk/__data/assets/pdf_file/0021/207228/third-bbc-annual-report.pdf,accessed 14 May 2021.

Ofcom (2020b) Small Screen: Big Debate, 20 December 2020. Available online at https://www.smallscreenbigdebate.co.uk/consultation, accessed 24 May 2021

Opinium (2021), UK Voting Intention, 8 April 2021. Available online at https://www.opinium.com/resource-center/uk-voting-intention-8th-april-2021/, accessed 10 May 2021.

Pickard, Jim (2021) Boris Johnson under fire for putting UK vaccine success down to 'greed', *Financial Times*, 23 March 2021. Available online at https://www.ft.com/content/f139aed7-619f-4ce6-88ac-50d798b924fc, accessed 27 April 2021.

ReNews (2021), Are culture wars co-opting the mainstream narrative? 14 January 2021. Available online at https://joinrenews.com/culture-wars-2020-01/, accessed 25 May 2021.

Reuters (2020) Digital News Report: United Kingdom. Available online at https://reutersinstitute.politics.ox.ac.uk/sites/default/files/2020-06/DNR_2020_FINAL.pdf, accessed 24 May 2021

Seaton, Jean (2015), 'Pinkoes and Traitors', the BBC and the Nation, 1974-87, London: Penguin.

Siddique, Haroon (2020) Idea of Charles Moore as BBC chair 'beyond the pale, says Tory MP, *The Guardian*, 29 September 2020. Available online at https://www.theguardian.com/media/2020/sep/29/idea-of-charles-moore-as-bbc-chair-beyond-the-pale-says-tory-mp, accessed 15 May 2021.

Tait, Richard (2008) Impartiality – why it must stay, in Gardam, Tim, Levy, David (eds) The Price of Plurality, Oxford: Reuters pp 110-115.

Tait. Richard (2020) Impartiality's last stand? In Mair, John et al, Brexit, Boris and the Media, Bury St Edmunds: Abramis pp 240-248.

Terms of Reference (2020), Public Service Broadcasting Advisory Panel, 10 November 2020. Available online at https://www.gov.uk/guidance/public-service-broadcasting-advisory-panel-terms-of-reference, accessed 22 May 2021.

Waterson, Jim (2020) UK's news channels shouldn't have to be impartial, says ex-BBC chair, *The Guardian*, https://www.theguardian.com/media/2020/nov/11/uk-news-channels-should-not-have-to-be-impartial, accessed 24 May 2021.

YouGov (2020) Do you think British television news channels should have to try to be politically impartial, or should they be allowed to express their own political views? 13 November 2020. Available online at https://yougov.co.uk/topics/politics/survey-results/daily/2020/11/13/605a0/1, accessed 16 May 2021

About the contributor

Richard Tait CBE is Professor of Journalism at the School of Journalism, Media and Culture, Cardiff. From 2003 to 2012 he was Director of the School's Centre for Journalism. He was Editor of *Newsnight* from 1985 to 1987, Editor of *Channel 4 News* from 1987 to 1995 and Editor-in-Chief of ITN from 1995 to 2002. He was a member of the 2004 Neil Review of the BBC's journalism after Hutton. He was a BBC Governor and chair of the Governors' Programme Complaints Committee from 2004 to 2006, and a BBC Trustee and chair of the Trust's Editorial Standards Committee from 2006 to 2010. He is a fellow of the Society of Editors and the Royal Television Society and a Board member (and former Treasurer) of the International News Safety Institute.

The populist press: Conservatism, 'common sense' and culture wars

It's no longer particularly controversial to talk of the 'Tory press'. But would it also be helpful to describe Tory papers as populist, or indeed authoritarian populist? And, if so, what more does it tell us about the political and ideological tenor of those newspapers? Professor Julian Petley

Now the *Sun*, *Mail*, *Express*, *Times* and, in particular, the *Telegraph* have become even more stridently partisan in their support for the Conservatives, with their steady transformation from newspapers into viewspapers now seemingly complete, reference to the 'Tory press' seems no longer to be considered a mark of extreme leftism or of being in thrall to conspiracy theory. But whilst it's gratifying such a notion is no longer the preserve of only media academics and those critical journalists not blinded by the myth that such papers represent a 'free press' or a Fourth Estate, I suggest we need to supplement the idea of a Tory press with that of a *populist* one – and, more specifically, an *authoritarian populist* press. First, however, we need to define populism and its authoritarian variant.

Populism

In recent years, there has been an explosion of writing about populism. Indeed, this book is part of it. There are, of course, different forms of populism and, equally, different theories about it. But there is broad agreement about the elements which are central to populism, however defined.

Firstly, there is the valorisation of 'the people', conceived of as a unified and homogenous entity. This is akin to the way in which right-wing American politicians since Nixon have habitually claimed to represent the 'silent majority'. A good example of this in the UK context would be Nigel Farage crowing on Brexit night that 'this will be a victory for real people, a victory for ordinary people, a victory for decent people' (BBC News 2016).

Second, 'the people' are defined in opposition to an out-of-touch, unrepresentative, overly-liberal 'elite' or simply the 'Establishment'. This typically includes the mainstream media ('fake news' in Trump-speak, the BBC in the case of those vociferously lobbying against it); elected politicians (in it only for themselves); public functionaries (unaccountable bureaucrats); intellectuals (pointy-headed inhabitants of the ivory tower); judges (the *Mail*'s 'enemies of the people'); and international organisations such as the EU or UN (interfering busybodies subverting national sovereignty).

Third, populism almost always involves the identification of out-groups: stigmatised Others who are represented as a threat to 'the people' – for example asylum seekers, migrants, people of colour, travellers, gay and trans people, statue topplers, BLM supporters, the 'woke', and so on and on. In other words, those who are not part of 'us'. Indeed, what constitutes 'us' is largely defined in opposition to those who are not 'us'.

One might also note an admiration for charismatic leaders, feelings of *ressentiment* on behalf of 'ordinary people' or 'plain folk' and a belief in 'common sense' interpretations of social reality as opposed to fancy theories, isms and ologies. And in its right-wing incarnations, which are the dominant ones in the UK, populism may support democracy, at least in principle, but as Cas Mudde (2019: 30) argues: "It fundamentally challenges key institutions and values of liberal democracy, including minority rights, rule of law, and separation of powers." Thus it is anti-pluralist, refusing to recognise the existence of legitimate differences among 'the people', and hostile to cultural, religious, sexual and other kinds of diversity. In this respect it can be regarded as a form of democratic illiberalism with distinctly authoritarian overtones.

Authoritarian populism

In the UK, the term 'authoritarian populism' was used by Stuart Hall to conceptualise certain aspects of the Thatcher regime. What particularly interested Hall was how, under Thatcher, popular consent had been won for measures which weakened the public realm but, at the same time, considerably increased the coercive powers of the state. The latter was achieved largely by playing on people's fears of crime, disorder and 'permissiveness', which, greatly fanned by much of the national press, took on the contours of a major moral panic about 'the end of life as we know it'. (The classic account of this process is Hall et al., 1978/2013).

Meanwhile weakening the public realm involved mobilising people in favour of the 'free market', mainly through large scale privatisations ('popular capitalism') and the identification of 'Britishness' with the restoration of competition, profitability and 'sound money', along with the inculcation of the 'common sense' notion that the country's economy should be run along the same lines as the household budget. As Hall put it: "The essence of the British people was identified with self-reliance and personal responsibility, as against the image of the over-taxed individual, enervated by welfare state 'coddling', his or her moral fibre irrevocably sapped by 'state handouts'" (1983: 29). And in this discourse of petit-bourgeois moral and economic rectitude, the emotive image of a new folk devil, 'the scrounger', played a key ideological role in mobilising public opinion against what was in fact a reincarnation of the 'undeserving poor' of Victorian times. This mobilisation was effected mainly via the national press, as is made abundantly clear by Peter Golding and Sue Middleton (1982), whilst James Morrison (2019) has analysed how this process has continued in recent times

Reactionary 'common sense'

What particularly interested Hall was how Thatcherism succeeded in creating a new reactionary 'common sense'. As already noted, 'common sense' interpretations of social reality are central to populism's appeal, so it's important to understand that Hall always employs the term in a critical fashion, one which draws on the Italian Marxist philosopher Antonio Gramsci to indicate the uncritical and largely unconscious ways of perceiving and understanding the world that have become 'common' in any epoch. As Hall and Alan O'Shea explain, it is: "A form of 'everyday thinking' which offers us frameworks of meaning with which to make sense of the world. It is a form of popular, easily available knowledge which contains no complicated ideas, requires no sophisticated arguments and does not depend on deep thought or wide reading. It works intuitively, without forethought or reflection. It is pragmatic and empirical, giving the illusion of arising directly from experience, reflecting only the realities of daily life and answering the needs of 'the common people' for practical guidance and advice." (2015: 52-3)

Common sense then is a compendium of customary beliefs and popular prejudices expressed in the vernacular, the familiar language of the street, the home, the pub and the workplace, and its most familiar refrain is 'stands to reason, doesn't it?'

'Common sense' explanations of the world work by presenting themselves as the 'natural' wisdom of the ages, but of course they are no such thing. Rather they are the deep-rooted products of politics, culture and history (what Gramsci calls 'stratified deposits' and 'the folklore of philosophy') and thus very far from being ideologically innocent or neutral. Indeed, imbued as they are with fixed conceptions of the unchanging and unchangeable character of human nature, they are deeply conservative.

Constructing 'the people'

One of the many important aspects of Hall's work on authoritarian populism is that it shows how populist discourse actively *constructs* a particular definition of 'the people' and does not simply appeal to a 'people' that exists before it is represented in various forms of communication – in particular the media. Indeed, it cannot do so, since, whatever populists may claim, the multiplicity and heterogeneity of voices and identities within any given community would make this quite impossible. So, when populists claim to speak in the name of 'the people', what they are in fact doing is bringing a subject called 'the people' into being, and thus producing what they claim to be representing. As Carsten Reinemann et al. (2017: 19) put it: "Populist communication tries to create a new social identity among citizens or to prime certain aspects of their social identity in order to unite them and generate a sense of belonging to an imagined community charged with positive emotions."

Populism as spectacle

Market-driven changes in the media have encouraged modes of journalism that have traditionally been described as 'tabloid' but could equally well be termed 'populist'. These have in turn resulted in the ever-increasing mediatisation of the political sphere. The consequences of both processes have been the simplification of political discourse into soundbites and slogans ('Get Brexit Done', 'Take Back Control', 'Believe in Britain'), a concentration on politicians' 'personalities' and 'images' ('Boris'), and the representation of the political process in increasingly gladiatorial terms: in short, the rendering of politics as 'spectacle'. This has worked greatly to the benefit of populist politicians, not simply because such a media sphere is fertile ground for their anti-Establishment messages but because performance and style are such crucial elements of their man-of-the-people appeal – witness, for example, Nigel Farage's repeated media appearances in pubs with a pint of beer in one hand and a cigarette in the other.

As Benjamin Moffitt (2016: 94) has stated: "Media can no longer be treated as a 'side issue' when it comes to understanding contemporary populism. It must be put at the centre of our analysis". One study which has done just this is Reece Peck's *Fox Populism*, which analyses in detail how Fox News's style is crucial to the communication of its populist ideology. As this concerns a US cable news TV channel rather than the British press, detailed consideration of its findings is beyond the scope of this chapter, but Peck's drawing of distinct correspondences between political populism and tabloid journalism is worth noting here. These he groups into three categories, namely:

- *Analytical disposition*: In both cases the experience of the 'ordinary person' is treated as equally authoritative as professional expertise in accounting for social reality. For example, Michael Gove brushing off those economists opposed to Brexit with the words 'people in this country have had enough of experts' (Mance 2016) or the *Mail*, as part of the anti-lockdown campaign that it waged relentlessly with other populist papers, calling Sir Patrick Vallance and Professor Chris Whitty Dr Doom and Prof Gloom (Borland and Chalmers 2020). And this in a 'news' item, not an opinion column.

- *Presentational form*: Both give priority to affective forms of communication, such as immediate, visceral language and emotional, embodied performance.
- *Public sphere imaginary*: In both cases this is a distinctly 're-feudalised' and illiberal public sphere which speaks for 'the people' and against the 'liberal elite' (2019: 43).

Also relevant to the phenomenon of populism in the British national press in Britain is his observation that: "Rhetorical appeals to cultural taste, 'common sense', and 'traditional values' have become exceedingly useful in the politicised informational space of today's media. Unlike formal expertise, these populist sources of legitimacy do not require institutional verification. What populism does require, however, is a deep knowledge of traditional moral discourses, an astute awareness of the key social cleavages (e.g. race, gender and class) active in a given historical moment and, most importantly, an exceptional level of *performative skill*." (Ibid. 26)

The populist press and the culture wars

That the vast bulk of the national press in Britain supports the Conservatives is a well-established fact that needs no further elaboration here (see, for example, Greenslade 2003). But where the *populism* of the Tory-supporting press is particularly evident is in its endless stoking of the culture wars that the Tories have declared, although there is nothing particularly new in this, since these self-same newspapers were highly active in the 1980s onslaught against the 'political correctness' of the anti-racist and anti-sexist policies of the Greater London Council and the so-called 'loony Left' London boroughs (Curran, Gaber and Petley 2019).

However, if the target there was the Left, here it has broadened considerably into the 'liberal elite' – the BBC has already been mentioned, and the National Trust has recently become a prominent press target for its report on the links between slavery and colonialism and some of its properties. The March 2021 report of the Commission on Race and Ethnic Disparities may have been derided by virtually everyone who knows anything about the subject, but for the populist press it was a golden opportunity to disparage yet another manifestation of the 'liberal elite', namely the idea of 'institutional racism', something which it has bitterly opposed ever since the Macpherson Report on the Metropolitan Police was published in 1999 (ibid.: 193-201). For the populist press, this idea is doubly objectionable.

Firstly, because it draws attention to something whose existence in British society it has always strenuously denied, namely racism. Thus, for example, when Prince Harry accused the tabloid press of being bigoted and racist, the Director of the Society of Editors, Ian Murray, immediately rushed out a statement denying that it was any such thing and claiming that 'the UK media has a proud record of calling out racism'. However, the Prince was not criticising 'the media' but the tabloid press specifically, and the fact that very large numbers of journalists immediately and publicly disagreed with Murray's statement, which had been issued without any consultation, all too clearly disproved the point that the Society had been so keen to make (Tobitt 2021).

The second reason why the idea of institutional racism (or institutional anything else, for that matter) is so disagreeable to populist papers is that their 'common sense' view of the world is intrinsically hostile to any attempt to explain events in terms of the operations of social, economic or political forces and in particular as the consequences of fundamental structural inequalities in society. No wonder, then, that they so strongly endorsed the Thatcherite mantra that there is no such thing as society and have always been bitterly hostile to 'ologies' of all kinds, particularly sociology. As presenter Anne Diamond so memorably put it in the *Mirror*, December 1, 1993: "God protect us from the 'ologists' – because their hackneyed perception is dangerous. I sometimes think that a degree in some sort of 'ology' blinds you to common sense." Yes, Anne, that's precisely the point.

'The spreading slime of imbecility'

Just as Diamond's outburst demonstrates that populist attitudes are not entirely confined to the Tory press, so it's important to remember that the current war on 'woke' being waged by Andrew Neil has its antecedents in a broadsheet, namely the *Sunday Times*. When Neil took over as editor in 1983 he set out to destroy what he called its 'liberal-left collectivist consensus' (1997: 64) and to turn the paper into a proselytiser for market populism – as well as, incidentally, to use it as a weapon in his campaign to turn Britain into the 'low-cost, high productivity Hong Kong of northern Europe' (ibid.: 486). Battle with what Neil liked to call the 'chattering classes' was joined in an editorial on September 20, 1987. Headed 'Britain's Breed Apart', it complained that: "Britain's intelligentsia has become the lost tribe of the 1980s. As it wanders aimlessly between Islington and the Groucho Club, stopping now and then at Channel 4 or Broadcasting House to let the world know how much it despises what is happening to the country, it has become increasingly divorced from the land it lives in. It hates everything the Thatcher government stands for but realises that the nation is not listening. So it has retreated to its own left-wing laager, where erudite moaning is taken for wise critique… Rarely have the ideals of the country's intellectual elite been so out of kilter with the aspirations of plain folk [sic]."

This led Neal Ascherson in an article in *The Observer*, September 27, 1987, headed 'The Spreading Slime of Imbecility' to identify the sentiments expressed by the paper as 'populist imbecility nourished on the porridge of resentful prejudice', 'the voice of the populist boor through the ages' and an appeal to 'England's equivalent to the Nazi *gesundes Volksempfinden* – healthy folk instinct' (reproduced in Ascherson 1988: 37-8). However, more was to come on November 29, 1987, in an article by Brian Walden in which he appeared to endorse what he called the 'widespread view, faithfully reflected in the tabloid press, that our cultural and intellectual elites are inherently treacherous. They are seen as the enemies of what most people want and the friends of those who want to destroy Western values'.

Neil is now chairman of GB News and his various public pronouncements on the new channel lead one strongly to suspect he fully intends to introduce into broadcasting, via the newcomer, exactly the same kind of values that transformed the *Sunday Times* into a vehicle for market populism (McKnight 2009). For example, in the *Sunday Express*, February 7, 2021, he described the current state of broadcast news as 'increasingly woke and out of touch with the majority of its people' and 'too metropolitan, too southern and too middle class'. In his view, many 'sensible people' ('plain folk' in a different guise) who don't share what he claims are the 'liberal-left assumptions' of many broadcast journalists 'feel left out and unheard. There's a restlessness, a sense that they're being talked down to; that much of the media no longer reflects their values or shares their concerns. GB News is aimed squarely at those people'.

Although Neil endlessly whines that critics are pre-judging the new channel before it's broadcast anything, it's abundantly clear from his statements – let alone the calibre of many of his new recruits (for example, Tom Harwood and Dan Wootton) and his addiction to the boo-word 'woke'– exactly what its ideological complexion is going to be: "We will not operate on the assumption that every problem demands a government solution. Or that every solution must necessarily involve more taxpayers' money" (thus a bias towards the small state and 'free market'). "GB News will be proud of our country, even when revealing its shortcomings and its inequalities. Our default position will not be to do Britain down at every turn" (at best nationalistic, at worst jingo-ridden and flag-clad). "We believe the British appetite for endless gloom, doom, blame and divisive argument is waning. People feel battered and exhausted by it" (stand by for bread and circuses).

Of course, within the limits set by the Ofcom rules on impartiality, Neil and his investors are free to do with their channel as they please, and no-one who dislikes its ideological tenor is going to be forced to watch it. However, the fear is it may do to broadcast news in the UK exactly what Murdoch did to the UK press after he purchased the *News of the World*, *The Sun* and *The Times* and the *Sunday Times*, that is, lead other channels to try to compete with it on its own terms. This, in fact, is exactly what Fox News has done in the US, and although GB News is not of course owned by Murdoch, it could well spark off a similar chain of events here. There is already mounting concern that the news values of populist national newspapers are increasingly setting not only the news agenda of the BBC but also the tone of some of its coverage, and anything which further encourages this process – which is clearly what those behind GB News have in mind – would be a disaster for trustworthy journalism, informed debate and, ultimately, for democracy itself in this country. We need only to look around the world – India, Turkey, Poland,

Hungary, for example – to see that populism is no friend to democracy. Except, that is, of the illiberal variety.

References

Aalberg, Toril and de Vreese, Claes H. (2017) *Populist Political Communication in Europe*

Ascherson, Neal (1988) *Games with Shadows*, London: Radius

BBC News (2016) 'Nigel Farage says Leave win marks UK "Independence Day"', 24 June. Available at https://www.bbc.co.uk/news/uk-politics-eu-referendum-36613238

Borland, Sophie and Chalmers, Vanessa (2020) 'Where did Prof Gloom and Dr Doom get THAT chart? French and Spanish numbers suggest infections could only be ONE FIFTH of advisors' terrifying 50,000 a day prediction', *MailOnline*, 22 September. Available at https://www.dailymail.co.uk/news/article-8758879/Projection-versus-reality-Experts-say-Britain-fall-short-Prof-Vallances-warning.html

Curran, James, Gaber, Ivor and Petley, Julian (2019) *Culture Wars: The Media and the British Left*, 2nd edition, Abingdon: Routledge.

Golding, Peter and Middleton, Sue ((1983) *Images of Welfare: Press and Public Attitudes to Poverty*, Oxford: Martin Robertson.

Greenslade, Roy (2003) *Press Gang: How Newspapers Make Profit from Propaganda*, London: Macmillan.

Hall, Stuart, Critcher, Chas, Jefferson, Tony, Clarke, John and Roberts, Brian (1978/2013) *Policing the Crisis: Mugging, the State and Law & Order*, 2nd edition, Basingstoke: Palgrave Macmillan.

Hall, Stuart (1983), 'The great moving right show', Hall, Stuart and Jacques, Martin (eds) *The Politics of Thatcherism*, London: Lawrence and Wishart pp. 19-39.

Hall, Stuart, and O'Shea, Alan (2015) 'Common sense neo-liberalism', Hall, Stuart, Massey, Doreen and Rustin, Michael (eds) *After Neoliberalism: The Kilburn Manifesto*, London: Lawrence and Wishart pp. 52-68.

Mance, Henry (2016) 'Britain has had enough of experts, says Gove', *Financial Times*, 3 June.

Moffitt, Benjamin (2016) *The Global Rise of Populism: Performance, Political Style, and Representation*, Stanford, CA: Stanford University Press.

Morrison, James (2019) *Scroungers: Moral Panics and Media Myths*, London: Zed Books.

Mudde, Cas (2019) *The Far Right Today*, Cambridge: Polity Press.

Neil, Andrew (1997) *Full Disclosure*, London: Pan Books.

Neil, Andrew (2021) 'UK news debate is woke and out of touch – prepare for a huge TV shake-up, says Andrew Neil', *Sunday Express*, 7 February. Available at https://www.express.co.uk/comment/expresscomment/1394315/Andrew-Neil-GB-News-latest-comment

Peck, Reece (2019) *Fox Populism: Branding Conservatism as Working Class*, Cambridge: Cambridge University Press.

Reinemann, Carsten, Aalborg, Toril, Esser, Frank, Strömbäck, Jesper and de Vreese, Claes H. (2017) 'Populist political communication: toward a model of its causes, forms, and effects', Reinemann, Carsten, Aalborg, Toril, Esser, Frank, Strömbäck, Jesper and de Vreese, Claes H. (eds), Abingdon: Routledge pp. 12-25.
Tobitt, Charlotte (2016) 'Society of Editors boss Ian Murray resigns amid row over Prince Harry "bigoted" press claims', *Press Gazette*, 10 March. Available at https://www.pressgazette.co.uk/society-of-editors-diversity-meghan-harry/

About the contributor

Julian Petley is emeritus and honorary professor of journalism at Brunel University London, and proud to be an 'ologist' with three degrees. His most recent book is the second edition of *Culture Wars: The Media and the British Left* (Routledge 2019), co-written with James Curran and Ivor Gaber. He is a member of the editorial board of the *British Journalism Review* and the principal editor of the *Journal of British Cinema and Television*. A former journalist, he now contributes to online publications such as *Inforrm*, *Byline Times* and *openDemocracy*.

Journalism ethics in a populist age

How can journalists exercise ethical responsibility and fulfil their role as society watchdogs when democratically elected leaders tell lies on an epic scale, asks Sara McConnell

Donald Trump had just been inaugurated as President of the United States, with a visibly smaller audience than at Barack Obama's inauguration four years earlier. But he sent his spokesman Sean Spicer out to tell the media this was: "The largest audience to ever witness an inauguration. Period." This set the tone for a Trump presidency in which Trump told more than 30,000 lies, according to fact checkers at the *Washington Post* (Kessler, Rizzo and Kelly 2020).

On the other side of the Atlantic, 'Britain Trump' [sic] Boris Johnson had triumphed in the EU Referendum campaign in 2016 by lying repeatedly about the benefits of leaving the EU (£350 million a week for the NHS) and the dangers of remaining in the bloc (Common borders with Turkey). Aided and abetted by a Eurosceptic, right-wing press, Johnson achieved his ultimate goal of becoming World King (Prime Minister of the UK) in December 2019. His premiership has seen no let-up in the number of lies he tells. Assessing Johnson's record in his first year, *Guardian* writer Simon Hattenstone described the Prime Minister as an 'inescapable, comprehensive liar' (Hattenstone 2020).

Inveterate liars? We don't care
But both Johnson and Trump still have big fan bases. Trump lost the election (even though he still denies it) but he won 74.6 million votes, more than any other presidential candidate in history apart from his opponent Joe Biden. Johnson has an 80-seat majority in Parliament after running on a 'Get Brexit Done' ticket, and, thanks to the successful vaccination campaign in the first half of 2021, has seen his approval levels surge.

This suggests something very disturbing – large sections of the public in the UK and the US either do not know, or do not care their leaders are inveterate liars. The idea that there is a verifiable account of events and this is part of public discourse in a democratic society with a free press has increasingly become questionable, even naïve. For journalist Peter Oborne, this is a disaster. "Truth has been captured by the Government and turned into a political weapon. For centuries we have had an area of public discourse which belonged to everybody, a common ground where rival parties could exist" (Oborne 2021: 6).

A populist platform and a theft of democratic rights

Both Trump and Johnson came to power on a populist platform, promising to restore national greatness, to roll back the powers and involvement of supra-national groups like the EU, and to make the voice of ordinary people heard. A big part of their appeal was they told people what they wanted to hear, which frequently entailed lying on an epic scale. Oborne (2021) argues this constitutes a form of theft. "It takes away people's democratic rights. Voters cannot make fair judgements on the basis of falsehoods. Truth has been taken out of the public domain" (2021:6).

In this environment, mainstream journalists struggle to gain and maintain public trust. YouGov's regular survey into trust in journalists carried out in March 2020 showed only 40 per cent of respondents trusted broadsheet newspapers, with a tiny eight per cent trusting red-top tabloids (Ibbetson 2020). Competition from social media and the spread of fake news makes it more difficult for the public to distinguish truth from lies and, judging by the enthusiasm of voters for Trump and Johnson, many have given up trying.

A serious challenge for ethical journalism

This is a serious challenge to journalists who still put core ethical values of accuracy, truth-telling, balance and transparency at the centre of their work, and seek to call out government lies (Kovach and Rosenstiel 2007; Harcup 2009; Frost 2015). In a liberal democracy, part of journalists' roles is to act as watchdogs for the public and scrutineers of the powerful (Anderson and Ward 2007) and this is complicated by the refusal of politicians to submit to interviews, to be questioned in public and to answer truthfully. It is more difficult for journalists to act as 'guardians of democracy' (Anderson and Ward 2007:42) if they cannot obtain information voters can rely on to make decisions. More worryingly for journalists trying to get behind the bluster and the obfuscation are attempts to smear them and their industry as 'enemies of the people' who produce 'fake news'.

Ducking and weaving…

Populists like Trump and Johnson duck and weave to avoid scrutiny. They tell their followers that sections of the media who do not follow their version of the story are part of the problem because they are part of the elite who do not understand and engage with ordinary people, successfully turning people against journalists. Johnson consistently refuses to submit to questioning from journalists he knows will give him a grilling. He and his ministers have declined to appear on Channel 4 and *Newsnight* and have boycotted *Good Morning Britain*, with its former presenter, the combative Piers Morgan. Journalist Simon Kelner writes that the refusal to appear on GMB 'reveals the monumental historic arrogance of this government' (Kelner 2020).

In February 2020, journalists from a number of left-leaning UK press organisations including the *Daily Mirror* and *The Independent* were banned from a briefing at Number 10, a ploy which backfired as all the invited journalists promptly boycotted the briefing. More broadly, the Conservatives have threatened whole media organisations with loss of funding, claiming the BBC has a left-wing bias and is being taken over by the 'woke' brigade, so should lose its licence fee. Johnson has also threatened to privatise Channel 4, which is publicly funded and which frequently runs hard-hitting investigative news programmes.

In the US, Trump's labelling of any negative coverage of him as 'fake news' and his depiction of journalists as 'enemies of the people' has created a hostile environment for media outlets such as CNN, but also journalists generally, as Trump supporters follow him in attacking the media. In a grim illustration of the Trump effect on the media, and the shift from verbal to physical threats, the words 'murder the media' were scrawled on a door during the invasion of the Capitol in January 2021 (Wong, 2021).

Tragic and avoidable outcomes

Refusal to submit to rightful scrutiny and to listen to unwelcome but important advice has led to tragic outcomes both in the UK and the US during the Covid pandemic. Nearly 700,000 people in the two countries have died of Covid-19 as at March 23, 2021. Both Trump and Johnson have distinguished themselves by their disastrous belated response to the seriousness of Covid, which has led to unnecessary deaths. Johnson's refusal to fire his chief adviser, Dominic Cummings after it emerged Cummings had driven to County Durham with his family in breach of lockdown regulations in May 2020 seriously dented the credibility of the Government's message to 'Stay Home'. In a bizarre televised press conference, Cummings assailed the assembled journalists with a story about needing to drive to Barnard Castle to test his eyesight, and refused calls to resign. Taking a leaf out of the Trump playbook, Number 10 declined to respond to the revelations from *The Guardian* and *Daily Mirror*, dismissing them as 'false accusations' from 'campaigning newspapers'.

Professor Charlie Beckett comments in *The Guardian* that the Johnson Government's refusal to engage with legitimate questions from the media was an echo of Trump's approach: 'For example, attacking the fact-based revelations in the *Mirror* and the *Guardian* as 'inaccurate' (in what way? tell us!) and as 'campaigning' journalism (implying it is partisan and discountable). It is similar to Trump's cry of 'fake news' about any hostile coverage. By attacking the motive of the accuser, you avoid addressing the actual charge.' (Beckett 2020 in Waterson 2020).

Media attacks, propaganda and populism are not new..

Attacks on the media are not new. The emergence of a free press in the UK was hard won, with successive governments since the seventeenth century suppressing unwelcome criticism with censorship, taxes on everything from newsprint to advertising, and imprisonment for editors who refused to comply (Conboy 2010). Within recent memory, prime ministers have gone head-to-head with media outlets – consider Margaret Thatcher's Conservative administration clamping down on BBC coverage of Northern Ireland during the Troubles, or Tony Blair's Labour Government furiously attacking the BBC for alleging the Government 'sexed up' a dossier of evidence designed to encourage public support for war in Iraq, as just two examples.

Using the media to influence the public is not new. In the UK, for example, ever since mass media took shape at the end of the nineteenth century and the beginning of the twentieth, governments have used media to spread propaganda and generate popular support for causes such as wars and imperial expansion, helped by the press barons who shaped the tabloid and broadsheet newspapers of today (Conboy 2010).

Populism is not new, although the combination of Trump and Johnson in power at the same time has led to much discussion about why people are voting for them and in the UK, why they supported Brexit. Eatwell and Goodwin (2018) argue these are the wrong questions, asked by journalists and others who see populism as a short-term phenomenon, without understanding deep-seated and long term trends of distrust of politicians, a perceived destruction of national identity and established ways of life, relative deprivation and 'left-behindness' and de-alignment with mainstream political systems, all factors which led to Trump in the US and Brexit in the UK (Eatwell and Goodwin 2018).

But now governments are gaslighting us

But what is arguably new is the extent to which leaders like Trump and Johnson, running governments in sophisticated democracies in peacetime, habitually attempt to gaslight journalists and the public, tell lies which they must know will be called out and engage in a form of censorship by refusing to submit to scrutiny from all sections of the press, rather than just friendly media like Fox News in the US or the tabloid press in the UK.

Those journalists who still believe ethics are 'not some optional extra' (Randall 2000:134) might justifiably feel they are fighting an uphill battle to gain public trust in the face of distorted or frankly wrong information which some newspapers have been pouring out for years. Harding (2016) points out the UK has had the most Eurosceptic press in the bloc since Britain joined in 1973, particularly *The Sun*, *Daily Mail* and *Daily Express* (Sample headline: 'Now EU wants to ban our kettles'). Coverage by these newspapers contributed substantially to suspicion and hostility to Europe and to the Brexit vote, with the connivance and support of those now in power. A weak system of self-regulation allowed the lies to continue.

Not an insuperable challenge

From an ethical point of view, governments' refusal to engage with the media, creation of a hostile environment for media scrutiny and disregard for truth, are a challenge for responsible journalists. But not an insuperable challenge. As the discussion above suggests, both the UK and the US still have a free press, and journalists ready and willing to call out government lies and obfuscation. The *Washington Post* counted and exposed Trump's lies during his administration. *The Guardian* and *Daily Mirror* exposed Cummings. The *Sunday Times*, even though it is a Conservative paper owned by Rupert Murdoch, has carried a number of damning pieces by its Insight team of investigative reporters, exposing Johnson's cavalier behaviour during the Covid epidemic. A number of fact-checking operations, such as FullFact and the BBC's RealityCheck now work to check ministers' claims and highlight distortions and inaccuracies.

But as Oborne (2021) argues, these successes must be set against the collective failure of many media outlets to challenge Johnson, both for his role in the Brexit vote and his rise to the premiership. Far from challenging him, the mainstream press overwhelmingly supported him in his race to Downing Street on a Brexit platform and failed to hold his feet to the fire when he insisted his Brexit deal meant the UK had 'freedom in its hands'. As Oborne (2021) says: "Future generations are bound to ask why Johnson's record as a liar, a charlatan and a cheat did not prove fatal on his way into Downing Street… one reason is that the mainstream press ignored Johnson's lies" (2021: 116).

References

Anderson, Peter and Ward, Geoff eds (2007) The future of journalism in advanced democracies Aldershot and Vermont CT: Ashgate

Beckett, Charlie (2020) in Waterson (2020) "Daily Mail demand for Cummings to go poses challenge for UK PM" https://www.theguardian.com/media/2020/may/25/daily-mail-cummings-challenge-uk-pm-conservative-newspaper-boris-johnson

Conboy, Martin (2010) Journalism in Britain: a historical introduction London: Sage

Eatwell, Roger and Goodwin, Matthew (2018) National populism: The revolt against liberal democracy London: Penguin

Frost, Chris (2015) Journalism ethics and regulation London: Routledge

Harcup, Tony (2009) The ethical journalist London and Thousand Oaks CA: Sage

Harding, Gareth (2016) Media lies and Brexit: A double hammer blow to Europe and ethical journalism: Ethical Journalism Network

Hattenstone, Simon (2020) "In Boris Johnson's long history of lies, the Marcus Rashford is one of the strangest "https://www.theguardian.com/commentisfree/2020/jun/21/boris-johnson-lies-marcus-rashford-prime-minister

Ibbetson, Conor (2020) Do people trust journalists? London: YouGov https://yougov.co.uk/topics/politics/articles-reports/2020/03/26/trust-newspaper-journalists

Kelner, Simon (2020) "Boris Johnson's boycott of Good Morning Britain reveals the monumental arrogance of him and his ministers" https://inews.co.uk/opinion/comment/boris-johnsons-boycott-of-good-morning-britain-reveals-the-monumental-arrogance-of-him-and-his-ministers-656681

Kessler, Rizzo and Kelly (2021) "Trump's misleading claims total 30,573 over four years" https://www.washingtonpost.com/politics/2021/01/24/trumps-false-or-misleading-claims-total-30573-over-four-years/

Kovach, Bill and Rosenstiel, Tom (2007) The elements of journalism New York: Three Rivers Press

Oborne, Peter (2021) The assault on truth London and New York: Simon and Schuster

Randall, David (2000) The Universal Journalist (2nd edition) London and Sterling VA: Pluto Press.

Spicer, Sean (2017) First post-inaugural press briefing https://www.youtube.com/watch?v=PKzHXelQi_A

Wallace, Tim, Yourish, Karen and Greggs, Troy (2017) "Trump's inauguration vs Obama's: comparing the crowds" https://www.nytimes.com/interactive/2017/01/20/us/politics/trump-inauguration-crowd.html

Wong, Julia Carrie (2021)" "We're the news now": Pro-Trump mob targeted journalists at US Capitol" https://www.theguardian.com/us-news/2021/jan/07/capitol-attack-trump-targeted-journalists

About the contributor

Dr Sara McConnell is a University Teacher in the Department of Journalism Studies at the University of Sheffield. She has taught ethics at BA and MA level for 15 years. Previously she was a lecturer in journalism at Kingston University. As a journalist, she worked at *The Times*, before going freelance and working for publications including *The Guardian*, the *Evening Standard*, the *Sunday Telegraph* and the *Daily Mail*.

Journalism safety in the time of populism: A cautionary tale from the US

How did the home of freedom of expression become a very dangerous place to report the democratic process? Elena Cosentino, director of the International News Safety Institute, says the American experience is a lesson for us all

One week before the most controversial US presidential election in modern history, senior representatives from 40 leading news organisations from around the world came together for a confidential, and very alarming, online meeting.

The host was the International News Safety Institute (INSI). For nearly 20 years, INSI members meetings had been about keeping journalists safe by sharing information to identify and mitigate risk, mostly in so-called hostile environments. The term had traditionally applied to war zones, natural disaster regions, or authoritarian states with a penchant for arresting or even shooting at journalists.

But at the October 27, 2020 meeting, the hostile environment on the agenda was the United States of America and the dangerous assignment – covering the aftermath of the election of a US president.

Planning for the unthinkable

The virtual meeting room was packed when a seasoned US news manager kicked off the roundtable sharing his hunch for the days ahead. The worst-case scenario, he said in a tone of resigned foreboding, was one when there was no clear winner, and one side prematurely claimed victory. That, in turn, could lead to angry protesters pouring into the streets and clashing with police. Armed right-wing militia groups – he added – might come out to 'defend the White House' or, even 'storm state capitols'.

Journalists could potentially become prime targets, treated as 'traitors', just for doing their jobs. An awkward silence followed. This was not a meeting of easily impressed amateurs. The men and women in the room were used to sending news teams to war zones or to countries whose governments loved journalists as much as Duterte, Erdogan or Putin do. But this was the United States, a country whose much admired constitution guaranteed media freedom and where good journalism had long been a badge of honour for a healthy society. That it should have come to this – journalists planning for an election in the US as they would in Iraq – almost beggared belief.

Overt hostility to the mainstream media, which was eminently represented at the INSI meeting, had snuck up on everyone slowly at first. But, as in one of those now familiar graphs tracking the exponential growth of a contagious virus, by 2020 the curve had started shooting up nearly vertically. A perfect storm of pandemic denialism, emboldened white supremacy, and police brutality at Black Lives Matter protests, had led to a record 400 journalists being physically assaulted in the first ten months of the year. That was three times the total of 2017, 2018 and 2019 combined[1].

As an entire category, journalists in the US were probably now at greater risk than ever before.

Extraordinary measures

In INSI's virtual meeting room, each news outlet proceeded to share their contingency plans with colleagues and competitors alike: what was being put in place, just to *physically* protect journalists covering the ordinary business of democracy – was simply extraordinary.

Personal protective equipment (PPE) usually reserved for conflict zones, was now part of the kit for anyone attending election-related or any other protests. However, somebody warned, ballistic plates for bullet proof vests were sold out anywhere in the country. Usually plentiful, there was now up to a 12-week lead time on deliveries.

Some said they were planning to triage their limited PPE and carefully weigh staff deployment accordingly. One outlet, which had stocked up well in advance, offered spares in case of emergency. While the indispensable N95 masks and other Covid-19 protections were luckily widely available, the politicisation of Covid-19 meant that even just wearing a mask could put a journalist in someone's crosshairs.

A young female producer attending a recent rally had been heckled and harassed by Trump supporters to such an extent that she'd felt unsafe and removed the mask. One week later, she'd tested positive.

The general consensus in the room was that no journalist without prior hostile environment experience or full safety training should be deployed on the streets. But the pandemic had made in person training virtually impossible and some did not believe online training was enough to prepare inexperienced teams to violence of the level experienced in Minneapolis or Portland. With many more staff than usual needed to cover all possible flashpoints, photographers and tv crews usually working in war zones were being flown back to the US to contribute to the domestic frontline coverage.

Flashing a press pass was no longer believed to offer protection or elicit respect either. Logos identifying the news outlet were to be removed, including from crew vans. Where possible, small cameras or even mobile phones were to be favoured, in order to keep a low profile.

Foreign news organisations ought not to assume they were immune either, as one recounted their team being attacked at a Trump rally and told to 'go back home'. Many of the news outlets were resorting to employing professional backwatchers to accompany news teams. Others introduced a buddy system among colleagues, so no one would find themselves alone facing a possibly hostile crowd.

Finally, a news outlet shared their preparations for possible information security attacks, both domestically and from abroad. Journalists were asked to use DeleteMe or similar services to remove all their personal information online. The amount of abuse and threats received by US journalists via social media was at an all-time high and many were worried harassers may start turning up at theirs or their family's doorstep. If anyone thought these measures were overkill, nobody said.

Gunning for journalists

Looking back on how we'd gotten here, the case for laying the blame at Trump's door would be easily made.

His presidency-via-social-media purposefully obliterated, tweet by tweet, a large portion of Americans' trust in the news industry, raising to record highs the society's threshold of tolerance for violence against journalists.

Since first tweeting that the US news media was 'the enemy of the American people'[2], just one month into office in February 2017, Trump had been relentlessly goading his fans into taunting and heckling what he labelled the 'Fake News' media. He'd routinely verbally assaulted reporters, many of whom he'd single out by name, unleashing torrents of online abuse, trolling and even death threats to journalists[3]. Women journalists, particularly if of colour, were reserved the harshest display of contempt during press conferences or interviews[4].

Any news outlet who wasn't slavishly biased in Trump's favour would, at one time or another, incur his wrath.

Some, such as the *New York Times* or CNN, were recurring targets and gained as many detractors as Trump got fans. One of them was Cesar Sayoc, a mentally ill man, who was arrested for sending pipe bombs to CNN in October 2018. Sayoc's lawyers described him as a Trump 'super-fan'. He himself declared that Trump rallies were his 'drug'[5].

Warnings that Trump's rhetoric could inspire unstable people to lash out and harm journalists went unheeded. In fact, in 2019, when a congressional candidate body-slammed a *Guardian* reporter for asking a question he didn't like, Trump celebrated him and called him 'my kind of guy'[6].

As election day approached, his rhetoric sunk to new lows. In September 2020, at a Minnesota campaign rally, Trump went on to describe the rubber bullet shooting of NBC's reporter and anchor Ali Velshi at a protest, as a 'beautiful sight'[7].

Law enforcement's excessive use of force at protests was indeed a growing concern of news organisations. The militarisation of US police had started long before Trump. But many felt that the 'enemy of the people' rhetoric likely contributed to making quasi-acceptable for police to use a wide array of so-called 'less lethal weapons' against journalists, which accounted for the vast majority of the media injuries at protests.

For months now the police at rallies in Minneapolis, Portland or Washington DC, had appeared to regularly slip into a dangerous 'us versus them' pattern vis-à-vis the media. The intimidating effect of law enforcement on the media suited Trump, whose brand of populism – like Brazil's Jair Bolsonaro's, or Hungary's Viktor Orban's – regards evidence-based, independent news media as an existential threat to be neutralised at any cost.

In order to grow in power and influence, from early on, such leaders presented *themselves* to their supporters as the true purveyors of information. Something which their social media accounts, often with a far greater reach than any news outlet, gave them ample opportunity to do.

The normalisation of Nazi

Whether by accident or by design, these kinds of populist leaders help deliver new, huge audiences to forces and beliefs that are deeply rooted in the dark corners of many countries.

In the US, far-right, white supremacist groups had a long and infamous history, often overlapping with criminality, from the Aryan Nations to the Klan, but were previously confined by societal opprobrium to the fringe. Trump's presidency's biggest responsibility was to have emboldened, legitimised and brought some of their heirs into the open. Forces that are racist, xenophobic, misogynistic and homophobic and which, invariably, paint the news media, with its 'political correctness', as a threat to the white man.

As a result, the threat posed to journalists by the far-right, started becoming a real concern. Those news organisations that had the resources to monitor the dark web, said they would regularly find white supremacy threads spewing vitriol and threats about the 'Jewish-dominated media' or journalists who should 'get the rope'.

But trying to sort out empty threats from real ones remained difficult. The violent paramilitary neo-Nazi group Atomwaffen, for instance, was found to have adopted specific tactics of harassment with the stated goal to "erode the media [..] air of legitimacy by showing people that they have names and addresses, and hopefully embolden others to act."[8]

In one of several similar incidents in 2019, a US journalist who'd investigated Atomwaffen was 'swatted' in revenge. A fake call was made to 911 pretending there was an active shooter in the journalist's house. The caller's hope was to provoke a violent law enforcement response. When a swat police team stormed the journalist's house, he and his wife were both detained in front of their traumatised young child, before the hoax was sorted out.

It is difficult to overestimate the psychological impact of such an incident, particularly in a country where it's not uncommon for swat raids to end in a fatal shootout.

Throughout 2020, far-right groups, including QAnon and the Proud Boys, with their growing echo chambers in alternative social media like Parler, Gab, or 4Chan, were increasingly successful in disguising and re-packaging their propaganda and then pushing it into the mainstream, through Facebook, Twitter and YouTube.

As election day neared, Trump offered one such group a mainstream audience of at least 73m Americans when, asked to condemn white supremacy and their militias at a televised presidential debate, he did just the opposite. In a nod to the Proud Boys Trump name-checked them and asked them to 'stand back and stand by'[9]. Shortly afterwards, the Proud Boys leader duly replied on Parler, 'Standing by, Sir'[10].

Backwatchers at Westminster

It was clear to everyone at the INSI meeting how high the stakes in this election were, and not just in the US. For many non-American news organisations in attendance, particularly the European ones, there was a worry that such decline in journalism safety in America could be matched in their own countries.

The risk landscape for journalists covering domestic news in the UK, for instance, had already significantly worsened over the same period of time as in the US. After a toxic Brexit campaign during which a pro-Europe British member of Parliament, Jo Cox, was murdered by a far-right supporter, the 2016 referendum result had left the country bitterly split in two.

The political crisis that followed saw months of ugly scenes outside the Palace of Westminster with news crews (and some politicians) needing protection from far-right groups like the English Defence League (EDL) and supporters of its controversial former leader, Tommy Robinson[11]. Robinson was instrumental in bringing extreme far-right views and aggressive anti-media sentiments into the UK political discourse. Being a virulent Islamophobe with a criminal record proved no obstacle to him working with elected politicians in Ukip and the Brexit party. In a disturbing echo of the KKK's endorsement of Trump, Robinson asked all of his far-right supporters to endorse Boris Johnson in the 2019 election. Johnson did not disown him[12].

Echoing tactics used across the Atlantic, Robinson repeatedly targeted individual journalists and their families, harassing them even in their homes in the middle of the night, all the while livestreaming the incidents online, thus inciting further trolling and threats. As a result, one journalist left the country with his family[13], and another obtained a stalking ban against Robinson, as recently as March 2021[14].

While the current threat level towards journalists in the UK may not be comparable with the US one, news teams, particularly broadcasters, are still regularly insulted, spat on and, at times, attacked on the streets in Britain and the support of backwatchers is now widely considered necessary when covering protests or controversial public gatherings.

The British Prime Minister's ambivalence towards the profession he once practised may not be helping public perception either. In February 2021 Boris Johnson told a group of school children that while journalism was a 'great, great job' – journalists were 'always abusing people, attacking people'[15]. Only a few weeks later his government launched its first action plan to protect journalists. The plan follows years of reports "from journalists who have suffered abuse and attacks while going about their work, including being punched, threatened with knives, forcibly detained and subjected to rape and death threats"[16].

Putting pressure on social media companies to take tough action against online threats and harassment of journalists is one of the UK government's stated plans.

INSI has also been working on this particularly intractable problem, engaging with the social media platforms to speed up the processes and improve the tools that can help shield journalists, and particularly women and minority journalists, from the escalation of online abuse and threats[17]. A satisfactory solution is proving elusive.

No friends in high places

Back in the US, the worst-case scenario of the pre-election INSI meeting, conjuring up far-right militias rampaging the symbols of American democracy, actually came to pass. On January 6, 2021 a group, secretly led by the Proud Boys, stormed the United States Capitol in Washington DC. Five people died, including one policeman.

Twelve journalists were physically attacked on that day, including several INSI members. Many more were harassed and TV and photo equipment were destroyed[18]. Luckily, and likely thanks to preparedness, no journalist was seriously injured.

Now, with Trump gone from office and banned, at least for now, from his Twitter, Facebook and YouTube bully pulpits, the temptation to pull a sigh of relief is strong. But it would sadly be misplaced. The temperature in the US has gone down now that the leader of the country isn't calling the media 'Fake News' any more or berating individual journalists on live TV. But many in the US believe that the level of risk for journalists working in the country will remain high, possibly for years to come.

The deep mistrust in the media that exists in large parts of the populations, and which Trump stoked and inflamed, will probably deepen. Trump may have let the genie out of the bottle, but many others are positioning themselves, ahead of the next presidential election, to take advantage of the anger, grievances and hatreds that he nurtured.

Some in the US news industry fear they may reach a place soon where it will be difficult for certain media to even go to report from certain locations in the US without security. They also fear that black, Asian and other non-white American journalists will be increasingly harassed and threatened when working in the field.

But this is not just a concern for America. The way the Covid-19 measures have been politicised in many countries is also deepening pre-existing divides in society. And as the mainstream media becomes identified with one side or other of the 'culture war' divide, news organisations in many European countries will also need to start thinking about domestic security for their journalists, much more than ever before.

Before the rise of social media, governments might have hated journalists but they still needed them to pass on their messages, spin their truths or spread their lies. Now they can go straight to their audiences via the social media platforms.

Even politicians who are not overtly hostile to the news media, appear unwilling to stand up for it and the consequences of going after journalists, throwing them in jail or instigating violence against them are lower or sometimes non-existent.

While ostensibly more tolerant of the media, Joe Biden does not need the mainstream media any more than Trump did. That's maybe why among his first acts as the new president, he refused to sanction in any way Saudi crown prince Mohammed bin Salman in relation to the murder in Istanbul of Jamal Khashoggi, a journalist who in America sought protection.

This is certainly not a time for the media to be complacent. It's a time for journalists and news organisations to rally together and have each other's back, because no one else will.

Notes

[1] US Press Freedom Tracker, https://pressfreedomtracker.us/physical-attack/

[2] Michael M. Grynbaum, *The New York Times* (February 17, 2017), *Trump Calls the News Media the 'Enemy of the American People'* https://www.nytimes.com/2017/02/17/business/trump-calls-the-news-media-the-enemy-of-the-people.html

[3] Travis M. Andrews, *The Washington Post* (October 14, 2020), *Commander in Tweets, The Dispatches that define the Trump presidency* https://www.washingtonpost.com/graphics/2020/technology/trump-twitter-tweets-president/

[4] *NowThis News* (April 25, 2020) *President Trump Attacks Journalists of Color, A Supercut* https://www.youtube.com/watch?v=k66F9FzZthk,

[5] Benjamin Weiser and Ali Watkins, *The New York Times*, (August 5, 2019), *Cesar Sayoc, Who Mailed Pipe Bombs to Trump Critics, Is Sentenced to 20 Years* https://www.nytimes.com/2019/08/05/nyregion/cesar-sayoc-sentencing-pipe-bombing.html

[6] Ed Pilkington, *The Guardian* (October 19, 2018) *'He's my guy': Donald Trump praises Gianforte for assault on Guardian reporter* https://www.theguardian.com/us-news/2018/oct/18/trump-greg-gianforte-assault-guardian-ben-jacobs

[7] Mark Joyella, Forbes (September 19, 2020) *Trump Describes Journalist Hit By Rubber Bullet As 'A Beautiful Sight'* https://www.forbes.com/sites/markjoyella/2020/09/19/trump-describes-journalist-hit-by-rubber-bullet-a-beautiful-sight/?sh=2f5733d95dcb

[8] Paulina Villegas, *The Washington Post* (April 9, 2021) *Neo-Nazi group leader who threatened journalists and activists pleads guilty to hate crimes* https://www.washingtonpost.com/national-security/2021/04/08/atomwaffen-neo-nazi-shea/

[9] *Associated Press* (September 30, 2020) *Trump tells Proud Boys: 'Stand back and stand by'* https://www.youtube.com/watch?v=qIHhB1ZMV_o

[10] Matt Mathers, *The Independent* (September 30, 2020) *'Standing by, sir': Proud Boys respond to Trump presidential debate mention* https://www.independent.co.uk/news/world/americas/trump-presidential-debate-proud-boys-us-election-hate-group-b716510.html

[11] Chloe Chaplain, *iNews* (July 11, 2019) *Tommy Robinson supporters attack journalists and clash with police outside Parliament after he is jailed for contempt of court* https://inews.co.uk/news/uk/tommy-robinson-supporters-attack-journalists-and-clash-with-police-outside-parliament-after-he-is-jailed-for-contempt-of-court-312786

[12] Andy Gregory, *The Independent* (November 17, 2019) *General election: Boris Johnson condemned after Tommy Robinson endorses him for general election* https://www.independent.co.uk/news/uk/politics/boris-johnson-tommy-robinson-endorsement-conservatives-islamophobia-a9205701.html

[13] Aasma Day, *HuffPost* (January 12, 2020) *'Tommy Robinson Hounded Me Out Of My Home And Country'* https://www.huffingtonpost.co.uk/entry/tommy-robinson-hounded-me-out-of-my-home-and-country_uk_5dfd0e41e4b0b2520d0aae59

[14] PA Media, *Press Gazette* (March 19, 2021) *Tommy Robinson handed stalking prevention order over threats to Independent's Lizzie Dearden* https://pressgazette.co.uk/tommy-robinson-given-stalking-ban-after-threats-against-independent-journalists-partner/

[15] BBC News (February 23, 2021) *Boris Johnson on moving from journalism to politics* https://www.bbc.co.uk/news/av/uk-politics-56169588

[16] UK Government Press Release,*Department for Digital, Culture, Media and Sport (March 9, 2021) Government publishes first ever national action plan to protect journalists* https://www.gov.uk/government/news/government-publishes-first-ever-national-action-plan-to-protect-journalists

[17] Marcela Kunova, *Journalism.co.uk, Facebook and Google team up with INSI to fight online harassment of journalists*
(November 21, 2019) https://www.journalism.co.uk/news/facebook-and-google-team-up-with-insi-to-fight-online-harassment-of-journalists-/s2/a747721/

[18] US Press Freedom Tracker, https://pressfreedomtracker.us/all-incidents/?search=capitol

About the contributor

Elena Cosentino has been director of INSI since 2019. She has more than 20 years' frontline experience of news and investigative documentaries working as a reporter, producer and director for the BBC, ITN and CNN.

Insurrection or over reaction? One afternoon in Manchester

Was it a repeat of January's Washington's mayhem when football fans took to the pitch at Old Trafford in early May? Did Old Trafford's have its own Capitol moment? Or did the media and the public get it all wrong? Jim White compares the two events and believes the fans may have discovered something quite valuable

Peter Boyle has been going to Manchester United matches, home and away, for more than three decades. On Sunday May 2, he decided to join a gathering outside Old Trafford to protest about the owners of his club, the Florida-based Glazer family.

Accompanied by his 12-year old son George (named after George Best) he was surprised and impressed by the thousands of others who had fetched up, swarming the forecourt some three hours ahead of the scheduled kick off in United's home Premier League match with Liverpool. "There was a real buzz there," he recalls. "A lot of lads I knew were there. It was like being back at the match."

The pandemic had locked supporters out of following their team for more than a year. And here they were embracing the chance to gather in large numbers again, chanting and shouting, singing and dancing as if they were going to a game. Flares were lit, smoke billowed into the Manchester sky.

Quickly, the sense of intoxication rose. Finding there was precious little security in place, the protestors pushed towards the tunnel that runs under the south stand of the stadium. Once there, with no more than half a dozen stewards in hi-vis waistcoats blocking their way, a couple of hundred bundled their way into the ground itself.

It appeared after the event that one of the stewards had obligingly opened an access door. Another door had been kicked down. Once inside, the trespassers gathered on the pitch, an acre of greensward of significant cultural heft. It was clear from their behaviour this was not planned: they had little idea of what to do, other than take a few selfies, organise a penalty shoot-out and nick a corner flag as a souvenir. They were gone almost as soon as they had arrived.

Telling parallels on show

Watching it all unfold from afar, one thing quickly became apparent: how much this resembled the storming of Washington DC's Capitol building by supporters of Donald Trump four months earlier. The purpose and motivation may have been very different, but the execution and organisation had telling parallels. As did the response in the media.

'Anarchy at Old Trafford' was the *Daily Mirror's* take on the United insurrection, a headline which exactly recalled its report on the Capitol incident: 'Anarchy in the USA'. The *Telegraph's* headline – 'Rioters storm Old Trafford' – was a conscious echo of its 'Rioters storm Capitol' four months earlier. While the tone of Sky online's 'Outrage grows over Trump-inspired mob's storming of Congress' was reflected in the *Daily Mail's* view of the Manchester mob: 'Day protest turned to mayhem'.

Like the Capitol assault, the Old Trafford demonstration had been artfully orchestrated on social media.

The previous week, the proposed Super League breakaway by 12 of Europe's wealthiest clubs had collapsed in disarray after it had been roundly condemned by everybody from retired footballer turned pundit Gary Neville to Prince William. The idea of creating a competitive closed shop had outraged the British sporting sensibility, with its historic commitment to the idea – however fond – of meritocracy.

It is an idea that American sports followers, used to closed competitions, find hard to comprehend. More than that: for the American billionaires who own several of England's grandest footballing institutions, it is a concept close to economic illiteracy.

To a sizable section of United followers, the discovery that Joel Glazer had been a driving force in the Super League plans came as no surprise. For them it was indicative of the manner in which his family had long treated the club's heritage and tradition as a personal cash machine.

It was not hard to rally dissenters to gather to make their feelings known. Moreover, it was the perfect, media-savvy time to do it: the match with Liverpool was to be broadcast live, with coverage spinning across the globe. The idea was that points they wished to make could be amplified far and loud.

The role of social media

Just as they had in advance of the Capitol march, all week ahead of the Manchester demonstration, social media networks thrummed with arrangements. This was not a secret operation. Yet, just like the Capitol, nobody in authority seemed to notice the build-up. Which was an appropriate irony at Old Trafford: in the wake of the fury against the Super League, Joel Glazer had issued a statement saying he would from now on 'pay attention to the fans'. A week on and he was apparently blind to the fact that the self-same fans were preparing to march on his property in large numbers.

It meant, just as had happened in Washington, when the marchers arrived at their destination they discovered precious little standing in their way. Nobody thought to up security. Suddenly both sets of demonstrators found themselves able to gain entry to places previously reckoned accessible only to a privileged elite: the floor of Congress and the Old Trafford pitch.

And it was this ingress that changed the tenor of the reporting. The moment it happened, this became less a demonstration and more a trespass on territory infused with emotional heft. Even those sympathetic to the United protestors' cause – like Neville and his fellow Sky Sports pundit Jamie Carragher – felt obliged to add the caveat that breaking on to the pitch and forcing the postponement of the fixture the media had come to report, was beyond the pale.

On the BBC's flagship football show *Match of the Day* that evening, its pundit Alan Shearer was unequivocal in his disdain about the pitch invaders: "This was just unacceptable." Meanwhile, the *Daily Mail* – whose columnists, even those of robust views like Richard Littlejohn, had previously praised the demonstrations which had brought down the Super League as a wholesome affirmation of the power of the little man – was damning about the encroachment. Its back-page headline was 'Pitched battle', illustrated with a picture of a snarling fan wielding a corner flag. 'Gruesome injury: one of the victims of yesterday's carnage' was the caption under a photograph of a bloodied policeman.

A few hotheads, was the consensus, had undermined everything. Even those sympathetic to the tenor of the protest were obliged to frame their comments with the caveat: 'While I cannot condone'. In the week since the Super League collapsed, football had become, as it were, a political football. And politicians were invariably asked about the Old Trafford business and required to have an opinion.

The Foreign Office minister James Cleverly, speaking on *Sky News,* was the exemplar: "I cannot condone the images that we have seen about storming the ground," he said. "But we do need to understand the frustrations that fans have, not just with Manchester United but with a number of clubs across the game."

Was it really mayhem?

Closer analysis, however, suggests objectively it was hard to categorise what had happened inside Old Trafford as the mayhem implied in the media coverage. There were five deaths in the storming of the Capitol. In Manchester, the entirety of the toll of violence was a cop who received a gash under the eye when someone hurled a traffic cone at police lines; he was not 'one of the victims' of the *Mail*'s caption, he was the only one. Not that anyone can condone that. One is too many.

And the transgression had practical ramifications on the transmission of what was happening. When the first invaders arrived on the pitch, Sky TV was already in place, broadcasting its pre-match build up.

Precluded by the pandemic from using an indoor studio, the presenter and pundits were perched on an outdoor platform built across the unoccupied seats at the Stretford End of the stadium. Neville, ahead of his stint as co-commentator, was there too. The producer recommended the Sky team get out immediately. Neville said there was nothing to worry about: the demonstrators wouldn't harm them. And indeed he saw a group of protestors making their way past the platform up into the stands, taking selfies with him and fellow pundit Roy Keane, former United stalwarts both, in the background.

But, despite Neville's call for common sense, safety protocols prevailed and all Sky staff – from pundits to cameramen – were told to evacuate.

As the team left the platform, they were propelled on their way by someone hurling a lit flare in their direction (it landed at some distance). Inadvertently, the hasty escape deprived the protestors of immediate coverage. The cameras stopped rolling. And a pitch invader took out his ire at Sky's long involvement in the broadcast of the game, by smashing the lens of one of the cameras left unattended.

The lack of pictures, however, did not dilute the condemnation.

What had made the fans' action more transgressive was the fact they had, like the Capitol stormers before them, stepped on hallowed turf. That immediately changed the complexion of the protest. The fact they didn't do anything to damage the playing surface (unlike those behind the campaign to free the south London gangster George Davis who, in 1975 broke into Headingley and carved up the cricket square the night before an Ashes test match) did not mitigate the offence.

What's more, for the first time in the history of the Premier League – and for generations before that – direct supporter action had led to the suspension of a match. That had never happened, even in the dark days of hooliganism. And for many media outlets the association between supporter action and hooliganism was a simple one to make. In the immediate aftermath, the similarity with the Capitol incident was reinforced in the coverage: things had gone way too far.

How the British media saw it

'Generations of United fans turned out to fire a defiant message to the owners and the world', was the subheading in the *Daily Mirror* above their reporter David McDonnell's eye-witness account. 'But it all blew up and heaped shame on the biggest club on earth'.

The day after the demonstration, however, after it became clear the damage to person and property was not extensive (there were even pictures doing the rounds on social media of protestors picking up litter left outside the stadium) the tone in the reporting shifted gear once more.

On the newspaper sports pages, there was growing evidence of support for the demonstrators' intent largely missing from any of the coverage from Washington. While the American mischief-makers were almost universally dismissed in both the US and UK as a bunch of loony conspiracy theorists, there were plenty of voices in the British media who reckoned the Old Trafford 'mob' had a point.

While still delivering the standard anti-violence message, Miguel Delaney, the *Independent's* football correspondent, put it like this: "Many might find some of the elements distasteful or ugly, such as bottles and flares being thrown, as well as the stadium being invaded. Violence of course should not be tolerated, or condoned. The pictures of officials with their faces slashed was a disgrace, and those responsible for such violence should be condemned. But that should not preclude the right of fans for civil protest. That is what most of this was, and pretty much all that was left to them."

While Martin Samuel in the *Daily Mail* reckoned: "There was nastiness, as there so often is on these occasions; there are people who abuse the right to dissent for their own ends. Yet for all this, for all the disruption, disturbance and inconvenience around Old Trafford on Sunday, this was not the worst day for football. It was a good day, one might even argue.

"Good, even with no match. Good, despite the bad. It was a day when many supporters made their feelings known in a way that truly encapsulated the anger around the Super League sell-out. It was a day that owners ignore at their peril. This was football's *Network* moment. The fans were as mad as hell: and they weren't going to take it anymore."

Samuel's column was clear. A fundamental corollary of what makes a successful demonstration had been fulfilled: the fans' voice had been heard. Until the insurrection, it appeared they were effectively powerless. Now their views were all over newspapers, television vox pops and radio phone-ins. The media was the most important conduit for their purpose and a sympathetic media was more likely to deliver it.

"This is about the Glazers' utter disregard for the fans since they took control of the club," Peter Boyle was quoted in the *Daily Telegraph*. "The Super League was just a typical part of the way they have always viewed us. They just think they can get away with anything they like. Well maybe now we have given them pause." Boyle had made his point. It was there in black and white, in print in a national newspaper.

But there was another thing too. The Premier League had reacted to assumed menace by quickly moving to postpone the game, even though the threat to the safety of those involved was minimal. Now, the ease with which they had succumbed has given fans a potential route to prominence that had not been available to pursue in the past.

From now on, whatever the cause, whatever the purpose, groups of supporters know how to communicate their intent: get on the pitch and get the game postponed. That might be the most challenging lesson of the Old Trafford insurrection.

About the contributor

Jim White is a sports writer for the *Daily Telegraph*. Previously he wrote for *The Independent* and *The Guardian*. He is an ardent Manchester United supporter and writes a regular column for the fanzine *United We Stand*.

Over here, over there: Lessons from the USA on why British TV journalism needs to be fair and impartial

Clive Myrie, British TV Journalist of the year, draws lessons for the UK from the rampant jungle that is cable news in the USA where the First Amendment rules, but alongside does deeply partisan broadcast journalism

Who, what, where, when and why? Five questions at the heart of our trade. Answer those questions in relation to any news story and we're doing our jobs as journalists. They underpin everything we do, what we write in a newspaper or online, what we say on TV or the radio.

But it feels to me one of those questions we sometimes need to ask of ourselves; why? It doesn't have to be everyday or all the time but given the power we have, it's important. What is the point of the media in a democracy? What are we here for? We can influence massive societal changes. Indirectly we even wield political power, able to influence policy, perhaps even able to help change governments. And with power, as we're all well aware, comes great responsibility

But who should police this? Is it enough to let the industry itself be the gatekeeper of how far a broadcaster or newspaper should go in trying to make a profit or build an audience or are independent regulators the only way to ensure media companies use the power they have wisely?

Let's focus on the broadcasting sector and specifically television and contrast the situation here in the UK, where there is a robust, and for some, choking regulatory framework, with the United States where oversight in one crucial respect is non-existent – the requirement to fairly represent the views of opposing sides in news and current affairs broadcasts. Could that lack of a check on how America does news actually imperil democracy itself?

I love America but...

I love America and its endless possibilities. In the 1990s I was the BBC West Coast correspondent based in Los Angeles but I frequently made trips to Washington. I will never forget the first time I went inside the White House. I was in awe. To be at the heart of global power. I later spent quite a bit of time at 1600 Pennsylvania Avenue as the full time BBC Washington Correspondent while George W Bush was in residence. I've covered every Presidential election since 1996 including Joe Biden's recent victory.

The fact the richest democracy on the planet cannot quite get it right and promote the interests of all its citizens, is what's endlessly fascinating about America. The gap between its ideals and the reality. It's the country of Silicon Valley and the internet, of democratic ideals and dreamers and astronauts, of tens of millions convinced they can secure their American Dream and tens of millions who believe they already have.

The nightmare on Cable Street...

Opinion hosts are why people switch on cable TV, the straight news bulletins are by the by. It's the opinion hosts who can mould and shape minds, with many millions of viewers every week. They make the money for their networks because their followers are loyal and TV news providers in America aren't under any legal obligation to be fair and impartial.

But broadcasters in the UK are forced to be honest, fair and impartial in their news coverage, in order to hold a licence. The rules come under section five of the regulator Ofcom's codes, covering due impartiality, accuracy and opinions. Similar rules did exist in America but were thrown out almost 40 years ago when Ronald Reagan was president and attempts since to revive the legislation have always stalled on the altar of the First Amendment, the right to free speech.

In the US you can say what you like, your opinion is protected and you can use all your power and might to beam that opinion right across the land, without giving any counter arguments, without reporting the opposing point of view. Opinion can be dressed up as news.

There are many in America, horrified by the opinion hosts on both the right and the left. Whether it be Fox News or MSNBC. Yet a study last year showed both channels were in the top five of the most trusted news brands for viewers, symbolising the country's political polarisation. It's clear many Americans want their views affirmed, not challenged.

Can a regulator tame that TV Wild West?

But there is absolutely no reason why an independent regulator would materially damage the consumer. The study conducted last year which showed Fox News and MSNBC in the top five most trusted news brands for American viewers also had as third most trusted new brand PBS, Public Broadcasting Service, whose nightly *Newshour* was deemed in a study by the University of California 'the most centrist news program on television and the closest news show to holding a truly objective stance'. That's because it has to be fair and balanced as PBS is technically not a network but a programme distributor which provides television content and related services to its member stations across America, blue states and red states

But what's the 'news brand' that beats them all – Fox News, PBS, Bloomberg, and MSNBC – when it comes to public trust? It's the heavily regulated British Broadcasting Corporation. The BBC, subject to independent rules on impartiality and accuracy, is the most trusted news brand in America.

The BBC and public trust

Look at the figures, they are revealing and clearly suggest an ambition to be impartial, watched over by independent regulation, does make a difference for the better in helping to increase levels of public trust. The BBC isn't perfect by any means. Trust levels are under pressure especially after the terribly divisive Brexit campaign. Its system of funding is under scrutiny like never before and the giant tech companies with seemingly bottomless pockets of cash are now big media players. Yet the news division of this ancient institution, which will be 100 years-old next year still commands levels of trust for which many other media organisations would die.

Research last year by the independent thinktank the Reuters Institute for the Study of Journalism at Oxford University suggests the BBC is the most popular source of news in the UK among both Conservative and Labour voters and among Leave and Remain voters even after Brexit. This research showed while the BBC is slightly less trusted by people who identify with the political right than people in the centre and on the left, it is still as trusted on the right, as the major Conservative newspapers.

US TV has a trust deficit

That is America's fundamental problem which I witnessed first-hand during last year's presidential election – the trust deficit at the heart of American democracy. For the first time ever Edelman's annual trust barometer shows fewer than half of all Americans have trust in traditional media with 56 per cent of Americans believing journalists and reporters lie and 58 per cent believing most news organisations are more concerned with supporting an ideology or political position, rather than informing the public. A Gallup survey from last year showed a third of Americans had 'no trust at all' that the media reported the news 'fully, accurately and fairly'. Almost another third said they had little trust and confidence in the media. Unregulated social media is at the bottom of the pile when it comes to public trust. This is a state of affairs with serious consequences for the fabric of US society, and the future of American democracy.

The storming of the US Capitol Building on January 6, 2021, shamed America, but was partly the logical conclusion of a toxic media environment with no rules, promoting public distrust. It was one consequence of a media free-for-all and was years in the making. And where there is a void of fact and truth and public trust, conspiracy theories can live and breed.

What's been interesting to gauge is the effect of Fox News and MSNBC on the traditional news networks. Their news operations are now shadows of their former selves and came sixth, seventh and eighth respectively in the table of most trusted news brands. The coverage in nightly news programmes of major topics or foreign news often lasts less than a couple of minutes and deeper analysis is hard to find. The first time I heard the phrase 'news you can use', known in the UK perhaps as 'soft news' was when I went to live in America in 1997. Tough, gritty topics receive scant attention – poverty in America, racial conflict, the everyday struggles of the working and middle class. It is little wonder audiences for BBC World News America have rocketed in recent years, with so many hungry for in depth analysis turning away from their own home-grown broadcasters.

Over there, over here? Soon?
Back in the UK, I travelled around the country during the 2019 General Election campaign from County Durham to Southampton, Enniskillen to Pembrokeshire, and I came across people on the political right who'd be very happy to get their news from a UK equivalent of Fox News, and some on the left who'd be very happy to watch a British equivalent of MSNBC. Some Brits want their own opinions reaffirmed too. They don't want discussion. They don't want debate. It's in this atmosphere that two new TV channels are coming on stream. *GB News* under the leadership of the brilliant Andrew Neil, and a new venture backed by Rupert Murdoch. The *New York Times* quotes Andrew Neil as saying British news broadcasting is pretty much a one-party state. "They all come at stories from various shades of left," he says. "*GB News* would come from the centre, perhaps the centre right, not the hard-right approach of *Fox*. *GB News* will offer diverse voices and stick to the facts."

But, Ofcom, the regulator, is watching. Impartiality rules and strong regulation are the bulwark against the disaster of the American media jungle being replicated here, with its attendant detrimental effects on democracy.

I began with who, what, where, when and why, the basic ingredients of our trade as journalists. And I suggested from time to time we needed to ask ourselves why do we do what we do? I'll end with the words of the Fairness Doctrine, now consigned to history in America, but alive and well in the regulations of Ofcom: "Licensees must not use their stations for the private interest, whims or caprices of licensees, but in a manner which will serve the community generally as a whole. Broadcasters must provide adequate coverage of public issues and ensure that coverage, fairly represents opposing views."

The maintenance of democracy and a just and fair society – that is why, I think, we do what we do.

The is an edited version of the speech in honour of Sir Harold Evans. It was supported by the Society of Editors and the London Press Club, produced by John Mair. The full version is on Youtube https://youtu.be/VucKN2112eU

References
TV brands – https://brandkeys.com/wp-content/uploads/2019/06/073018Mediapost-TVs-Most-Trusted-News-Brands.pdf
Reuters – https://reutersinstitute.politics.ox.ac.uk/risj-review/bbc-under-scrutiny-heres-what-research-tells-about-its-role-uk

About the contributor
Clive Myrie is a BBC News presenter and correspondent of 30 years standing. He is the 2021 RTS Television Journalist of the Year and the 2021 RTS Network News Presenter of the Year. He will present *Mastermind* on the BBC from autumn 2021.

Misinformation and the decline of shared experience

Canadian Ken Goldstein looks at how the under-threat mainstream media have contributed to our collective view and knowledge of the world. He is concerned that short-term solutions will not address fundamental structural change

'Misinformation' has become one of today's media buzzwords, as audiences fragment, and the internet and social media make possible not only alternative opinions, but also what often appears to be alternative information claiming to be facts.

At the outset, we have to understand that the current situation is not only a result of the addition of the new 'media' of all types, but also the result of the subtraction of the old media that once served as a common core for information about public affairs.

The growth of misinformation is partly the result of the fact that the new alternative media have, for many people, replaced, rather than just supplemented, our traditional media. In other words, the nonsense being peddled by some of those new sources might have less of an impact if they were co-existing with our previous mass media. But the collapse of the traditional media model – for newspapers in particular – has created a vacuum that now is being filled by the purveyors of 'alternative facts'.

How did we get here?
For much of the 20th century the tangible form of the daily newspaper provided a mix of continuity and familiarity, while at the same time, for a few moments each day, it also provided the illusion that the events of the previous day had been frozen in time. Community (weekly) newspapers and magazines were also part of the mix of print media.

As the century progressed, we added radio, and then television, in both cases, initially in limited numbers – a byproduct of a mixture of technology, economics, and regulation. So, the mass or mainstream media were characterised by three important characteristics:

- First, the coincidence of oligopoly;
- Second, the economic benefit of protectable scarcity; and
- Third, an unplanned, but very real, role in helping to shape our shared experience.

In 1991, Newton Minow, former chairman of the US Federal Communications Commission, made the following observation:

> *We see 400- and 500-channel systems on the horizon, fragmenting viewership into smaller and smaller niches, and we need to remember that for all their presumed benefits these developments undermine the simultaneous, shared national experiences that comprise the nation's social glue.*[1]

In 1991 the fragmentation of media was just starting. The internet had not yet become a consumer-facing platform. But a few years later it did – and challenged not only the economics of local journalism, but also the parallel role of local media in contributing to our shared experience.

What the internet changed

In the pre-digital, pre-internet era, local media benefited from the scarcity premium, from the ability to define territories, and from the ability to earn revenue from a gatekeeping function for content produced in other places. All of that helped to subsidise local coverage.

When that internal cross-subsidy was challenged by the new technology, most local newspapers did not respond well. Some adopted the slogan of 'digital first' – but that did not always take into account that 'digital' meant no boundaries, and increased competition for enough of the pieces of the bundle to make what remained less profitable.

The internet unbundled the traditional media model, and one of the early challenges came from the free classified advertising services, which shattered what had been one of the most profitable sources of revenue for local newspapers.[2]

And while there was the obvious negative economic impact, the classified ads, in their own way, also told the story of their community – help wanted, houses for sale, apartments for rent, furniture to put in that house or apartment. And who was born. And who had died.

At the same time, the internet created an opportunity for a limited number of titles to transform themselves into national (or international) news brands, by leaving their local roots behind, in an attempt to aggregate enough users across wider geography to achieve viability (*The New York Times*, *The Washington Post*, and *The Guardian* are three examples).

And, of course, it created an enormous opportunity for tech platforms, like Google and Facebook, to become new intermediaries in the information business, through a combination of search functions, algorithms that reinforced specific interests, and advertising that used data to promise greater targeting.

By the mid-2010s, all of those changes were disrupting the local media model – particularly for newspapers. And along with that decline came a decline in shared experience.

Death of the daily (newspaper)?

While many comments on misinformation or fake news deal with the role of social media in spreading that false information, it might also be argued that the rise of fake news and the decline of the daily newspaper – and its physical, printed form – are (to some degree) connected.

Not much more than a generation ago, paid print daily newspaper circulation in Canada still reached about two-thirds of our households.[3] The tangible physical presence of the daily newspaper, in addition to the specific content in the newspaper, was part of the nation's shared experience.

The physical presence of the newspaper meant that most people knew the broad scope of the material that their fellow citizens were also seeing. That does not mean we all read the same thing, but it does mean that we all had access to, and were aware of, a similar menu of information.

And the implicit assumption that many others might be reading the same content could motivate argument as well as agreement – but, unlike the current situation, such arguments would be more likely to start from the same point.

Even earlier than the rise of fake news, the changes in the physical distribution of metropolitan daily newspapers may have been a factor in a growing divide between urban and rural areas, particularly in the United States.

The problem was rooted, at least in part, in pressure from advertisers for daily newspapers to focus their circulation on the suburbs, which led to cutbacks in statewide coverage and circulation in smaller towns and rural areas. And that, in turn, led to a situation in which both metro and non-metro residents were learning less and less about each other.[4]

With the advent of the internet, of course, the ability to receive information from anywhere increased, but, in many cases, that electronic connection did not provide the same sense of general community connection as did the physical presence of the newspaper.

Within those broader trends, something else was happening – a dramatic change in the way that citizens, particularly younger citizens, interact with media.

Perhaps most important, the last 30 years have seen the emergence of a new fundamental reality of media content – the means of production and distribution, once in the hands of intermediaries, now are also in the hands of individuals.

Today, anyone can be a publisher/broadcaster, or – another current buzzword – an 'influencer'. By lowering the threshold for celebrity, fragmentation has also contributed to the fulfilment of a prediction attributed to Andy Warhol that in the future 'everyone will be world-famous for 15 minutes'.

The rise of the smart phone

Not only is there a new platform (the internet) with many new participants, there is also a new method of news consumption. A food analogy might be useful. In the old routine, reading a newspaper, or listening to or watching a newscast on radio or television, might be thought of as a meal – professionally-prepared, usually consumed at a fixed time, and containing a number of different elements. Increasingly, however, and for younger news consumers in particular, the new approach to news might be characterised as a series of 'snacks', consumed in a very different context than traditional news presentations.

In Statistics Canada's 2016 General Social Survey, a number of important questions were asked about the way Canadians get the news, and particularly about the relationship between getting the news online (from any source) and getting it from print newspapers. And the answers indicated that whether you got your news online or in print was clearly linked to two factors – your age, and whether you had a smart phone. (And smart phones are even more ubiquitous now than they were five years ago.)

In terms of age, the younger the consumer, the greater the likelihood that reading news online daily would exceed daily reading of a print copy of a newspaper.

In terms of smart phone ownership, the survey indicated that, compared to those without smart phones:

- Smart phone owners were almost twice as likely to read news online daily; and
- Smart phone owners were less than half as likely to read a print copy of a newspaper daily.

Can we consider the smart phone a news medium? That depends on what we mean by media, of course. There are many overlapping definitions in today's media world. Years ago, media were viewed in separate silos, based on formats – print, radio, television, etc.

And those separate media formats were often received on separate devices with the same name – for example, radio on a radio, television on a television set. Then the internet emerged, allowing numerous formats to be received on a single device, and from far more sources than was previously the case.

To the extent that we include devices as part of our definition, and because the nature of the device – portability, size, etc – can influence the formats, then it might be argued that the smart phone has emerged as an important news medium in Canada. (Which raises another question: if 'local' is difficult, and 'digital first' is an incomplete answer, might 'smart phone first' be part of the solution?)

Now for the hard part – what do we do about it?

The focus of that discussion has had many ebbs and flows in the last decade, with most current attention directed at finding some way of getting Google and Facebook to compensate traditional media – sometime based on competition law principles, and sometime based on copyright principles. And there are significant questions around the degree to which the large tech platforms should or should not be shielded from issues involving libel.

Various other forms of economic assistance for traditional media have been proposed, including government assistance for journalism, tax credits for digital subscriptions, and an expanded role for philanthropy.

And there is also a variety of proposals aimed at dealing directly with misinformation and fact-checking.

Many of those proposals have merit. But it is important to ask whether some of them are (a) too focused on specifics, and/or (b) of insufficient scope to make a long-term difference. If that is the case, then we run the risk of thinking we have solved the problem, only to find that we have not.

So here is a suggestion – while pursuing the specifics, let's also add a broader, holistic view of the future of the media industry. Because that is what seems to have been missing from too many of the proposals currently under consideration.

In short, we need to spend more time on what comes next, including:

- A range of possible futures – where the industry might be in five or 10 years;

- Determining which of those possible futures are best for public policy goals (like local news and trusted content relevant to the community); and

- Determining the best combination of corporate structures and public intervention that might bring us closer to the most positive of the possible futures that appears to be achievable.

Let's not fall into the trap of proclaiming that some specific solution has solved the problem, while losing sight of the bigger picture. Because there is an important question that urgently needs an answer: How will a modern democracy function if we all have less in common?

Notes

[1] Newton N. Minow, address to the Gannett Foundation Media Center, Columbia University, New York City, May 9, 1991, p. 17.

[2] In 2005, classified advertising revenue in Canadian daily newspapers totaled C$875m. By 2019, that had fallen to C$69m – a decline of 92 per cent.

[3] Sadly, today, paid print daily newspaper circulation in Canada is equivalent to only about 10-12 per cent of Canadian households.

[4] Bob von Sternberg, 'Rural areas feel information gap, blame metro media', Minneapolis *Star Tribune*, July 15, 1990, p. 1B.

About the contributor

Ken Goldstein is President of Communications Management Inc, based in Winnipeg. He is one of Canada's leading authorities on media economics and media trends. He has a MSc in Journalism from the Medill School of Journalism at Northwestern University, and has served as Associate Deputy Minister of Communications for the Province of Manitoba..

If you have enjoyed this book, why not read
the first two books in the series...

Brexit, Trump and the Media
ISBN: 978-1-84549-709-5

Brexit, Boris and the Media
ISBN: 978-1-84549-764-45

Published by Abramis Academic Publishing and available from Amazon and other book retailers.

www.ingramcontent.com/pod-product-compliance
Lightning Source LLC
Chambersburg PA
CBHW071955220426
43662CB00009B/1133